KNOWLEDGE-BASED SOFTWARE ENGINEERING

Frontiers in Artificial Intelligence and Applications

Series Editors: J. Breuker, R. López de Mántaras, M. Mohammadian, S. Ohsuga and W. Swartout

Volume 62

Previously published in this series:

Vol. 61, E. Kawaguchi et al. (Eds.), Information Modelling and Knowledge Bases XI
Vol. 60, P. Hoffman and D. Lemke (Eds.), Teaching and Learning in a Network World
Vol. 59, M. Mohammadian (Ed.), Advances in Intelligent Systems: Theory and Applications
Vol. 58, R. Dieng et al. (Eds.), Designing Cooperative Systems
Vol. 57, M. Mohammadian (Ed.), New Frontiers in Computational Intelligence and its Applications
Vol. 56, M.I. Torres and A. Sanfeliu (Eds.), Pattern Recognition and Applications
Vol. 55, G. Cumming et al. (Eds.), Advanced Research in Computers and Communications in Education
Vol. 54, W. Horn (Ed.), ECAI 2000
Vol. 53, E. Motta, Reusable Components for Knowledge Modelling
Vol. 52, In production
Vol. 51, H. Jaakkola et al. (Eds.), Information Modelling and Knowledge Bases X
Vol. 50, S.P. Lajoie and M. Vivet (Eds.), Artificial Intelligence in Education
Vol. 49, P. McNamara and H. Prakken (Eds.), Norms, Logics and Information Systems
Vol. 48, P. Návrat and H. Ueno (Eds.), Knowledge-Based Software Engineering
Vol. 47, M.T. Escrig and F. Toledo, Qualitative Spatial Reasoning: Theory and Practice
Vol. 46, N. Guarino (Ed.), Formal Ontology in Information Systems
Vol. 45, P.-J. Charrel et al. (Eds.), Information Modelling and Knowledge Bases IX
Vol. 44, K. de Koning, Model-Based Reasoning about Learner Behaviour
Vol. 43, M. Gams et al. (Eds.), Mind Versus Computer
Vol. 42, In production
Vol. 41, F.C. Morabito (Ed.), Advances in Intelligent Systems
Vol. 40, G. Grahne (Ed.), Sixth Scandinavian Conference on Artificial Intelligence
Vol. 39, B. du Boulay and R. Mizoguchi (Eds.), Artificial Intelligence in Education
Vol. 38, H. Kangassalo et al. (Eds.), Information Modelling and Knowledge Bases VIII
Vol. 37, F.L. Silva et al. (Eds.), Spatiotemporal Models in Biological and Artificial Systems
Vol. 36, S. Albayrak (Ed.), Intelligent Agents for Telecommunications Applications
Vol. 35, A.M. Ramsay (Ed.), Artificial Intelligence: Methodology, Systems, Applications
Vol. 34, Y. Tanaka et al. (Eds.), Information Modelling and Knowledge Bases VII
Vol. 33, P. Pylkkänen et al. (Eds.), Brain, Mind and Physics
Vol. 32, L. de Raedt (Ed.), Advances in Inductive Logic Programming
Vol. 31, M. Ghallab and A. Milani (Eds.), New Directions in AI Planning
Vol. 30, A. Valente, Legal Knowledge Engineering
Vol. 29, A. Albert (Ed.), Chaos and Society
Vol. 28, A. Aamodt and J. Komorowski (Eds.), Fifth Scandinavian Conference on Artificial

ISSN: 0922-6389

Knowledge-Based Software Engineering

Proceedings of the Fourth Joint Conference on
Knowledge-Based Software Engineering
Brno, Czech Republic, 2000

Edited by

Tomáš Hruška
Brno University of Technology, Czech Republic

and

Masa-aki Hashimoto
Kyushu Institute of Technology, Japan

IOS
Press
Ohmsha

Amsterdam • Berlin • Oxford • Tokyo • Washington, DC

ISBN 1 58603 060 4 (IOS Press)
ISBN 4 274 90391 5 C3000 (Ohmsha)
Library of Congress Catalog Card Number: 00-106150

Publisher
IOS Press
Nieuwe Hemweg 6B
1013 BG Amsterdam
Netherlands
fax: +31-20 620 3419
e-mail: order@iospress.nl

Distributor in the UK and Ireland
IOS Press/Lavis Marketing
73 Lime Walk
Headington
Oxford OX3 7AD
England
fax: +44 1865 75 0079

Distributor in the USA and Canada
IOS Press, Inc.
5795-G Burke Centre Parkway
Burke, VA 22015
USA
fax: +1 703 323 3668
e-mail: iosbooks@iospress.com

Distributor in Germany
IOS Press
Spandauer Strasse 2
D-10178 Berlin
Germany
fax: +49 30 242 3113

Distributor in Japan
Ohmsha, Ltd.
3-1 Kanda Nishiki-cho
Chiyoda-ku, Tokyo 101
Japan
fax: +81 3 3233 2426

PRINTED IN THE NETHERLANDS

Preface

This book contains the proceedings of the Joint Conference on Knowledge-Based Software Engineering (JCKBSE) held in Brno, Czech Republic on September 12th – 14th, 2000. It was the fourth in a series of biannually organised conferences of this kind.

JCKBSE generally aims to provide a forum for researchers and practitioners to discuss the latest developments in the areas of knowledge engineering and software engineering. Particular emphasis is placed upon applying knowledge-based methods to software engineering problems. The conference originated in order to provide a forum in which the latest developments in the field of knowledge-based software engineering could be discussed. Although initially targeting scientists from Japan, the CIS countries and countries in Central and Eastern Europe, JCKBSE warmly welcomes participants from all countries. JCKBSE 2000 continued with this tradition and achieved a truly wide international participation. Furthermore, the scope of the conference as indicated by its topics was updated to reflect the recent development in all the three covered areas, i.e. knowledge engineering, software engineering, and knowledge-based software engineering.

The JCKBSE 2000 proceedings are a collection of contributions of authors from different countries to a wide range of topics related to knowledge-based or automated software engineering. The papers, which were selected after a standard refereeing process (at least 2 reviewers for each paper), tackle some of the major open research issues of the field, such as architecture of knowledge, software and information systems, requirements engineering, domain analysis and modelling, formal and semiformal specifications, knowledge engineering for domain modelling, intelligent user interfaces and human machine interaction, data mining, automating software design and synthesis, object-oriented and other programming paradigms, knowledge-based methods and tools for software engineering, including testing, verification and validation, process management, maintenance and evolution, CASE, applied semiotics for knowledge-based software engineering, knowledge systems methodology, development tools and environments, practical applications and experience of software and knowledge engineering, information technology in control, design, production, logistics and management, enterprise modelling, workflow, and learning of programming.

For JCKBSE 2000, we first received 68 full size submissions, from which the Programme Committee finally selected 26 to be included in the proceedings as full papers and 23 as short papers. The original submission came from 22 countries spread over 4 continents. Quality was the principal selection criterion for selected papers but the Programme Committee also wanted to ensure that the papers presented included both advanced academic research and the practical use of automated software engineering technology. Here, we gladly acknowledge the responsible work done by the reviewers and the Programme Committee members.

The whole volume is structured into the following sections which reflect the major themes of the JCKBSE 2000 event:

- Software Architecture, Applied Knowledge Engineering,
- Knowledge Modelling and Reasoning,
- Program Understanding, Reuse, Knowledge Discovery,
- Knowledge-Based Methods and Tools for Software Engineering,

- Knowledge Management for Business Processes,
- Intelligent User Interfaces,
- Learning and Education.

As editors of this volume, we would like to thank IOS Press for publishing the proceedings. The authors of the papers are to be thanked not only for contributing their ideas and research results, but also for their effort in elaborating the final versions in electronic form. However, to produce a camera ready version of the whole volume required still an immense effort. Here, the editors would hardly be able to complete the task in time without a substantial help of Tomáš Vojnar and Vladimír Janoušek from Department of Computer Science and Engineering, Brno University of Technology.

Many people helped us to make the conference as convenient as possible for the participants. The local organising committee recruited from the Department of Computer Science and Engineering of the Faculty of Electrical Engineering and Computer Science at the Brno University of Technology and from VEMA Computers and Systems Brno, Ltd. They deserve a full credit for their excellent work.

Tomáš Hruška and Masa-aki Hashimoto
Editors

Conference Organisation

Steering Committee

Christo Dichev, Bulgaria
Morio Nagata, Japan
Pavol Navrat, Slovakia
Vadim L. Stefanuk, Russia
Haruki Ueno, Japan

Programme Chairs

Tomas Hruska, Czech Republic
Masa-aki Hashimoto, Japan

Programme Committee

Bailes P., Australia
Banaszak Z., Poland
Benczur A., Hungary
Bielikova M., Slovakia
Brusilovsky P., USA
Devedzic V., Yugoslavia
Dichev Ch., V., USA
Dicheva D., USA
Dochev D., Bulgaria
Ehrlich A., Russia
Eisenecker U., Germany
Far Behrouz H., Japan
Fukazawa Yoshiaki, Japan
Gams M., Slovenia
Gladun V. P., Ukraine
Hashimoto Masa-aki, Japan
Hori Masahiro, Japan
Hruska T., Czech Republic
Kaijiri Kenji, Japan
Kang Kyo-Chul, Korea
Khoroshevsky, V. F., Russia
Komiya Seiichi, Japan
Koyama Teruo, Japan
Kumeno Fumihiro, Japan
Lozovskiy V. S., Ukraina
Moessenboeck H., Austria
Molnar L., Slovakia
Nagata Morio, Japan
Navrat P., Slovakia
Okamoto Toshio, Japan
Oomori Yasumasa, Japan
Osipov G.S., Russia
Pechersky Y., Moldova
Stefanuk V. L., Russia
Sugawara Kenji, Japan
Tan Chew Lim, Singapore
Ueno Haruki, Japan
Welzer T., Slovenia
Williams M., United Kingdom
Yamamoto Shuichiro, Japan
Yamada Hiroyuki, Japan
Young Gilbert H., Hong Kong
Zendulka J., Czech Republic

Organising Committee

Tomas Hruska
Vladimir Janousek
Tomas Vojnar
Jaroslav Zendulka

(Brno University of Technology, Czech Republic)

Vera Burdova

(VEMA Brno, Computers and Projects, Ltd., Brno, Czech Republic)

Reviewers

Bailes Paul
Banaszak Zbigniew
Benczur Andras
Benes Miroslav
Bielikova Maria
Brusilovsky Peter
Devedzic Vladan
Dicheva Darina
Dochev Danail
Eisenecker Ulrich
Far Behrouz
Fujita Shigeru
Fukazawa Yoshiaki
Galbavy Miroslav
Gams Matjaz
Hanacek Petr
Hashimoto Masa-aki
Hirashima Tsukasa
Hirota Toyohiko
Hori Masahiro
Hruska Tomas
Inoue Tomo'o
Janousek Vladimir
Kaijiri Kenji
Kaiya Haruhiko
Kolar Dusan
Komiya Seiichi
Koyama Teruo
Kumeno Fumihiro
Lim Tan Chew
Lozovskiy Vitaliy
Moessenboeck Hanspeter
Nagata Morio
Navrat Pavol
Okamoto Toshio
Oomori Yasumasa
Osipov Gennady
Pechersky Yuri
Peringer Petr
Rabova Zdena
Saloun Petr
Schwarz Josef
Stefanuk Vadim
Sugawara Kenji
Ueno Haruki
Vojnar Tomas
Welzer Tatjana
Yamada Hiroyuki
Yamada Keizo
Yamamoto Shuichiro
Yoshida Takaichi
Zendulka Jaroslav

Organisers

Czech Society for Computer Science
Department of Computer Science and Engineering, Faculty of Electrical Engineering and Computer Science, Brno University of Technology
SIG-KBSE, The Institute of Electronics, Information and Communication Engineers, Japan

Co-operating Institutions

IEEE Tokyo Section Computer Chapter
Japanese Society of Artificial Intelligence
Russian Association for Artificial Intelligence
Slovak Society for Computer Science
The Institution of Electrical Engineering – Slovakia Centre
VEMA Brno, computers and projects, Ltd., Brno, Czech Republic

Sponsors

SIG on Knowledge-Based Software Engineering, Institute of Electronics, Information and Communication Engineers, Japan

Contents

Knowledge Modelling and Reasoning

Program Understanding, Reuse, Knowledge Discovery

Knowledge-Based Methods and Tools for Software Engineering

Learning and Education

Knowledge-Based Software Engineering
T. Hruška and M. Hashimoto (Eds.)
IOS Press, 2000

Project Structure and Development Methodology Toward The IT Revolution — Lesson from Practice —

Masanobu UMEDA, Isao NAGASAWA
Kyushu Institute of Technology, Iizuka 820-8502, Japan

Abstract. In the face of the Information Technology (IT) revolution, knowledge-based systems are going to play an important role in the advancement of information services. However, the development and maintenance of a knowledge-based system generally take much time and require intensive labor. It is not easy for a small research project to achieve a great degree of success.

We have been introducing a new project structure and a new development methodology based on the experiences with developments of practical knowledge-based systems since about 7 years before. The fundamental idea is to allow domain models, modeling techniques, software tools, and whatever else possible to be shared by making all possible effort to generalize them. This concept is relevant to the research and development methodologies of general information systems which support the IT revolution.

This paper describes the project structure and the development methodology that we have adopted. The concept of Information-Driven Systems is also introduced. It is a natural generalization of this approach regarding overall research on information systems.

1 Introduction

The Information Technology (IT) revolution represented by the Internet is going to change industry, economy, and society drastically as if it has come to symbolize the beginning of the new century. Knowledge-based systems that involve expert knowledge of design, medical, and financial domains are strongly expected to advance information services all the more. However, the development and maintenance of a knowledge-based system generally take much time and require intensive labor. It is not easy for a small research project to achieve a great degree of success.

We have been developing knowledge-based systems in several application domains, such as design and medicine, and putting them to practical use. For example, the Health Care Support System [1] is a knowledge-based diagnosis system involving about 6000 rules for the detection protocol of chronic diseases. It has been in use for more than 10 years and was applied to 120 thousand people last year. Similarly, DSP [2] is a programming language with a supporting environment dedicated to design calculation problems. It has been applied to actual product designs such as cameras.

Although we have had experiences with the development of these practical systems, our initial development style was almost the same as that of other research groups in universities and companies, that is, an ad hoc development style. However, lessening of the costs of both development and maintenance became more and more important due to the small number

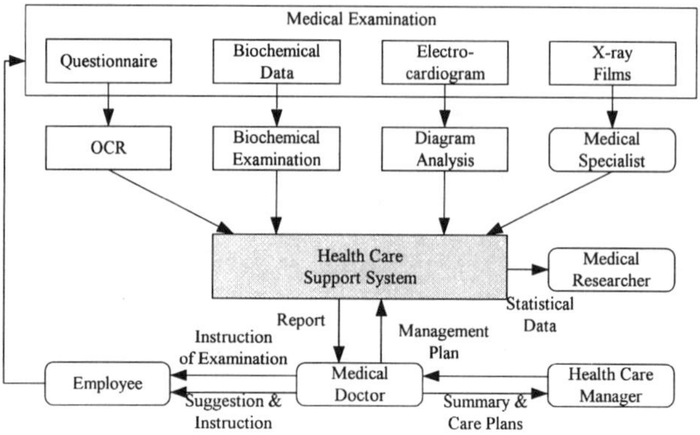

Figure 1: Model of Health Care Management.

of people involved in the research group. Thus, a new project structure and a new development methodology were introduced since about 7 years ago. The fundamental idea is to allow domain models, modeling techniques, software tools, and whatever else possible to be shared by making all possible effort to generalize them. The idea is relevant to research and development methodologies of general information systems which support the IT revolution.

This paper describes the project structure and the development methodology that our research group has adopted. The concept of Information-Driven Systems which is planned as a new department of Kyushu Institute of Technology is also introduced. It is a natural generalization of this approach regarding overall research on information systems.

2 History and Structure of the Research Project

2.1 History of Health Care Support System

Let's describe a brief history and problems encountered using the Health Care Support System (HCS) [1] as an example of a knowledge-based system. The HCS is a knowledge-based diagnosis system which supports the health care management of employees in a company. Figure 1 illustrates a model of health care management by using the HCS. The HCS evaluates the conditions of an employee's health based on biochemical data, electrocardiogram, X-ray films, and questionnaire, and explains the evaluation result in natural language. The HCS involves about 6000 rules for the detection protocol of chronic diseases.

Development of the HCS began in 1987, and took about 3 years. The HCS was initially developed and operated on a Lisp machine. However, the Lisp machine lost support after several years. The HCS was then developed again in Common Lisp and Prolog on a Unix workstation. During these changes, most of the rule compiler, inference engine, and GUI had to be rewritten. Furthermore, since the first Common Lisp system chosen lost support after several years, the HCS had to be moved again to yet another Common Lisp system which had different GUI tools and a different external language interface from the first one.

¿From these experiences, the costs of not only development but also maintenance became significant. Therefore, development of a stable development environment was recognized as one of the major tasks of the research project. The development of the environment was started in 1994, and the project structure was reorganized in response to it.

2.2 The Project Structure

The fundamental idea is to allow domain models, modeling techniques, software tools, and whatever else possible to be shared by making all possible effort to generalize them. According to this idea, the research group is organized into several subgroups arranged in a layered structure as shown in Figure 2, and each subgroup is tightly coupled with others.

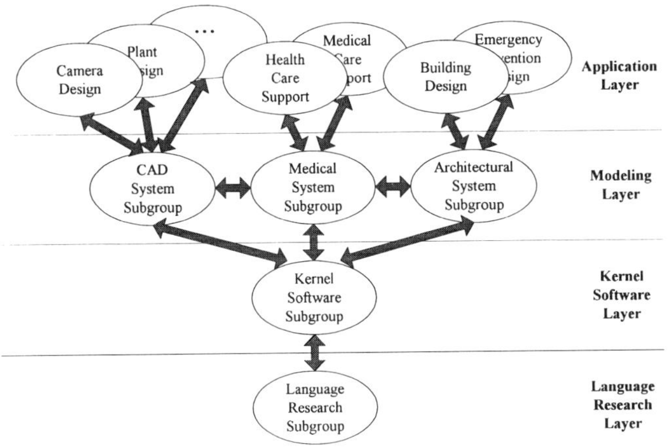

Figure 2: The Project Structure.

Language Research Layer The language research subgroup in the first layer focuses on research on language design and implementation techniques suitable for knowledge processing, and it is intended to provide fundamental ideas for the upper layers. The subgroup has proposed a Prolog abstract machine ATOAM and its faster implementation techniques [3, 4], and has also proposed a generalized lazy evaluation mechanism which enables the implementation of various types of constraint solvers on a Prolog-based system [5]. B-Prolog is a widely used and well-known Prolog system containing these features.

Kernel Software Layer The kernel software subgroup in the second layer is intended to provide a common programming environment for all other subgroups. The softwares developed by these subgroups are all intended to be used in practical application domains including commercial purposes. Thus, it is expected that the development of a program is supported from an early prototyping phase to the final commercial production phase in the same environment. The subgroup has developed an integrated development environment named INSIDE [6]. It is based on a multi-threaded abstract machine TOAM. Prolog with many extended features required for the development of a knowledge-based system has been implemented on it. INSIDE has been applied to the developments in the upper layers for more than 5 years.

Modeling Layer The modeling layer is composed of several domain-oriented research subgroups [1, 7, 8, 2, 9, 10]. Each subgroup focuses on one application domain, but information of each is exchanged with others, and efforts are made to share domain models, modeling techniques, and software tools between them. A software tool developed by a subgroup may be swallowed up that of another subgroup by generalizing the tool. Functions which turns out to be useful and universal may be incorporated into INSIDE. For example, DSP which was initially developed for representing design knowledge by the CAD system subgroup is now extended to represent knowledge in different application domains, such as medicine and commerce.

Application Layer The application layer is a place of collaboration with experts in application domains, such as camera designers associated with a company and physicians from a hospital. Since collaboration between experts in an application domain and experts in a software domain, i.e. a subgroup in the modeling layer, is essential for the development of knowledge-based systems [7], a collaboration framework has to be initially established and maintained continuously. Experts in an application domain provide a research subgroup with knowledge about the domain as well as good examples [11]. The research subgroup systematizes the knowledge and proposes a framework of knowledge processing as a prototype system. The experts describe their knowledge using the prototype system and return the evaluation results to the research subgroup for succeeding improvements.

3 Development Environment INSIDE

3.1 An Overview of INSIDE

INSIDE [6] is an integrated development environment for knowledge-based systems. Figure 3 shows the organization of INSIDE which is composed of three layers: an abstract machine layer, programming language layer, and application layer. The abstract machine layer is composed of a multi-threaded abstract machine TOAM and fundamental functions. Taking into account that both Prolog and Lisp, which are adequate to knowledge processing, can be realized, Prolog abstract machine ATOAM [3] is made as basis of TOAM and extended. Fundamental functions are implemented in the abstract machine layer and differences between platforms are absorbed in this layer for the sake of portability. Programming languages such as Prolog and Lisp are intended to be realized over the abstract machine layer. Prolog is currently implemented as an application programming language. All of applications are intended to be developed using these programming languages.

The lower 2 layers are written in C, and INSIDE runs on several types of Unix and Windows.

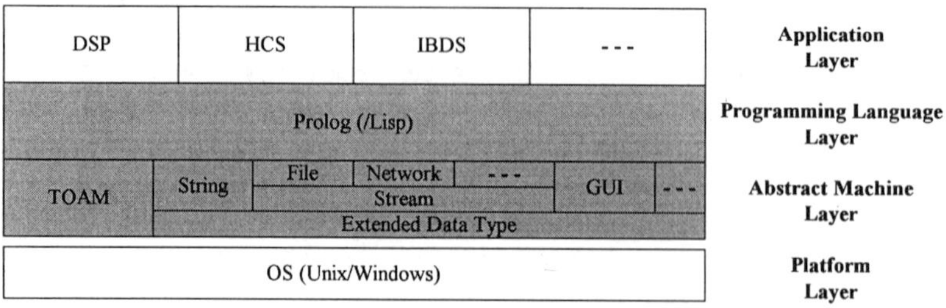

Figure 3: System Organization of INSIDE.

3.2 Essential Features of INSIDE

INSIDE is intended to support the development of knowledge-based systems from an early prototyping phase to the final commercial production phase in the same environment. For this purpose, INSIDE has the following essential features.

Prolog-based Environment Easiness of both rapid-prototyping and symbol processing is essential for the development of knowledge-based systems. Prolog is chosen as an application programming language for this reason. Prolog is based on ISO/IEC 13211-1 [12] with various extensions. Lisp is also intended as a yet another programming language of INSIDE.

Multi-threaded Environment Multi-thread capability is useful for preventing an application from being locked or frozen while performing operations such as blocking I/O. It is also effective to speed a processing in appearance. INSIDE is based on a multi-threaded abstract machine TOAM, and a POSIX-like thread interface is provided to write a multi-threaded application in Prolog.

Platform-independent Environment Most of operations to files and printers and GUI usually depend on an operating system and hardware. If an application uses these functions naively, it is quite difficult to move it to a different platform. Once a knowledge-based system is developed, it may be used for a longer time than the life cycle of a computer system. INSIDE implements most of the fundamental functions in the abstract machine layer for the sake of the portability of INSIDE, and provides these in a platform-independent manner for the sake of the portability of its applications.

Integrated Environment Prototypes written in Prolog or Lisp have sometimes been rewritten using conventional procedural languages, such as C and C++. This is because required performances are not only satisfied, but also all of the required functions are not provided by the development environment used for prototypes. However, this is not desirable for both development and maintenance. INSIDE provides all of the required functions not only for prototype development but also for practical application development. These functions include OLE [13], ODBC, OpenGL, Parasolid [14], and so on.

4 Information-Driven Systems

4.1 Background and Purpose

Information technology (IT) is composed of fundamental theories of Computer Science (CS), constitutive technologies of Computer Engineering (CE), and systematization technologies of Information Systems (IS). Information systems used to be developed mainly based on CS and CE, and IS used to play a role only in the system's implementation. However, IT is going to be introduced rapidly into a wide range of application domains, such as manufacturing and finance. Automobiles, home equipment, and production lines are going to gain more and more intelligence. For these reasons, a gap between the need for information systems and the domains of CS and CE has widened, and it has become more difficult for IS to provide exact solutions quickly. Especially, ordinal development methodology for information systems, which develops systems one by one according to the current needs of a customer, cannot follow the needs of the marketplace. It is time to restructure a development methodology for information systems.

Information-Driven Systems (IDS) constitute a new approach to this problem. It shifts the development of information systems from a seeds-oriented approach to a needs-oriented approach. The main features of IDS are summarized as follows:

Analysis and solution based on needs The technologies of CS and CE used to be applied directly to the development of unique information systems. In IDS, the technologies are applied to a model that is created by both analysis and solutions that are based on needs.

Restructuring of economy, politics, and society based on IT Globalization of human activities and environmental problems require the restructuring of organizations, systems, and processes related to all human activities. IDS is expected to enhance IT's ability to provide reasonable solutions to these problems.

Systematization based on standardization Information systems are expected to be reconstructed based on the standardization of data, tools and knowledge instead of based on ad hoc development. This contributes the improvement of productivity, maintainability, reliability, and applicability of the system.

4.2 The Structure of Information-Driven Systems

As shown in Figure 4, the structure of IDS can be described as a layered structure in a circle which is divided into four application domains. This is a natural extension of the structure in Figure 2. The application domains are (1) electrical equipment involving computers, (2) computer-supported operation of various technologies, (3) computer-supported organization management, and (4) computer-supported personal activities. Most human activities can be realized by combining some of these domains. For example, the manufacturing industry involves activities such as planning, design, production, sales, maintenance, and management. Actual production is performed by automated machinery, while design is supported by computer systems. Management of organization and individual activities are also supported by computer systems.

The layers of technologies in Figure 4 represent layers of implementation abstraction.

CS and CE Layer CS and CE are involved in this layer. The layer provides fundamental technologies for the upper layers.

Kernel Technology Layer All of the softwares developed in the upper layers are developed by combining the kernel technologies in this layer. Databases and computer networks are such examples since they are used in most information systems. The solid modeler used in CAD and CAM can be recognized as a kernel technology since it also can be applied to medical purposes. These technologies are common to several application domains, and can be used to construct applications in the domains by combining knowledge with data.

Modeling Technology Layer In this layer, a concept which is required for solving the problems of the upper layer is generalized by using an information model. For example, a business model on which an information system for a company is based should be as independent from the organization as possible. This is because information sharing and deployment of the system are much easier in the future.

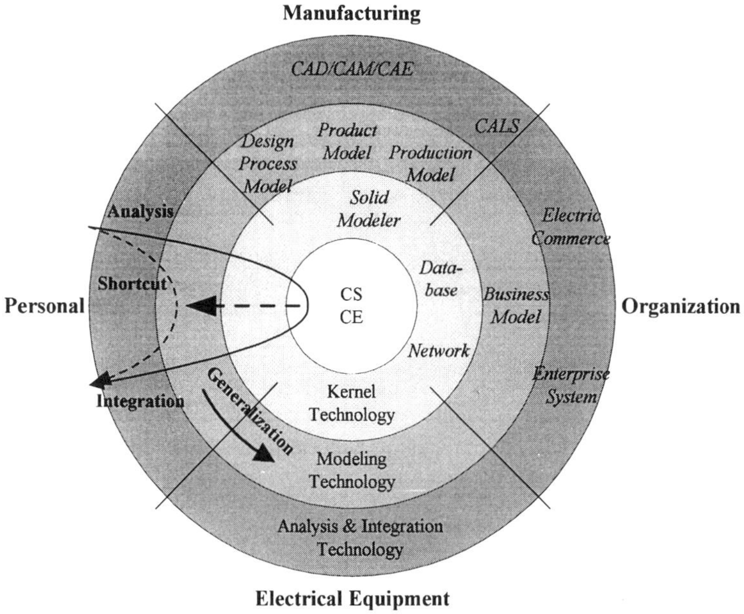

Figure 4: The Structure of Information-Driven Systems.

Analysis and Integration Technology Layer This layer involves analysis and integration technologies which actually solve the problems in application domains. For example, the reengineering of a company is accomplished by analyzing the work, structures, and functions of the organization, proposing an ideal solution, and restructuring the organization and functions using information systems. CALS (Commerce at Light Speed/Continuous Acquisition and Life-Cycle Support) is a typical example of restructuring the design, logistics, assembly, operation, and maintenance of a manufacturing process by standardization and sharing of the information regarding them.

In case of solving a problem of an application domain, a conventional approach used to analyze the problem, propose domain models, examine required tools, and look for the foundations on CS and CE. Then, it used to create tools and models based on the foundations, and solve the problem by integrating them. On the other hand, the approach of IDS turns domain models, modeling techniques and tools into reusable things by exhaustive generalization, and solves the problem by a shortcut without going down to the CS and CE layer every time. If these domain models, modeling techniques and tools are generalized by spreading them on different domains, they drive further the efficiency of the research and development forward.

5 Conclusion

In this paper, the history of practical knowledge-based system development is briefly reviewed, and the project structure and the development methodology applied to that process are described. Though the development and maintenance of knowledge-based systems generally take much time and require intensive labor, this approach enhances the efficiency of small research groups. The concept of Information-Driven Systems is also introduced, which is generalized from our approach regarding overall research on information systems. We hope this activity contributes to the evolution of an information-oriented society in the next century.

Acknowledgements

The authors would like to thank members of Information-Driven Systems Working Group and colleagues who have provided suggestions regarding this concept.

References

[1] Furukawa, Y., Nagasawa, I. and Ueno, M.: HCS: A Health Care Support System, *Journal of Information Processing Society of Japan*, Vol. 34, No. 1, pp. 88–95 (1993).

[2] Umeda, M., Nagasawa, I. and Higuchi, T.: The Elements of Programming Style in Design Calculations, *Proceedings of the Ninth International Conference on Industrial and Engineering Applications of Artificial Intelligence and Expert Systems*, pp. 77–86 (1996).

[3] Neng-Fa, Z.: Parameter Passing and Control Stack Management in Prolog Implementation Revisited, *ACM Transactions on Programming Languages and Systems*, Vol. 18, No. 6, pp. 752–779 (1996).

[4] Katamine, K., Hirota, T., Zhou, N.-F. and Nagasawa, I.: On the Translation of Prolog Program to C, *Transactions of Information Processing Society of Japan*, Vol. 37, No. 6, pp. 1130–1137 (1996).

[5] Neng-Fa, Z.: A High-Level Intermediate Language and the Algorithms for Compiling Finite-Domain Constraints, *Proceedings of Joint International Conference and Symposium on Logic Programming*, pp. 70–84 (1998).

[6] Katamine, K., Umeda, M. and Nagasawa, I.: Design and Implementation of Integrated Development Environment for Knowledge-based System, *Proceedings of the Symposium on Industrial Applications of PROLOG*, INAP'97 Organizing Committee, pp. 28–35 (1997).

[7] Hirota, T., Hashimoto, M. and Nagasawa, I.: A Discussion on Conceptual Model Description Language Specific for an Application Domain, *Transactions of Information Processing Society of Japan*, Vol. 36, No. 5, pp. 1151–1162 (1995).

[8] Mochizuki, M., Nagasawa, I., Umeda, M., Higuchi, T. and Ojima, T.: Design Verifications using Knowledge Representation Language KOSA, *Proceedings of Computer Applications in Production Engineering '95*, pp. 566–575 (1995).

[9] Umeda, M., Nagasawa, I. and Ito, M.: Knowledge Representation Model for Engineering Information Circulation of Standard Parts, *Transactions of Information Processing Society of Japan*, Vol. 38, No. 10, pp. 1905–1918 (1997).

[10] Efendy, L., Hashimoto, M., Katamine, K. and Hirota, T.: A Reference Model of CAD System Generation from Various Object Model-Based Specification Description Languages Specific to Individual Domains, *Transactions of IEICE*, pp. 713–721 (2000).

[11] Nagasawa, I. and Suzuki, H.: Roles in the Development of Intelligent CAD systems, *Journal of Advanced Automation Technology*, Vol. 7, No. 1, pp. 13–16 (1995).

[12] ISO/IEC: *13211-1 Information technology – Programming Languages – Prolog* – (1996).

[13] Brockschmidt, K.: *Inside OLE*, Microsoft Press, second edition (1995).

[14] Unigraphics Solutions: Parasolid V10.1 PK Programming Reference (1999).

Knowledge-Based Software Engineering
T. Hruška and M. Hashimoto (Eds.)
IOS Press, 2000

Informal, Formal and Operational Modelling of Medical Guidelines

Vojtěch SVÁTEK[1], Antonín ŘÍHA[2], Tomáš ZÍKA[2],
Jana ZVÁROVÁ[2], Radim JIROUŠEK[1], Zdeněk ZDRÁHAL[3]

[1] *Laboratory for Intelligent Systems, Faculty of Informatics and Statistics, University of Economics, Prague, W.Churchill Sq.4, 13067 Praha 3, CR*

[2] *European Centre for Medical Informatics, Statistics and Epidemiology of Charles University and Academy of Sciences, Pod Vodárenskou věží 2, 182 07 Praha 8, CR*

[3] *Knowledge Media Institute, The Open University Walton Hall, Milton Keynes MK7 6AA, UK*

E-mail: {svatek,radim}@vse.cz, {riha,zika,zvarova}@euromise.cz, z.zdrahal@open.ac.uk

Abstract. Formal representation and automatic processing of medical guidelines is one of the foremost challenges in applied knowledge engineering. We describe a new, flexible model of medical guideline, which seems to be particularly suitable for analysis of guidelines with respect to patient records. To provide for clear transition between the analysis and design phases of development of guideline–processing software, we formulate the model at various levels: informal, formal and operational. For the first one, we use structured text plus diagrams, while for the latter two, the OCML (Operational Concept Modelling Language) seems to be suitable, since it enables both formal checking of concept definitions and execution of operational specifications. The model is currently being tested in the hypertension domain.

1 Introduction

Medical guidelines (MG) are a standard means for dissemination of medical knowledge and for putting through healthcare standards in various areas of medicine. In addition to the textual (be it paper or electronic) form of MGs, attention is currently paid to the possibility of their *formalisation* and *computational processing*. In the European project MGT (Medical Guidelines Technology) of the 4th framework programme, we attempt to convert medical knowledge hidden in the textual form of MGs into a simple yet rich and flexible representation, and to connect it with *electronic patient records* (EPR). The interaction between MGs and EPRs can then have different forms, such as:

- support of a physician in the course of decision–making
- posterior comparison of the actions undertaken by a physician with the MG
- critique and suggestion of revision of the MG based on analysis of multiple EPRs
- comparison of several MGs from the same domain, with respect to their impact on a target population (and thus, indirectly on the EPRs).

Each of these "modes of work" requires a different computational model but all should rely upon the same representation of medical knowledge and format for data. In designing this representation, several characteristics of MGs should be taken into account.

MGs aim at supporting the diagnostic and therapeutic activities of a physician. This is done in both *prescriptive* (or, procedural, algorithmic...) and *descriptive* (or, declarative) manner. In ordinary cases, the interpretation of *prescriptive* knowledge, such as decision trees or tables, is *relatively straightforward*, but *vague* statements[1] still have to be instantiated by concrete values. *Descriptive* knowledge (such as causal relationships) is, again, hard to interpret. Furthermore, the use of background knowledge not present in the text but common to physicians is *implicitly* assumed[2]. Also, the guidelines are often inapplicable on *rare*, untypical cases. Finally, most guidelines describe *sequences* of events in the course of *time*; they can thus not be easily captured by means of shallow situation–action rules.

The construction of guideline models, formalisation of concrete MGs, as well as the development of algorithms for processing such models, require a combination of skills pertaining both to *knowledge engineering* and to general *software* (and database) *engineering*. An important issue is that of *reusing* knowledge from previous projects from the same or similar domains. It is also clear that each step has to be carefully validated from the *medical* point of view.

In this paper, we describe the output of the first phase of this effort: a generic model for representation of the MG (domain ontology and representation ontology), as well as particular tools and formalisms used to express this model. In section 2 we describe the model at an *informal* level, using structured text and diagrams. In section 3 we proceed to the *formal*[3] level of description, which is, thanks to the properties of the OCML language, closely related to *operationality* (executability) of parts of the model. Section 4 is devoted to examples taken from our pilot domain of *hypertension* treatment. Finally, section 5 points at related work, and section 6 summarises the results and outlines perspectives for the future.

2 Informal Modelling: Structured Text and Diagrams

The first phase of any knowledge modelling activity is focused on informal and semi–formal representation of knowledge. Such representation may be textual or graphical, but highest expressivity can be achieved through a combination of both. We will present our model both as *structured text* and as diagrams more–or–less compatible with the UML graphical language[4].

Our informal model consists of two parts:

- A guideline *domain ontology*, which describes the most important *concepts* dealt with in the guideline text, their *attributes*, and *semantic relations* among them
- A guideline *representation ontology*, which defines how the concepts (not necessarily all of those listed in the ontology) can be embedded, aggregated and linked so as to make up the overall *syntactic* structure of the guideline. The informal representation ontology is a starting point for a prospective formal language in which guideline knowledge will be input into target applications.

---

[1] E.g. "There is a *good response* to the treatment".

[2] E.g. the primary goal of hypertension treatment is declared to be "to lower the blood pressure", but this does not mean that blood pressure should ideally drop to zero!

[3] This notion of formality has to do with predefined syntax of a language rather than with strict mathematical formality.

[4] Note that UML starts to play an integrating role for knowledge and software engineering. Being a well established format in software engineering, four of its component–diagrams (class, activity, state and use–case) have been also incorporated into the notational standard of the CommonKADS methodology, which is a de facto standard for knowledge system development in business environment, see [3].

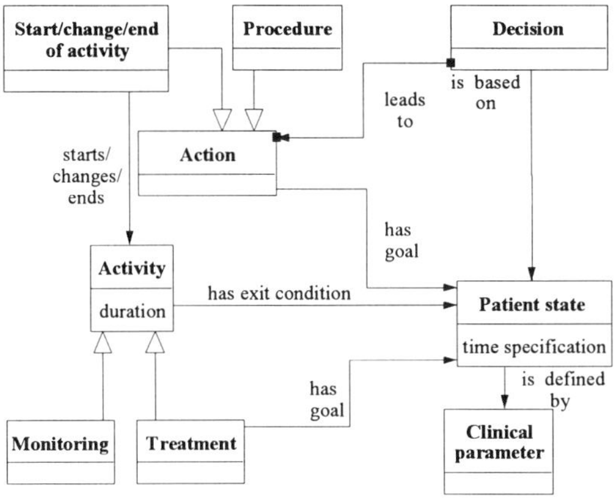

Figure 1: Diagram of the guideline domain ontology

2.1 Guideline domain ontology

The diagram[5] at Figure 1 depicts the most important classes from the guideline domain ontology, and the relations among them. As an example of textual description, for the "activity" class, see Table 1. Due to complexity constraints on diagrams, several classes are described in the textual form of the ontology only.

The prescriptive knowledge in an MG consists of elements determining „what" should be done and „under what condition" it should be done, which correspond to classes *action* and *decision*, respectively, in the domain ontology. Actions and decisions follow each other *in time*, either immediately or with a delay. Main subtypes of action are one–shot therapeutic (or diagnostic) *procedure*, as well as the *start*, *end* or *change* of a long–term process (therapy or monitoring); we call this process *activity*, consistently with the recent proposals within the commonly used EON Protocol Model [8]. The difference between an action and an activity is based on time: while an action (as well as decision) takes place within a single *time point* (such as patient's visit), the activity has measurable duration and is delimited by actions of type "start" and "end", respectively. A "snapshot" of activities in a given time point can e.g. give information on the drugs currently administered, without having to scan the database retrospectively and seek their prescription. An activity can be ended regularly, as its assigned time expires, or can be interrupted, if its exit condition is evaluated as satisfied. The exit condition can be related to the goal of the treatment (e.g. if there is surprisingly good response to the treatment and the blood pressure is sufficiently lowered, the drug treatment can be ended before than expected). It can also describe undesirable conditions (adverse effects of drugs, which force their administration to be terminated). In addition to prescriptive information ("how" to proceed), we also want to capture *descriptive* information – the goals to be reached by the treatment. This is done by means of the *patient state* class, which associates *clinical parameters* with time specifications, such as "patient has had normal blood pressure for at least three weeks".

[5] In accordance with the UML notation for edges in class diagrams, triangular arrows in our diagrams correspond to the generality relation, empty diamonds to aggregation and filled diamonds to composition. Ordinary arrows correspond to named relations.

activity
Process which has duration; its temporal aspect is described by means of a time specification. An ACTIVITY can be either TREATMENT or (passive) MONITORING.
Note: We do not consider an activity of type "waiting", as it is implicitely defined by a GUIDELINE ELEMENT with timing different from „now".
Attributes:

- description (long string)
- generic time (time specification)
- actual start (time point)
- actual end (time point)
- exit condition (relation to PATIENT STATE)

Table 1: Fragment from the semi-formal version of the guideline domain ontology

2.2 Guideline representation ontology

The guideline, as a complex object, is supposed to be represented as consisting of four types of descriptive elements: goals, scenarios, causal relationships and concept definitions.

- *goals* express desirable states (of the whole treatment, or within a certain context)
- *scenarios* express relations between conditions (as patient states and history) on the one side, and recommendations of steps to be taken (as simple action steps, as well as decision steps which again lead to action steps) on the other side
- *causal relationships* express relations between actions/activities and clinical parameters on the one side and clinical parameters on the other side; they may include information on time delays
- *concept definitions* define the criteria for being an instance of a certain concept, and prescribe how the values for variables (clinical parameters or the like) can be computed.

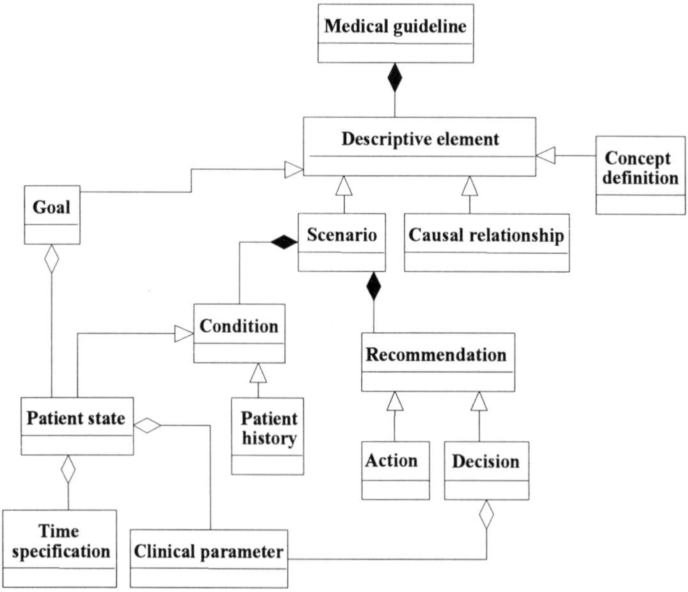

Figure 2: Diagram of the guideline representation ontology

In addition, two higher–level structures will be superposed on the descriptive elements: a network of scenarios, which reflects the order of steps (prescriptive aspect) recommended by the guideline, and a network (lattice) of patient states defined by the guideline, which reflects the similarity of states. Since the order of steps is defined only as a secondary structure upon scenarios, the model can be applied flexibly in the sense that a deviation from the recommendations does not entail its subsequent inapplicability on the patient.

Figure 2 depicts some aspects of the representation language graphically.

3 Formal and Operational Modelling: OCML

OCML (Operational Conceptual Modelling Language) has been developed at the Knowledge Media Institute of the Open University, UK. It is destinated for formalization and operationalization of knowledge models such as ontologies or problem–solving models. Its representation combines a relational approach with object–oriented[6] approach and with basic procedural constructs such as loops and conditioning. The OCML inference engine, which serves for evaluation and „execution" of models, combines three main strategies:

- theorem–proving analogical to Prolog, including backtracking on failure
- inheritance of attributes along class hierarchies
- procedural calls to the functional language CommonLisp [7], on the top of which the OCML engine is running[7].

Our way of using OCML is concentrated on building a *library* of data structures, procedures and functions that correspond to constructs (and ways of their evaluation) typically occuring in MGs. Elements of this library can later be used by MG–processing applications.

As first, rather simplified, examples, we can introduce the *classes* „person" and class „visit". The latter corresponds to the event of the patient visiting the physician, and includes measurements of temperature and blood pressure as its *attributes*.

```
(def-class person ()
          ((ID :type string)
           (name :type string)
           (smoker :type string))).
(def-class visit ()
          ((date :type string)
           (ID :type string)
           (temperature :type real)
           (sbp :type integer)
           (dbp :type integer))).
```

Individual persons then can be defined as *instances* of the class „person":

```
(def-instance pat_1 person ((ID 123456)(name John)(smoker YES)))

(def-instance pat_2 person ((ID 234567)(name Joseph)(smoker NO)))
```

Information on visits of a particular person can be obtained using the *query*

```
ask (visit ?a
  ID (the ?q (person ?w ID ?q name John))
  date ?b temperature ?c sbp ?s dbp ?d ))
```

[6] To be correct, relations are internally used even to express object–oriented constructs, such as classes and attributes.

[7] The elementary syntax of OCML therefore obeys that of Lisp, as its underlying language.

The query combines instances of the two classes using the function „the", which picks up the value of variable „?q". The „ask" query mechanism enables to make the inference engine backtrack; we can thus obtain multiple instances relevant to the query, in turn.

Surprisingly enough, an attribute can have multiple values at the same time – the reason is that classes are internally defined as unary relations and attributes as binary relations. As an example, let us define the class „variable" with a single attribute „value":

```
(def-class variable ()
           ((value :type real)  )).
```

All values of this variable can be obtained via defining a *function* which has the predefined function *setofall* in its body:

```
(def-function GetAllValues (?p)
:body (setofall ?x (variable ?p value ?x))).
```

Finally, we will introduce an example of *relation*, which formally defines a difference between two dates (e.g. of encounters):

```
(def-relation  date-difference (?date-1 ?date-2 ?diff ?diff1))
(def-rule date-difference
  ((date-difference ?date-1 ?date-2 ?diff ?diff1)
     if
   (and
    (date ?date-1 day ?d1 month ?m1 year ?y1)
    (date ?date-2 day ?d2 month ?m2 year ?y2)
    (not (== ?date-1 ?date-2))
    (= ?diff1 (+ (* (- ?y2 ?y1) 365) (* 30 (- ?m2 ?m1)) (- ?d2 d1)))
    (> ?diff1 ?diff))))
```

For more details on OCML, see [3].

4 Application in the Hypertension Domain

Hypertension treatment is an example of medical task in which patients are observed for a long period, measurements (in particular, of blood pressure – BP) are repeatedly taken, and activities (most often in the form of drug administration) are carried out.

In our example, let us start with a text from a particular hypertension MG. According to the 1999 WHO/ISH Hypertension Guidelines for the Management of Hypertension [1], "the primary *goal* of treatment of patients with high blood pressure is… treatment of all reversible risk factors as well as restoration of blood pressure to normal or optimal levels." The representation of the guideline should thus contain the above two *goals* (treatment of risk factors and lowering of BP), as well as the definitions of the *concepts* of high BP, reversible risk factors, and normal or optimal BP. In addition to textual and graphical representation, the guideline model can be expressed in OCML.

As an example, let us take the general definition of *blood pressure level*. We will express it as ternary relation among systolic BP, diastolic BP, and a term denoting the level (such as normal, optimal, hypertension, etc.):

```
(def-relation bp-level (?systolic-bp ?diastolic-bp ?level))
```

If we want to use this relation for determining the level for a given pair of systolic/diastolic BP, we further need a rule (note that there could be several such rules for a given relation):

```
(def-rule bp-level-determ
   ((bp-level ?systolic-bp ?diastolic-bp ?level)
    if (and
      (bp-level-table ?bp  bp-level ?level defining-condition or
                         systolic-min ?syst-min systolic-max ?syst-max
                         diastolic-min ?dias-min diastolic-max ?dias-max)
          (or (between ?syst-min ?systolic-bp  ?syst-max)
              (between ?dias-min ?diastolic-bp ?dias-max))))
```

The rule states that BP level can be computed from systolic and diastolic BP, through comparison with values taken from the "bp–level–table", which is another relation.

The representation of the guideline further contains a large number of *scenarios*, which can be exemplified in a semi–formal way e.g. as:

- CONDITION: patient is in *state* "eligible for hypertension treatment"; RECOMMENDATION: perform *action*: *start–activity* "Lifestyle measures"; perform *decision*: according to patient's prognosis, decide if drug treatment is to be started.
- CONDITION: patient is in *state* "medium risk prognosis"; patient's history shows that "BP monitoring" *activity* is going on for less than 3 months; RECOMMENDATION: continue with "BP monitoring" *activity*.

Causal relations among BP, various clinical parameters and associated conditions are also present in the guideline text and can be thus included into the representation.

5 Related work

Since medical guidelines are one of the hot topics in up–to–date (applied) knowledge engineering, several projects have emerged, which aim at their formalisation and exploitation. Beyond the MGT project, it is, in particular, the Asgaard project [6], conducted in co-operation between the Stanford University and the Austrian Research Institute for Artificial Intelligence. The main ideas of Asgaard are to discover implicit *intentions* of the guideline and of the healthcare provider, and to compare them at an abstract level. For this, powerful mechanisms for conceptual as well as temporal abstraction have been devised. Among the European projects of the 4th framework programme, we should mention HC-REMA, its follow–up PatMan, PRESTIGE, PROGUIDE and PROMPT. The main targets of the first two is to create a mapping between the rather vague directives of MGs and more concrete requirements imposed by day–to–day assignment of (both human, technical and financial) resources in a hospital environment; the representation of MGs is based on the formalism of Petri nets, in which patients correspond to tokens moving between the nodes[8]. The aim of PRESTIGE is to develop infrastructure for dissemination and application of medical guidelines based on up–to–date medical knowledge and to contribute to the development of standards for clinical practice. The PROGUIDE project aims to improve the availability of medical guidelines by means of a WWW server that provides information on existing guidelines, as well as persons and institutions involved in their implementation and quality assurance. The PROMPT project aims to create a clinical workstation, combining components like EPR, decision support and protocol development software, multimedia knowledge reference system and telematic technology. From the above mentioned projects, the MGT is close to Asgaard in its aiming, since it attempts to surpass the "procedural" view of an MG toward a "goal–oriented" view. The guideline model contains fewer primitives than that of Asgaard,

[8] Interestingly, the OCML language has been used in both HC–REMA and PatMan, but, as it seems, mostly as ontology–modelling language without immediate operationalization.

which is motivated by the need of comparison with large volumes of data. The use of OCML also provides a smoother transition from abstract models to executable code.

6 Conclusions and Future Work

We have presented a generic *model of medical guideline*, and its application in a specific domain (hypertension treatment). Construction of the model was the first step in designing a complex of software tools for guideline–based support of treatment, healthcare evaluation, and guideline analysis and critiquing. The elaboration of *algorithms* for the above tools is the next task to be solved within our project. In the model itself, certain parts need to be deepened, so that it covers all important concepts and relations. In particular, the area of *drug treatment* (drug groups, indications, interactions, costs) requires further elaboration.

More attention should be also paid to the connection with *electronic patient records*. Multimedia patient record ORCA (Open Record for CAre) is a system that integrates the possibility of structured patient data entry including history, medication, symptoms etc. with multimedia objects as ECG, angiography or laboratory data [3]. Structured data can be entered either using custom–prepared forms or directly using a "knowledge tree". The structure on data makes subsequent statistical processing and translation of entered data into other languages easier. The ORCA system has been validated in two Czech hospitals and in one Slovak hospital [8]; we are currently investigating how structured data extracted from the database can be processed with the operational code in OCML. When this problem is solved, we can proceed to more extensive tests on real medical data.

In a longer term, our project should involve processing of *uncertain information* (by means of probabilistic models) and *induction* of hypotheses from large patient databases.

Acknowledgement

The work on this paper has been supported by the Copernicus PL973121 (MGT – Medical Guidelines Technology) Project within the 4th Framework Program of the European Union, by the grant no.VS96008 (Laboratory of Intelligent Systems) of the Czech Ministry of Education, and by the grant no.201/00/D045 (Knowledge model Construction in Connection with Text Documents) of the Grant Agency of the Czech Republic.

References

[1] WHO/ISH Hypertension Guidelines for the Management of Hypertension. Journal of Hypertension 17, 1999, 151-183
[2] Dazzi L., Fassino C., Saracco R., Quaglini S., Stefanelli M.: A Patient Workflow Management System Built on Guidelines. Proceedings of AMIA'97, Nashville 1997, p.146-150.
[3] Motta E.: Reusable Components for Knowledge Modelling. IOS Press, 1999.
[4] Pierik F.H., van Ginneken A.M., Timmers T., Stam H., Weber R.F., Restructuring Routinely Collected Patient Data: ORCA Applied to Andrology. Methods Inf Med 36, 1997 184 - 190.
[5] Schreiber, G. et al.: Knowledge Engineering and Management: The CommonKADS Methodology. MIT Press, 1999.
[6] Shahar Y., Miksch S., Johnson P.: The Asgaard Project: A Task-Specific Framework for the Application and Critiquing of Time-Oriented Clinical Guidelines. *Artificial Intelligence in Medicine* 14:29-51, 1998.
[7] Steele, G.: Common Lisp the Language, 2nd edition. Digital Press, 1990.
[8] Tu S. W., Musen M. A.: A Flexible Approach to Guideline Modeling. 1999, Stanford Medical Informatics Technical Report SMI-1999-0789.
[9] Zvárová J., Hanzlíček P., Přibík V.: Application of Orca Multimedia EPR in Czech Hospitals. In: Proceedings of the EuroRec '99 Conference, Sevilla, 1999

Knowledge-Based Software Engineering
T. Hruška and M. Hashimoto (Eds.)
IOS Press, 2000

Object-Oriented Database System G2

Tomáš HRUŠKA[1], Michal MÁČEL[2]

[1]*Department of Computer Science and Engineering, Faculty of Electrical Engineering and Computer Science, Technical University of Brno, Božetěchova 2, 612 66 Brno, Czech Rep.*
tel.: ++420-5-4121 2219, e-mail: hruska@dcse.fee.vutbr.cz

[2]*VEMA Computers and Projections, Ltd., Výstavní 13/15, 603 00 Brno, Czech Republic*
tel.: ++420-5-43215524, e-mail: macel@vema.cz

Abstract. The object-oriented database system G2 was designed and developed in the VEMA Brno, Computers and Projections, Ltd. in the period 1994 – 2000. G2 is not only an object-oriented database system, but also the case environment for an application development. At present, G2 system is used for several commercial information system implementations with many components. This paper gives us a short overview about the G2 system, mostly in examples. The detail descriptions of the formal model, definition languages, case system etc. exceed the range of this paper and they are published separately [8, 9, 10].

1 Introduction

The G2 object-oriented database system serves for development and maintaining of network object-oriented database applications. The G2 development system was designed for a work in large groups of application designers. The system supports design and implementation of:

- *conceptual model* of an application,
- *documentation* and helps,
- *presentation* toward the user,
- *printed reports* and also
- tests, menus etc.

We will describe mainly the conceptual model in this paper.

2 Conceptual Model

2.1 Concept Definition

CDL (**C**oncept **D**efinition **L**anguage) is the specification language for the conceptual object modelling of G2 system applications. It exists in two syntax forms - the textual form and UML.

The object model consists of *objects*. An object is an ordered tuple of property values. Each property possesses a *name* and a *data type*. We call *concept* the Cartesian product of the named property data types. For the time being, the concept is equivalent to the well-known notion of *class*, but we have expanded it in its semantics. Each property can be parameterised, i.e. each property can have an arbitrary number of parameters. Each parameter must also have some *name* and *data type*.

We start our examples with an object of *persons*. Each person can have a *list of names*, a *family name* and a *birth date*. Objects are define in the form of concepts. The following concept defines the names `Name`, `Family` and `DateOfBirth` for such properties and their data types **`String`** and **`Date`**. The property `Name` is parameterised. The parameter `Order` is used to designate the order of person names.

```
Concept Person
Properties
  Name(Order: Integer):  String
  Family:                String
  DateOfBirth:           Date
End Concept
```

We do not say whether the property is a date or an algorithm. The concept defines the interface of the object for a user communication. The implementation is defined otherwise.

We define a basic set of elementary data types **`Byte`**, **`Integer`**, **`Long`**, **`Single`**, **`Double`**, **`Currency`**, **`Date`**, **`String`** and **`Boolean`**.

Relationships and Collections

We said that the model consists of objects. But objects do not exist separately. In opposition to the relational model, each object can define possible relationships to other object or objects. We distinguish two kinds of relationships: *relationships 1:1* and *relationships 1:N*.

The 1:1 kind of relationship definition expresses that one object - *owner* of the relationship is bounded with one another objects – *member* (for example a person has usually one father). The kind 1:N expresses that one owner is bounded with the (possibly empty) set of members (a person and its kids). Our model expresses such relationships in the following way. First of all we define *collection* of objects.

The natural purpose of objects is establishing of collections. For example, some person has a collection of children or some document has a collection of lines etc. Generally, the collection of objects can have another properties as the only one object.

We will define an object and a collection of such objects in one concept (here the notion of concept starts to distinguish from the class).

```
Concept Person/Persons
Properties
  Name(Order: Integer):  String
  Family:                String
  DateOfBirth:           Date
  Father:                Person
  Children:              Persons
  AverageAge:            Integer [Where=Col]
End Concept
```

Because concepts can define both separate objects and collections, they can have two names and property kinds (for single object definition and for collection definition). In our example, we define *one person* under the name `Person` and the *person's collection* under the name `Persons`. To be able to distinguish between properties for single object and collection, we can use an attribute `Where` behind the property definition. This attribute can have values `Alone`, `Col` or `(Col, Alone)`. It means that the property belongs to single object, to collection or to both definitions. Most properties belong usually to single object. Therefore, we need not use the attribute `Where = Alone`.

Very important collection type of the model is an *extent*. An extent is the collection of all the objects of the same concept. The database system maintains this collection automatically. Extents are the main entry points to the object-oriented databases.

After the collection description, the definition of relationships is easy. We will use concept names for single objects and collections as new data types of concept properties. If we use the name for single object, we establish the kind 1:1 of relationship. If we use the name for collection, we establish the kind 1:N of relationship.

In our example, the relationship `Father` is of kind 1:1 to the object `Person` and the relationship `Children` is of kind 1:N to the collection of `Persons`.

Inheritance

The inheritance is the binary relation over the set of concepts. The notion of inheritance is explained for example in [9]. G2 model defines multiple inheritance of concepts. The successor in the inheritance relation contains all the properties of its predecessors and also its own contribution to the property list. Because we define multiple inheritance, the number of predecessors is not limited. Remark that we speak about interfaces and about the interface definition. The implementation inheritance definition will not be discussed in this paper.

The object `Student` will contain all the properties of the object `Person` (and similarly for collections) and more the property of an identification number `IDNumber`. The object `Reader` will have the same properties as `Person` and more the relationship of kind 1:N `Loans` of loans (the concept `Loan/Loans` is not defined here). The object `LibraryMember` contains all the properties of `Person`, `Student` and `Reader`. Here we use multiple inheritance. Each property will occur only ones in the successor.

```
Concept Student/Students
Inherits
  Person
Properties
  IDNumber: Integer
End Concept

Concept Reader/Readers
Inherits
  Person
Properties
  Loans:    Loans
End Concept

Concept LibraryMember/LibraryMembers
Inherits
  Student
  Reader
End Concept
```

Attributes

Till this time, we have described the basic structure of the model, i.e. concepts, inheritance, properties and parameters. It is clear that this level of definition does not satisfy all the application needs. Moreover, we would like to define the model as open to be able to expand it in the future without redefinition of the CDL language syntax.

Therefore, all the basic elements of the model can be decorated by attributes. The set of attributes is not closed and could be expanded in the future. In this time, we have about fifty attributes.

Each attribute possess a *name* and a *data type*. For example, we have used the attribute `Where` to define a pertinence of a property to one object or to a collection. The type of this attribute is the potential set of elements `Col` and `Alone`. We will define attribute values inside of brackets. An attribute definition consists of `name = value`, for example `Where = col.`

The following features describe an attribute:

- name,
- part of the model for this attribute (concept, inheritance, property or property parameter). One attribute can be defined for more that one part of the model,
- data type,
- implicit value,
- for no implicit value, the necessity to define this attribute value and
- specification of the attribute inheritance.

If the attribute is of type `Boolean` and its value is `True` then we can omit this value. For example the definition `[Label = True]` is same as `[Label].` It is impossible to show all the G2 attributes here, although the big part of G2 semantic is hidden there. The complete set of attributes is defined for example in [8]. We show for example the attribute Kind.

Attribute name	Part of model	Data type	Implicit value	Obligation	Inherited
Kind	property	(Set, Get, Setget),	Setget		Yes

This attribute defines whether we can to set the value of a property (set) only or we can to get the value only (get). The implicit value of the attribute is setget (normal behavior of a variable).

We suppose that the property `Average` gets the value only. The property `Tutor` can be set and it gets also values. Therefore, the attribute `Kind` has the value `SetGet` here. Because this value is implicit for this attribute, we could omit this attribute value definition.

```
Concept Student/Students
Inherits
  Person
Properties
  IDNumber:                  Integer
  Average(Year: Integer):    Single [Kind = Get]
  Tutor:                     Person [Kind = SetGet]
End Concept
```

2.2 Concept Implementation

Concept implementation is realised under the COM system. From the concept definition, two COM classes are generated, for single object and for collection. They implement the concept properties interface and the common system interface. We have two types of data containers: *persistent* and *transient*.

We control the selection of the implementation model by the **Data** attribute of the concept. It can have two values:

- `ref` (implicit value) – implementation of persistent objects,
- `value` – implementation of transient objects.

The concept definition determines the data segment structure for the implementation. An implementation is an algorithm, which give to a user a property value. The algorithm can be also a constant (i.e. data).

The program frame for implementation is generated automatically for the MS Visual Basic in the G2 system. If the user wants to store and restore data only, it is not necessary to expand the generated code. But every special property implementation (in the Visual Basic, the functions set/let a get are generated for each property) could be instrumented.

The next example shows us a generated code structure. For the concept

```
Concept Person
   Properties
      Name :  String
      Family: String
End Concept
```

we will generate the following Visual Basic code

```
Option Explicit
Implements G2Object
Private myData As G2PersistData     'a container for lasting data
Private clsIdIdx As Integer         'index of data segment
Private Enum pidPerson              'identification of a segment item
   pidName
   pidFamily
End Enum

Public Property Get Name() As Variant         'string
Name = myData.AsString(clsIdIdx, pidName)     'object implementation
      If Name = Empty Then
         'here, we can to write our own implementation
      End If
End Property

Public Property Let Name (ByVal vNewValue As Variant) 'string
myData.AsString(clsIdIdx, pidJmeno) = vNewValue
End Property
```

3 Documentation

The core of the G2 documentation is generated directly from CDL definition. In the G2 development system, the user can describe all the application components documentation.

The documentation structure is synchronized with the CDL definition during the whole time of the application development. The documentation text is stored in the HTML form.

From this form, the G2 system generate

- all types of printed documentation,
- .chm on-line MS Windows help file,
- html pages.

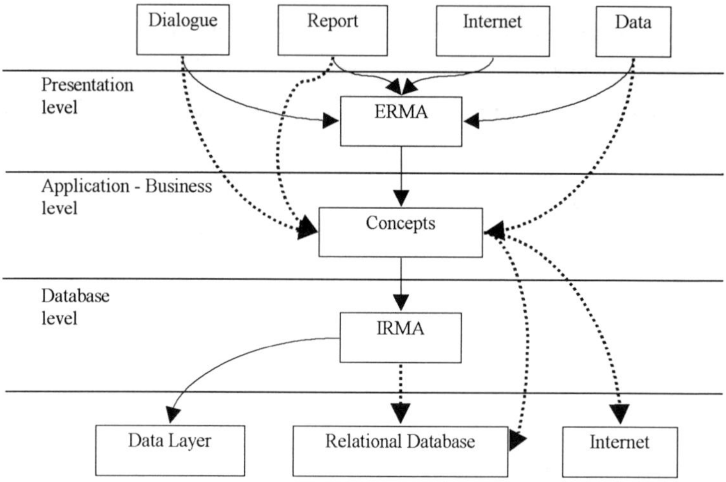

Figure 1. G2 – Three Tier Architecture

4 System Architecture

The G2 is implemented under the COM technology (the main implementation language is MS Visual Basic). Both the system components and application elements are regular COM components. Therefore, they are widely usable in the Windows COM environment.

4.1 Three-Tier Architecture

In the Fig.1., we can see the schema of the G2 application architecture. The G2 application environment consists of three levels:

- presentation level,
- business level (also called application level) and
- database level.

The presentation level is realised by the *ERMA* component (ERMA – **ExteRnal MAnager**). The business level consists of application components generated by the G2 development system. The database level is realised by the *IRMA* component (IRMA – **InteRnal MAnager**).

4.2 ERMA – Presentation Level

ERMA transmits selected values of objects into various presentation environments. The content of the presentation is independent on a presentation form. The application level objects communicate through a universal component interface. ERMA builds *a binder*. The binder is a tree of **A**bstract **D**ata **E**lements (ADE).

4.3 Presentation Environment

ERMA supports unlimited number of presentation environments. The presentation environment is an abstract medium for the presentation of a structured value. The basic presentation environments are:

- dialog on the display,
- Active X documents,
- reports,
- data files,
- Internet page,
- XML files.

4.4 Application Level

The application or business level contains components. Each component describes the behaviour of several objects - concepts. We can write components in arbitrary language, which supports COM technology. The main system support was developed for MS Visual Basic. To ensure unification with the other levels, each object must realise the G2 system interfaces. Except these system components, the object has interfaces generated from their own properties. Using these interfaces, objects can communicate together and can be controlled from a G2 system environment.

4.5 IRMA – Database Level

IRMA is a database machine. At present, we have two database machines now:

- IRMA G2 as the specialised database machine for object-oriented databases and
- IRMA ADO as the database machine for the relational data storage.

Using of IRMA ADO, an *arbitrary relational database* can be used as the low-level database machine. It could be interesting for more users, which use the relational database till this time.

5 G2 and other Object-Oriented Systems

In this paper, we could introduce basic concepts of the G2 system only. At this level, G2 shows all the basic features of standard persistent object-oriented system. But the notion of collections is expanded. In standard systems (ODMG for example [2]), collections cannot have their own properties and their own behaviour.

The power of G2 is hidden in attributes. Using of new attributes, the system can be (and is) expanded. According our opinion, the concept of multiple class objects [3,9] is quite new. It allows defining roles of objects not only in the definition time, but also in the whole life of the persistent object.

6 Conclusion

At present, the release 1.04 of G2 system is in use. It serves for VEMA commercial applications development and for many student projects. According to VEMA plans, the G2 system will be available for other users next year.

References

[1] Chaudhri,B. A., Loomis, M.: Object Databases in Practice, Hewlett-Packard Professional Books, Prentice Hall, New Jersey 1998, p. 312, ISBN 0-13-899725-X

[2] Cattell,R.: The Object database Standard ODMG-93, Release 1.2., Morgan Kaufmann Publishers 1996

[3] Hruška,T. - Kolenčík,P.: Extending an Object-Oriented Model: Multiple Class Objects. In: Proceedings of 16th International Conference ER 97 on Conceptual Modelling, D. W. Embley and R. C. Goldstein, Eds., vol. 1331 of LNCS, Springer Verlag 1997, pp. 229-242

[4] Hruška,T. - Kolenčík,P.: Comparison of Categorical Foundations of Object-Oriented Database Model, In: Proceedings of the 5th International Conference, Deductive and Object-Oriented Databases DOOD '97, Montreux, Switzerland, December 8-12, 1997, Lecture Notes in Computer Science 1341, Springer Verlag 1997, pp. 302-319

[5] Anquetil,N. - Vaucher,J.: Expressing Opposition in the Object Model, First Step towards Negation, In: ACM SIGPLAN Notices Volume 33, number 1, January 1998, ACM Press 1998, pp. 48-55

[6] Bancilhon,F. - Delobel,C. - Kanellakis,P.: Building an Object-Oriented Database System – The Story of O2, Morgan Kaufmann Publishers San Mateo, California 1992, p.618, ISBN 1-55860-169-4

[7] Rogerson,D.: Inside COM - Microsoft's Component Object Model, Microsoft Press, Redmont - Washington 1997 p.376, ISBN 1-57231-349-8

[8] Máčel,M. - Hruška,T.: Programmer's manual G2, VEMA Brno, Brno 1999, p. 54

[9] Hruška,T.: Multiple Class Objects, In: Proceedings of the ISM 98 Workshop, MARQ Ostrava, Sv. Hostýn 1998, pp. 15-22

[10] Hruška,T. - Máčel,M.: G2 - Component Architecture of Object-Oriented Database System, In: Proceedings of the ISM 99 Workshop, MARQ Ostrava, Sv. Hostýn 1999, pp. 119-124

Knowledge-Based Software Engineering
T. Hruška and M. Hashimoto (Eds.)
IOS Press, 2000

Knowledge-Based Approach to Risk Analysis Modelling

Petr HANÁČEK, Petr PERINGER, Zdena RÁBOVÁ

Department of Computer Science and Engineering,
Faculty of Electrical Engineering and Computer Science
Božetěchova 2, 612 66 Brno
e-mail: { hanacek, peringer, rabova }@dcse.fee.vutbr.cz

Abstract. The article deals with methodology framework for creating risk analysis models of diverse heterogeneous systems. Risk analysis, which refers to the study of threats and their potential impacts, is modelled with the use of knowledge-based models. From a broad range of different knowledge-based approaches we have chosen the fuzzy description for expressing the knowledge base. The fuzzy description suits best the nature of knowledge that we use.

1 Introduction

During design, implementation, and operation of different heterogeneous systems it also might become necessary to choose from different alternatives or options, which can bring some risks. All these risks have to be identified, analysed, and reduced to the minimum by implementation of suitable measures or controls. The process of identification, analysis, and reduction of risks is called *risk analysis*. For risk analysis process automation we proposed the approach of risk analysis modelling.

We are searching an optimal internal structure of the risk analysis model that is capable of expressing a variety of different assets with various values that bring a broad range of vulnerabilities into the system. The *vulnerability* is a weak point in a system that can be exploited and can consequently lead to a malfunction of the system or to a security incident. The intention or potential of the outside world (called environment) to exploit the present vulnerabilities is called a *threat*.

A clear understanding of the concept "risk" is necessary to establish a common frame of reference for further discussions in this paper. For the purpose of this paper, a risk is viewed as:

- the adverse effect if a threat is realised
- the adverse effect if vulnerability is exploited

Viewing a risk with the use of these dual, but parallel, concepts enhances the comprehension of the concept, which is essential for the effective modelling of the risks within a computing facility.

By using the above concept of a risk, risk analysis can be viewed as a systematic examination of:

- all the possible vulnerabilities and the probability that these vulnerabilities will be exploited
- all the possible threats and the likelihood that these threats will be realised

This view of the risk analysis process will now be used to describe a framework for a systematic analysis of computer related risks.

The risk analysis process has three main input values - assets, threats, and vulnerabilities.

Assets

Assets include hardware (computers, memory devices, peripheral equipment), software (operating systems, application programs), data, networks (transmitting equipment and media), and personnel (operators, users, managers). From a risk viewpoint, the assets within a computing environment are interrelated. A vulnerability can affect more than one asset or cause more than one type of loss.

Threats

Threats to all types of assets include people (who may intentionally damage assets), natural events (such as earthquakes, floods, and tornadoes), and accidents (such as fire, burst water pipes, and human mistakes).

Vulnerabilities

Vulnerabilities are physical (unprotected entrances, unreliable environmental control, unreliable power, and weak fire protection). Personnel vulnerabilities are those that can be caused by personnel (mistakes, fraud, theft, blackmail, bribery), and those that can happen to the personnel (injury, death). Hardware vulnerabilities include environmental effects on hardware, failures, and design mistakes. Software has also some vulnerabilities because of the storage media used, and because of unreliability or poor design. Network vulnerabilities include physical and hardware vulnerabilities, as well as insufficient protection against tapping, eavesdropping, and other forms of interception.

The output of the risk analysis process is a set of recommended countermeasures. These countermeasures should be as specific as possible.

As the risk analysis procedure is a creative, intuitive and systematic process, the tools that are used to model this process must likewise be flexible, to be able to reflect the real-world scenario as truly and effectively as possible. Risk analysis often relies heavily on producing numbers, and does not rely sufficiently on human analysis and a common sense to interpret the results. The model must place a minimal hindrance on the intuitive, common sense and creative spirit necessary for the risk analysis process.

As it is not possible to establish the correctness of a risk analysis procedure, it is necessary to ensure that the model is as understandable and comprehensible as possible. Risk analysis should not be a black box system which "magically" provides answers that are to be trusted. It is necessary for the user to be able to intuitively follow the modelling and reasoning the process of the risk analysis, and in this way to verify the correct functioning of the model.

The proposed risk analysis methodology internally contains two models (see Fig. 1). The first one is a knowledge based *behaviour model*. This model is fixed (it does not change in the risk analysis process) and it is based on a *reality knowledge base*. This model describes relations among assets, threats, vulnerabilities, and countermeasures. The second model is a *system model*. This model is system-dependent and it is based on a *system knowledge base*. It is created in the first phase of the risk analysis process. This model describes the structure of the analysed system and the interdependencies among the assets in the system.

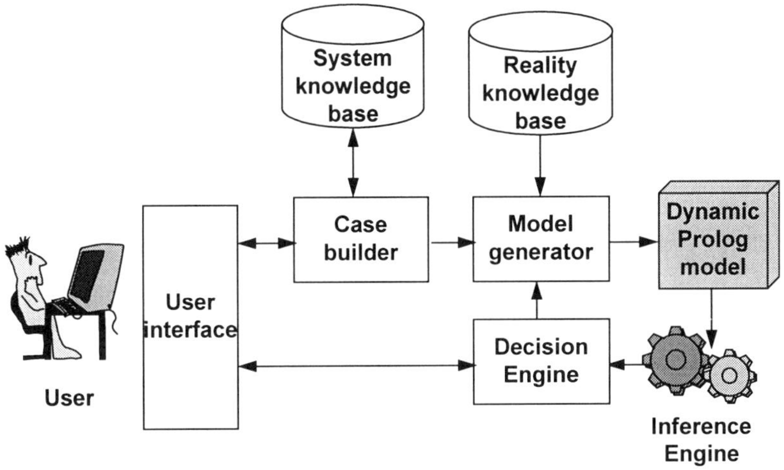

Figure 1. The structure of the risk analysis system

Most of the above factors are difficult to be quantified and they are usually expressed using vague estimates. The probability of occurrence of threat is not a single value that could be determined with an absolute certainty, but it can be expressed in terms as „low", „middle", „high", or „unknown". This uncertainty can be modelled in fuzzy logic with the use of fuzzy sets.

2 Design of risk analysis model

Because of the complexity of the problem being solved and due to the incompleteness of the input information, we have decided to build a methodology of risk analysis as an integration of a number of different methods and tools. The basic part of the system is an object-oriented environment of the programming language C++. In this environment, the simulation library SIMLIB/C++ is implemented. The SIMLIB library contains tools for different kinds of system description, including fuzzy logic description.

In a heterogeneous simulation system, we need a fuzzy description each time we do not know an exact description of the model, or we need a simple (fast, but less accurate) solution of the problem.

In SIMLIB/C++, the fuzzy part of the model needs suitable interfaces. The developed fuzzy block has continuous/fuzzy input and output, it can be used as any other continuous block.

The fuzzy representation of a model encapsulated in a fuzzy block should implement the following operations: optional fuzzification of inputs, application of fuzzy operators and implication methods for all the fuzzy rules given, aggregation of outputs from all the rules, and optional defuzzification of outputs. This process is shown in Figure 2 together with the types of the processed data.

- **Fuzzification** is the conversion from a continuous input value (real number) to a fuzzy set value. We use *membership functions* to determine the degree of membership for a given numerical value.
- **If-then rules** are defined by the user in the general form

  if (antecedent) consequent

These rules allow computing outputs as the consequence of a user-defined antecedent. The problem here is the partial degree of membership of the antecedent, which should be applied to the consequent with the given weight of the rule. This process is called an *implication.*

Both the antecedent and consequent can have multiple parts. In the antecedent, we can use fuzzy && (AND), || (OR), and ! (NOT) operators. The method of computing the result of an AND operator is usually the minimum of both operands (which are numbers), the OR operator uses a maximum of the operand values, and NOT operator computes *1-x*. There are other algorithms to be used for the fuzzy operator evaluation, too.

- **Aggregation** is the method used for evaluating a single output value (for each output variable) from partial outputs of many if-then rules in the description of a fuzzy block. The output value is computed using one of the suitable algorithms (maximum, sum).
- **Defuzzification** is used for conversion from a fuzzy set to a single numerical value. There are many applicable methods, where most often the method of *centroid* is used. Other possible methods are for example: *bisector, middle of max, largest max, smallest max.*

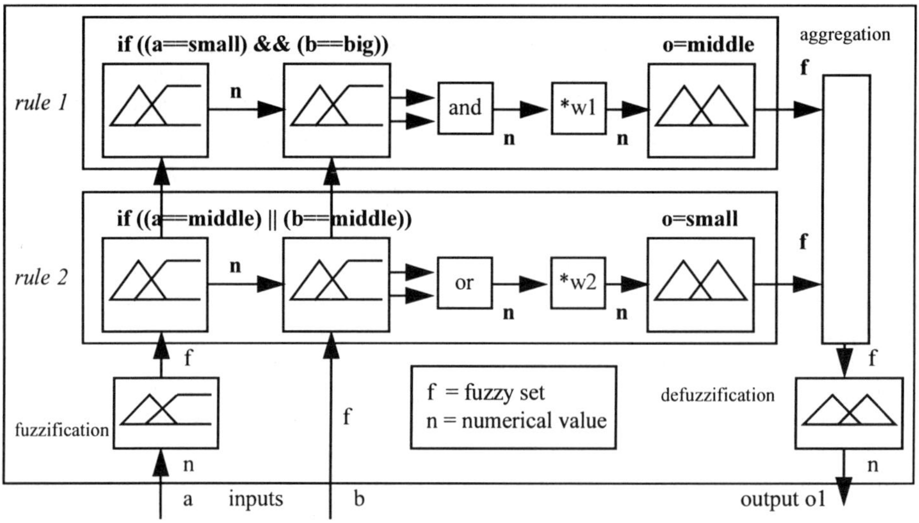

Figure 2. Fuzzy inference diagram

3 Implementation

We use the C++ language for the fuzzy inference system implementation. This language allows the use of encapsulation, polymorphism, and operator overloading.

Fuzzy set

The class *FuzzySet* implements the description of a fuzzy set value. It contains a reference to a set of membership functions and the associated values in the range <0,1>. Each fuzzy set contains a range of possible numerical values, which can be fuzzified to this fuzzy set.

Fuzzy set membership functions are defined as subclasses of the abstract base class *FuzzyMembershipFunction*. The user can add any kind of membership functions by inheriting this class and defining a suitable methods.

The correct value of a fuzzy set can be created by the fuzzification method or by an assignment. Each membership value can be obtained using operator [].

The class *FuzzyOutput* is defined for a fuzzy output specification. This class has a method for defuzzification and some special behaviour used by the aggregation phase of the fuzzy inference, but other characteristics are inherited from *FuzzySet*.

Fuzzification and Defuzzification

Fuzzification is a method of a fuzzy set. It assigns a new value to a fuzzy set object. If the input value does not fall into the range of possible values, an error is reported.

Defuzzification is implemented as a method of class *FuzzyOutput*. It computes the numerical value of the output. Various defuzzification methods can be used.

Inference rules

The inference rules implementation uses operator overloading. The operator == computes the degree of membership and the operators && (AND), || (OR),! (NOT) allow for rule combinations. All those operators return the object of the class *FuzzyValue*, which represents real number.

We use *FuzzyValue::operator bool* for some actions at the end of the *if-condition* evaluation. Those actions include storing of the condition result in a special variable used later by the operator = and setting the rule weight to 1.0. In the statement after *if(condition)*, we can use the function *weight* to change the weight of the rule. The operator = should be used for an output value specification.

The next examples show the use of overloaded operators:

```
if(in=="small") weight(0.9), out="big";
if(in=="big" || in == "medium") out="small", o2="zero";
if(in=="big" || in == "medium") { out="small"; o2="zero"; }
```

where *in* is a fuzzy input variable, *out* and *o2* are fuzzy output variables, *"small"*, *"big"*, *"medium"* are fuzzy values, which can be members of fuzzy set *in*.

The rules are evaluated in the given order, results are stored to the output variables *out*, *o2* and can be aggregated later. We can use any number of rules. As the output variables should be initialised before the execution of fuzzy rules, we defined the abstract class *FuzzyBlock* with the method *Evaluate*, which is suitable for a fuzzy rules definition. The evaluation of the block (performed automatically) ensures the initialisation, evaluation of inputs, fuzzification, inference of rules, aggregation, and defuzzification.

4 The structure of the knowledge base rules

The expert system used will allow easy orientation in the large amount of information and will compare the results of simulation experiments with similar cases and their consequences that are stored in the knowledge base. The expert system creates new questionnaires with questions for gathering input data for new simulation runs.

The behaviour model knowledge base contains the following types of knowledge:

1. Relevancy of an impact/threat, vulnerability and countermeasure to the asset type, such as:
   `"An impact I applies to the asset type A."`

2. A relation between an impact/threat and the vulnerability, e.g.:
   `"A threat T exploits the vulnerability V with factor x."`
3. A relation between a countermeasure and vulnerability, e.g.:
   `"A countermeasure C minimises the vulnerability V by factor x."`
4. A relation between a countermeasure and impact/threat, e.g.:
   `"A countermeasure C minimises the probability of threat T by factor x."`

These rules have to be expressed in the fuzzy logic notation. The rules of type 1 are exact logic rules that can be expressed in the conventional logic and they do not need the use of fuzzy logic. The rules of type 2, 3, and 4 need the fuzzy logic to be used. Now we will show some examples of fuzzy logic rules:

`"If Quality_of_password_management is low then Probability_of_user_masquerade is high."` (type 2 rule)
`"If Authentication_calculators_are_used then Probability_of_user_masquerade is low."` (type 3 rule)

5 Conclusion

The design of the described system for the risk analysis of information systems is based on extensive experience of the authors in this area. The experience includes classical modelling, building knowledge based models, and information system security.

Although the areas of simulation of systems and knowledge-based methods were developed separately, we can find a lot of similarities and common principles in both of these scientific areas. These similarities show close methodological relations between these areas and the techniques and tools used.

The SIMLIB library used for an implementation of a fuzzy logic inference engine was previously tested with other applications. This simulation library is not only limited to the fuzzy logic operations, but supports a wide variety of other simulation primitives that can be used for modelling other aspects of target system as well.

Acknowledgements

This work was supported by the research intention No. CEZ:J22/98: 262200012 - „Research in Information and Control Systems" and by the Grant Agency of Czech Republic grant No. 102/98/0552 " Research and Application of Heterogeneous Models".

References

[1] Courtney, R.: Security risk assessment in electronic data processing, AFIPS Conference Proceedings of the National Computer Conference, AFIPS, Arlington, Va., 97-104

[2] Zadeh, L.A.: Fuzzy Logic, Computer, Vol 1, No. 4, 1988

[3] Hanáček P.: Information System Security Models, XVI. Moravo-Silesian International Colloquium "Selected Problems of Simulation Models", CSS, SCS, EUROSIM, Brno 6.-8.9. 1994, pp. 35-39

[4] Hanáček, P., Rábová, Z.: Processing of Input Data for Risk Analysis, In: Proceedings of Conference ASIS'97, MARQ, Krnov, 1997, s. 91-96, ISBN 80-85988-17-8

[5] Hanáček, P., Rábová, Z.: Knowledge-Based Simulation in Risk Analysis, In: Proceedings of ASIS 1998, MARQ, Krnov, 1998, s. 79-84, ISBN 80-85988-26-7

[6] Jenkins, B.: Security risk analysis and management, Norman Data Defense Systems, Inc., 1995

[7] Ru, W.G., Eloff J.H.P.: Risk analysis modelling with the use of fuzzy logic, Computer & Security, Vol. 15, No. 3, pp. 239-248

Knowledge-Based Software Engineering
T. Hruška and M. Hashimoto (Eds.)
IOS Press, 2000

Support System for Distributed Collaborative 3-D Graphics Design

Takehiko TANAKA, Kenji FUKIMBARA, Junko KAWASAKI,
Shikari MATSUMOTO, Makoto MATSUSHITA, Masaru NAKAGAWA
Faculty of Systems Engineering, Wakayama University
930 Sakaedani, Wakayama 640-8510, Japan

Abstract. We have been developing a support system which realizes collaborative designs of 3-D computer graphics through a computer network. When a collaborator sends a 3-D graphic, a 2-D image or a plain text to the server, the other collaborators will correctly obtain it without being aware of concurrency. By using this function, the collaborators can hold unfinished or finished graphics data in common. Using the Web mechanism, users can store the database server with the design products to retrieve and reuse them subsequently. This system helps design request persons and designers who works at distant places to produce, review and modify 3-D graphics with their creative ideas.

1 Introduction

To develop the timely goods accepted by consumers, the design environment is required which can reduce a design period and makes use of designers' creative ideas. The computer network can be a hopeful environment. Therefore, we are aiming at the realization of the support system with which design request persons and designers in the remote places cooperate on the design of the 3-D graphic, using their own computers and a computer network. In this system called the *network collaboration system*, the finished or unfinished design data are communicated through the computer network (the Internet or the intranet). Each user can watch the image of the same content at the same time in the remote place. Since the graphic data are stored in each user's local computer, every user can see the image in their own points of view. Moreover a user may modify the graphic data, which can be distributed to the other users at his or her choice. According to the classification in [1], our system is concerned with a real time, different place CSCW (Computer Supported Cooperative Work).

There have been proposed various network collaboration systems, say [2, 3, 4]. In our understanding, most systems have provided the users with small size data, such as numerical values and characters. Even if a network collaboration system has a graphical user interface, users' client computers receive message composed of numerical values and characters to indicate the information graphically. Still, the advance of network technologies in recent years enables us to send or receive large size data instantaneously. We conjecture that it is possible to actualize a practical network collaboration system for communicating image files.

Through the development of the system, we attempts to solve several problems of network collaboration. Firstly, consistency of the data is maintained by the project server bound to the project. Furthermore, since the project manager takes charge of the user authentication, each user need not pay attention to his or her project. Secondly, to distribute the modified data to other users successfully, the distribution right is introduced. Lastly, for the users who has

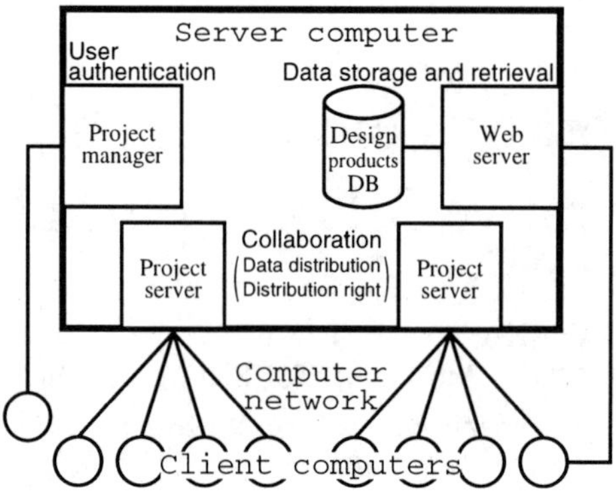

Figure 1: System Architecture

little skill in manipulating 3-D grapchic, the communication using 2-D images and text is available.

Users employ the existing softwares to view and modify 3-D graphics or 2-D images and to communicate with the other users, while we provide several application programs of user authentication, collaboration, and data registration and retrieval.

2 The System

Figure 1 shows the overview of the system. The server computer runs several project servers and one project manager. The client computers are connected by the star configuration in which the center is the project server.

The functions of this system are partitioned into (1) user authentication, (2) data distribution, (3) granting the distribution right and (4) data storage and retrieval. The details are described in Sections 2.1 to 2.4, respectively.

2.1 User Authentication

Our system carries out the user authentication for two purposes. One is the user authentication in a usual sense, that is, to judge from the user's inputs whether he or she is qualified for this system. The other is to determine the *project* in which the user participates. Our system solves the problem of project management by preparing as many *project servers* as projects, and one *project manager* which starts and stops every project manager. Each project server takes charge of a collaboration, and its details are described in the following two sections. On the other hand, the project manager takes charge of the user authentication. Specifically, the job of the project manager is to receive a user name and a password from a client computer, determine the project by the inputs (if they are wrong ones, then the project manager returns a error message to the client computer.), and return to the client computer a message called *ticket*, which includes the project name and the port ID of the corresponding project server. In carrying out this job, the project manager refers to two lists. One is called the *user list*, each line of which consists of a user name, a password, and the name of the project in which the user participates. The other is the *project list* and each line consists of a project name and a port ID.

One of the benefits of this method is that each user has only to remember his or her user name and a password. To the contrary, the project name and the way of connecting with the project server are the information that client computers and the server computer, not users, should know.

2.2 Data Distribution

The project server and the client computers connecting with it hold a 3-D graphic, a 2-D image and a design concept by text in common. We adopt Shade as the 3-D graphic viewing and processing software, since the file generated in the standard format of Shade contains all the data (outline data, texture images, etc.) to express a 3-D graphic, which makes our system simple with regard to the distribution of graphic data. The 2-D image is intended for a visual communication; for example, a design request person generates the 2-D image by looking at the 3-D graphic from a point of view, marks it up and sends it to the other collaborators. Additionally users make use of Internet Relay Chat (IRC) to communicate with other participants by text.

We must pay attention to the way of holding the data in common. In our system, each user decides whether the modified data are distributed. Actually, our system provides an "send" button on each client program dealing with the data distribution. When a user pushes the send button after specifying a file (a 3-D graphic, a 2-D image or a design concept), the data is distributed via the project server. Each client computer except the sender receives the file and stores it. If it is a 3-D graphic or a 2-D image, then the client computer executes 3-D or 2-D viewing and processing softwares to open the file. Otherwise, since the transmitted information is a design concept, the client computer replace the design concept with the latest one.

After a distribution is finished, the project server delivers a *renewal notice* to every client computers. Each client computer receives the notice and indicates it on a window called *renewal notice window* to inform the user.

2.3 Granting Distribution Right

As for the data distribution, nevertheless, a naive implement would cause a trouble. That is, if two users modified the graphic separately and pushed their buttons at the same time, then the data of either user would be lost. We solve the problem of such concurrency by the *distribution right*. The rules of the occurrence and the lapse of the distribution right are as follows.

Rule 1. The client computer which has just joined in a collaboration does not hold the distribution right, even if there exists no participant until then.

Rule 2. When a client computer send a request of the right to the project server, it holds the right while the client computer with the right (if exists) lapses it.

Rule 3. When the client computer which holds the distribution right leaves the collaboration, the right disappears.

Rule 4. When a client computer which does not hold the distribution right leaves the collaboration, there is no change of the possession of the right.

It follows from these rules that any client computer can hold the distribution right, but that no more than one client computer holds the right at any time.

2.4 Data Storage and Retrieval

Users can store the database server running in the server computer with the finished or unfinished data to retrieve and reuse them subsequently. In our system, the mechanism of the data storage and retrieval is constructed with a Web server and CGI.

In the data storage, the user specifies keywords for retrieval together with the file. When the user pushes the submit button, the client computer sends the file and the keywords to the Web server with the mechanism of CGI. The Web server stores the received data in the server computer.

The stored data are maintained with a text file called the *registration file*. Each line of the file represents a record of a piece of registered information. The line contains the location of the data file, keywords for retrieval, a timestamp and the project name. Note that the type of information is obtained by the extension of the file name. The timestamp is generated by the Web server. Since the project name is sent from the client computer through the "cookie" mechanism, users can register the data as the products of their project without inputting the project name.

To search and retrieve data in the database server, the user inputs keywords in the Web page for search. By means of the output, he or she can obtain a file. Since the search program is described by Perl, the input permits a expression (e.g. a regular expression) available to Perl. In other words, a user who little knows Perl may input a few words for search, while a user who is acquainted with Perl can specify the keyword using a Perl expression. With the cookie mechanism again, the output are limited to the items registered as the products of the project to which the searcher belongs.

3 Conclusions

We have described the support system which enables the users to produce 3-D graphics in a collaborative way using a computer network. Our system deals with a 3-D graphic, a 2-D image and a plain text. We consider that these types of data are indispensable for the collaborative 3-D graphic design. Furthermore, if these data can be communicated satisfactorily, then it will not be hard to improve the system to deal with other types of data. In this system several useful softwares are used, while we have implemented functions necessary for the collaboration.

A preliminary experiment in the authors' laboratory shows that 3-D graphics of about 100 kilobytes can be distributed before the users feel stress. From now on, we intend to improve the system through plenty of experiments. For example, distribution time will be reduced when the difference of data instead of the data themselves are transmitted. It is under study to add the function to the system so that the users can specify the types of data required in the collaboration of their project.

References

[1] Pfeifer, J., Koo, K. and Yin, P: "Electronic Meetings - CSCW & GDSS", `http://ksi.cpsc.ucalgary.ca/courses/547-95/yin/groupware.html`

[2] Li, D. and Muntz, R.: "COCA: Collaborative Objects Coordination Architecture", Proceedings of ACM CSCW'98, November 1998.

[3] Takeda, H., Takaai, M. and Nishida, T.: Collaborative Development and Use of Ontologies for Design", Proceedings of IFIP International Conference PROLAMAT'98, September 1998.

[4] Teege, G. and Koch, M.: "Integrating Access and Collaboration for Multimedia Applications", Proceedings of the East-west International Conference MHVR'94, 1994.

Knowledge-Based Software Engineering
T. Hruška and M. Hashimoto (Eds.)
IOS Press, 2000

Knowledge Sharing for Web Information Retrieval

Kenji MATSUNAGA
Senshu University, 2-1-1 Higashi-mita, Kawasaki, Kanagawa, 214-8580, Japan
E-mail: matunaga@isc.senshu-u.ac.jp

Abstract. In order to support novice Web searchers that feel difficult to find the meaningful information from huge Web information space, we have developed the tools that share the searching knowledge among the members of a group. The knowledge consists of two databases. One includes a list of directory/word-searching services with usefulness score for a specific topic. The other includes users' recommendations. These databases are modified while users engage in the searching activity. Depending on a user's profile and interests, the tool can support a user to find the meaningful Web pages.

1 Introduction

As the number of Web pages is increased, it becomes more difficult to retrieve the meaningful information on the Internet. We usually use directory services and word-searching services to overcome the difficulties. Some people can efficiently find the information with these services. On the other hand some people waste time to obtain the information. Formers have the knowledge to search them efficiently. A novice searcher will improve his ability by sharing the searching knowledge the experts have. Since 1997 we have developed software tools to share such knowledge among the members of a group [1, 2]. This paper describes which knowledge human expert searchers have. Then it shows what items the knowledge database of the tools should include and how it should give/take him the meaningful information by using the tools.

2 Human searching on the WWW

Skillful searchers can find some of the meaningful information by using directory/word-searching services. We observed their searching behavior and then noticed the below process. (1) They remember some of effective directory services for particular subject. (2) When they don't know useful directories they try to find a useful directory first. (3) If they know a person who knows a lot of useful Web pages, they ask him. (4) After they find a few useful Web pages, they try to extract some keywords from the pages and then use word-searching services with the keywords in order to find related pages.

(1), (2) and (3) are the activities to find the high-level information for searching the required information. Two types of knowledge are necessary for the above activities.

- Meta-information. For example, which directory service is the best for a specific topic?
- Searching process. When we use those services?

It is clear that the difference of the skillful searchers and novices is related to how much these knowledge they have.

3 Our Earlier Works

CBA (Case-Based Assistance of web information retrieval) [1] is a tool that has knowledge on meta-information to find useful information for a certain subject. For each subject, meta-information consists of a set of links to directory/word-searching service, returned page format description and usefulness score of the service. A user selects a subject first. Then he types a keyword related to what he would find. CBA passes the keyword to the directory/word-searching service with the highest score and shows him the returned results on the screen. If he does not satisfy the results, CBA does in the same way to the second highest service. When he obtains the meaningful Web pages from the service, CBA increases the usefulness score of the service. When a database manager needs to create knowledge base for a new subject, he copies a related subject and may add new meta-information and changes usefulness scores.

SKI (Sharing Knowledge of web Information) [2] is a tool that shares recommendation about Web pages among a certain group. SKI has message boards to which users can write recommending Web pages for a certain subject. SKI separately shows the fact (URL, title, frequently appeared words etc.) and the comments of a page. When a user attempts to find the meaningful information for a subject, he selects the subject and finds a page that the fact and comments of the page look useful. He may write a new comment about the comment he refers to. He designates relation type between the new and referring comment (agree, disagree, annotation etc.). He votes whether the referring comment is useful. Other users can easily understand the page's usefulness from its relations and its score without reading comments in detail.

Two tools we developed have the common concept that they support information-retrieving activity by advising which information is useful. CBA is effective when a user will find the information that other users have never found because it shares meta-information. SKI shares the information that someone has found. Users can use the two tools complimentarily.

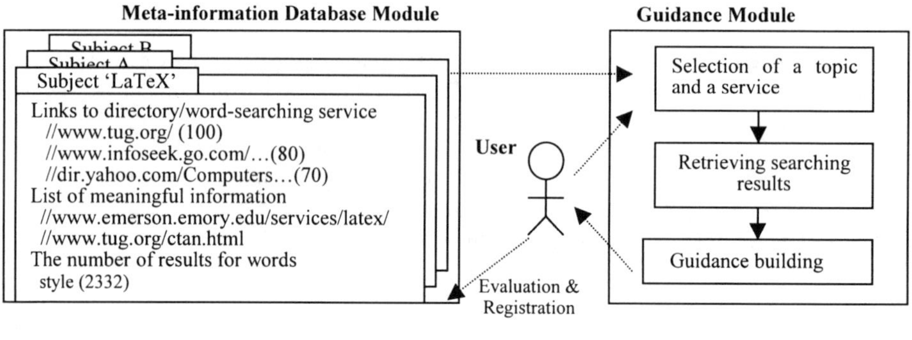

Figure 1. The model of CBA

4 Design of the Unified Tool

In this section, we describe the design of the new tool unifying CBA and SKI. After we review the tools with the users, we set the following objectives:

1. To decrease seams between the SKI module and the CBA module.
2. To prepare interface that prompts a user to write his comments.
3. To make a user get more quickly the meaningful information to him.

4.1 Seam

SKI is combined with CBA as one of meta-information since it shares information about Web pages that include concrete contents. CBA must know the value of each meta-information. The value of SKI is computed from the number of recommended links and comments about them.

4.2 Commenting Functions

A user is guided to write his comment on a Web page or other's comments. The users of SKI complained that it is time-consuming to write a comment. Since more comments make the tool valuable for other users, better interface to describe his comments must be prepared.

The earlier SKI implementation displays the window to describe a comment and then another window to designate its relation. The format of comments was free. We redesign SKI that it shows a user the relation window first and then comment windows. The format of comments window are decided from the designated relation type. If the relation is 'Agree', the following comments should be required:

- To whom the page is meaningful?
- What is his purpose when the page is meaningful for him?
- How should he use the page for it to become more meaningful?

If the relation is 'Related Recommendation', the user describes the URL of the recommending page and the same three kinds of comments for 'Agree'. If the relation is 'Disagree', the user should describe what he expects to get from the page.

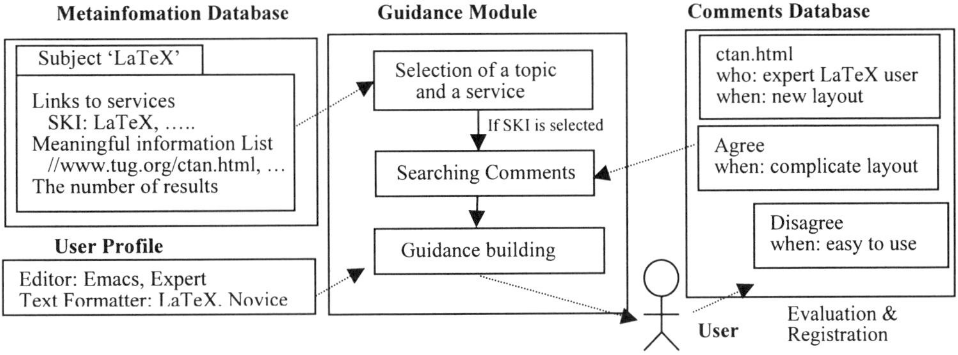

Figure 2. Model of the new system

4.3 Comment Viewing Functions

SKI should have better interface that user can easily search comments. We have introduced the following functions:

1. Comments grouping. If typical sequence of relation types is appeared (for example, 'Agree' relations are appeared in a row), those comments are gathered together. This function has been introduced in our developed asynchronous discussion system [3].
2. Searching from user's profile. The usefulness of the page depends on the user's profile. For example, when a user tries to find information on 'LaTeX', a page about 'LaTeX mode of Emacs' is meaningful only if he is an Emacs user. SKI searches registered comments that match with the user's profile.

5 Related works

Our system is one of recommender systems [4]. Most of those systems used content-based analysis and browsing-path based analysis [5]. These analysis methods may be valuable when the recommended pages are described about a special topic in detail. It is possible, however, to hide pages a user needs. We consider a searcher should determine whether a detailed page is useful. Our system supports him by sharing meta-information to find the useful information.

6 Conclusion

In this paper, we describe the tools that share Web searching knowledge within members of a group. They support a user to efficiently find the meaningful Web pages. Registered knowledge consists of the pages that are useful in order to find the necessary pages. It also includes usefulness score and recommended users. The user can view for Web pages fitting for him by using his profile. The tools are examined for several subjects within the laboratory members. The profile matching mechanism should be improved in order to expand the number of users.

References

[1] Matsunaga, K., Itabashi, N., Kaneko, I. and Torii, S.: Support System of World Wide Web Information Retrieval, T.R. Institute of Information Science, No. 49, Senshu University, Mar. 1999 (in Japanese).

[2] Abe, M. and Matsunaga, K.: SKI: Knowledge Sharing in Web Information among a Group, T.R. Institute of Information Science, No. 51, pp. 11-18, Senshu University, Mar. 2000 (in Japanese).

[3] Sugimoto, K. and Matsunaga, K.: An Asynchronous Discussion System using Statement Types, The 57th Annual Conference of Information Processing Society of Japan, Oct. 1998 (in Japanese).

[4] Resnick, P and Varian, H. R. Varian: Recommender Systems - Introduction to the Special Section. CACM, Vol. 40, No. 3(1997), pp. 56-58.

[5] Chalmers, M., Rodden, K. and Brodbeck D.: The Order of Things: Activity-centered Information Access, 7th International World Wide Web Conference, April 1998.

Knowledge-Based Software Engineering
T. Hruška and M. Hashimoto (Eds.)
IOS Press, 2000

A Discussion on Abstract Structure of Design Knowledge for Space Arrangement in Architectural Design

Masaaki HASHIMOTO[1], Takeshi MATSUOKA[1], Tomonori MIURA[1], Kiyomitsu GOTANJI[2], Toyohiko HIROTA[1]
Keiichi KATAMINE[1]

[1]Kyushu Inst. of Technology, [2]Gotanji Architect and Associate
[1]680-4 Kawazu, Iizuka, 820-8502 Japan

Abstract. This paper proposes an abstract structure of the design knowledge of space arrangement in architectural design, and discusses the abstract structure itself. By means of a prototype implementation of CAD system, we obtain the entire concrete knowledge which is proved by architects. Then, we extract an abstract structure which is mainly composed of space inclusion and connection associations by analyzing the knowledge. Then, we discuss the comprehensibility of the abstract structure.

1 Introduction

Software reliability and productivity is one of the main concerns in the development of the information society. Software reliability demands that the software requirements are precisely analyzed. Since the domain experts have exact knowledge of their domain in industry, it is desirable that they describe the requirement specifications of their systems by themselves. Therefore, we have been studying *domain-specific specification description languages* such as BDL (Building Design Language) which is comprehensible to the domain experts of the architectural structure design [1]. Moreover, for the sake of software productivity, system software should be automatically generated from the specification descriptions in the same manner to IBDS (Integrated Building Design System) [2].

In order to develop such a language, *an abstract structure* of the domain knowledge must be extracted. The abstract structure provides the semantics of the language. Therefore, we have been analyzing various actual domains mainly in the architecture industry, and have been studying the methodology of domain knowledge analysis. In the technique of analysis pattern, reusable concrete parts are cut off from object models. On the other hand, an abstract structure is extracted from object models by considering tacit knowledge of a domain.

This paper proposes an abstract structure of the domain knowledge of space arrangement in architectural design. Section 2 makes clear the requirements of abstract structure of industry knowledge. Section 3 describes a prototype system. Section 4 proposes the abstract structure. Section 5 discusses it.

2 Requirements of Abstract Structure

Industry knowledge can be classified into well-defined explicit knowledge, ill-defined explicit knowledge and tacit knowledge. The first is expressed formally using such tools as formal methods, arithmetic expressions, diagrams, and charts, all of which can be processed using computers. The second cannot be described without natural languages. This knowledge is difficult for computers to adequately implement. The above-mentioned explicit knowledge can be described in documents such as specifications, manuals, drawings, and tables. On the other hand, the third cannot be expressed in documents. This knowledge is obtained via training such as OJT (On the Job Training), and remains within the minds of domain experts.

Abstract structures should satisfy the following four requirements: Firstly, abstract structures have been being studied in order to provide a semantics of language which can describe industry knowledge and which is comprehensible to domain experts. Since domain experts are not information engineers, abstract structures should be simple to comprehend. Secondly, tacit knowledge is more basic and greater in scope than explicit knowledge in the minds of domain experts. With explicit knowledge highly dependent on the former, the thinking of domain experts is controlled by tacit knowledge. Therefore, abstract structures should depend on tacit knowledge. Thirdly, the computer implementation of ill-defined knowledge will become an important focus in the near future development of sophisticated information systems. Therefore, abstract structures should make ill-defined knowledge well-definable. Lastly, average staff members must be able to apply, maintain, and inherit the knowledge in industry. Therefore, abstract structure should make the entire knowledge of a domain comprehensible to average staff members.

3 Prototype Implementation

We have implemented a prototype system for supporting space arrangement design with the aid of domain knowledge provided by an architect on our research team. Almost all CAD systems start an architectural design with a drawing called a floor plan. The drawing shapes the rooms by dividing the floor with the walls. However, architects draw *a bubble chart* prior to the floor plan. In the chart, a bubble corresponds to a room. A line connecting two bubbles shows transition of persons between the rooms. The bubble chart is more basic than the floor plan.

Therefore, our CAD system has adopted the bubble chart. Moreover, our bubble chart has adopted an important concept of zone. A zone including some rooms is a space within which persons participating in the same activity such as library users or staff members.

In order to specify the transitions between rooms more precisely, our CAD system has adopted *the work flow diagram*. In the work flow diagram, time flows from the upper to lower side. The vertical regions correspond to rooms. In the regions, a vertical rectangular box specifies an activity. A horizontal line connecting two activities in different rooms determines a transition event. Of course, the transitions are automatically transferred to the bubble chart.

We have implemented the CAD system using the constraint-relieved version of the above-mentioned BDL. The system has been completed with 1,000 BDL description lines and 1,800 BDL procedure description lines. An object model specifying the BDL description has been made. An abstract structure is extracted mainly from the model.

4 Abstract Structure

In the space arrangement domain of architectural design, an abstract structure of the domain knowledge is proposed for further discussion. The abstract structure is obtained by restricting the object model and by imposing constraints on it as follows:

4.1 Object Class

Many object-oriented technologies such as OMT (Object Modeling Technique) use object classes as their conceptual frameworks. This approach is also useful for framing concepts in the domain of space arrangement design.

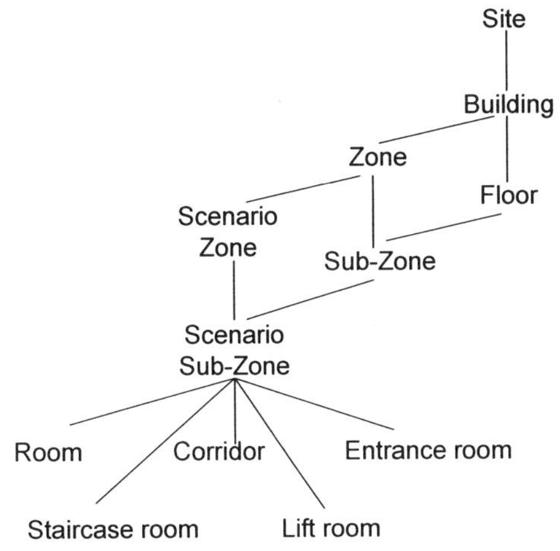

Figure 1 Space inclusion association.

Space is one of the main concepts in space arrangement design. Space is a super class of such classes as room, zone, floor, corridor, site, and road. These classes can have implied meaning as spaces by hiding the definition of super class "space" as language semantics. This implication is familiar to architects.

In the domain of space arrangement design, architects grasp various important concepts in terms of space. Each of the physical spaces, such as room, corridor, staircase room, lift room, entrance room, lobby, floor, and building, corresponds to a component in building structure.

Architects also grasp the following high level spaces: *a zone* including some rooms, corridor, and so on is a space within which objects of the same kind usually move about. For example, users and staffs usually move about within user and staff zones, respectively. A zone within which one of its typical occupants moves about for his/her purpose is called *a scenario zone*. A zone can be divided into *sub-zones* for arranging them on different floors.

4.2 Association

The definition of associations is an important aspect of making the entire knowledge of a domain comprehensible, since the structure is made of associations that link all classes. Therefore, the abstract structure is mainly provided by the definition of associations. The knowledge of space arrangement design uses the following associations:

Space inclusion is an association between a space and other spaces contained in it. A typical example of this association is shown in Figure 1. The association is binary and one-way. It is a "one to many" relation. Moreover, It is transitive. Suppose that space "a" includes space "b", and space "b" includes space "c". Then, "a" includes "c". The one-way, binary, and transitive feature denotes a hierarchy. Therefore, the association is comprehensible. The implied meaning of the association is that the spaces included in the same space are arranged near each other.

The association can have the attribute of specifying whether the spaces included in the same space overlap or not. If the spaces have no overlap, the area of a space is obtained by summing up the area of spaces included in it.

Class "building" has two kinds of association: the inclusion of zones and floors, respectively, as shown in Figure 1. For distinguishing both the kinds from each other, different role names must be specified in the association.

Space connection is an association between two spaces in the same level of the above-mentioned hierarchical association of space inclusion. The space connection specifies that two associated spaces have a certain relationship to each other. The detail content of the relationship is specified in terms of its attributes such as transition of persons or things, visibility, audibility, and so on. The detailed content of the transition can indicate a direction from one space to another. Therefore, two different role names must be specified in the association.

4.3 Constraint

The following constraints can be imposed on the above-mentioned classes and their attributes and associations:

Object existence dependency of an association specifies that the existence of an object depends on another object and that object's attributes. "Space inclusion" association described in the previous subsection has natively the existence dependency in which a space depends on its including spaces. Of course, object existence dependency can be arbitrarily specified in a "space connection" association.

Link existence dependency of an association determines that the existence of a link between two associated objects depends on the attributes of both the objects. The dependency can be arbitrarily specified in an association.

Attribute dependency determines that the value of an attribute of an object depends on the values of the object's other attributes and its associated objects. The dependency can be arbitrarily specified in an object class or association.

5 Discussion and Conclusion

This paper has proposed an abstract structure. It is discussed in the following: Architects think of space arrangement design mainly in terms of the concepts of space, space inclusion association and space connection association. Therefore, the abstract structure depends highly on the tacit knowledge of architects. Hierarchical structure is one of the main modes of understanding large complicated bodies of knowledge. Abstract structure demonstrates hierarchy by means of the space inclusion association. It is also significant in the sense of hierarchical structure that the space connection association and the hierarchical space inclusion association are interrelated as follows: The space connection links which concretely show the transition of the same object, such as a user or staff, are enclosed within a zone. Conversely, the links determine the zone.

Using the abstract structure as a semantic system, a language for describing the knowledge of space arrangement design will be designed and implemented. Moreover, our prototype system will be re-written using the new language. Further enhancement of space arrangement CAD systems will then be implemented by architects themselves.

References

[1] T. Hirota, M. Hashimoto and I. Nagasawa, A Discussion on Conceptual Model Description Language Specific for an Application Domain (in Japanese), *Trans. IPS Japan,* **36(5)** (1995) 1151-1162.

[2] E. Lukman, M. Hashimoto, K. Katamine and T. Hirota, A Reference Model of CAD System Generation from Various Object Model-Based Specification Description Languages Specific to Individual Domains, *IEICE Trans, Inf. & Syst.*, **E83-D(4)**(2000) 713-721.

Knowledge-Based Software Engineering
T. Hruška and M. Hashimoto (Eds.)
IOS Press, 2000

The Design and Application of the KODAMA System

Guoqiang ZHONG, Tsunenori MINE, Tarek HELMY, Makoto AMAMIYA

Dept. of Intelligent Systems, Kyushu University
6-1 Kasuga-Koen, Kasuga, Fukuoka 816-8580, Japan

Abstract. In this paper, both the design and application of a new multiagent system called KODAMA (Kyushu university Open & Distributed Autonomous Multi-Agent) are presented. We consider our research on KODAMA as an endeavour to advance both the *science* and *engineering* of the well-known multiagent technology. The key aspects of KODAMA are decided as: distributed, autonomous, cooperative, scalable and secure. Furthermore, KODAMA agents are different from their precedents because they are designed as fine-grain and plug-and-play agents. So far, we have devoted a lot of efforts to designing an agent architecture, an agent domain structure, as well as developing an "Agent Communication Zone" (ACZ) to facilitate agent communication. We ensure KODAMA's promising abilities to build the Internet applications through the experience of developing a distributed database retrieval application.

1 Introduction

With the explosion of the Internet, the surged challenge is the next evolutionary technology for the Internet-oriented applications. KODAMA (Kyushu university Open & Distributed Autonomous Multi-Agent) system is developed for this demand. In particular, KODAMA agents can interconnect disparate and distributed agents together to solve some problems whose solutions are typically beyond any singular agent's capabilities [6]. Therefore, from the beginning of this project, we have noted that:

- both agents and data may reside on anywhere over the network,
- agents should percept their environment by themselves,
- agents should make decision by themselves,
- each agent is designed to fulfil a limited, specific task,
- agents need to coordinate their actions with each other,
- interactions among agents can not be foreseen at design time [1],
- individual agents would be developed, and then added into or removed from the agent community in a free manner.

To meet all these requirements, our major efforts have been devoted to three fields: designing an agent architecture, defining an agent domain structure, and developing a new application-independent middle-tier for agent communication. The main aim of this paper is to introduce our researches on these areas and evaluate KODAMA by a practical distributed database-retrieval application.

2 Agent Architecture of KODAMA

Figure 1 provides a general description of the KODAMA agent architecture. Basically, a KODAMA agent is constituted by a *Kernel Unit* and an *Application Unit*. This highly modular structure separates application-level issues from agent-level issues. The latter, referred to as a *Kernel* of agent, only encapsulates a few modules. And each of them is necessary and common to all agents.

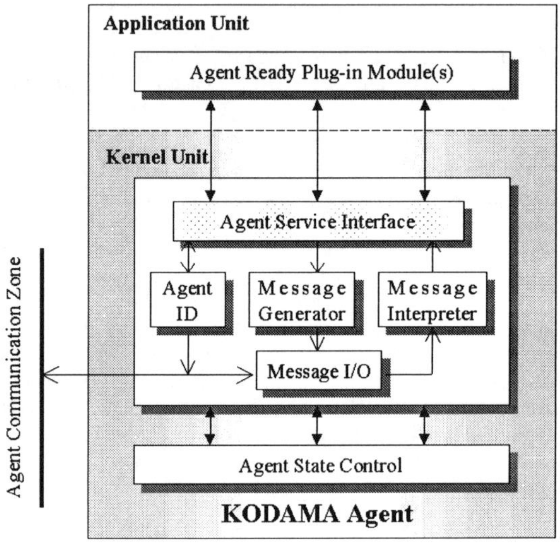

Figure 1. The Agent Architecture of KODAMA

- *Agent State Control*: One of the characteristics that distinguish agents from other software pieces is that agents have control over their internal state. An agent, for example, can move to another new place by itself.
- *Agent ID*: A unique identification of the agent.
- *Message I/O*: It is only a simple message I/O because we move the major functions of agent communication to the *Agent Communication Zone* (ACZ in short), which is fully described in Section 4.
- *Message Interpreter & Generator*: Since KODAMA emphasizes ACL (Agent Communication Language) communication, both the message interpreter and generator are indispensable functions. Otherwise, it is impossible for agents to understand with each other.
- *Agent Service Interface*: It is a standardized interface, which defines the interaction between the kernel unit and application unit. With the help of this interface, any application-oriented module can be removed, upgraded, or replaced without rewriting the kernel unit.

Meanwhile, the *application unit* encapsulates the application-oriented functions. One of the goals of its design is scalability. That is, the application unit can be easily set up by installing one or several relevant components from a pool of general components. This set of components is extendable, that is, new components can be created and used if they are following the common *Agent Service Interface*. In this sense, they are called as *Agent Ready Plug-in Modules*, or simply *Plug-in Modules*.

With this clearly defined agent architecture, we can easily facilitate the reuse of code and enlarge the system's capabilities by developing new plug-in modules. It is worth noting that both kernel unit and application unit are lightweight, so that KODAMA agents can be developed with impressive flexibility.

3 Agent Domain Structure of KODAMA

As a distributed and autonomous multiagent system designed for the Internet applications, KODAMA agents are required to be suitable for a full "open" environment where both agents and data are distributed and dynamic [2]. In order to make it more efficient and easier for agents to communicate with each other, all agents in KODAMA are organized by a hierarchical, domain-based structure, called Kodama Agent Domain System (KADS). Conceptually, the agent community is divided into a number of top-level agent domains, where each one may cover many distributed agents or sub-domains. As Figure 2 shows, all these can be represented as a tree. Each domain is extended from top-level domains directly or indirectly, and named by the path upward from it to the unnamed root. For agents, they are categorized to various agent domains based on their own facilities. For agent domains, they consist of a number of agents with close relationships. In particular, those agents are in charge of a certain kind of task, and tend to talk with agents within local domain more often than other outside agents. Agents can, however, belong to two or more different domains if they can do different jobs.

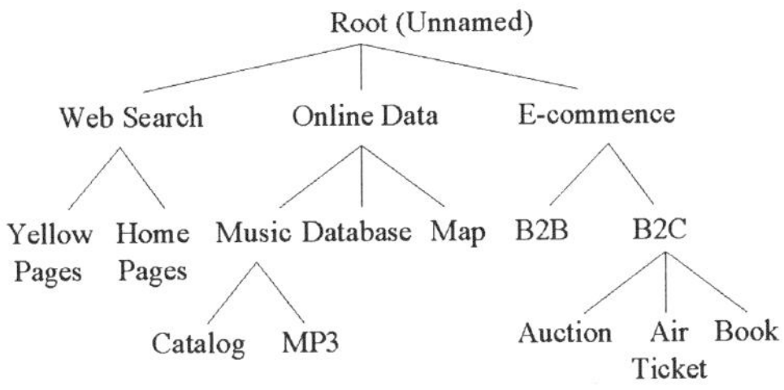

Figure 2. DNS-like Structure of KODMA Agent Domain System

In principle, each agent domain has full control over how it allocates the agents and sub-domain(s) under it without getting centralized permission. For example, if the B2B agent domain wants to be known as *B2B.E-commence*, it only needs permission from *E-commence* domain. Thus, the entire KADS uses client-server interaction to aid the agent name resolution, and it operates on a distributed and coordinated naming database for both agents and agent domains. In the worst case, the location of an agent can be specified through the "root".

When a new agent is created in KADS, it must be uniquely identified. This is done by the KODAMA Naming Interface (KNI). Instead of naming an agent after its network address, which is changeable from time to time, we give a "global name", which is unchangeable, to each agent at the moment of its birth. In order to follow the agent domain structure, a qualified "global name" looks like:

[<title>/<agent ID>/<domain qualifiers>]

The title is used to indicate what kind of entity it is. For instance, agents may have the title as "AGT", while ACZ may have the title as "ACZ". The domain name is simply used to represent which agent domain it stays. The agent ID, however, should be exclusive within its domain. The global name is much like a logical name, and the following global names would be valid for an agent and an ACZ respectively:

[AGT/Alice/database.info]

[ACZ/Davy/mp3.music.info]

If an agent belongs to two agent domains, it may have two global names with different domain qualifiers, but the same agent ID and title.

While global names are useful for agent identification and categorization, "transport addresses" are used to indicate the physical network addresses. The transport address is much like a physical name, and a qualified transport address looks like:

[<protocol>://<title>/<agent ID>/<network address>:<port number>]

where protocol, network address (e.g., IP address) and port number are amenable to changing. For instance, the transport address of one agent can be changed while using different protocols, as shown in the following:

[http://AGT/Michael/35.35.35.35:2020]

[tcp://AGT/Michael/35.35.35.35:2020]

On the other hand, it always requests recursive agent name resolution in which a global name can be resolved to an equivalent transport address. Given a global name, say,

[AGT/Japan/map.online-data]

its resolution process may start from the top-level domain, *online-data*, where it gives the location of its sub-domain, *map.online-data*. Finally, the given global name can be translated into an equivalent transport address in *map.online-data* domain.

4 Agent Communication Zone

Interaction among agents is one of distinguished properties of multiagent systems. Agent communications are kind of interactions that respect the heterogeneity and preserve the autonomy of agents [6]. This is largely due to the fact that the solution to the system task is typically beyond any singular agent's capabilities. Rather, the task solving process can be an incremental process involving coordination among agents [3]. Basically, coordination among agents is decentralized and heterogeneous, because agents can even dynamically enter or leave the system. This makes it difficult to maintain consistency over the system.

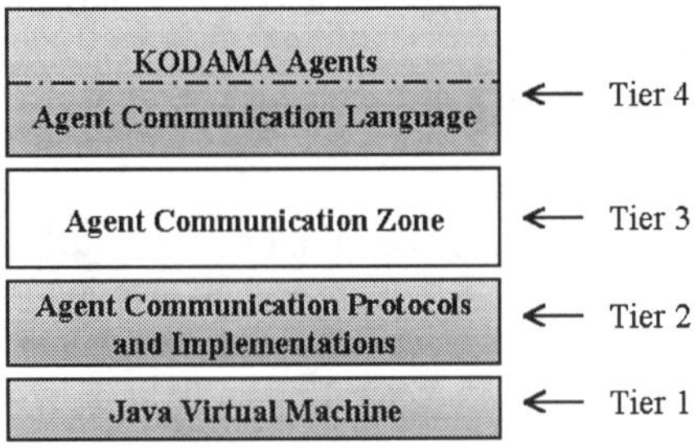

Figure 3. Four-tier Mechanism for Agent Communication in KODAMA

Originally, the agent systems exploit the client-server mechanisms of the agent interaction [6]. Unfortunately, the complexity of delivering interaction services directly to every agent and the dynamic administration of agent community on individual agent level have proved to be major limitations. In KODAMA, these limitations are avoided by implementing a four-tier model of agent communication [5], as shown in Figure 3. From the tier 4 to tier 1, they are ACL tier, ACZ tier, agent communication protocols & implementation tier, and Java VM. This four-tier mechanism separates the communication functions into tiers due to their levels of abstraction, complexity and characteristic. Each tier performs a related subset of the functions. Also, it relies on the next lower level to perform more primitive functions, as well as to conceal the details of those functions. Ideally, each tier can be independently extended, updated, or modified. Java VM comes to the lowest level because the current KODAMA system is developed in Java language. Next, the rest three tiers are discussed separately from high one to low one.

4.1 Agent Communication Language Tier

In KODAMA agent system, agent communication can be modeled as the exchange of declarative statements. The salient feature of the declarative language used by agents is its expressiveness because it allows agents to communicate complex information and goals, directly or indirectly triggers each other in efficient ways. In order to attack the problem of inconsistencies in the use of syntax and vocabulary, a universal communication language should be used. Although, there is no universally accepted ACL, two prominent ACLs are KQML (knowledge query and manipulation language) [4] and FIPA (foundation for intelligent physical agents) [www.fipa.org]. Belief in that KQML are enough for common purpose, our agents use it as their primary ACL. Another reason is that KQML is designed as a universal language, which can meet our requirement to exchange something more than pre-defined or fixed statements.

4.2 Agent Communication Zone Tier

ACZ is placed between the ACL tier and agent communication protocol & implementation tier. Thus, the agent-level issues can be separated from the primitive communication protocol and implementation. It is important to note that ACZ itself is naturally distributed to every computer where might have KODAMA agents. From each agent's point of view, it therefore always talks with a local ACZ, which acts like a gateway or proxy of agent itself, and any information is either coming from or sending to the local ACZ. From all ACZs' point of view, they work together to form a unified virtual agent communication zone where agents can talk with each other freely, as Figure 4 shows. Furthermore, the design of ACZ should be open so that it can be independently extended, updated or modified according to the practical communication needs of the system. For instance, the support of a new ACL or network connection protocol can be added to the ACZ. To a large extension, ACZ can help our KODAMA system to interact with agents created by other projects, taking full advantage of flexibility through the network.

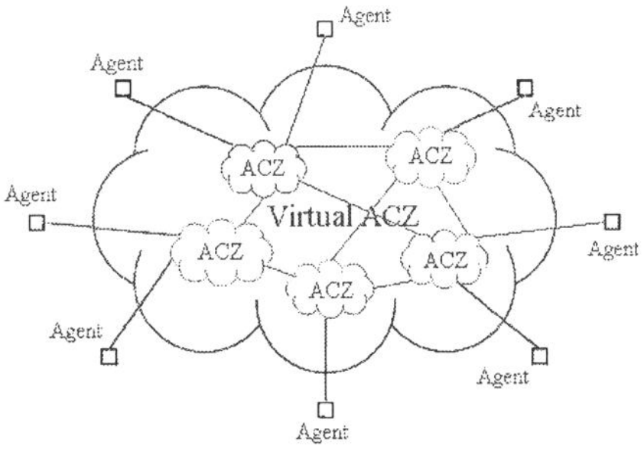

Figure 4. Virtual ACZ

According to its internal design (see Figure 5), the decentralization of ACZ can be guaranteed. That is, ACZ can be prevented from causing message traffic or becoming a bottleneck. (Most central blackboards may have such trouble as the size of the system scales up.) In a summary, ACZ has the following functions:

- Agent Communication Mediator: ACZ is designed to facilitate agent interactions, as well as to hide the low-level implementation details of network connections from the high-level development of multiagent systems.
- Agent Categorization: ACZ supports agent categorization by providing agent name registration and agent name resolution services. In fact, the hierarchical agent domain structure is maintained and managed by all ACZs. For instance, when an agent is created, deleted or moved, it simply (un)registers itself in a local ACZ, which has the responsibility to broadcast this news to other ACZs. Consequently, the translation of a global name into an equivalent transport address (agent name resolution) is also done by ACZ.
- Multithreading: Sophisticated agents often include several concurrent processes performing various kinds of tasks. To optimise computing resources and speed up overall performance, multithreading is an effective way. In ACZ's design, for example, message dispatch and receiver threads can dispatch outgoing messages and listen for incoming messages concurrently.

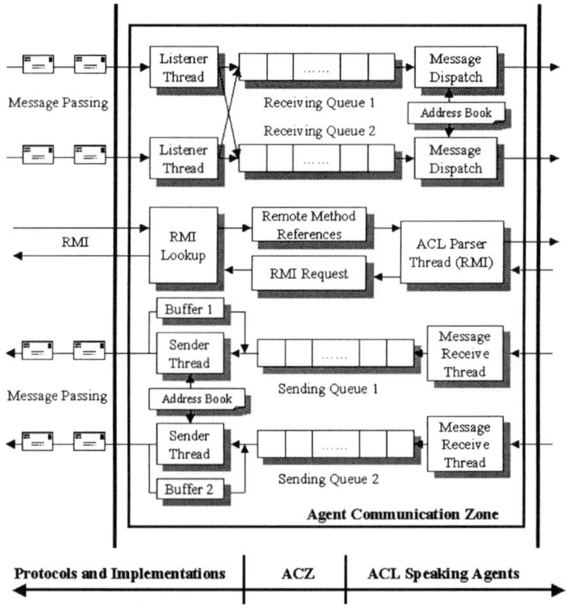

Figure 5. Agent Communication Zone
(RMI and message passing are two examples of network connection protocols)

4.3 Agent Communication Protocols and Implementations Tier

In this layer, the physical network connection can be specified. There are large varieties of protocols available now, such as TCP/IP, UDP, SMTP, HTTP, Java RMI, CORBA and so on. So far, TCP/IP, UDP and Java RMI have been used in the KODAMA system. TCP/IP is widely used in the Internet. It is a kind of low-level communication protocol, and does not need much network bandwidth. Above the TCP/IP, UDP allows the delivery of a message to multiple recipients, but it makes no guarantees about delivery of packets, or the order in which packets are delivered. UDP sockets are typically used in bandwidth-limited or multicasting cases. On the other hand, Java RMI allows us to do remote method calls in a natural way, and RMI takes care of all of the network-level details of the remote method calls. RMI may be needed in a complex application because it becomes difficult to maintain a protocol of message passing in such a system. It is also more complicated to extend an existing message-passing based system if new objects and operations should be added dynamically.

5 KODAMA System applied to Distributed Database Retrieval

In this section, we present an example of implemented KODAMA systems, which involves database retrieval in a distributed environment where both users and databases may spread over the network. The KODAMA system is suitable for this scenario in several aspects:

- Reducing the network load: Instead of moving large amounts of data to the user's terminal, a user agent can interact with remote agents to ask them to carry out a certain task. Later, the query result can be shipped back to the user.
- Autonomy: The KODAMA system provides higher-level abstractions than traditional distributed programming, and gives the system more autonomy and flexibility in making decision. Rather than hardwiring a specific behaviour for a given problem, agents might negotiate with one another to determine the best course of action for each situation.
- Decentralization and concurrency: Distributed database retrieval often involves a variety of heterogeneous entities, and probably takes expensive computing resources. The KODAMA system is good for doing this kind of job because distributed agents can operate it independently and concurrently while keeping interactions asynchronously.
- User-centric: A user can simply give out his/her query without knowing either the site or the content of available databases.

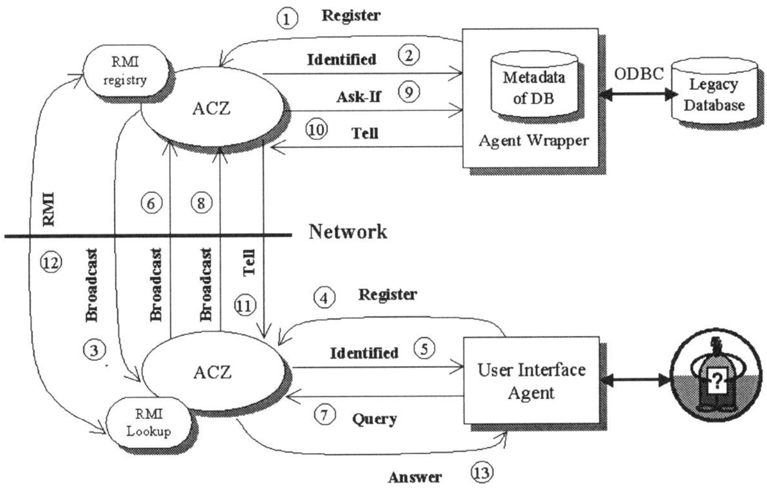

Figure 6. KODAMA system applied to distributed DB retrieval

Figure 6 shows an example of exchanged messages in sequence for agent registration and database retrieval. After the user can give out his/her query by keywords, the user interface agent tries to find out the appropriate database, which has relevant information to the query, by cooperating with database agents. If it is found, the result(s) are transferred to user side by using RMI. Note that, ACZ always acts like a gateway or proxy of agent.

6 Conclusion and Future Work

In this paper, we described the design and implementation of KODAMA system. In order to build an effective distributed multiagent system, KODAMA agents are organized by a hierarchical "agent domain" structure with the "Agent Naming Interface". KODAMA is actually distinct from other multiagent systems by its application-independent layer called "Agent Communication Zone". This additional layer makes the low-level network connection protocol and implementation be hidden from the agent-level development. Through the development of a distributed database retrieval system, we believe that the KODAMA system is naturally suitable for the Internet applications that usually require both intelligence and distribution, such as online information retrieval, e-commerce, scientific computing, personal assistant system, wrapper of legacy systems and so on.

The KODAMA system is still far from a sophisticated multiagent, and there are a lot of works remained for further study. First, we will try to enlarge the current implementation of KODAMA system, that is, more agents and agent domains will be involved. Second, we will enhance the design of plug-and-play agent. This idea is much like the key concept behind the Jini technology [7]. That means, enabling the intelligent agent as an instantly connected computing service on the network. Moreover, network security is a lasting concern in an Internet-oriented application. To enhance our agents' security, we will add the support of SSL (secure socket layer) protocol, use message cryptography, and apply authentication and authorization services for agents.

References

[1] N. R. Jennings, "On Agent-based Software Engineering", *Artificial Intelligence*, March 2000, Vol. 117, pp. 277-296.

[2] M. N. Huhns, "Networking Embedded Agents", IEEE *Internet Computing*, Jan./Feb. 1999, pp. 91-93.

[3] M. J. Wooldridge and N. R. Jennings, "Software Engineering with Agents: Pitfalls and Pratfalls", IEEE *Internet Computing*, May/June 1999, pp. 20-27.

[4] T. Finin, Y. Labrou, and J. Mayfield, "KQML as an Agent Communication Language", In *Software Agents*, MIT Press, 1997, pp. 291-316.

[5] G. Zhong, T. Mine, T. Helmy and M. Amamiya, "The Design and Implementation of Agent Communication in KODAMA", to appear in the *Proceedings of the 2000 International Conference on Artificial Intelligence*, Computer Science Research, Education, & Application Press, June 2000.

[6] V. R. Lesser, "Reflections on Nature of Multiagent Coordination and Its Implications for an Agent Architecture", In *Autonomous agents and multiagent system*, Kluwer Academic Publishers, 1998, No.1, pp. 7-38.

[7] J. Waldo, "The JINI Architecture for Network-centric Computing", *Communications of the ACM*, July 1999, Vol.42, No.7, pp. 76-82.

Knowledge-Based Software Engineering
T. Hruška and M. Hashimoto (Eds.)
IOS Press, 2000

A Problem Knowledge - Based Evolutionary Algorithm KBOA for Hypergraph Bisectioning

Josef SCHWARZ, Jiří OČENÁŠEK
Brno University of Technology, Faculty of Engineering and Computer Science
Department of Computer Science and Engineering
CZ - 61266 Brno, Božetěchova 2
e-mail: schwarz@dcse.fee.vutbr.cz, ocenasek@dcse.fee.vutbr.cz

Abstract. This paper is an experimental study on an utilization of additional knowledge about the decomposition problem to be solved. We have demonstrated this approach on the hypergraph bisectioning that can serve as a model of system decomposition in common, data base decomposition etc. We have focused on the extension of the Bayesian Optimization Algorithm BOA. The extension of the original BOA algorithm is based on the usage of a prior information about the hypergraph structure. This knowledge is used for both setting initial Bayesian network and the initial population using injection of clusters to improve the convergence of the decomposition process. The behaviour of our version KBOA is tested on the set of benchmarks, such as grid and random geometric graphs as well as real hypergraphs.

1 Introduction

The decomposition of the system such as communication networks, complex data base system and VLSI layout are usual tasks to be solved. These tasks can be often formalized as a hypergraph partitioning into *k* partitions – it is a well known problem of graph theory. This paper deals with the case of 2-way partitioning called bisectioning. If necessary the k-way partitioning can be realized by a series of the hypegraph bisectioning.

Many heuristics are used to solve this NP-complete problem. We can refer to the well known paper [1], where a good overview of the efficiency of known local search techniques as well as simulated annealing is presented. A very good survey about netlist partitioning techniques was done in [2], where the geometric representation, combinatorial formulations, move-based and clustering approaches are discussed. The interesting hybrid genetic algorithm is described in [3]. The authors have used a simple genetic algorithm (GA) [4], with reordering of graph nodes to receive shorter schemata/building blocks so as to prevent the disruption of schemata mainly of large defining length.

The problem of schemata disruption has been intensively studied in GA community during few last years. As a result a new class of promising approaches based on an estimation of the joint distribution of promising solutions (EDA) was proposed in [5], [6] and recently new ideas in [7], [8].

We focus in this paper on an extension of Bayesian Optimization Algorithm BOA [5], [9], [10] based on the problem knowledge to speed up the convergence of optimization process during hypergraph bisectioning.

The paper is organized as follows. In chapter 2 and 3 the problem formulation is declared and cost function is defined. Chapter 4 presents the original BOA algorithm which allows to understand the ideas of knowledge based approach presented in chapter 5. In chapter 6 benchmark tests are specified and experimental results are discussed. In chapter 7 the conclusions and research activities for the future are summarized.

2 Problem formulation

More formal, the particular bisectioning problem can be defined as follows: Let us assume a hypergraph $H=(V,E)$, with $n = |V|$ nodes and $m = |E|$ edges. We are supposed to find such a bisection $(V1,V2)$ of V into equal sized parts ($|V1| = |V2|$, $V= V1 \cup V2$) that minimizes the number of hyperedges which have nodes in different set $V1$, $V2$. The set of external hyperedges can be labelled as $E_{cut}(V1,V2)$. The primary objective function/cost of the hypergraph bisectioning is the number of external hyperedges, shortly called cut size:

$$c(V_1,V_2) = |E_{cut}(V_1,V_2)| = |\{e \in E \,/\, e \cap V_1 \neq 0,\ e \cap V_2 \neq 0\}| \quad (1)$$

This is the case of strongly balanced bisectioning. Next, we define the set $M(v)$ of hyperedges incident to node v and the set $N(v)$ of nodes that are neighbours of node v:

$$M(v) = \{e \in E \,/\, v \in e\} \quad (2)$$

Using the previous equation the cost can be expressed as

$$c(V1,V2) = \Big|\bigcup_{v \in V_1} M(v)\Big| + \Big|\bigcup_{v \in V_2} M(v)\Big| - m \quad (3)$$

The immediate/first neighbours of a node v:

$$N(v) = \{u \,/\, \exists e \quad v, u \in e,\ v \neq u\} \quad (4)$$

The degree of node v is defined as $D(v) = |N(v)|$.

An example of the hypergraph with 8 nodes and 5 hyperedges is shown in Fig.1. The bisection of the hypergraph resulted in $V_1=\{v_1, v_2, v_7, v_4\}$, $V_2 = \{v_5, v_6, v_3, v_8\}$. The external hyperedges $E_{cut}(V_1,V_2) = \{e_3, e_4\}$, cut size $c(V_1,V_2) = 2$.

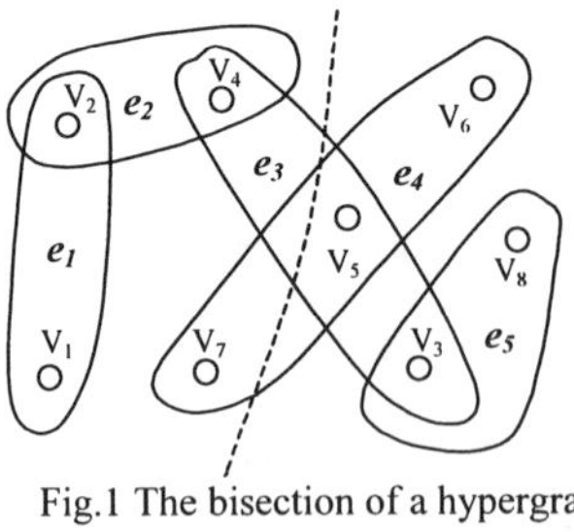

Fig.1 The bisection of a hypergraph

3 Solution encoding

For the BOA algorithm the following ordinary encoding of the solution is used:

Table 1. The ordinary solution encoding for bisection of hypergraph.

Chromosome/String		Meaning
gene value	**1 1 0 1 0 0 1 0**	Partition number
locus value	1 2 3 4 5 6 7 8	Hypergraph nodes

Each solution of the bisection is represented by a chromosome, which is a binary string $X=(x_1, x_2, \ldots, x_n)$. The gene value x_i represents the partition number, the index of locus specifies the node in the hypergraph. It is possible to express the cost function using the string encoding. In case of hypergraph bisectioning the cost function can be expressed using the equation (3):

$$c(V1,V2) = |\bigcup_{\forall x_i=1} M(i)| + |\bigcup_{\forall x_i=0} M(i)| - m, \quad for\ i=1,\ldots,n \qquad (5)$$

In case we define a dummy node v_0 with $M(v_0)=\varnothing$, we can transform the last equation into:

$$c(V1,V2) = |\bigcup M(i\ x_i)| + |\bigcup M(i\ (1-x_i))| - m, \quad for\ i=1,\ldots,n\ , \qquad (6)$$

where $M(i)$ is a set of hyperedges incident of node i.

4 BOA algorithm

In the simple genetic algorithms the standard crossover and mutation operators for offspring generation are used. In the last few years there has been a growing interest in the field of Estimation of Distribution Algorithms (EDAs) also called probabilistic model-building genetic algorithms, where crossover and mutation operators are replaced by probability estimation and sampling techniques. They use statistical information contained in the set of selected parents to detect gene dependencies. The estimated probability model is used to generate new promising solutions according to this distribution. The process can be described as follows:

Generate initial population of size N (randomly);
While *termination criteria is false* **do**
  begin
    Select parent population of S individuals according to a selection method (S≤N);
    Estimate the distribution of the selected parents;
    Generate new offspring (according to the estimated model);
    Replace some individuals in current population by generated offspring;
  end

There are various probability distribution models with different complexity.

In BOA (Bayesian Optimization Algorithm) [5] Bayesian network (BN) is used to encode the structure of a problem. Each gene in the chromosome is treated as a variable and represented by a node in the dependency graph. For each variable X_i it is defined a set of variables Π_{X_i} called parents it depends on, so the distribution of individuals is encoded as

$$p(X) = \prod_{i=0}^{n-1} p\left(X_i \mid \Pi_{X_i}\right) \qquad (7)$$

Generally, the existence of oriented edge from X_j to X_i in the network implies that the variable X_j belongs to the set Π_{X_i}. To reduce the space of possible networks, the number of incoming edges into each node is limited to k. According to results in [10] we have limited the parameter k in our experiments to be three.

Example of Bayesian network for 5 variables:

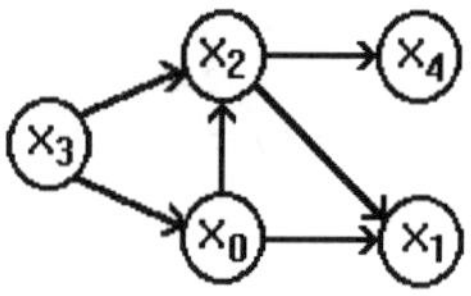

The corresponding joint probability distribution is

$$p(X) = p(X_3)\cdot p(X_0 \mid X_3)\cdot p(X_2 \mid X_0, X_3)\cdot p(X_1 \mid X_0, X_2)\cdot p(X_4 \mid X_2) \quad (8)$$

The Bayesian Dirichlet metric (BD) [11] is used to measure the quality of the network:

$$p(D, B \mid \xi) = p(B \mid \xi)\prod_{i=0}^{n-1}\prod_{\pi_{X_i}} \frac{m'(\pi_{X_i})!}{(m'(\pi_{X_i}) + m(\pi_{X_i}))!}\prod_{x_i}\frac{(m'(x_i, \pi_{X_i}) + m(x_i, \pi_{X_i}))!}{m'(x_i, \pi_{X_i})!} \quad (9)$$

where ξ is the prior information about the problem, D is the population of parents and $p(B \mid \xi)$ is the prior probability of the network B. The product over x_i runs over all instances of the variable X_i and the product over π_{X_i} runs over all instances of the set of its parents Π_{X_i}. The term $m(\pi_{X_i})$ stands for the number of occurrences of the tuple π_{X_i} in the population D and $m(x_i, \pi_{X_i})$ stands for the number of individuals in D having both X_i set to x_i as well as Π_{X_i} set to π_{X_i}. The prior knowledge on the probability distribution is represented by numbers $m'(\pi_{X_i})$ and $m'(x_i, \pi_{X_i})$ representing the expected $m(\pi_{X_i})$ and $m(x_i, \pi_{X_i})$ values. The detailed description of the prior parameters is in the next section.

If no prior information is available, the simpler K2 metrics can be used. It is a special case of BD metrics having all prior counts $m'(x_i, \pi_{X_i})$ set to 1 and all prior counts of parent configurations $m'(\pi_{X_i})$ set to number of possible values on i-th position (equal to 2 for binary chromosome).

Many algorithms can be used to build up the network. The optimal search is NP-hard, thus in the implementation a simple greedy algorithm was used with only one edge addition in each step. The algorithm starts with an empty network B and the edge giving the highest increase of metric value is then added to the network B. This process is repeated until no more addition is possible.

After network is constructed, new instances/solutions are generated. First, the variables/nodes of BN are ordered in the topological order and each iteration, the nodes whose parents are already calculated are generated using the conditional probabilities. This is repeated until all the variables are generated.

5 Knowledge based KBOA algorithm

For many combinatorial problems the information about the structure of the problem is available. If the information is complete, the dependence graph can be constructed in-hand by the expert. This method is used in the FDA (Factorized Distribution Algorithm) [6]. In our case, the structure of the problem is given by the list of edges between hypergraph nodes but the decomposition of the problem in the sense of FDA is not simple because the variables of the cost functions are overlapping. We can only expect that adjacent nodes in the hypergraph are dependent but we have no exact knowledge about the degree of independence between non-adjacent nodes.

The goal of our approach is to use modified BOA algorithm to investigate the structure of the problem together with the partial (local) information about the linkage to improve the performance of that algorithm. Three possible approaches were tested:

- The first one was based on the prior information about the problem in the BD metric. The term $p(B \mid \xi)$ represents the prior probability of the network *B*. We use a simple assignment $p(B \mid \xi) = c\kappa^{\delta}$, where *c* is a normalization constant, $\kappa \in (0,1]$ is a penalty constant factor and δ is the number of edges in the final Bayesian network having no match in the hypergraph to be bisected. The greedy algorithm that constructs the dependency graph using only one edge addition in each step, prefers edges existing between adjacent nodes of hypergraph (local information about the problem) with the setting δ to be zero. When no such edge exists, a penalization is used by setting $\delta = 1$.
- The prior knowledge about the optimized problem is also represented by numbers $m'(\pi_{X_i})$ and $m'(x_i, \pi_{X_i})$. It can be shown, that the values of $m'(\pi_{X_i})$ and $m'(x_i, \pi_{X_i})$ express our belief in the accuracy of the values $m(\pi_{X_i})$ and $m(x_i, \pi_{X_i})$. When these values increase, the BD metric will tend more towards the prior assignment of distribution, when those numbers decrease the influence of sampled values $m(\pi_{X_i})$ and $m(x\ , \pi_{X_i})$ becomes more significant. Our experiments with this type of information were not too promising, so we used the original uniform assignment.
- The standard BOA uses the random set of solutions in the initial population. We have tested the usage of the initial population based upon the knowledge of the hypergraph structure. Initial solutions are affected by injection of clusters of predefined size. The detection of such a cluster in a hypergraph is shown in the Fig. 2:

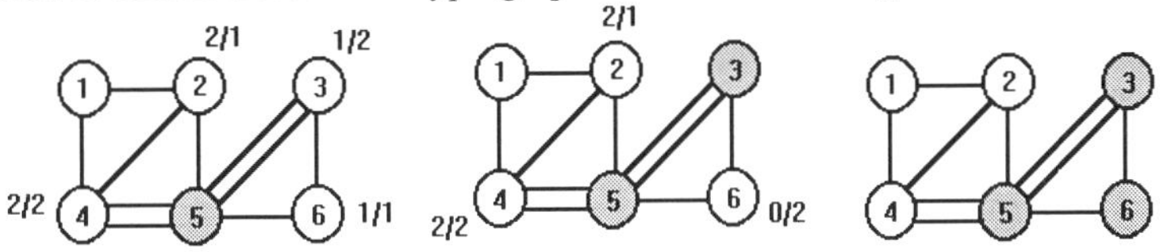

Fig.2. Clustering technique

First, a random node is selected to be the seed of the cluster. Then the effect of addition of each neighbouring node is expressed by the number of external and internal hyperedges incident of this node. Each step the node having minimal ratio external/internal edges is selected. When maximum size of cluster is reached or all neighbours are selected, next cluster is created. The cluster injection serves as a source of low-order building blocks.

6 Experimental results

6.1 Test graphs

The four types of graph structures are used:

1. Regular graphs *Gridn.c* with grid structure [3], [10] where the notion *n* specifies the number of nodes, *c* specifies the minimal cut size. As an example a bisection of graph *Grid100.2* is represented in Fig.3a having a 2-edge bottle-neck in the dashed cut line.
2. Random geometric graphs *Un.d* [1], [3]. Random geometric graph on *n* vertices is placed in the unit square and coordinates of its nodes are chosen uniformly.

There exists an edge between two vertices if their Euclidean distance is l or less, where the expected vertex degree is specified by $d = n\pi l^2$.

3. Caterpillar graphs *CATk_n* [3], with *k* articulations, six legs for each articulation, and *n* nodes, see Fig. 3c with *k=3* and *n=21*. This type of graph serves as a hard benchmark.

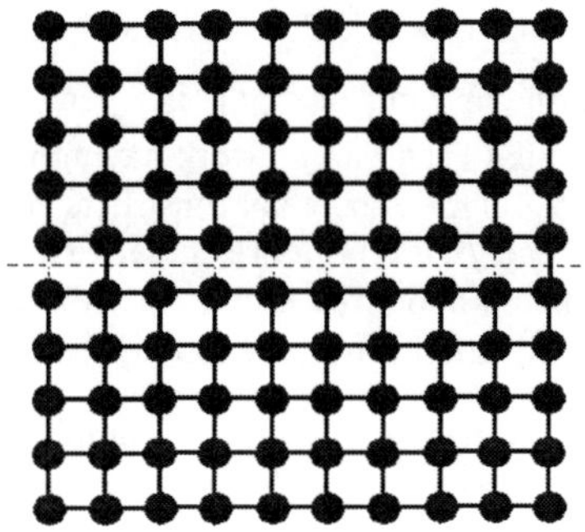

Fig.3a Grid graph

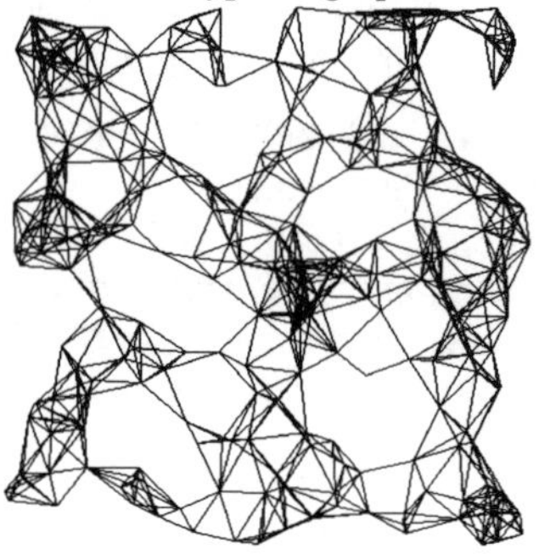

Fig.3b Geometric random graph

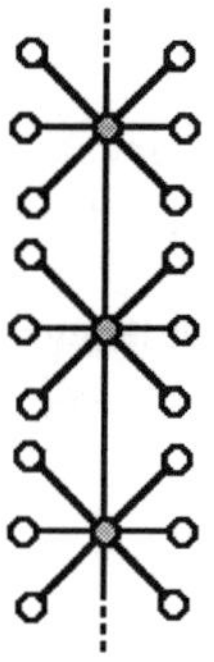

Fig.3c Caterpillar graph

4. Hypergraphs representing real circuits labelled by *ICn* [12]. The global optima is not known. The hypergraphs can be also specified by pair nodes/edges: *IC67/138, IC151/419, IC116/329, Fract149/147*. The structure of these circuits can be characterized as a random logic.

6.2 Results of the hypergraph and graph bisectioning

We have performed various experiments to demonstrate the efficiency of the developed algorithm KBOA comparing to the original BOA algorithm.

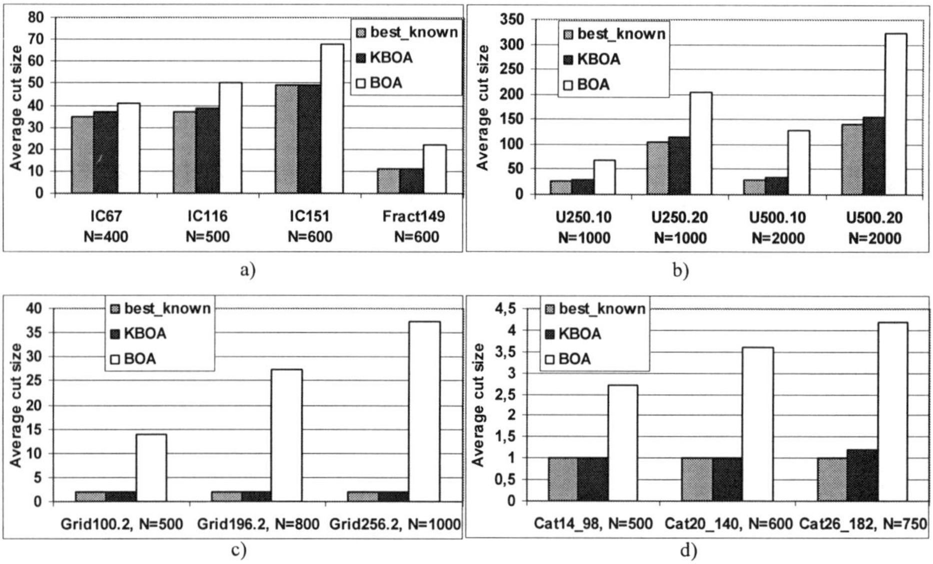

Fig.4 Average and best known cut size for BOA and KBOA a) on real hypergraphs, b) on geometric random graphs c) on grid graphs, d) on caterpillar graphs

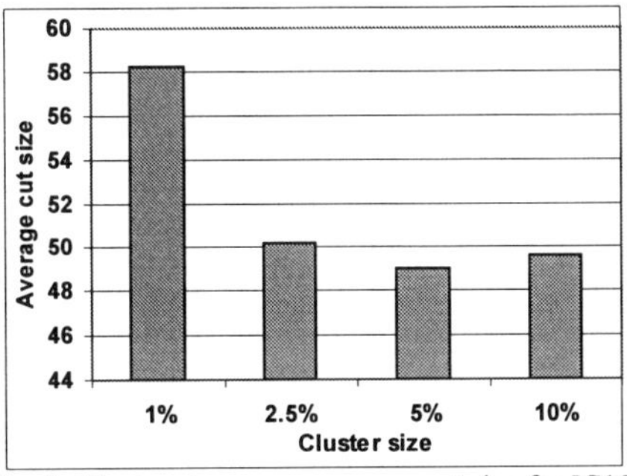

Fig. 5 Cluster size versus average cut size for IC151

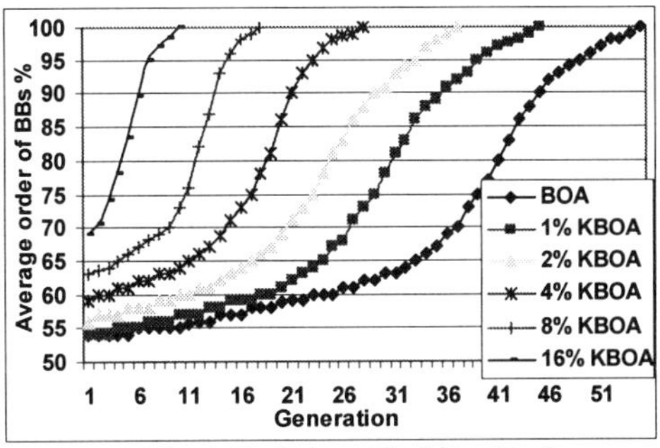

Fig. 6 Evolution of building blocks

In Fig. 4 the comparison of BOA and KBOA is shown for four groups of graphs. The best known solutions are determined by KBOA itself or well known hMetis program[13]. We performed ten independent runs for KBOA and BOA on each of the 14 test graphs of various type and size. The population size is the same for BOA and KBOA and it is set to the value for which the KBOA was successful for all ten runs for the case of grid graphs. Generally, for other types of graphs the population size was increased linearly with the size of the problem (as suggested in [8]). The KBOA outperforms BOA in all tests of hypergraph bisectioning. The time consumption for both algorithms is comparable due to equal population size. Let us note that BOA algorithm is theoretically capable to reach the similar cut size as KBOA but with about five times greater population size (for our test graphs) and thus with a rapid increase of computation time.

In Fig. 5 the performance of KBOA algorithm on the hypergraph IC151 for different sizes of injected clusters is shown. The size of clusters is expressed as a percentage of the number of hypergraph nodes. The proper value about 5% is used in all our trials. In the case of the smaller cluster injection, the growth of proper building blocks is weak and the opposite case of the injection of too large clusters leads into local optima.

In Fig.6 the growth of average value of building blocks order (ABB) in the population is depicted. This experiment is done for grid graph Grid100.2 with cluster size as a parameter. For the experiment the population size is set to N=300-2400 for KBOA and to N=2400 for BOA to get the global optimum for all sizes of cluster. Because two symmetrical optimal solutions exist, we separate all the chromozomes into two groups according to their similarity to each of the possible solution and the calculation of ABB based on the Hamming distance is summarized. It is clear that for small cluster size and BOA the average order of BBs in the first generation is about 50% which is typical for initial random population. A strong influence of the cluster size on the speed up of the evolution is evident. Let us note that in the 1% KBOA the cluster injection is not used and it is affected only by the phenomenon of prior probability (penalization) of the Bayesian network (see chapter 5) and only this phenomenon differentiates 1% KBOA from the BOA.

7 Conclusions and future works

In this paper we presented KBOA algorithm as a promising enhancement of the original version of probabilistic model-building genetic algorithm BOA [8], [9], [10]. The both algorithms use Bayesian network to model multivariate data as a mean of estimation of distribution of promising solutions. Although the BOA is powerful tool for solving hard optimization problems inclusive class of deceptive problems there are open questions to be solved e. g. the time complexity for very large problems, the setting of population size and parameter *k* (the complexity parameter of BN) for current problem, etc.

Our goal was to incorporate a problem knowledge into the whole process of BN construction. Firstly we applied the prior probability of the Bayesian network expressed by the term $p(B \mid \xi) = c\kappa^{\delta}$. The essence of this approach lies in the penalization of edges of BN having no match in the hypergraph. The influence of this phenomenon can be recognized in Fig.6 on the comparison of 1%KBOA and BOA as a slight increase of convergence speed for 1% KBOA. The concept of cluster injection into the initial population detected on the hypergraph structure seems to be a really promising tool for enhancement of the population genotype. This phenomenon leads to the meaningful reduction of cost function and population size. This approach can be used for another optimization problems but with particular problem knowledge.

Future activities will be directed towards an efficient construction of the dependency graphs using the techniques of parallel processing and on a hybridizing of KBOA algorithm using local improvement to enhance genotype not only in the initial population but also during the evolution.

Acknowledgements

This research has been carried out under the financial support of the Research intention No. CEZ: J22/98: 262200012 – "Research in information and control systems" and it was also supported by the Grant Agency of Czech Republic grant No. 102/98/0552 "Research and Application of Heterogeneous Models".

References

[1] Johnson, D. S., Aragon, C., McGeoch, L., & Schevon, C.: Optimization by Simulated Annealing: An experimental Evaluation, Part 1, Graph Partitioning, Operations Research, vol.37, pp. 865-892, 1989.

[2] Alpert, C. J., Kahng, A. B.: Recent Directions in Netlist Partitioning: A Survey, Integration: The VLSI Journal 19 (1995), pp. 1-81.

[3] Bui, T. N., Moon, B. R.: Genetic Algorithm and Graph Partitioning. IEEE Transactions on Computers, Vol.45, No.7, July 1996, pp. 841-855.

[4] Goldberg, D. E.: Genetic Algorithms in Search, Optimization, and Machine Learning, Addison-Wesley, 1989.

[5] Pelikan, M., Goldberg, D. E., & Cantú-Paz, E.: Linkage Problem, Distribution Estimation, and Bayesian Networks. IlliGal Report No. 98013, November 1998,pp. 1-25.

[6] Muehlenbein, H., Rodriguez, A. O.: Schemata Distributions and Graphical Models in Evolutionary Optimization. GMD Forschungs Zentrum Informationstechnik, 53754-St. Augustin, 1998, pp.1-21.

[7] Pelikan, M., Goldberg, D. E., & Lobo, F.: A Survey of Optimization by Building and Using Probabilistic Model, Illigal Report 99018, September 1999, pp. 1-12.

[8] Pelikan, M., Goldberg, D. E., & Cantú-Paz, E.: Bayesian optimization Algorithm, Population Sizing, and Time to Convergence, Illigal Report 200001, January 2000, pp. 1-13.

[9] Pelikan, M.: A Simple Implementation of Bayesian Optimization Algorithm in C++(Version1.0). Illigal Report 99011, February 1999, pp. 1-16.

[10] Schwarz, J., Očenášek, J.: Experimental Study: Hypergraph Partitioning Based on the Simple and Advanced Genetic Algorithm BMDA and BOA, In: Proceedings of the Mendel'99 Conference, Brno University of Technology, Faculty of Mechanical Engineering, Brno, 1999, pp. 124-130, ISBN 80-214-1131-7.

[11] Heckerman, D., Geiger, D., & Chickering, M. (1994). Learning Bayesian Networks: The combination of Knowledge and Statistical Data (Technical Report MSR-TR-94-09, Redmont, WA: Microsoft Research, 1995, pp. 1-53.

[12] A benchmark set, University of California, Los Angeles, VLSI CAD Laboratory, http://vlsicad.cs.ucla.edu/~cheese/benchmarks.html.

[13] Karypis, G., Kumar, V.: Hmetis - A Hypergraph Partitioning Package, version 1.5.3, University of Minnesota, Department of Computer Science&ENGINEERING, Army HPC Research Center Minneapolis, http://www-users.cs.umn.edu/~karypis/metis/hmetis/download.shtml.

Knowledge-Based Software Engineering
T. Hruška and M. Hashimoto (Eds.)
IOS Press, 2000

Applying of Character-Preserving Mutation to Scheduling Problem

Mitsuaki HIGUCHI[1], Morio NAGATA[2]

[1]*Niigata University of International and Information Studies, 3-3-1 Mizukino Niigata, 950-2292, Japan, hig@nuis.ac.jp*

[2]*Dept. of Administration Engineering of Science and Technology Keio University, 3-14-1 Hiyoshi Yokohama, 223-0061, Japan, nagata@ae.keio.ac.jp*

Abstract. The author has conducted research mainly into the use of genetic algorithm as a problem solving method applied to scheduling and combinational problem. A main feature of both kinds of problems is that their research objects do not permit multiple selection, therefore genetic manipulation has been carried out using order expression. However, when "crossover" and "mutation" are carried out in the order expression this breaks the good gene sequence from the previous generation. Therefore "crossover" and "mutation" do not necessarily produce a very good individual.

In another paper a different method called the "sub tour crossover" method was proposed [3]. This method makes it possible to preserve the genotype as the genetic expression, therefore allowing the good genes from the previous generation to be kept. We wanted to make a mutation which emphasized characteristic heredity and devised and experimental with a new "swap type mutation". We tested this new genetic manipulation method on the problem that was announced at JCKBSE'96. [4]

Then we examined the degree of difference in results between the new method and the previous are. Also we examined the effectiveness of the character preserving mutation.

1 Introduction

The trial of the scheduling problem application using GA is interesting research field. In previous paper, the new concept of "the penalty difference" was introduced [1], and manufacturing scheduling of the synthetic resin factory was made.

Then, the result of being better than the expert system carried out in the factory the present was obtained. However, this research object has the large property that the multiple selections are not permitted.

Therefore, in making the individual to be the order expression, the genetic manipulation has been carried out. However, it often has trouble with the good gene, when "crossover" and "mutation" are manipulated in the order expression. Therefore, it was considered that "crossover" and "mutation" might not always produce the excellent individual.

In the different paper, "sub tour crossover" in which the good gene might also remain was proposed [3]. "sub tour crossover" is possible for it in as of genotype.

We also regarded it as a necessity "mutation" which emphasized the characteristic heredity. Then, new "swap type mutation" was devised, and the experiment was tried. Switching cost smallest problem of the synthetic resin factory of the existence was taken up as an object.

Then, the following were done : The result that it carried out the experiment by new genetic manipulation "swap type mutation" and tried of the mutation by the order expression and comparison consideration.

2 Genetic algorithm

The genetic algorithm is one of the generation test method for the various plan design.

The good result may come out, when it is applied to the case that it has the means for evaluating the plan though that it did not prove it, that it completed the procedure for making the plan. First by making much plans by some methods. These were made by the random numbers arising, in this research.

The plan of one piece is called "individual". The individual cluster is called "population". Then, the content of the plan is called "gene". For example, they are the manufacturing order, etc..

It calls "gene locus" there, when the what number in the gene is made to be a problem. The individual (plan) which not become completely a problem removes the existence by the process for the generation. This is called "lethal gene".

Next, whether it is the result which each individual suited the purpose is evaluated. The result of evaluating is called "fitness".

By doing the contrivance so that the individual with the low fitness may not grow so that the individual with the high fitness may grow abounding, very much, next generation is made. This is called "selection".

Two operations are done here, because it is merely a copy of the old generation in the new generation, if it consists only in the selection. Those one's are to change gene column of two individuals in the middle point. Then, the new individual which there was no in the old generation grows. The individual of which the fitness is higher than the old generation may grow. This operation is called "crossover".

Different one is to change a part of gene in the individual for the result of completely differing. Not had individual appears in a past. It is equal to crossover. This operation is called "mutation".

New population is called "generation". On the new generation, the following are also repeated : selection crossover and mutation.

After the much generation, the possible plan (individual) of the satisfaction may arise. Such operation resembles the occurrence of the living world. Then, it was named the genetic algorithm (GA).

3 The outline of the scheduling problem

3.1 The general definition of the scheduling problem in this study

We make the scheduling problem handled here to be optimization problem with the property like the following. In some fixed periods, multiple products are produced only at the once.

The solution of the problem: It is to decide the manufacturing order of the product.

The objective function: That the switching cost is minimized.

Constraints: The difference between the switching costs by the difference between the manufacturing orders of the products.

3.2 The property of the scheduling problem in this study

Certainly the product must be once made in the period. And, the product once made is not made in the period over it. The products which must produce have already been decided. They are not problem of the profit maximum type but problem of the cost minimum type.

There is an inconvenience here in order to take the general fitness proportion strategy. The ratio between correct answer and cost is not proven, as the value of the correct answer does be not proven. It is difficult to regard fitness. It is easy to be considered of that the absolute value of the cost is reduced. Then, the fitness was not used as it is, and the cost was caught as a penalty, and the absolute value of the penalty would be evaluated. It also converted the loss which could not be attempted at the cost into the cost, it was given.

In this paper, it is meant that the value is small for the fitness being high, because the penalty is made to be the fitness.

By regarding above property, the following was designed.

3.3 Production scheduling of the job shop type production factory

Products as an object are some synthetic resin. The variety consists of 18 brands. The cost depends on the manufacturing order of the product. In giving the consecutive number to producing brand, it is made to be the manufacturing order. An individual is made to be one schedule plan. The arrangement of the gene shows the order of the manufacturing.

The gene length becomes a number of the manufacturing object product.

On the fitness, after all individual penalties were calculated, the penalty of each individual is subtracted from the individual which has largest penalty value in the generation, and it is made to be the fitness of each individual.

By this operation, the fitness becomes 0 for the individual with the largest penalty. The selection strategy is the roulette system. Therefore, the probability in the next generation of this individual is 0. This is named the anti elite strategy.

In this method, the fitness value is different even in the equal plan by the generation. Therefore, the following were used in the evaluation of the plan : Not fitness but penalty.

In the plan with the large loss which can not be calculated at the cost, large penalty is given in arbitrary like. For example, the cleaning of the polymerization tank is required, when some different products behind some products are made, and it is to become the closure in a few days, etc.. Such large penalty was named the penalty difference.

On GA parameter and other condition, it is according to the following.

(A) The population includes 100 individual. Number of generations is 1000.

(B) By initial population, it is also considered that the result greatly differs. Then, 10 times are executed by changing generation of the random number.

(C) Switching degree of difficulty (switching cost) is divided into group from 0 to 129 and the 100, 000 (100k) groups in which full face cleaning of reaction chambers are necessary.

(D) On the brand produced in beginning of month, the penalty in the delivery date delay was made to be 1, 000, 000 (1000k). It wants to limit such switching. The penalty had the difference for the reason. However, plan itself may be not possible, when it removes them in all as a lethal gene.

(E) 18 brands are produced.

(F) Early must brands are the 4 brands. The penalty (D) was imposed, if those 4 brands were not made to first 6 brands.

Under the above common condition, following 3 cases ("mutation by the order expression", "swap type mutation" and both combined use) were executed.

In present system (Expert system) which worked actually, the penalty was 400038. Execution program of the above was written in C language.

The program is shown in "http: //www.nuis.ac.jp/~ hig/jckbse.html".

3.4 The execution of the system

3.4.1 The mutation by the order expression

The mutation rate is 50%. In short, the half of generated individual does the mutation. This is the mutation by phenotype. Because, it becomes a lethal gene, when it was mutate by genotype. Which part mutated, was decided in the random number. Generally, crossover and mutation are pairs. However, only the mutation was manipulated for the comparison this time.

By all experiments, the fitness became "under 200037". This is a result of being better than the practical system of ES. It was proven that it was used as a sufficient practical use.

3.4.2 "Swap type mutation"

In the scheduling problem in which the multiple selections is not possible, the same product will be produced to two times, when the mutation by genotype is done, and it becomes a lethal gene.

Generally the mutation by phenotype like (3-4-1) is done.

However, the gene list of the origin has been broken with that especially, the gene length is long.

For example, there was a problem in search of the production sequence of 10 products.

"A B C ... J" is assumed description of product. "I A C D F J H B G E" means the production sequence.

For example, the mutation happened in the third Locus.

This is shown in the order expression "9 1 2 2 3 5 4 1 2 1 ".

This changed to "9 1 7 2 3 5 4 1 2 1".

It becomes that this is returned in genotype for "I A H C E J G B F D".

Gene column "D F J H B G E" there is completely no characteristic.

Then, the individual mutates in as of genotype.

The third Locus changed, and it became "I A H D F J H B G E".

In this as, it becomes a lethal gene. Then, the seventh Locus H is replaced with the third Locus. The third Locus is the thing before it mutates.

The individual is "I A H D F J C B G E".

It becomes able to exist. Moreover, "D F J" and "B G E" have left "the characteristic before it mutates".

Sub tour crossover is not possible, if the subset does not agree. Merit of this method are not only that it leaves the genetic material before it mutates but also that it accomplishes the mutation certainly. This genetic manipulation was named "swap type mutation".

Then, the mutation rate was defined as 50% in order to compare under the condition equal to 3.4.1.

The result was unexpectedly worse than the mutation by the order expression, and the maximum was 300031. Being better than the practical ES system, also stayed in 5 cases in 10 cases.

3.4.3 Both combined use

The result of independently applying "swap type mutation" was not so good. Following reason is considered from the character of the mutation.

It is meant that the effect of the old gene is strong for doing the mutation leaving characteristic of the old gene. This method is effective, when it leads to the result which may inherit the characteristic, as the old gene has the good characteristic.

However, there is no meaning, even if the characteristic of the gene which is not excellent in the applicability is left.

Then, next trial was carried out by both utilizing features. "swap type mutation" was applied to the individual with high fitness, and the order type mutation was applied to not so individual.

"Swap type mutation" was chosen when the individual has the small penalty (under 400k). And mutation by phenotype was chosen when the individual has the big penalty (over 400k).

In all results, the solution was got fitness under 200034. The experimental result is shown in (table 1).

With this, there is no a remarkable difference, because both also have the satisfied fitness on the final result to 1000 generation. Then, it is considered that fitness decreased from 300k and is the practical solution. The latter be reaching it in 226 generation, though the former has been taken in the about 310 generation.

And, it was proven that the number of practical solutions which are included in the inside was also abounding in the case of equal number of generations.

For example, though in this example, the practical solution was merely obtained the former by 6 cases in the time to 400 generation, in the latter, 9 cases became the practical solution.

4 Conclusion

The result that the mutation by the order expression was better than the interchange mutation came out. It is meant that the good result of that completing mutation was accomplished is deduced without sticking the old characteristic.

However, it can not be said of that the characteristic of which all genes are old is not left good. However, it was proven that the good result of that the characteristic was left came out on the gene of the high fitness.

In this paper, whether it chose which mutation only in the fitness was decided.

Though it was not tried this time, it will be considered as following.

The for example, individual which partially has gene list which it wants to leave (result which switching cost of the part is approximate minimally).

It is to devise in leaving the characteristic, even if the fitness is bad, etc., and it is considered that more and more effective genetic manipulation may be possible.

And, the fact is to also adapt to application field of other (for example, traveling salesman problem, etc.) of leaving the characteristic of the list of the gene.

By using two mutation properly, the good result came out. By searching such object in future too, further it wants to obtain the utility of this Swap type Mutation.

(Table 1) The execution results

Init. rand. num.	Phenotypye Mutation G	F	Arrive at Under 300k G	F	Swap type Mutation G	F	Both use G	F	Arrive at Under 300k G	F
1	626	200031	202	200084	543	300084	558	200027	50	200049
3	917	200036	292	200097	206	300031	246	200034	226	200051
5	786	200032	657	200046	451	300096	514	200029	397	200049
7	528	200031	432	200099	737	500040	389	200031	114	200107
11	952	200033	435	200036	753	500029	427	200031	122	200107
13	499	200031	476	200043	218	400098	738	200032	453	200114
17	861	200032	262	200107	88	400027	321	200029	311	200107
19	849	200037	214	200111	796	400095	917	200029	146	200111
23	55	200036	55	200036	297	500031	606	200029	55	200036
29	78	200031	78	200031	637	400035	597	200027	382	200111
ave.	615	200033	310	200065	473	400057	531	200030	226	200084

G: Generation number, F: Fitness Value

References

[1] M. Higuchi, M Nagata: *An application of the genetic algorithm to the scheduling problem of a plant producing many item of small quantities.* Information Processing society of Japan, Lecture papers book2, pp53-54, the latter term 1995

[2] M. Higuchi, M Nagata: *An application of the genetic algorithm to flight scheduling problems.* The Institute of Electronics, information and Communication Engineers, Technical report of IEICE, pp9-14, AI95-58, KBSE95-46 (1996-03)

[3] M.Yamamura, T.Ono, S.Kobayashi: *Character-Preserving Genetic Algorithms for Traveling Salesman Problem.* Journal of Japanese Society for Artificial Intelligence, pp117-127, Vol7, No.6 (1992-11)

[4] M. Higuchi, M Nagata: *An application of the genetic algorithm to scheduling problems using the concept of differential penalty.* Proceedings of JCKBSE'96, pp202-205, (1996-9)

Knowledge-Based Software Engineering
T. Hruška and M. Hashimoto (Eds.)
IOS Press, 2000

Knowledge-Based Design for Autonomous Humanoid Service Robot HARIS

Haruki UENO

Intelligent Systems Research Division, National Institute of Informatics
2-1-2 Hitotsubashi, Chiyoda-ku, 101-8430 Tokyo, Japan
E-mail: ueno@nii.ac.jp

Abstract. This paper presents the concepts and methodology of knowledge-based design of the autonomous humanoid service robotic arm/hand system HARIS, based on Cognitive Science. The HARIS robotic system consists of model-based 3D vision, intelligent scheduler, computerized arm/hand controller, humanoid HARIS arm/hand unit and human interface, and aims to serve aged and disabled persons on desk-top 3D-object manipulations. A world model, i.e., a shared knowledge base, is introduced to work as a communication channel among these software modules. The key idea is to use "*words*" in describing a scene, scheduling tasks, controlling an arm and hand, and interacting with a human. The world model plays a key role in fusing a variety of distributed functions. The generalized frame-based knowledge engineering environment ZERO++ has been effectively used as a software platform in implementing the world model. The experimental system is working within a limited situation successfully. The introduction of Cognitive Science-based knowledge modeling has resulted in useful hints for realizing human-robot symbiosis, that is our long-term goal of the project.

1 Introduction

Due to increasing of average age and decreasing of young people *Autonomous* service robots are required for helping the aged and disabled [6, 10]. By "autonomous" we mean that a robot achieves a higher level request by itself, i.e., receiving a request in a natural sentence, planning a task sequence, making motion and path plans, and controlling the robot to achieve the request [1]. This type of abilities could be realized by a fusion of knowledge-based AI technologies [2], vision technologies [3] and humanoid robotic technologies. The HARIS project aims to make a break through in the field of service robots by demonstrating the high performance and flexibility of an autonomous human-like robotic arm/hand system. The HARIS robot system consists of a model-based 3D vision, an intelligent task and motion scheduler, an arm controller, a human-like robotic arm, and a human interface as an all-in-one system. In this paper we propose an effective knowledge-based system modeling based on Cognitive Science for a humanoid service robot which works in a situation of desk-top object manipulations. The concepts and methodology of World Model is applied to integrate a variety of functions to achieve the autonomy.

We have developed a highly flexible human-like robotic arm for the project [4]. The design policy is to realize a human-like arm/hand functions in manipulating a variety of 3D objects for assisting human beings. The structure and functions of human arms, hands and fingers have been analyzed and evaluated in this direction. Usage of multiple tactile sensors results in higher flexibility in manipulating a variety of objects with simpler control mechanisms. The embedded local intelligence arrows to control the HARIS hand at a symbol level.

Cognitive Science is considered in designing the software architecture of HARIS, i.e., "*word*"-oriented scene description and task scheduling [5, 6]. Motion-level processing is embedded within the word-based model. We think that this method is similar to human's way of task scheduling in manipulating his/her own arms in achieving ordinary tasks in daily life. We are trying to mimic a human's way in realizing an autonomous human-type robot arm as much as possible. This is because a human friendly interface should be one of key issues in realizing service robots for serving human beings and our approach would be quite natural for a human who needs robot's services.

All the functions in integrating the HARIS software system have been realized in the generalized frame-based knowledge engineering environment ZERO++ [7], which is a re-implemented version of ZERO [8] in C++ to improve performance for the HARIS project. It must be noted that a powerful platform like ZERO++ is absolutely important in developing integrated intelligent robots under distributed computing environment with LAN.

2 Design Concept

As mentioned above the concept of Cognitive Science is considered in modeling the software architecture of the HARIS system, i.e., a human's way of cognition is introduced in designing the system. It should be noted that our approach would be different form those of cognitive scientists. They seem to consider deeper structure of human's cognition in identifying objects as well as solving problems. The key idea in our approach here is to use *words* in designing a robotic system, i.e., term-oriented semantic network in representing an image of a scene, term-oriented task scheduling, and term-oriented arm and hand control in manipulating objects. Detailed procedures have been embedded within the background of the model. We think that a combination of the term-oriented task scheduling and arm/hand control is similar to human's way in manipulating his/her own arms in achieving ordinary tasks in daily life. We are trying to mimic a human's way in realizing an autonomous human-like robot arm as much as possible. A natural human-robot interface is one of issues of this project.

Figure 1 shows an abstraction hierarchy including the level for "words" in designing an information model of an autonomous humanoid robot. As shown in the figure the hierarchy could be divided into two contrastive worlds, which are so-called a knowledge-based world and a sensor-based world. The former consists of three levels, i.e., concepts, words, and tasks. The latter consists of two levels, i.e., actions and sensors. This hierarchy tells that a concept could be expressed in a combination of words, which could be replaced by a combination of tasks, in the knowledge-based world. A task could be achieved by a combination of actions, which could be controlled and monitored by means of sensory information.

Behavioral models of robots are designed within the sensor-based world. Our robot is designed based on both worlds. A request given by a human-being is expressed in natural sentences at the word level. The request is translated into actions and achieved in the sensor-based world. The sensory information is monitored within the sensor-based world for behavior-level control, and feedbacked to the knowledge-based world for higher level monitoring and re-planning for achieving the request.

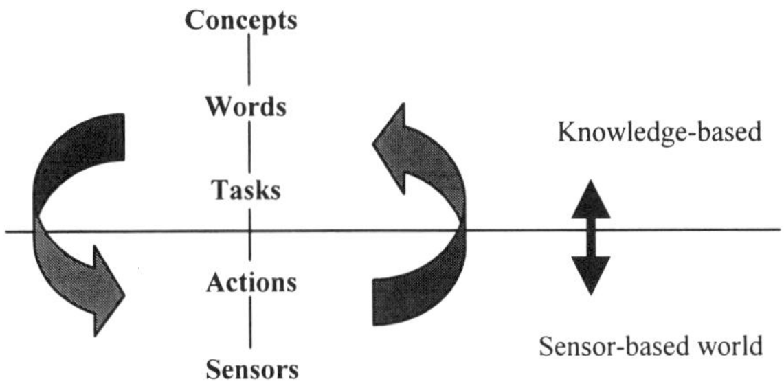

Figure 1. An ideal image of a fusion of a knowledge-based world and sensor-based world into an integrated system in our trial.

3 HARIS Arm

The HARIS arm has three jointed-arms with 8 d.o.f. and a hand with 17 d.o.f.. Arm 1 and 2 consist of three bar-link mechanisms to obtain high torque and are connected by universal joints for easy positioning. Third arm works like a human wrist, by rotation of forearm and by flexion, extension and rotation with differential gear mechanism. The hand has five fingers like a human hand. The embedded arm control system achieves efficient and flexible manipulations.

For holding an object we have established a tactile sensing system introduced with new recognition method for multi-tactile sensors. The hand for this project has advanced mechanism of the prior one [9]. Every finger surface has a set of 4 to 10 tactile sensors in a diamond array distribution, in total 128 sensors are installed in the finger surfaces. In addition, in order to nip an object with pointing and middle fingers each side face has 7-10 sensors, 50 in total. Therefore, 178 tactile sensors are installed in total. Every sensor is connected to a 8-bit microcomputer chip installed within the hand unit, which recognizes an object by detecting a pattern of contacts with sensing switches. Each finger is able to detect slippage by detecting the deformation of the skin within a time unit.

A human hand is capable of performing a variety of holding actions. Typical holding actions are named as grasping, nipping, picking and so on. Our robot hand is designed to achieve something human-like actions in holding an object by means of sophisticated finger structures, motion controls and tactile sensors. The three-jointed plastic finger is designed to twist an object by single micro-motor. The feedback signals from the tactile sensors are used to recognize an object, stop the actions of holding it and lift it with least torque. By this mechanism our robotic arm is expected to be able to grasp an egg, hold a paper cup and lift a glass cup without troubles by simple control commands.

In addition, in order to achieve sophisticated manipulations by simpler actions some fingers have special mechanisms as follows. Pointing and middle fingers are able to move in side-to-side directions up to 20 degrees and they can nip a small pipe as humans do. The thumb is actuated with a differential gear mechanism with a micro-motor and an electromagnetic clutch, so that it can out-rotate and flexion/extension. The thumb rotates first, then twists until it meets the object. Change of motion is controlled mechanically. The sensory system and an examples of object holdings by the HARIS hand are shown in Figure 2.

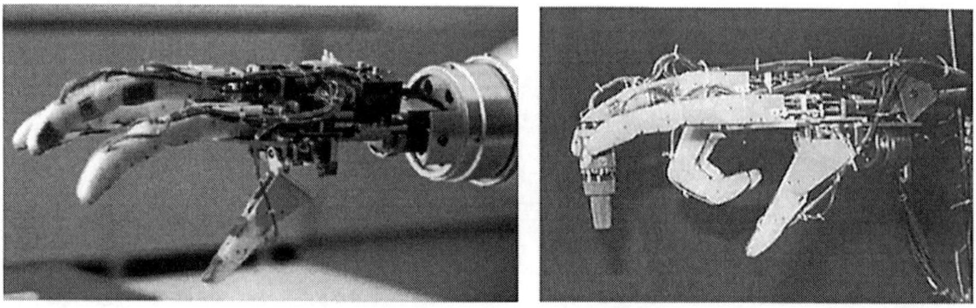

Figure 2. Tactile sensory system (left) and an example of object holding type "nip" by the HARIS hand (right).

4 Outline of HARIS System

As shown in Figure 3, the HARIS software system consist of a 3D vision system, intelligent task and motion schedulers, command generator, robotic interface, a monitor system, a human interface and two knowledge bases which are a world model and a scheduling model.

The world model is a knowledge base to represent a scene by a combination of a shape model, a functional object model and a spatial model. The world model plays a key role as the communication channels among the software modules of the system. The shape model is used to identify an object in 3D using the shape-related attributes of each object within a scene. The functional model, which is used for task scheduling and motion controls, represents functional attributes of each object. The spatial model describes the spatial relationships among the objects in a semantic network by means of relational operators and distance descriptors. The spatial model generated by the scene undestander is used for task and motion scheduling and monitoring.

Figures 4 shows a part of the red cup frame stored within the functional model.

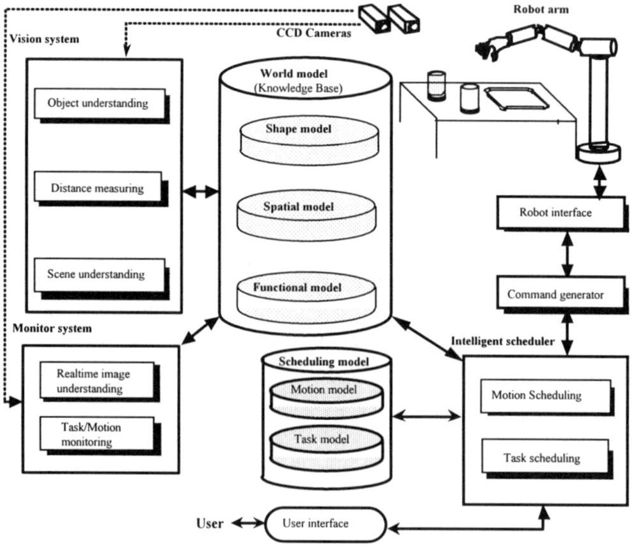

Figure 3. An overall view of the HARIS software system.

```
Frame: Red-cup
  a-kind-of       Cup
  hasparts        (container)
  state           (empty half full)
  roles           (contain_drink)
  color           red
  accept_tasks    (reach hold lift carry put release leave)
  accept_htypes   (hook grasp nip)
  default_htype   nip
  accept_prepos   (in into)
  held_form       ((nip (held_space *[nip[globe [0 0 50] +-10 +-10 +-10]])
                   (vcondition (posturep approach_vector *[nip[0 0 1]] 5))))
    ..............
```

Figure 4. An example of a part of the red cup frame as a class frame in the Functional model.

The user interface receives a user's request in a natural language sentence, such as "Put a red cup onto a white tray", understands it and sets a goal task. In this example "put" is the target task.

The scheduling model is another knowledge base to represent the knowledge about tasks and motions. The task scheduler receives the goal as a request from the user interface, makes a sequence of primitive tasks to achieves the goal by means of the task model as a sequence of transitive verbs, such as, "reach", "hold", "lift", "move", and so on. Since the HARIS system is designed based on the concepts of Cognitive Science a human-robot interaction could be achieved smoothly by means of verbal terms. Then the scheduler makes a sequence of motion primitives to achieve the tasks by means of the motion model, and generates a set of commands to execute the motions by the command generator, which are sent to the robot interface to control the robotic arm. The path plans are generated as a part of the motion scheduling using the knowledge stored in the functional model and spatial model.

The vision system, i.e., a model-based 3D scene understander, receives stereo color images through two CCD color cameras, identifies objects, measures distances, and generates the scene description in the world model. Since the knowledge of every candidate object is pre-defined as a template in a class frame the scene understanding can be achieved by generating instances for identified objects using partial information of them.

The robot interface receives the commands one by one in a sequence from the command generator, and executes them in a real-time mode. During the execution situation is monitored by the monitor system, which is consisted of a combination of computation-based virtual monitor and a real-time image recognizer.

5 Vision System

At first, color image data through two CCD cameras are preprocessed with an image processor to minimize noises. Then object regions are localized by means of color information such as red, black and white. By color-oriented localization object recognition time could be extremely decreased. Since specific color attribute is attached to associated knowledge of every candidate object within the knowledge base at class frames, top-down based object understanding can be applied. For example, if the color attribute of region "p" is identified as "red", then "a red cup" is supposed to exist there. In this case, only a couple of parallel lines is recognized by means of straight line identifier, which is one of 2D-primitive identifiers. This can be simply decided using the knowledge stored in the shape model of the knowledge base, i.e., World Model.

The trigonometric measurement method is applied next in order to both assure the objects and measure distances. Next, spatial descriptions are created in the spatial model using the results of distance measurement and the shape model. At last, the functional object model is generated by instanciating associated class frames. Automated calibration is done beforehand.

```
Frame: Spatial-description
a-kind-of        Spatial-model
hasparts         (Red_cup_1  Black_cup_1 Tray_1)
Red_cup_1        ([150 110 0] ([100] [010] [001]))
Black_cup_1      ([250 310 0] ([100] [010] [001]))
Tray_1           ([-200 250 0] ([100] [010] [001]))

Frame: Objects-relations
a-kind-of        Spatial-model
Red_cup_1        ((left-of Tray_1) (left-of  Black_cup_1))
Black_cup_1      ((Right-of Tray_1) (Right-of Red_cup_1))
Tray_1           ((right-of Red_cup_1) (left-of Tray_1))
```

Figure 5. An example of spatial descriptions of a scene in the Spatial model.

Using the results of the distance measurement, geometric positions of the objects and spatial relations among them are recognized, which are attached to associated descriptors of the associated frame of the spatial model. The spatial relations among the objects are represented by means of the semantic network model, and the geometric positions of the objects are described by the world coordinate system. In order to represent the spatial relations we have introduced nine description primitives which are 'left-of', 'right-of', 'in-front-of', 'behind-of', 'on', 'under', 'above', 'below' and 'contact-with'. Figure 5 shows a part of the spatial model generated as the results of the understanding.

6 Intelligent Scheduler

The method of task/motion scheduling is a revised version of the earlier system [5]. A task schedule is a static system, i.e., complete task schedule is generated before beginning robotic motions. While, motion scheduling is real time-based, i.e., the tasks are sent to the motion scheduler one-by-one, which generates motions, which in tern converted to a sequence of robotic commands. The sequence of robotic commands are sent to the robot interface one-by-one, which executes the command and returns signals to the interface to execute next command. At the end of execution the motion scheduler requires next task to the task scheduler to continue execution. While, a motion schedule is generated as a sequence of primitive motions according to the generated task sequence using the knowledge in the motion model to the knowledge on environment and manipulations.

The primitive tasks and motions are pre-defined as the templates and stored in the task knowledge base, i.e., task model. The attributes for a task template include such as an agent, an instrument, a manipulation object, a destination, prior tasks, next tasks, pre-conditions, post-conditions and acting constraints. These attributes are stored in associated slots of associated task frame in the task model. The knowledge on prior tasks and next tasks is used to generate a reasonable task sequence in scheduling. The attribute values of initial tasks and terminal tasks are "nil", which terminate the process of the task scheduling automatically. As the result of the task scheduling the sequence of associated tasks is instanciated from the templates. The pre-conditions and post-conditions give the initial and terminal conditions for the motion of the task, which are used in the robot control.

The primitive tasks consist of basic manipulations of the robot arm at word level such as 'reach' the arm for an object and 'grasp' an object. The current task knowledge base stores the task-related knowledge for seven primitive verbs, which are 'reach', 'hold', 'lift', 'carry', 'put', 'release' and 'leave' in class frames. While, six primitive motions are defined which include 'hform (hand_form)', 'approach', 'hold', 'lift', 'move' and 'leave'. Some primitive motion identifiers are same to those of primitive tasks, since these tasks are one-to-one relations to associated motions.

The basic strategy of task scheduling is a kind of term-based goal-oriented. That is, a target task is identified as a goal from a request sentence first. The target task is easily extracted from a user's request using the Case grammar-based method of natural sentence analysis. Then a sequence of primitive tasks is generated as a sequence of terms, each of which is directly connected to specific primitive task, in order to achieve the goal. In the current system we are dealing with simple request such as "Put a red cup onto a white tray". In this case the target task, i.e., goal, is "put".

Generation of a task sequence starts with the "put" task, i.e., goal task, which results in generation of the goal frame. For examples, the "put" task needs the "carry" task as the prior task, which needs the "lift" task as its prior task, and so on. This sequence should terminate with the "reach" task as the first task since the value of the prior task slot of the "reach" task frame is "nil". A sequence of the following tasks is generated in a similar way using the values stored in the next task slots. In cases where plural tasks are allowed for prior or next tasks the shortest sequence of tasks should be assigned for a proper task schedule.

Pre- and post-conditions for each task are generated during the process by means of the information stored in the pre- and post-conditions slots of an associated task template, the information of the associated objects in the functional model, the information stored in the spatial model and the knowledge to instantiate task frames. The task scheduling procedure is discussed a little more detailed in [11]. Figure 6 shows an example of generated pre-condition for the "Put" task as an instance frame.

The command sequence is generated finally to control a manipulator. Since the HARIS hand is under tuning-up for tactile sensors and grasping controls, a Movemaster which is a commercially available robotic arm is used for feasibility study. Since the Movemaster has own control interface to connect to another computer and has functions to accept relatively higher level robotic commands such as "open hand", "close hand" and "contain object in hand", it is easier to control by simply sending commands in sequence. However, "nip" is only available in holding an object. Figure 7 shows an example of generated commands for Movemaster. It should be noted that the generation of commands must be adjusted to positions of objects on the tables as folloes. 1) If a black-cup may exist in the action path for carrying a red cup, the black one, i.e., an obstacle, must be avoided from the path by producing a suitable action path. 2) If a black-cup exists on the tray, then a suitable task sequence must be generated to make a room for the red cup. The current scheduler can solve these problems.

```
Task "put":
pre_condition:    ((freep white_tray[on[qprism [0 0 0] +-210 +-150 +5]])
                   (abovep red_cup white_tray)
                   (hand_inp
                     red_cup[nip[globe [0 0 50] +-10 +-10 +-10]]
                     MMEX_hand[nip[globe [0 0 0] +-100 +-100 +-100]])
                   (posturep MMEX_hand[nip[0 1 0]] red_cup[nip[0 0 1]] 5)
                   (liftp MMEX_hand red_cup)
                   (inp
                     red_cup[globe [0 0 0] +-35 +-35 0]]
                     white_tray[on[qprism [0 0 50] +-210 +-150 +5]])
                     (posturep white_tray[#[0 0 1]] red_cup[#0 0 1]] 5)
                     (posturep white_tray[#[0 0 1]] world[#[0 0 1]] 5))
```

Figure 6. An example of the generated pre-conditions for task "put".

Program for **MoveMaster**.	**- Semantics -**
OG	Initialize Arm and Hand.
~ **REACH** ~	~ REACH ~
PD 1, 100, 66, 50, 0, 0	Assign an action-path 1.
PD 2, 200, 132, 100, 0, 0	Assign an action-path 2.
MC 1, 2	Move Hand to Position 2 through Position 1.
PD 3, 300, 200, 150, -90, 0	Assign a sub-goal.
MO 3	Move Hand to the sub-goal (above a cup).
MT 0, 0,-50	Move Hand by 5 cm in keeping direction.
~ **HOLD** ~	~ HOLD ~
GC	Close Grip.
~ **LIFT** ~	~ LIFT ~
DW 0, 0, 50	Move Hand by 5 cm up.
~ **CARRY** ~	~ CARRY ~
PD 1, 190, 240, 150, -90, 0	Assign an action path 1.
PD 2, 80, 280, 1500, -90, 0	Assign an action path 2.
PD 3, -30, 320, 150,-90, 0	Assign an action path 3.
MC 1, 3	Move Hand to position 3 through positions 1 and 2.
PD 4, -150, 360, 150, -90, 0	Assign a sub-goal.
MO 4	Move Hand to the sub-goal.
~ **PUT** ~	~ PUT ~
MT 0, 0, 50	Move Hand by 5 cm in the direction.
~ **RELEASE** ~	~ RELEASE ~
GO	Open the grip.
~ **LEAVE** ~	~ LEAVE ~
MT 0, 0, 50	Move Hand by 5 cm in the inverse direction (up).
~ **INITIALIZE** ~	~ INITIALIZE ~
OG	Initialize Arm and Hand.

Figure 7. An example of generated commands for "Put a Red cup onto a white tray".

7 Concluding Remarks

1. Current system deals with very simple objects such as cups without a handle and boxy tray. Sophisticated objects like coffee bottles and spoons are next targets.
2. A fusion of knowledge-based AI technologies, model-based 3D vision technologies and mechatronic arm technologies has resulted in a possibility of highly flexible hu-

man-like autonomous service robot HARIS for assisting the aged and disabled in desktop object handlings. This technology should also be applicable to next generation industrial robots in handling complex objects.

3. By introducing Cognitive Science the integration of scene understanding and task/motion scheduling has been smoothly achieved. This approach would be useful for a human-robot interface in realizing service robots for the handicapped[Saito94]. For example, we will be able to imagine a future situation, where autonomous service robots and a handicapped person would exist to collaborate each other. In such a situation a robot should serve him/her by inferring his/her intentions from body actions and/or simple requests in terms during execution. This is true for communications between human beings as well.
4. Usage of frame-based software platform ZERO++ in conjunction with the concept of World Model plays undoubtedly important roles in realizing integrated autonomy for the HARIS robotic system. Module-based software development and maintenance have been easily accomplished by this approach. This is very helpful in such a university-like development environment, where students are joining and leaving every year, while the system must be progressive continuously. We are planning to develop distributed system via LAN and Internet for further flexibility and performance.

Acknowledgment

The HARIS project is a joint work with Prof. Y. Saito's group Tokyo Denki University, and supported in part by the Research Promotion Foundation of Tokyo Denki University, and Japan Ministry of Education for international collaborative research with Intelligent Robotics Laboratory at Vanderbilt University .

References

[1] Ueno, H. and Saito, Y., An Autonomous Robot Arm with Visual and Tactile Sensors, Proc. Mechatronics '94, pp.448-451, 1994.

[2] Ueno, H., Object Model for a Deep Knowledge System, Springer-Verlag, Lecture Note in Economics and Mathematical Systems 286, pp.11-19, 1986.

[3] Hasegawa, T. Model-based Vision for Robotic Manipulation, Journal of the Robotic Society of Japan, Vol.10, No.2, pp. 153-158, 1992.

[4] Ohnishi, K., Saito, Y., Ihashi, T. and Ueno, H., Human-type Autonomous Service Robot Arm: HARIS, Proc. 3rd France-Japan Congress on Mechatronics, pp.849-854, 1996.

[5] Ueno, H. and Saito, Y., Model-based Vision and Intelligent Task Scheduling for Autonomous Human-Type Robot Arm, Special issue on Robotics and Autonomous Systems 18, pp.195-205, Elsevier Science Journal, 1996.

[6] Ueno, H., Intelligent Task and Motion Scheduling for Autonomous Human-Type Service Robot Arm, Artificial Intelligence: Methodology, Systems, Applications (Ed., A.M. Ramsay), Frontieers in Artificial Intelligence and Applications, Vol. 35, pp.239-248, IOS Press, 1996.

[7] Ueno, H., Kogure, S. and Ookuma, Y., Implementation of Frame-based Knowledge Engineering Environment ZERO in C++, Lecture Note on Software 15, pp.101-110, Kindaikagaku-sha, 1995.

[8] Ito, H. and Ueno, H., "ZERO: Frame + Prolog", Logic Programming '85, LNCS221, pp.10-17, 1986

[9] Ooshima, T, Higashibara, T., Saito, Y. and Kubo, S., Holding Features of Multiple Tactile Sensors for Artificial Arm, Abstract of 11th Annual Conference of Japanese Society for Biomechanism, pp.5-6, 1990.

[10] Kawamura, K. and Thomas, E. D.(eds.), Proceedings of International Workshop on Biorobotics: Human-Robot Symbiosis, Tsukuba, Japan, 1995.

[11] Ueno, H., A Cognitive Science-Based Knowledge Modeling for Autonomous Humanoid Service Robot – Towards a Human-Robot Symbiosis, Proc. 10th European-Japanese Conference on Information Modeling and Knowledge Bases, 2000.

Knowledge-Based Software Engineering
T. Hruška and M. Hashimoto (Eds.)
IOS Press, 2000

Knowledge Representation and Reasoning with Transparent Intensional Logic

Leo HADACZ, Aleš HORÁK
Faculty of Informatics, Masaryk University Brno
Botanická 68a, 602 00 Brno, Czech Republic
E-mail: {hadacz,hales}@fi.muni.cz

Abstract. This paper describes the design of a system for knowledge representation and reasoning (KRR) based on transparent intensional logic (TIL). It depicts the basic principles of temporal version of TIL based on the extended type hierarchy and presents our suggested method of inference from facts based on natural language input. We show the advantages of using TIL for the knowledge representation of this kind of data and describe particular implementation strategy of KRR.

1 Introduction

In the last decade many researches have been involved in searching the best knowledge representation that would fulfill the need for a well behaving surrogate of the real world objects and situations. The approaches range from encoding the knowledge in some strictly specified procedures in procedural knowledge and logic representation through semantic networks and frames up to statistical and probabilistic knowledge (see [6]). However none of these approaches can claim itself to solve all the difficulties that are brought with objects described by means of natural language.

The most often discussed conceptions are various alternatives of the logic approach, mainly due to its declarativeness. The central problem of logic describing the real world lies in the low descriptiveness of the predicate logic. Though if we want to use logic for representing natural language knowledge, we need some more enhanced and sophisticated variants of logic. One of the most powerful logic is the Intensional Logic by Montague [10]. The transparent intensional logic (TIL) that we use in our system is at least as covering as the Montague's logic, while it is more declarative (hence the "transparent" in title). In the next section we shortly introduce the basics of TIL and in section 4 we enumerate the advantages that TIL brings to KRR field.

2 TIL Principles

There are various approaches to semantic analysis. Here we will discuss the use of the transparent intensional logic, or TIL. It is a logical system based on the typed lambda calculus. TIL was created by Pavel Tichý whose main work on this topic can be found in [1].

TIL is based on the objectual base which consists of the set of four basic types: o is the two-element class of truth-values (truth, T, and falsehood, F), ι is the class of individuals (universe of discourse), ω is the logical space and τ the time space (real numbers). The non-basic types are classes of special entities build upon this base. They form an infinite hierarchy. The classes are formed by mappings from and into the initial objects, mappings from and into those mappings, etc. For every type a countable set is given, whose members are called *variables*.

The members of types we call *objects*, i.e., if ξ is a type, $A \in \xi$ then A is called a ξ-object. We will often consider particular types. The most important of them are *propositions* and *properties of ξ-objects*. The first are $((o\tau)\omega)$-objects. For this type we use the abbreviation π. The latter are $(((o\xi)\tau)\omega)$-objects.

A TIL object that represents an entity described by the analyzed natural language expression is referenced not by some sort of name but rather as a construction of the object. The construction is a lambda term in a kind of the typed lambda calculus. Variables are the only simple constructions. The notion of the construction will be defined inductively. There are three modes of forming constructions (from non-constructions and other constructions): trivialization, composition and closure. Classes of all constructions form another basic types in the hierarchy. From now on we will consider as types also constructions involving those objects and mappings, mappings from and into those constructions, etc. We will formulate an inductive definition of this hierarchy.

Let **B** be a base.

1. (t_1i) Every member of **B** is a *type of order 1 over* **B**.

   ($t_1$ii) If $0 < m$ and $\alpha, \beta_1, \ldots, \beta_m$ are types of order 1 over **B** then the collection $(\alpha\beta_1 \ldots \beta_m)$ of all m-ary (total and partial) mappings from $\beta_1, \ldots, \beta_m$ into α is also a *type of order 1 over* **B**.

   ($t_1$iii) Nothing is a type of order 1 over B unless it follows from (t_1i) and ($t_1$ii).

2. (c_ni) Let τ be any type of order n over **B**. Every variable ranging over τ is a *construction of order n over* **B**. If A is an object of the type τ then ^0A is *construction of order n over* **B**.

   ($c_n$ii) If $0 < m$ and $X_0, X_1, \ldots, X_n$ are constructions of order n over **B** then $[X_0X_1 \ldots X_n]$ is a *construction of order n over* **B**. If $0 < m$, τ is a type of order n over **B**, and Y as well as the distinct variables $x_1, \ldots, x_n$ are constructions of order n over **B**, then $[\lambda_\tau x_1x_2 \ldots x_n Y]$ is a *construction of order n over* **B**.

   ($c_n$iii) Nothing is a construction of order n over **B** unless it follows from (c_ni) and ($c_n$ii).

Let $*_n$ be the collection of constructions of order n over **B**. The collection of *types of order $n+1$ over* **B** is defined as follows:

3. (t_{n+1}i) $*_n$ and every type of order n is a *type of order $n+1$*.

   (t_{n+1}ii) If $0 < m$ and $\alpha, \beta_1, \ldots, \beta_m$ are types of order $n+1$ over **B** then the collection $(\alpha\beta_1 \ldots \beta_m)$ of all m-ary (total and partial) mappings from $\beta_1, \ldots, \beta_m$ into α is also a *type of order $n+1$ over* **B**.

   (t_{n+1}iii) Nothing is a type of order $n+1$ over **B** unless it so follows from (t_{n+1}i) and (t_{n+1}ii).

The connection between a construction and the constructed object is fact-independent and is directed by the mechanism of typed lambda calculus. Constructions carry information about relations between the elementary parts of a language expression.

3 Inference in TIL

The basic entity, which we are working with, is a so called *match*, which is a pair of two components. The first component in the pair is an object (that means a member of some type, a constant) or some variable. The entity which is a constant or a variable we call an *atom*. The latter component is a construction. Intuitively, the atom in a match tracks the entity, which the construction constructs. A match is designated a : C.

The input facts and question are given through a set of matches $\mathfrak{P}1, \ldots, \mathfrak{P}n, \mathfrak{Q}$. We assume that the appropriate propositions are true in the reference world **W** and at the time of utterance **T**. This assumption is expressed through the constant T on the place of atoms in matches. The input facts are:

$$\mathsf{T} : \mathrm{P1}_{\mathrm{WT}}, \ldots, \mathsf{T} : \mathrm{Pn}_{\mathrm{WT}}$$

We use inference system similar to Gentzen's Sequent Calculus, which is well known from the propositional or predicate logic. That is why the inference rules have the following form:

$$\frac{\Psi_1 \vdash \mathfrak{M}_1; \Psi_2 \vdash \mathfrak{M}_2; \ldots; \Psi_k \vdash \mathfrak{M}_k}{\Psi \vdash \mathfrak{M}}(*)$$

The inference behaves like operations over sequents. Above the line there could be also an empty set of sequents. For more explanation and a particular system of inference rules see [2, 8, 1].

The questions can be divided into two classes. In the first class there are questions, which may be answered with "Yes" or "No". These are called yes-no-questions. In the second class there are questions, which start with words like "which", "who", "where", "what", "when". These are called wh-questions.

Inferring the answer to a question could be a very complicated task. At the moment we restrict the system only to those questions, which lead to finding some object or a class of objects declared in KB or finding some properties of these objects declared in KB.

Yes-no-questions are $o_{\tau\omega}$ objects. To answer the given yes-no-question involves inferring the sequent:

$$\mathsf{T} : \mathrm{P1}_{\mathrm{WT}}, \ldots, \mathsf{T} : \mathrm{Pn}_{\mathrm{WT}} \vdash \mathsf{T} : \mathrm{Q}_{\mathrm{WT}}$$

or

$$\mathsf{T} : \mathrm{P1}_{\mathrm{WT}}, \ldots, \mathsf{T} : \mathrm{Pn}_{\mathrm{WT}} \vdash \mathsf{F} : \mathrm{Q}_{\mathrm{WT}}$$

where Pi symbolize the starting constructions, Q symbolizes the question.

A wh-question Q is $(o\xi)_{\tau\omega}$ object. Answering such question involves inferring the sequent:

$$\mathsf{T} : \mathrm{P1}_{\mathrm{WT}}, \ldots, \mathsf{T} : \mathrm{Pn}_{\mathrm{WT}} \vdash \mathsf{T} : \mathrm{Q}_{\mathrm{WT}}(X)$$

and determining all evaluations of X, which yield the desired objects.

It can happen that it will be impossible to infer such sequents. In this case the inference machine should answer with *I do not know*.

The remarks above represent a theoretical background of the inference. We are currently working on an implementation of TIL Inference Machine, or TIM. The TIM system is being implemented in the CAML language, which is a functional language based on the ML language. TIM is being developed simultaneously with the implementation of the Normal Translation Algorithm (NTA). For more details see [5, 3]. NTA outputs TIL constructions of analyzed natural language expressions. These constructions form the basic data for the inference machine. All derivations made by TIM still could be viewed like a correct derivations in the declarative way introduced above.

4 Advantages

The main advantage of TIL is its intensionalistic feature, which is enabled through the possibility of denoting objects of complex type (that means not only objects of the universe (individuals), but also functions of individuals, functions of functions of individuals and so on). Let us explain the concept of intensionality on the following example of two expressions: *the capital city of Poland* and *Warsaw*. The latter expression is a label of an individual, which is independent on the state of the world and on the time moment. In the case of the first expression the situation is different. The dependency of this expression on time moment is clear: the capital city of Poland was not the same in every time moment of the history. It was, for example, also *Krakow*. The fact that *Warsaw* is now the capital of Poland is only one of many possibilities, that could have happened. Objects dependent on the state of the world and on time moment are called *intensions*, other objects are *extensions*. For example first order predicate logic, which is sometimes also used to represent real world facts, has no means to work with intensions.

Another powerful feature of TIL is based on the extended type hierarchy — TIL works with objects of higher order type. That means we can represent belief sentences in the same way as any other object and that representation does not lead to any inconsistencies in further processing. For instance, if we say *Paul counts the square root of 36*, usual representation would make the expression *the square root of 36* identical with the number *6*. However this approach does not reflect the reality properly — it is obvious that Paul does not need to really know what is the correct result of *the square root of 36* and thus he may not even think about *any* particular number here.

5 Knowledge Base Design

We can look at the knowledge base design as consisting of *the ontology* and the description of the way *inference* is performed. The ontology is used as specification of all concepts, that the inferring machine (TIM) knows about, only those concepts that commit to the ontology can ever be thought of as being processed by the machine. In our case the ontology is well defined by means of TIL. All objects that are stored in the knowledge base are derived directly from input constructions that reflect the meaning of facts that the user had implanted to TIM's memory. Every object has an equivalent type in the epistemic framework of TIL.

Our design of representation of TIL objects in computer is based on an implemented system ADAM, that is described in [8, 9]. ADAM's ontology came out of early versions of TIL, that had not used time in verb constructions and did not allow to use objects with higher order types, as it is in the extended type hierarchy. Even without these enhancements the system ADAM was able to catch quite complicated phenomena of natural language like the difference between implication and conditional.

In the system the knowledge is stored in a directed acyclic graph with several edge types. The designed knowledge base can then be viewed of as a semantic net, since the edges represent the structural semantics of subconstructions following Frege's compositionality principle in TIL.

The best way to shortly present the KB structure is followed in the next example of representing the facts arised from input sentence

Tom brought flowers to his mother yesterday. (P1)

The equivalent construction in Normal Translation Form (the output of NTA) is written in the λ-calculus notation

$$\exists f.\mathsf{Class}_{W_{\text{TIM}}T_1}(\mathsf{flower}, f) \wedge \exists m.\mathsf{mother\_of}_{W_{\text{TIM}}T_1}(\mathsf{Tom}, m)$$
$$\bigwedge \mathsf{who}_{W_{\text{TIM}}T_1}(\mathsf{Tom}) \wedge \mathsf{what}_{W_{\text{TIM}}T_1}(f) \wedge \mathsf{to\_whom}_{W_{\text{TIM}}T_1}(m)$$
$$\bigwedge \mathsf{P}_{T_1}(\mathsf{Onc}_{W_{\text{TIM}}}(\mathsf{Does}_{W_{\text{TIM}}T_1}(\mathsf{Tom}, \mathsf{Perf}_{W_{\text{TIM}}}(\mathsf{bring}_{W_{\text{TIM}}}(f, m)))), \mathsf{yesterday}(T_1)) \quad \text{(C1)}$$

This construction consists of three main parts that are separated with the $\bigwedge$ operator:

1. variable allocations
2. semantic operators
3. TIL construction with the TIM's world W_{TIM} and the fact's reference time T_1 applied

When storing the facts in KB the variable allocations are replaced with newly allocated constants of the appropriate type (skolemization) or linked to already allocated objects (see indexic quantifier later on).

The semantic operators are used when identifying the answer to a wh-question. They can be regarded roughly equivalent with Fillmore's deep cases [11], however they seem to be sufficient for the simple cases of inference we want to start with. Now we cannot foreclose the possibility that for the sake of imposing "incompatibility" on some objects that would otherwise be regarded as compatible, we will have to further divide these semantic operators and make them really equivalent with deep cases.

The part of KB that represents our construction consists of 17 basic objects (objects without subconstructions) and 11 structured terms. The whole net that represents this sentence is depicted in figure 1.

6 Inference Notes and Examples

Here we will demonstrate our suggested inference mechanism using the sentence (P1) and the following possible questions:

1. (Q1) What did Tom bring to his mother?
2. (Q2) What did Tom bring to his mother yesterday?
3. (Q3) What did Tom bring to his mother yesterday evening?
4. (Q4) Who brought flowers to his mother?
5. (Q5) To whom did Tom bring flowers yesterday?

The details of inference can be shown on the reasoning that answers the question (Q1). The reference time, i.e. the time when the question was asked, is labeled T_2. The construction that represents question (Q1) is:

$$\text{И}\, m.\mathsf{mother\_of}_{W_{\text{TIM}}T_2}(\mathsf{Tom}, m)$$
$$\bigwedge \mathsf{who}_{W_{\text{TIM}}T_2}(\mathsf{Tom}) \wedge \mathsf{what}_{W_{\text{TIM}}T_2}(F) \wedge \mathsf{to\_whom}_{W_{\text{TIM}}T_2}(m)$$
$$\bigwedge \mathsf{P}_{T_2}(\mathsf{Onc}_{W_{\text{TIM}}}(\mathsf{Does}_{W_{\text{TIM}}T_2}(\mathsf{Tom}, \mathsf{Perf}_{W_{\text{TIM}}}(\mathsf{bring}_{W_{\text{TIM}}}(F, m)))), \mathsf{anytime}) \quad \text{(C2)}$$

F is the variable, whose value we have to find. In the construction (C2) we can notice two new things — the quantifier И and the time interval anytime. The quantifier И is similar to the well-known $\exists$ quantifier, but we do not allocate a new constant here, like it is done in

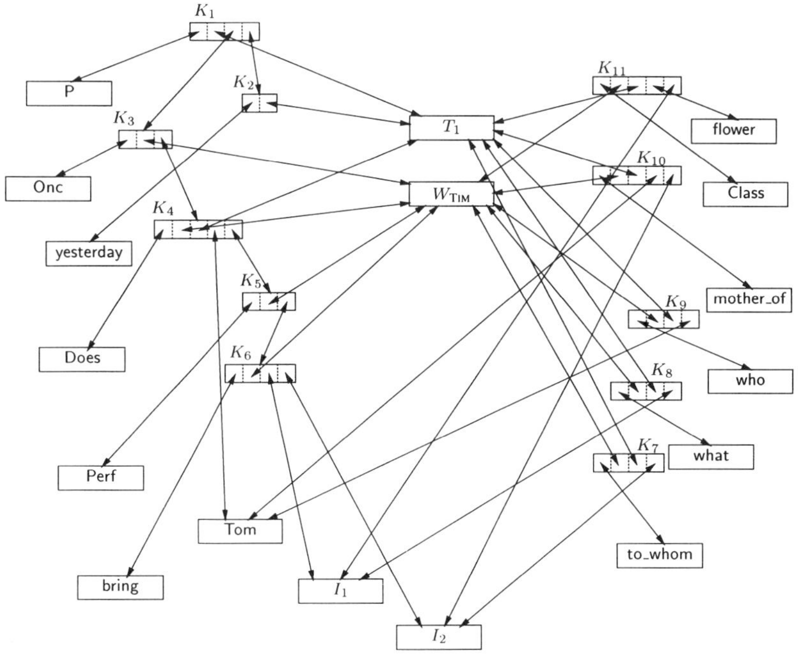

Figure 1: KB for sentence (P1)

skolemization. We assume that the quantified variable is a reference to an object allocated before. We call И the indexic quantifier. During the storing to KB the quantified variable is replaced with the object it pointed to, in our case it is the object labeled as I_2.

In the construction (C2) we have used the time interval anytime, that represents the whole class τ. This usage is implied by the fact, that the input sentence did not specify the time information.

The construction (C2) is first translated to the form similar to KB in picture 1. The value of the variable F is found by successive unification of subconstructions in (C1) and (C2). In terms of KB data structures objects labeled as K_n are subject to unification.

A special kind of unification is needed in case of the following constructions

$$\mathsf{mother\_of}_{W_{\mathrm{TIM}}T_1}(\mathsf{Tom}, I_2) \qquad \text{and} \qquad \mathsf{mother\_of}_{W_{\mathrm{TIM}}T_2}(\mathsf{Tom}, I_2)$$

Indeed we want these constructions to be unifiable for the sake of inference, because we can assume, that Tom's mother is the same person in both moments T_1 and T_2. Therefore we introduce a special unification procedure unifix, that extends the standard procedure unify by equalizing selected time moments or intervals and some other things needed for natural language reasoning.

The reference time T_q (and time interval t_q) of the question will be unified with time T_f (time interval t_f) of a fact if and only if $T_f \leq T_q$ ($t_f \subseteq t_q$). We can do it in this straightforward way only in case we work with positive facts and questions. Otherwise the unifix operator has to take the negation into account.

The inference of the answer to question (Q1) leads to unification of following subconstructions:

$$\mathsf{P}_{T_1}(\mathsf{Onc}_{W_{\text{TIM}}}(\mathsf{Does}_{W_{\text{TIM}}T_1}(\mathsf{Tom}, \mathsf{Perf}_{W_{\text{TIM}}}(\mathsf{bring}_{W_{\text{TIM}}}(I_1, I_2)))), \mathsf{yesterday}(T_1))$$

and

$$\mathsf{P}_{T_2}(\mathsf{Onc}_{W_{\text{TIM}}}(\mathsf{Does}_{W_{\text{TIM}}T_2}(\mathsf{Tom}, \mathsf{Perf}_{W_{\text{TIM}}}(\mathsf{bring}_{W_{\text{TIM}}}(F, I_2)))), \mathsf{anytime})$$

After skolemization and removing the И quantifier the variables f and m were replaced with constants I_1 and I_2. The comparison leads to the unification of the variable F and the constant I_1 which is the requested value.

The question (Q2) differs from (Q1) only in the specification of the time interval, which is now the same in the question and in the corresponding fact. Therefore the condition $t_f \subseteq t_q$ is satisfied, so that the unification also leads to finding the object I_1.

For question (Q3) the time interval is more specific than in fact (P1), that is why the subconstructions cannot be unified. For the question (Q3) TIM gives the answer *"I do not know"*. That follows the intuition — Tom could have brought the flowers in the afternoon or in the evening, but there is no way to infer this from fact (P1).

Answers to questions (Q4) and (Q5) are derived in the same way as in previous cases, only the free variable F is now argument of who or to_whom functions.

7 Conclusions

We expect our system for knowledge representation and reasoning to be a jumping board for new natural language analyser and inference machine based on the very powerful apparatus of transparent intensional logic. This logic comprises the techniques for analysing intensions, belief sentences, verb tenses, time sliding discourse and other difficult phenomena of natural language. The possibility to infer new facts from represented knowledge can also improve the correctness of semantical analysis of text, text disambiguation or speech analysis.

References

[1] Tichý, Pavel: *The Foundations of Frege's Logic*, de Gruyter, Berlin, New York, 1988.

[2] Tichý, Pavel: Foundations of Partial Type Theory, *Reports on Mathematical Logic 14*, pp. 52-72, 1982.

[3] Hadacz, Leo: Using TIL for Semantic Analysis of Text, *Proceedings of TSD 1998*, pp. 363-368, Brno, 1998.

[4] Hadacz, Leo: Semantic Inference in the Human–Machine Communication, *Proceedings of TSD'99*, pp. 353-356, Springer Verlag, Berlin, 1999.

[5] Smrž, Pavel and Horák, Aleš: Implementation of Efficient and Portable Parser for Czech, *Proceedings of TSD'99*, pp. 105-108, Springer-Verlag, Berlin, 1999

[6] Luger, George F. and Stubblefield, William A.: Artificial Intelligence: Structures and Strategies for Complex Problem Solving, 3rd edition, Addison Wesley Longman, Reading, MA, 824 p., 1998

[7] Materna, Pavel, Pala, Karel and Zlatuška, Jiří: Logická analýza přirozeného jazyka, Academia, Prague, 1989.

[8] Chrz Tomáš: *Reprezentace znalostípři komunikaci člověk–stroj* (The Knowledge Representation in the Human–Machine Communication), PhD thesis, Prague, 1984.

[9] Chrz, Tomáš: A System for Knowledge Representation Based on Intensional Logic, *Computers and Artificial Intelligence*, 3 (1984), No. 3, pp. 193-209, No. 4, pp. 305-317

[10] Montague, R.: *Formal Philosophy*, editor R. H. Thomason, Yale University Press, New Haven, 1974

[11] Fillmore, C.: The Case for Case, *Universals in Linguistic Theory*, pp. 1–88, New York, 1968.

Knowledge-Based Software Engineering
T. Hruška and M. Hashimoto (Eds.)
IOS Press, 2000

A Measuring Dependent Degrees among Class Members and Structural Complexity

Hirohisa AMAN, Torao YANARU, Masahiro NAGAMATSU, Kazunori MIYAMOTO
Dept. of E.E. and Computer Eng., Kyushu Institute of Technology,
Sensui-cho 1–1, Tobata, Kitakyushu 804–8550, Japan
aman@soft.comp.kyutech.ac.jp

Abstract. We represent a class structure as a directed graph which is called class structure graph, and quantify the dependent relationships among class members using the class structure graph. Then we propose a measurement of a class structural complexity attribute so as to be more flexible and more suitable for OO software rather than we previously proposed measurement.

1 Introduction

It is generally believed that object oriented (OO) methodologies bring some benefits (e.g. high re-usability, maintainability) to a developed software. However such benefits might be missed, since most processes of design and development are achieved by software engineers, then the processes depend on the each engineer's ability and experience in a software development. So software metrics will be of great significance; software metrics measure and/or predict some properties of software development processes, resources and products. Indeed some metrics have been proposed for OO software or design(e.g.[1]–[4]). Most metrics have, however, a lack of consideration for directions of class members couplings. So we have proposed a metric for a class structural complexity attribute (SC) which has a concept of directed coupling, then discussed not only direct relations between class members but also indirect relations[3]. The contribution of this paper is to improve the metric SC to be more flexible and more suitable for OO software.

2 Class Structure Graph

Let us introduce the notion of *class structure graph*[3]. A class structure graph is a directed graph to represent the couplings between class members, on which each of members and couplings corresponds to each of nodes and edges, respectively. On a class structure graph, we could represent class member couplings according to the following 1) — 4): 1) If a method m writes some data to an attribute a, then we represent it as the edge (m, a) on the graph; 2) If a method m reads some data from an attribute a, then we represent it as the edge (a, m) on the graph; 3) If a method m_1 calls a method m_2, which has no return value, then we represent it as the edge $(\mathsf{m}_1, \mathsf{m}_2)$ on the graph; 4) If a method m_1 calls a method m_2, which has some return values, then we represent it as two edges $(\mathsf{m}_1, \mathsf{m}_2)$ and $(\mathsf{m}_2, \mathsf{m}_1)$ on the graph.

The notions of inheritance and aggregation have been supported as well[4].

If a class is a sub-class of another class, the sub-class structure graph includes all nodes and edges of the super-class structure graph, since a sub-class inherits its features from the super-class.

When a class is a part of another class, the part-class will be treated as one member of the whole-class, that is, the part-class will become one node on the whole-class structure graph. Then all couplings with the part-class members will be concentrated upon the node. So the part-class structure could be separated from the whole-class structure.

For a simple example, we consider *intStack* class shown in Fig.1(written in Java^{TM}). Now we can obtain the class structure graph for *intStack* class (see Fig.2).[1] Note that *java.lang.Object*[2] is the super-class of *intStack* class, so Fig.2 contains the class structure graph of *java.lang.Object* as the sub-graph(see broken line area in Fig.2).

```
public class intStack {
  private int sp;
  private int[ ] data = new int[100];
  public intStack(){ sp = 0; }
  public void push(int x) {
    if ( sp < 100 ){
      data[sp] = x;  sp = sp + 1;
    }
  }
  public int pop(){
    if ( sp > 0 ) {
      sp = sp − 1;
      return data[sp];
    }
    return 0;
  }
}
```

Fig. 1 *intStack* class declaration

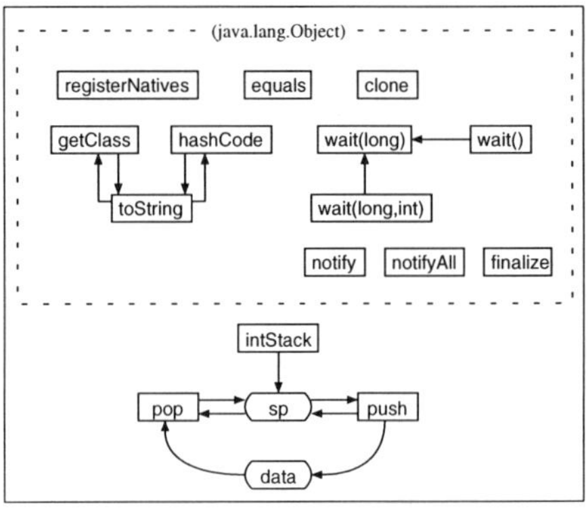

Fig. 2 Structure graph of *intStack* class

3 Dependent Relationships and a Class Structural Complexity Attribute

In order to consider dependent relationships among class members, we might evaluate the reachability on the class structure graph. However some strongly connected components appear often on the structure graph. Since all members within a strongly connected component are reachable each other, it will be regarded as a mass of members, then be difficult to analyze the class structure. Consequently we will evaluate not only reachability but also the degrees of dependent relationships among class members[3].

Definition 1 (weighted closure) Let A be the adjacency matrix of a class structure graph. We define the *weighted closure* of A as $A_w^* := \sum_{k=1}^{\infty} w_k \, A^k$, $(w_k \geq 0, \ \sum_{k=1}^{\infty} w_k > 0)$,where w_k is the weight coefficient corresponding to k-length path on the structure graph. ■

The above weighted closure represents the degrees of dependent relationships between class members. The degrees are based on the distances and the number of paths between members on the class structure graph. The distances depend on the weight coefficients $\{w_k\}$, so we may make various analysis by adjusting $\{w_k\}$. Some methodologies as to the *decision making problem* (e.g. the *paired comparison method*[3]) will be helpful to decide $\{w_k\}$.

[1] For instance, method *push* 1) reads attribute *sp*, 2) writes a value to *data* in the corresponding position, and 3) increase *sp* by one. Thus the three edges (*sp*, *push*), (*push*, *data*) and (*push*, *sp*) are appearing in Fig.2.

[2] we omit the source code of *java.lang.Object* for the lack of space.

Definition 2 (dependence index between class members) Let $a_w^*(i,j)$ be the element in the i-th row, j-th column of A_w^*. We define the *dependence index* as $p(i,j) := a_w^*(j,i)$. Moreover we call the matrix $P = (\ p(i,j)\ )$ as *dependence matrix.* ■

$p(i,j)$ represents the degree of which the i-th member[3] depends on the j-th member as an external factor to behave correctly (in the case of method), or to be stored correct value (in the case of attribute). An external factor[4] means a method-call or a data reading/writing on an attribute. In order to see the total degree of dependent relationships, we now consider $\sum_{i=1}^{N} p(i,j)$ and $\sum_{j=1}^{N} p(i,j)$, where N is the number of rows (columns) in P. $\sum_i p(i,j)$ represents the total degree of which all members depend on the j-th member; $\sum_j p(i,j)$ denotes the total degree of which the i-th member depends on other members. Then we define the following vector.

Definition 3 (dependency vector) Let $p(i,j)$ $(i,j = 1,2,\ldots,N)$ be a dependence index in a class. Then we define the *dependency vector* as $\boldsymbol{p}_k := \left(\sum_{i=1}^{N} p(i,k),\ \sum_{j=1}^{N} p(k,j)\right)$, $(k = 1,2,\ldots,N)$. ■

We believe that the dependency vector reflects a summarized dependent relationship as to the k-th member within the class. In [3], we proposed a metric for a class structural complexity attribute using the above dependency vector. It had, however, a lack of flexibility since it restricted the method complexity metric to *Halstead's effort equation*[5], and had a loss of suitability for OO because the consideration for aggregation (a-part-of relation) were not sufficient. We now propose an improved metric for a class structural complexity attribute.

Definition 4 (metric for class structural complexity attribute) Let *cls* be a class. We define the class structural complexity of *cls* as $SC(cls) := \sum_{k=1}^{N} |\boldsymbol{p}_k|\ C(k)$, where N is the number of class members; $\boldsymbol{p}_k$ and $C(k)$ is the dependency vector and the complexity of the k-th member, respectively $(k = 1,2,\ldots,N)$. If the k-th member is a method, then $C(k)$ is a method complexity metric[5]; otherwise $C(k)$ has the unit of complexity. ■

On this metric, we can consider each member's complexity using not only itself but also the relations around it, although WMC[1], a famous class complexity metric, has been the sum of the method complexities. This notion is from the *moment of force* in the field of dynamics. When we regard $C(k)$ as the mass at $\boldsymbol{p}_k$, SC can be interpreted as the moment of force about the origin; Figure 3 shows this concept image.

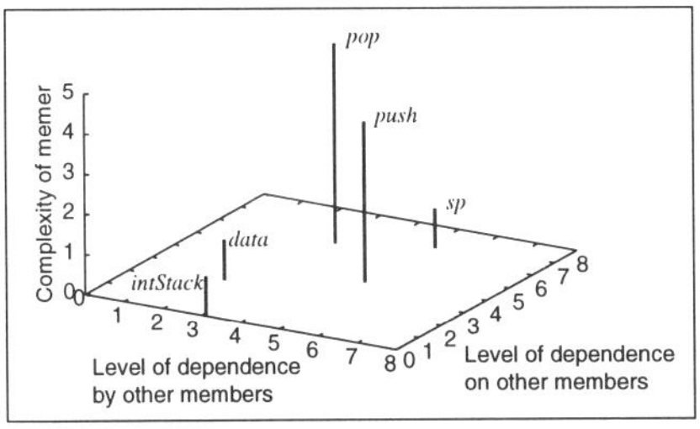

Fig. 3 Dependent relationships and complexities of members within *intStack* class (without super-class members)

[3] the k-th member denotes the member corresponding to the k-th row of A.

[4] On the other hand, "internal" factor is the structure or description of the member itself.

[5] Although the method complexity metric could be an existing metric such as *Halstead* metric[5], *McCabe* metric[6] and so on, we avoid specifying the metric especially so as to be useful in several cases.

This metric SC has the monotonicity with respect to inheritance.

Theorem 1 (monotonicity) Let X_1 be a class, and X_2 be a sub-class of X_1. Then $SC(\mathsf{X}_1) \leq SC(\mathsf{X}_2)$.

Proof. Let A_1 and A_2 be the adjacency matrix of the structure graph corresponding to X_1 and X_2, respectively. Then we can write $A_2 = \left[\begin{array}{c|c} A_1 & S \\ \hline T & U \end{array}\right]$, where S, T and U is matrix of $(N_1, N_2 - N_1)$-type, $(N_2 - N_1, N_1)$-type and $(N_2 - N_1, N_2 - N_1)$-type, respectively; N_1 and N_2 denotes the order of A_1 and A_2, respectively. Now we can obtain $A_2^n = \left[\begin{array}{c|c} A_1^n & O \\ \hline O & O \end{array}\right] + R_n$, with $R_n = Y^{n-1}Z + Y^{n-2}ZY + \cdots + Z^{n-1}Y + \cdots + Z^n \geq O\ (n = 1, 2, \dots)$, where $Y = \left[\begin{array}{c|c} A_1 & O \\ \hline O & O \end{array}\right]$, $Z = \left[\begin{array}{c|c} O & S \\ \hline T & U \end{array}\right]$; O denotes zero matrix. So we get $P_2 \geq \left[\begin{array}{c|c} P_1 & O \\ \hline O & O \end{array}\right]$ from Def.1 and 2. Since $P_1, P_2 \geq O, \forall k |\boldsymbol{p}_2(k)| \geq |\boldsymbol{p}_1(k)|$, so $\sum_{k=1}^{N_1} |\boldsymbol{p}_2(k)| C(k) \geq \sum_{k=1}^{N_1} |\boldsymbol{p}_1(k)| C(k) = SC(\mathsf{X}_1)$. With $\forall k\ |\boldsymbol{p}_2(k)| \geq 0\ \forall k\ C(k) \geq 0$, we now see $SC(\mathsf{X}_2) = \sum_{k=1}^{N_2} |\boldsymbol{p}_2(k)| C(k) = \sum_{k=1}^{N_1} |\boldsymbol{p}_2(k)| C(k) + \sum_{k=N_1+1}^{N_2} |\boldsymbol{p}_2(k)| C(k) \geq \sum_{k=1}^{N_1} |\boldsymbol{p}_2(k)| C(k)$. Therefore $SC(\mathsf{X}_1) \leq SC(\mathsf{X}_2)$. ■

4 Conclusion and Future Work

We improved the metric SC proposed in [3]. Although we currently have a confirmation that SC satisfies Weyuker's properties[7] with a small number of conditions[6], it seems not sufficient theoretically because Weyuker's properties have some criticisms(e.g. [1],[8]). In the future, in order to evaluate the validation of SC, we intend to experiment with other existing metrics and investigate some related works (e.g. Fenton's work[8]).

Acknowledgements

We would like to thank the anonymous referees for their helpful comments on this paper.

References

[1] S.R. Chidamber et al., A Metrics Suite for Object Oriented Design, *IEEE Trans. Software Eng.*, vol.20, no.6, pp.476–493, June 1994.

[2] E.M. Kim et al., A New Metric for C++ Program Complexity and Its Evaluation in Academic Environment, *IEICE Trans.* vol.J79-D-I, no.10, pp.729–737, Oct. 1996.

[3] H. Aman et at., A Metric for Class Structural Complexity Focusing on Relationships among Class Members, *IEICE Trans. Inf. & Syst.*, vol.E81-D, no.12, pp.1364–1373, Dec. 1998.

[4] H. Aman et al., A Study of Class Structural Complexity in Object Oriented software, through a Fuzzy Graph Connectivity Analysis, *Journal of Japan Society for Fuzzy Theory and Systems*, vol.11, no.3, pp.521–527, June 1999.

[5] M.H.Halstead, *Elements of Software Science*, Elservier North-Holland, 1977.

[6] T.J. McCabe, A Complexity Measure, *IEEE Trans. Software Eng.*, vol.SE-2, no.4, pp.308–320, Dec. 1976.

[7] E.J. Weyuker, Evaluating Software Complexity Measures, *IEEE Trans. Software Eng.*, vol.14, no.9, pp.1357–1365, Sep. 1988.

[8] N. Fenton, Software Measurement : A Necessary Scientific Basis, *IEEE Trans. Software Eng.*, vol.20, no.3, pp.199–206, March 1994.

[6] They are the following two conditions. For the lack of space, we omit the details.
1) The class member complexity metric $C(\cdot)$ satisfies Weyuker's properties 1, 2 and 8;
2) For the series of weight coefficients $\{w_k\}$, $w_1 \neq 0$ and [$(\exists n \geq 2)(\exists M \geq n)$ s.t. $w_n > 0$ and $w_k = 0$ $(\forall k > M)$].

Knowledge-Based Software Engineering
T. Hruška and M. Hashimoto (Eds.)
IOS Press, 2000

The Analysis of a Planning Task

Marcos ROMERO-CASTRO, Abraham RODRÍGUEZ-RODRÍGUEZ

Departamento de Informática y Sistemas
Universidad de Las Palmas de Gran Canaria
Canary Islands, Spain
Tlf: + 34 928 458 700, Fax: +34 928 458 711
E-mail: mromero@teror.dis.ulpgc.es, arodriguez@dis.ulpgc.es

Abstract. In this paper we present how a planning domain can be analysed in order to allow reusability. We propose a lineal task decomposition with a global control task. The *control task* is modelled using a generic problem solving method (PSM) for planning. We have selected a PSM that fits the main characteristics of this *control task*. We have applied these ideas and we have obtained the analysis in the RCC (Rescue Center Co-ordination) and SAR 802 Squadron of the Spanish Air Forces in Las Palmas (Canary Islands). We have applied the problem solving methods that provide the CommonKADS methodology and we have modified some of them following this philosophy. We have developed a prototype of the Knowledge Based System (KBS) that it works fine, and this fact validates the analysis we have performed. The clear advantages of reusability are the decrease in development time and effort.

1 Introduction

The number of domains in which the decision making is supported by means of computers has been increasing during the last years. At the same time, it has generated an interest in the topic, causing a growth of the artificial intelligence in this area. This requires a development of the Knowledge Based System (KBS) methodologies. However, this is not enough for developing this field so much as Software Engineering has done. One of the bases is, in our opinion, the capacity of generating, developing, applying, modifying and, finally, reusing the analysis of a specific domain in a similar and generic one. The reuse is only important if the effort accomplished in the application of reusable components is smaller than the necessary effort to build the components again from the beginning [3]. Considering this, we will propose an approach to analyse similar planning domains.

Among the methodologies that have a great relevance to implement the analysis of some domain, we find DESIRE, PROTEGE-II, MIKE [8] and CommonKADS [8][9][17]. One of the main differences is that CommonKADS performs a deep context modelling. Furthermore, it applies a selection and refinement process of available template models of different generic environments. CommonKADS performs it through an approximation to the life cycle. PROTEGE-II makes a more complete use of the tools for the knowledge acquisition and considers the reusability as an integral part of the methodology. MIKE also applies an approximation through a life cycle. CommonKADS is in period of summit, since there are several work groups that use this methodology for the development of the Knowledge Based Systems.

CommonKADS facilitates the specification of a particular system through the use of some model templates that contain the formal descriptions and operationalizations of generic common systems [4]. These templates are known as Problem Solving Methods (PSM). They are selected according to the aim of the system that we wish to model, and then, they are completed. This way, these standards allow reusing the developed systems. There is a wide range of available templates, so that practically all the environments can be modeled through the election of the most similar template, according to its nature. They are classified by its goal: those of analysis, and those of synthesis [12].

The Search and Rescue domain (SAR) develop an important task in which the faster the time response to an emergency, the better the result of the mission. The SAR has to act in all accidents or emergencies that occur in a predefined zone known by all Rescues Center Coordination (RCC), each of them have their own responsibility zone. It is primordial optimize the resources in order to obtain the best results. The reusability allows us to use planning tasks in this domain. There are many people working and studying the reusability through template models, seeking for the adaptability of the studies accomplished in a field to other [2][11] and developing architectures that permits the reusability of the existing components. Methodologies like CommonKADS facilitate this idea of reusability, which is considered as a powerful tool for the development of KBS. The problems emerge when trying to re-use the solutions built from one domain to another.

Most of the planning models have been derived from the Open Planning Architecture, known as O-PLAN [7]. Parts of our studies were focused on projects that were accomplished by other authors. We were interested in knowing which template model was chosen, why they selected that template and studying the reusability degree of their analysis and projects. Firstly, we made an exhaustive study of Knowledge Level of Planning System with the works done by Valente [14][15] in background, and in other way, the planning which use O-PLAN. The introduction of a knowledge-based system was studied by the Defence Research Agency Flight Systems Division [6][10] in the Edinburgh Rescue Co-ordination Centre of the RAF. The approach given in that environment was to use a generic-planning template. Such template was envisaging all the possible processes involved in the course of a mission. This template was adapted for that particular system, which prevents that solution from being used in other domains.

2 Analysis of SAR domain

We used the CommonKADS methodology for the analysis of different tasks. In this paragraph, we consider the conceptualisation of domain, focused on the SAR domain. Our goal was to perform an analysis that could be reused in other Planning domains.

The idea of developing an analysis of a Planning domain is related to an architecture fragmented in tasks with not overlapped competencies. Each task can be a subtask of a process in a higher level. Each one of them is modelled following a generic standard (PSM) that is repeated in similar tasks from different domains. The advantage of this approach is already visible. Applying this idea, other similar Planning domains would be able to use the developed analysis that we outline. However, if we want to perform a reusable analysis, it is necessary to make use of specification structures extensible to any domain. The generic templates that CommonKADS provides for modelling (PSM) have this mission [2]. To study how these systems represent and use available knowledge to solve the problem is a valuable way to realise a high level analysis of a particular domain [1]. Due to this, we have made an analysis using the templates that best fulfill the Knowledge requirements, according to its nature. Then, we can split the planning domain in different parts that could be analysed separately. This way, a less generic system remains, but the subtasks are reusable. These subtasks carry on different functions, therefore, the conceptualisation modelling is made by different template functions. This is a first step, but the objective is to apply it in multiple domains without requiring further efforts. That is the reason why we make incidence in the reusability. Building reusable systems imply the improvement of the applications, thus obtaining a better analysis and facilitating the subsequent design. We could then focus our efforts in this point.

Once our purpose is stated, we reflect it in a real domain, the SAR domain. The main activity of the SAR domain is to accomplish searches and rescues. It mainly consists of planning the different events in order to co-ordinate them in an optimum way. We propose to divide the systems in subtasks, among which there are intensive communications to solve the problem of the dependencies.

Planning environments in which we can apply the analysis performed for this system without having to change drastically are maritime rescue, the emergency service, the fire department, etc. There are tasks that should be planned, due to their complexity and to the fact that they use, in their activities, devices and resources that must be coordinated.

2.1 Ontology of the SAR domain and Task Ontology

The ontology can be seen as a specification of the knowledge explicit level of a conceptualisation [16]. 'It is considered as a representation vocabulary, typically specialised to some domain or subject matter. More precisely, it is not the vocabulary itself what qualifies an ontology, but the conceptualisations that the terms in the vocabulary are intended to acquire. The identification of those terms and the intended conceptualisations generally require a careful analysis of the object classes and relationships that exist in the domain' [5]. Because of this, an ontology does not vary when translated into another language. It requires quite dedication to accomplish a stable ontology and it is a continually changing incremental process. We have used the following ontology tools to develop the analysis: terms glossary, hierarchy tree concepts, graphs of relationships, knowledge model, inference model, representation of the tasks sequence and data flow graphs. We have considered the order in which the resources are chosen to avoid dependencies, restrictions, or preferences that could influence to different final solutions and the necessary functions of the domain that have been studied.

2.2 State and knowledge of the Problem Solving Method. Method Ontology

We have studied the different suitable templates for modelling the system and the interaction among them [12]. The solution is evaluated so that it does not introduce neither dependencies nor restrictions in the outputs of the different tasks, since the solution is the result of each subtask's having reached its own goal.

2.3 Generic and Specific Domain Ontology. Domain Knowledge

In this point, we describe and write in CML (Conceptual Model Language) the objects, relationships and rules obtained from the domain. A part of this specification is shown in the figure 1.

```
Concept Aircraft;
  Sub-Type-Of: Resources;
  Has-Part-Of: Fuel-Tank, Stuff, Crew;
  Attributes:
    ...
End Concept Aircraft;
```

```
Rule-Type Yyyyy;
 Antecedent: Associated-With;
 Consequent: Xxxxxxx;
 Connection-Symbol: Make-A-Formation;
End Rule-Type Yyyyy;
```

Figure 1. Specification in CML.

3 Description of the split reusable subtask

There are some ways to model a planning domain, other authors have developed it by means of a generic template that agglutinates all the actions and events that have to be carry out by the task [6][7]. However, we think that a valuable way to make this task is by means of doing an exhaustive analysis in order to capture the subtask that compound a whole domain. The control subtask is responsible for the designed plan. Its mission is to give an order to the different events and actions that are produced by other subtasks and external agents of the system.

Information Management is in charge of collecting the information that has been introduced by the user or external sources to the system. Information Processing task is splitted in a set of subtask that have to be performed to achieve the plan, and Operations Control subtask that is modeled with a planning template. The operation control is responsible for analysing all the new information and controlling that the mission is following the right course of action. On the other hand, Information Management task is also entrusted of generate new information by means of abstracting the previous acquired information. The data that contain the location of the accident must be acquired, how many passengers should be recovered (if it is necessary), whether it is a task of rescue, and in this case, whether the mission must be co-ordinated with other rescue teams, data about the wrecked ship, etc. In figure 2, we show how are connected these tasks.

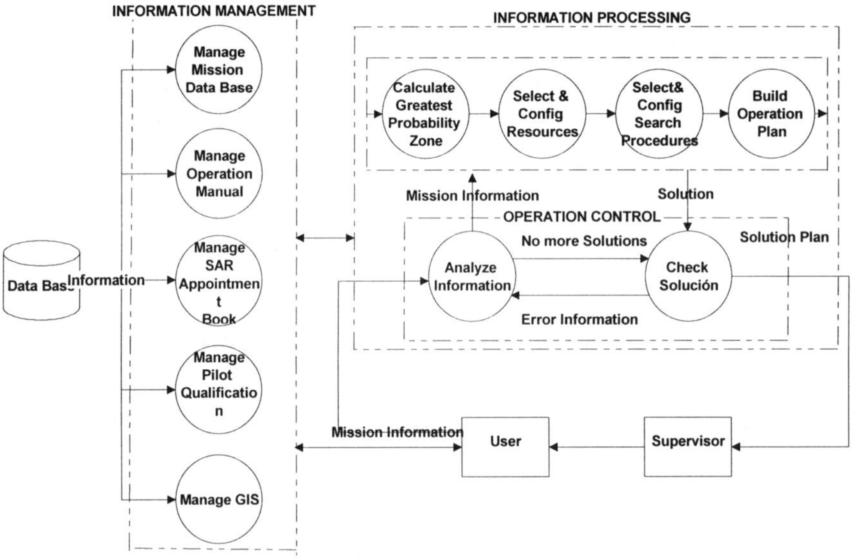

Figure 2. A detailed tasks decomposition.

The subtasks that have to be performed to achieve the plan are:

Calculating the greatest probability zone: it has to calculate those areas in which the injured element will be most probably found. In that area will be made searches if resulted with large dimensions. The user can modify this area if it is considered convenient. Among the things that must be considered are: size of the search area, maximum probability zone, atmospheric conditions, precision of the co-ordinates where the injured element has been reported, other accidents in the location (historical). Within these tasks, the calculations from the current drifts have a special importance. This calculation is based on complex mathematical studies. We focus on it as numerical models in which the obtained information acts as a variable of a function. The following data are necessary to calculate these expressions: Environmental conditions, force and direction of the current drifts, force and direction of the wind, state of the sea, and other characteristic as the depth, presence of rocks in the zone, characteristics of the body in current drifts, etc. We have built a prototype to validate the outputs of this subsystem. It is based on the Geographical Information Systems (GIS) in which the user introduces data about the characteristics of the accident and meteorological information.

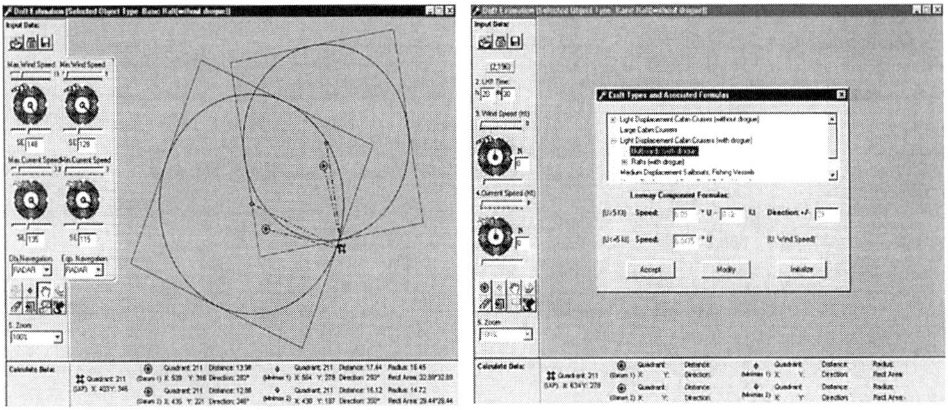

Figure 3. Snapshots of the prototype. It contains the limits of the search area for a lost raft. It is calculated using the domain knowledge elicited from the human expert and combined with numeric standard methods.

Selecting and Configuring Resources: This task takes into account the selection of the aircraft, the selection of the material to be carried and the configuration of the fuel deposits, due to the fact that it is variable for the helicopters. The data that should be considered are: active and inactive resources, situation or location, state in which concerning fuel is found, how many units of search and rescue are necessary, and generic characteristics of the ship. About the configuration, we should consider how the inactive means could be configured, how the active means are configured, characteristic with this given configuration, etc. These three subtasks have been modeled separately. We have used a template similar to configuration design but we have accomplished the template with some modifications to adjust it to reality.

Selecting and configuring the search procedure: the search procedure adapted for such conditions is selected with the information about the characteristics of the accident and with the data generated by the previous tasks. The configuration of the search procedure consists of giving the concrete values to accomplish it. Among these values are: the point within the area in which the search must start, the number of travels, the distances between passes, the width and height of the area, speed, height, configuration of the procedure, time between the sign emission if it is necessary, angle, etc. The chosen template has been classified according to the available templates by the CommonKADS library. We use the classification template to choose the best candidate search method according to the characteristics of the mission.

Building the operations plan: It consists of establishing the most advantageous route to accomplish the mission. Within this task, the possibility of doing refuelling in different points is studied. Moreover, a mission could be coordinated with other entities, so that some aircraft should be displaced to some particular available enclaves with the greater briefness.

Synthesis has been the chosen template to model this task. It is very auspicious to model the planning processes.

Operations Control: It must control that all the processes are being accomplished according to the established plan, and it must take decisions so that the mission follows its right course according to the planning. The characteristics of the subtask sign that the inference model of a non-linear planner is suitable for accomplishing this subtask. In Table 1 we show these characteristics.

Application domain characteristics	The goals are actions Interaction between actions
Static Role	World Description Plan Composition Plan Assessment knowledge
Domain-Model characteristics	MTC Total Order Propagation Constraints
Task	Select Goal Test-for-unachieved-Goals Critique Modify
Realizing Method	Linear/Smart MTC Backtracking
Type of PSM	MTC Total Order Propagation Constraints

Table 1. SAR domain characteristics.
MTC = Modal Truth Criterion.

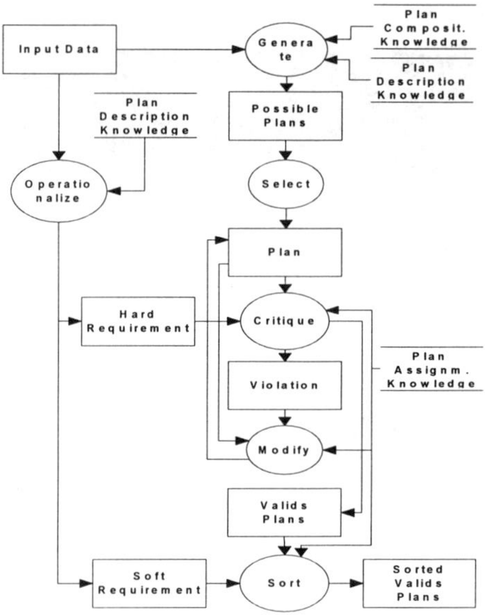

Figure 4. Inference Model of a non-lineal Planner.

Control Structure:

```
Operationalize (Input-Data, WDK->Hard-Requirement, Soft-Requirement)
Generate(PCK,PDK,Input-Data->Possible-Plans)
While (Possible-Plans) do
   Select(Possible-Plans->Plan)
   Repeat
     Critique(Plan,Hard-Requirement,PAK->Violation)
     If Violation= true then
       Modify(Plan,PAK,Violation->Plan)
     Else
       Valid-Plans:=Valid-Plans +Plan
     End If
  Until Violation=False
End While
Sort (Valid-Plans, Soft-Requirement->Sorted-Valids-Plan)
```

WDK = World Description Knowledge; PCK = Plan Composition Knowledge
PDK = Plan Description Knowledge; PAK = Plan Assessment Knowledge

This method can be viewed as a specialization of Chandrasekaran method propose-Critique-Modify (PCM). It initially was proposed for design tasks, however, it could be used in planning domain since we can see it as a planning design (synthesis) [15].

The Planning Process step by step is the following:

1. Depending on the information of the mission, the constraints (preferences and restrictions) that affect the actual mission are activated.
2. Using the information of the mission, the Plan Composition Knowledge and Plan Description Knowledge, the planner presets the length of the skeletal plan and begins to generate possible plans.
3. A plan is selected and is criticized by restrictions. In this way, if a possible plan does not satisfy all the restrictions it has to be modified using the plan assignment knowledge and try to pass again all the restrictions with the new variations.
4. If the plan does not violate any restrictions, it will be part of the valid plans. The steps three and four are repeated until there are not more possible plans.
5. The valid plan solutions are sorted by the soft requirements.

The method used to implement this PSM was the Forward Checking Algorithm [13]. We selected this method because of the high number of possible combinations of plans in the SAR domain. The main idea of this method is to avoid all the possible candidates that do not contribute to the plan solution. In this way, the system does not have to try all the possible combinations in the solutions tree. We used this algorithm to solve all the planning subtasks mentioned above.

4 Conclusions

We outline the reusability as an important concept in which future works could be based. We have shown how a planning domain can be analysed in order to allow reusability. We propose a way in which the analysis of a particular planning domain could be totally or partially reuse in other similar domains. Different to other research groups which have approached the planning problem with the use of a global template of planning, or by means of a general form that agglutinates every planning sub-problem, we have performed an exhaustive analysis in which every subtask have been studied and modeled separately. This allows to reuse each part that we need in similar processes. In addition, we can use the same architecture to implement another system, cutting the subtasks that do not match with the new domain. Moreover, we can use the ontology in similar tasks. The method ontology is a good point to start the problem. The ontology is another way to exploit reusability.

We have applied these ideas and we have obtained the analysis in the RCC (Rescue Centre Co-ordination) and SAR 802 Squadron of the Spanish Air Forces in Las Palmas (Canary Islands). Following the reusability ideas we have taken the PSM that CommonKADS provides. We have started from PSM templates and we have reused them, by modifying some of them. We have developed a prototype of the KBS that it works fine, and this fact validates the analysis we have performed. The clear advantages of reusability are the decrease in development time and effort.

Acknowledgements

To all different members of the RCC and SAR squadron 802 for their patience in the difficult task of the knowledge acquisition. To Francisco R.Teruel Alberich, co-worker in this project for his valuable comments and discussions on the research reported here. This work has been partially founded by European Commission and the Comisión Interministerial de Ciencia y Tecnología of Spain through the project SARPA id. 1FD97-0612.

References

[1] Barros, L., Valente, A., Benjamins, V.R. Modeling Planning Tasks. In Third International Conference on Artificial Intelligence Planning Systems, AIPS-96, pp. 11-18. American Association of Artificial Intelligence (AAAI). 1996.

[2] Benjamins, V. R., and Fensel, D. : Editorial: Problem-Solving Methods, International Journal of Human-Computer Studies (IJHCS), 49(4):305-313,1998.

[3] Beys, P., Benjamins, V.R., van Heijst, G., Remedying the Reusability -- Usability Trade-off for Problem-Solving Methods. In proceedings of KAW'96 (Banff), pages 2.1-2.20, 1996

[4] Breuker, J., Van de Velde, W.. CommonKADS Library for Expertise Modelling. IOS Press, Amsterdam, 1994.

[5] Chandrasekaran, B., Josephson, J. R., Benjamins, V. R. "Ontology of Tasks and Methods," 1998 Banff Knowledge Acquisition Workshop. Two versions, "What are ontologies and why do we need them?," IEEE Intelligent Systems, Jan/Feb 1999, 14(1), pp. 20-26; "Ontology of Task and Methods," IEEE Intelligent Systems, May/June, 1999.

[6] Cottam, H., Shadbolt, N., Kingston, J., Beck, H., Tate, A. Knowledge Level Planning in the Search and Rescue Domain. In Research and development in expert systems XII edited by M. A. Bramer, J. L. Nealon and R. Milne, Information Press Ltd, Oxford, England, 1995. pp.309-325. ISBN-1-899621-04-0. 1995.

[7] Currie, K., Tate, A.: O-Plan: The Open Planning Architecture. Artificial Intelligence 52(1):49-86. 1991.

[8] Frances M.T. Brazier and Niek J.E. Wijngaards. In KAW'98 Proceedings - Evaluation of knowledge-acquisition methodologies A Purpose Driven Method for the Comparison of Modelling Frameworks. 1998.

[9] Hoog, R.de, Martil, R., Wielinga, B.J., Taylor, R., Bright, C., & Van Der Velde, W. The CommonKADS Model set, Deliverable ESPRIT project P5248, KADS-II/WP I-II/RR/UvA/6.0.(Ext.r.no.). Amsterdam: Universiteit van Amsterdam, 31 pp. 1994

[10] Kingston, J., Shadbolt, N., Tate, A. CommonKADS Models for Knowledge Based Planning. AIAI-TR-199. Extended version of an article published in Proceedings of AAAI-96. 1996.

[11] Motta, E., Fensel, D., Gaspari, M., Benjamins, V.R. Specifications of Knowledge Components for Reuse. In the Eleventh International Conference on software Engineering and Knowledge Engineering (SEKE-99). 1999.

[12] Schreiber, Akkermans, Anjewierden, de Hoog, Shadbolt, Van de Velde, Wielinga. Engineering and Managing Knowledge. The CommonKADS Methodology. 1998.

[13] Shanahan M., Southwick R. Search, inference and dependencies in artificial intelligence. Ellis Horwood Series in Artificial Intelligence, 1989.

[14] Valente, A. Knowledge Level Analysis of Planning Systems. SIGART Bulletin, Vol. 1, N.6, 1994.

[15] Valente, A. Planning. In J.Breuker and W. Van de Velde, editors. Reusable Problem Solving Components: The CommonKADS Library for Expertise Modelling. Chapter 10, pages 213-230. IOS Press, Amsterdam, 1994.

[16] Van Heijst. The role of Ontologies in Knowledge Engineering. PhD thesis, 1995.

[17] Wielinga, B.J., A.Th. Schreiber, J.A. Breuker; KADS: A Modelling Approach to Knowledge Engineering. Knowledge Acquisition, Special issue "The KADS Approach to Knowledge Engineering", 4, 1, 1992, p.5-53.

Knowledge-Based Software Engineering
T. Hruška and M. Hashimoto (Eds.)
IOS Press, 2000

Representation of Complex Structures Extracted from Object Databases, and Access to their Components

Dmitry A. ZASTAVNOY, Alexander A. BUKATOV
Rostov State Uviversity, Center of IT, Russia

Abstract. The article presents the ways for representation of composite data structures, extracted from object databases as results of queries and the access to their components. In previous works we described the object data modal and a high-level navigational query language. The data stored in object databases are of complex structure (composite objects, relationships, etc), therefore a query result, that is cashed outside the database, inherits the complex structure of the origin data. We provide the sub- language based on the notion of secondary navigation, intended for accessing data of cached results from convenient programming languages.

1 Introduction

The contemporary applications of information systems involve complex data structures. Object databases are aimed to represent such data structures; their data models are based on notions of relationships and composite objects. The origin data can be composed by sets of complicatedly linked objects, especially in such domains as CAD systems and CASE systems. For example, the tasks of program transformation [5] often deal with an extraction of representation of enclosed operators, or, on the contrary, distributed in program between other operators. The manipulation with these data requires special means, i.e. a query language that suppose to identify and extract complex structures (not flat sets) from object database.

In previous papers [1,2,3,4] we introduce object data modal and high-level query language, that is aimed to get facilities to extract and access data from object database in high-level manner. In the current work we present the following important tasks:

1. The representation of query results outside database, i.e. in cache.
2. The ways for accessing cached components of query result.

This access should be provided in accordance with the same goal that we followed to when developing data modal and query language, that is the high-level of data engineering. From another point of view, while the data are fetched from the cache into environment of conventional programming languages, the suitable means are required. Then, the third suggestion is a sub-language for manipulating components stored in cache.

The preliminary results of our investigations have been presented at works [1,2,3,4]. The works [2,4] propose examples of applying our approach to data modelling for CASE systems and program transformation systems.

Authors assume that the problem concerned with representation of data in a cache outsize database is quite important, especially for object databases that are intended for storing data of complex structure. However, this field has not been investigated properly from conceptual point of view; the main researches deal with more technical aspects of data caching.

The structure of our paper is the following. In Section 2 the main features of data model are sketched: objects, types and type elements. Section 3 describes our query language. At first we provide the conceptual origin of the languages, that get facilities to identify the set of paths (chains) of objects linked by relationships. Then the basic operators and rules for forming expressions are introduced.

In Section 4 the authors introduce a concept of contexts. This notion is involved for two aims: to provide the way for execution of query expressions and the way for keeping data that are cached. We describe rules for execution of expressions.

At last, we present sub-language for manipulating with components of executed queries, in Section 4. While an expression of high-level query language has specified a set of object chains, the representation of these chains can be accessed by expressions of our sub-language and fetched from environment of host programming language.

2 Object data model

The entities of application domain are represented as object database. These objects are instances of *object types* that form database schema. Each type includes definitions of *elements* that are:

1. Fields, that describe actual data values associated with each object and are stored in database. All values of object fields are of basic types, such as numbers and strings. Fields cannot keep objects.
2. Relationships, that link objects of this type with other different objects of database. In general case, any object can be related to many other objects. A relationship instance is a ordered pair of two linked objects.
3. Templates of collections, that are intended for filtration of object sets by some conditions.
4. Functions and predicates, that can be applied to objects to derive new values.

Element declarations of a type include element names and groups of attributes that define the elements in accordance with their semantics. We address readers to our previous papers [4,5] for additional details.

An object has a real or substitute name and an internal identifier (which is not used in query language expressions and cannot be accessed externally). If an object has a name, the pair <object type, object name> uniquely identifies this object in database.

Object types form "type – subtype" hierarchy. The list of supertypes is declared in type definitions. If a type has supertypes, each of its instances has its "parent" objects that are instances of supertypes. Also, polimorphic elements (functions, for example) can be declared in a type and its supertypes.

All relationships are divided into two kinds: static (real) and calculated (virtual) ones. Instances of the relationships of the first kind are stored in object database and are created by commands of object manipulation language [3,4], while the other instances are constructed at execution time when some conditions on objects are checked.

3 Primary navigation in database and high-level navigational query language

A state of object database can be visualized in the form of an extensional graph that represents objects and relationship instances linking these objects. The graph nodes and hedges are corresponded with database objects and instances of relationships between them. The pairs <objects type, object name> and relationship names label nodes and hedges of the graph. The hedges are directed.

The main feature of our approach is that we specifies the whole paths (chains) in the graph instead of single objects for all the three activities: schema engineering, query specification and accessing query result. The means intended for identifying database objects by specification of their relations to other objects are introduced as *primary navigation.*

An *elementary path* in intentional graph is an ordered list of linked nodes; any path is described by names of objects and names of relationships in the graph.

A *query* to object database specifies a set of elementary paths in object database and, therefore, all objects that belonging to these paths and relationships between the objects. Specification of a query includes the three tasks:

1. An object or a set of objects that start the paths.
2. The structure of paths that is described by a lists of relationships (i.e. graph hedges) names.
3. The conditions on the path objects.

The specifications of a query as a description of a *general path* in extensional graph. We also will say that a general path produces a set of elementary paths. The first node of an elementary path, the second node, etc, are levels of the elementary paths. When a general path produces a set of elementary paths, a set of objects of the their first levels construct the first level of the general path; the other levels are constructed simultaneously.

The Figure 1 shows an example of a database for a university timetable.

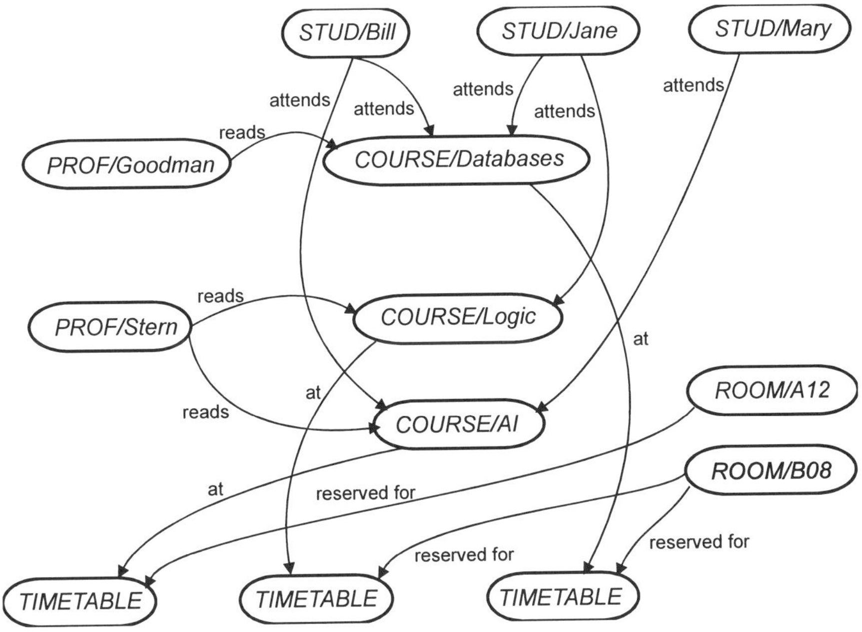

Figure 1. An example of university database

We distinguish three kinds of a query value: *common*, *partial* and *mixed*. The common value is the set of whole elementary paths specified by a query. The partial value is the objects that finish the elementary paths. While different paths can lead to the same object, the notion of object multiplicity is involved as a number of these paths. At last, j-mixed value is defined as a set of tails of elementary paths starting from objects of j-level.

From conceptual point of view, if a user wants to specify a set of database paths, he should specify the starting objects in the paths, describe the structure of paths (i.e. relationships that are passed through), and conditions on objects. Also user can specify functions and fields on each level of these paths.

Formal description (specification) of sets of database paths is given by expressions of proposed query language. The expression syntax is provided below. Their operands are type names, relationship names as well as names of other type elements, and object names. Expressions of operators are the following:

1. Direct navigation operator, denoted by "." symbol
2. Reverse navigation operator, denoted by ".'".
3. Operator of filtering by object name, "/"
4. Operator of getting values of fields and applying functions to objects, ":"
5. Operator of collectors, "-".
6. Operator of type resolution, "~".
7. Union operator, ",".

Here is syntax of expressions of query language:

query :- first_section { [section] } ["," query]
first_section :- simple_section / (query "," query) | context_name
simple_section :- type_name conditions action
section :- ("." | ".'") relationship_name conditions action
conditions :- ["-" collection_name { "-" collection_name}]
["/" object_name_list]
action :- [":" field_name_list] | [":" function_name]

Let's consider an example for the database shown on Figure 1. The expression

STUD . attends / {Databases, Logic} . at .' reserved_for

specifies **students** that attend some **courses** from **timetable**, and the **rooms** where the courses are held. These paths consist of four levels of objects. This query generates the following set of elementary paths that are the common value of it.

{ (STUD/Bill)°attends(COURSE/Databases)° at(TIMETABLE/)° 'reserved_for(ROOM/B08),*
(STUD/Jane)°attends(COURSE/Databases)° at(TIMETABLE/) °'reserved_for (ROOM/B08),*
(STUD/Jane)° attends(COURSE /Logic) ° at(TIMETABLE/) ° 'reserved_for (ROOM/B08)}*

As each of direct relationships always determines the type of objects of the following level, the names of types for these levels can be omitted:

{ STUD/Bill ° attends/Databases ° TIMETABLE/ ° ROOM/B08,*
STUD/Jane ° attends/Databases ° TIMETABLE/ ° ROOM/B08,*
STUD/Jane ° attends/Logic ° TIMETABLE/ ° ROOM/B08 }*

This form of elementary paths is quite similar to the notion of original query. Partial value of this query is a multiset

{ $ROOM/B08^3$ }

where 3 – a multiplicity of object *ROOM/B08*.

Here symbol ° is used to separate objects in elementary paths in formal notion of query results; and * symbol substitutes names for unnamed objects. Note that the object type is specified for the first level only.

A special kind of queries is called context queries. After a query was executed, the objects of its partial value can be used as starting nodes for another query. This query is named context one. The specification of such query starts from a context name (see the Section 4). Data structure where this partial value is stored is named a *context*.

4 Query evaluation

Here we discuss the way of execution of query expressions that is based on the notion of contexts. This notion is involved for the purposes of understanding what is a cache of objects extracted from database and how these objects are accessed.

Let's describe briefly the internal structure of data stored in object database. All objects (names and values of fields of each) of each type are represented by the flat table, that is similar to tables of relational databases. The values of static relationships are sets of associative pairs of linked objects; these sets are also represented by tables. Such representation provides an appropriate and effective way for data management.

Every context includes a *result set* of tuples. All tuples are of the same structure that is formed by object name, values of object fields and derived values.

Now let's consider the evaluation of query expressions, that do not include union operator. These expressions are called linear. Each of these expressions can be decomposed into series of binary operators. The most left operand of each operator is a type name or a context specification. The right operand can be a name of element of object type (relationship, collection, and so on), or object name, depending on semantics of this operator. By formal notion, every linear expression $T *^1 C_1 *^2 C_2 * \ldots *^n C_n$ are calculated as $(((\ldots(T *^1 C_1) *^2 C_2) * \ldots)*^n C_n$ composition of sub-expressions, here * denotes any of operators except union.

All operators are divided in two groups. The first group includes operators that generate new contexts, as it is shown below. These are operators of direct and reverse navigation. The other operators, that perform filtration of result sets by object names or conditions of collections, get values of fields and applies functions, do not produce new contexts, but modify result sets of existing contexts.

The first sub-expression $T *^1 C_1$ is calculated, and its value is a set of object of type T. These objects are placed in a result set of a new-generated context, that is denoted as K_1.

The second sub-expression $(T *^1 C1) *^2 C_2$ is evaluated as context query $*^2 C_2$ in the context K_1. If $*^2$ is an operator of filtering, the result set of K_1 context is modified in accordance with semantics of the operator. By other words, objects that do not match the conditions are removed from result set. If $*^2$ is operator of direct navigation, the new context is generated, and its result set is filled with objects that is linked with objects of K_1 context. The other sub-expressions are calculated by the same way. The new context is pushed on top of context stack.

If each operator is context-generating, the steps required to perform the query are:

rest of expression	*stack of context*
$T *^1 C_1 *^2 C_2 * \ldots *^n C_n$	$\varnothing$
$*^2 C_2 * \ldots *^n C_n$	K_1
$*^3 C_3 * \ldots *^n C_n$	$K_1\ K_2$
....	....
$*^n C_n$	$K_1\ K_2 \ldots\ K_{n-1}$
$\varnothing$	$K_1\ K_2 \ldots\ K_{n-1}\ K_n$

Non-linear expression, that includes union operators, can be decomposed into linear parts; and these parts must be evaluated separately. As a result, each part produces its own stack of contexts. Rules for merging result sets of these contexts are difficult and complicated, and we do not discuss them in this paper.

5 Representation of query results and sub-language for manipulating with the representation

In this section we present a sub-language that provides access to components of results of complex query that have been extracted from object database and kept in cache and that are to be fetched from an environment of host programming language. It is obvious that the convenient programming languages supports sequential extraction of data of elementary structure, while a high-level query language is intended for specifying sets of complex data in conceptual manner. Therefore, we strictly distinguish the two style of data access, and provide the notion of *secondary navigation* that is means for manipulation with data extracted from database by high-level queries (i.e. *primary navigation*).

We show in the previous section that the result of complex query is represented by a stack of contexts, and each of the contexts keeps the result set of objects for each level of paths. So, these result sets have the same flat structure. The Figure 2 shows a stack of contexts, which represent result of query expression provided in Section 3.

So, the representation of data in database and in cache is the same. But there is the main difference: data are extracted from database by an expression of high-level query language. This expression specifies the set of paths at once. When data are placed in the cache, they are accessed by operators of sub-language that is aimed for extraction of simple components from the cache. We name such facilities of our sub-language as "secondary navigation".

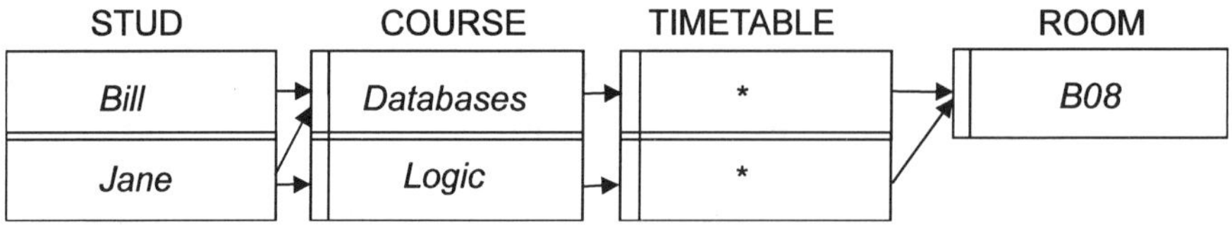

Figure 2. The context stack

The operators of this language can be executed from an interactive shell as well as from environments of C language.

There are four groups of the operators:

1. Creating, dropping context and making it current.
2. Moving current element forward and backward trough result sets.
3. Extracting data stored in the current element (tuple).
4. Reconstruction of paths.

The operators of the first group are proposed to manipulate with contexts. Before executing any query expression, an initial context must be created. After the query has been performed, some of new contexts are pushed on the stack. Each context has a name to be referred by it (the contexts created internally by system have names derived from name of the initial context). Afterwards any context can be dropped, and its resources are released. A user may make each context current.

A pointer to current element is posed in a result set of any contexts. This pointer can be moved forward and backwards in a result set. Data of current elements are fetched by names of fields specified in query expression or by order.

Each result sets can be scrolled, and fetch the data from it. To access data from non-current contexts, the name of required context should be qualified.

The operators of the fourth group are involved when a user wants to deconstruct database paths from objects, which are distributed in result sets of contexts. Reconstruction of database path can be performed by two ways. The first of them is to produce all paths that come through the object that is current in the current context.

The operator

SET { LEFT | RIGHT } { FIRST | NEXT | PREV }

poses pointer to next/previous linked objects in neighbor contexts (makes them current).

For example, if the record for object "Database" is current in the second context (see Figure 2), we are able to scroll result sets for STUD and TIMETABLE objects by the operators and access values from these contexts. The following code demonstrates how operators of our sub-query work.

Let's assume that the initial context is named $CONT, then the other contexts created by system are $CONT1, $CONT2 and $CONT3.

```
SET CONTEXT $CONT1 ;    -- the context is current
SET FIRST;              -- set pointer to first record
SET RIGHT FIRST;        -- second record is current in $CONT2
SET LEFT FIRST;         -- record for "Bill" is current in $CONT
SET LEFT NEXT;          -- record for "Jane" is current there
```

Now one path is reconstructed, and we can fetch data from the three contexts.

```
SET RIGHT NEXT;         -- fails because there is no other object in $CONT2 that
                           is linked to "Database" objects.
```

These operators reconstruct local sections of paths. Other way for path reconstruction is provided by operator

SET { FIRST | NEXT | PREV } PATH

that generates the whole paths. It means, these operators order objects in all result sets of contexts to produce the first or the next paths every time. In our example, the three clauses form three paths that are the common value of the query (Section 3):

```
SET FIRST PATH;
SET NEXT PATH;
SET NEXT PATH;
```

The execution of these operators does not depend on current context, and pointers to current records are set internally in each context.

6 Conclusion

The system presented in this paper is being implemented in Center of IT, Rostov State University. We decided to use some of existing database systems (Oracle7) as a basis for object database. Therefore, the main tasks of the implementation are the translation of clauses of proposed languages (data definitions, queries and the sub-language for contexts) to SQL clauses.

The descriptions of existing standard (ODMG 2.0, Oracle8) are published in [9,10]. The notable work [6] supposes a near approach. The main distinction of our approach is that the proposed means are targeted for dealing with database paths instead of flat sets. Besides, after query execution, the result of existed systems listed above is flat sets too, while a query of our language produces a group of result sets that keep the representation of database paths. The authors do not have any information about approaches that provides the similar means.

The authors are going to advance our system and to develop its model power and convenience of data model and query language. We expect to apply this system for tasks of CASE technologies and program transformations.

References

[1] Zastavnoy D.A.. "High-level Declarative Query Language for Object-Oriented Database". In: "Advance in Databases and Information Systems. St.Petersburg, 1997, V.2,pp. 26-28.

[2] Zastavnoy D.A. "A Concepts of Polymorphism for High-Level Query Language for Object Databases" (in Russian). In: "Computer Technologies for Engineering and Management". Taganrog.1997.

[3] Bukatov A., Zastavnoy D.. "High-level Navigational Language for Querying Complex Data Objects and its Application to CASE Systems". In: Pavol Navrat. Haruki Veno (ed) "3th Joint Conference on Knowledge-Based Software Engineering". Pp. 103-107. (IOS Press, Amsterdam. 1998).

[4] Bukatov A.A., Zastavnoy D.A. Specification and Result Representation of Complex Navigational Queries for Object Databases. In Proceedings of The Workshop on Computer Science and Information Technologies (CSIT99). (Electronic Edition hppt://msu.jurinfor.ru/CSIT/BukatovZ.htm).

[5] Bucatov A.A. Development of Tools Intended for Creation of Source Program Transformation Systems. Information Techologies. Moscow, 1999, N22-25.

[6] Barclay P.J., Kennedy J.B.. "A Conceptual Language for Querying Object Oriented Data". In Proceedings of BNCOD-94.

[7] Cattell R.G.G, Barry D.K. (ed) "The Object Database Standart: ODMG 2.0". Morgan Kaufmann publ. San Francisco, 1997.

[8] David A.Arstey. "High Performance Oracle8 Object-Oriented Design". Coriolis Group, 1998.

Knowledge-Based Software Engineering
T. Hruška and M. Hashimoto (Eds.)
IOS Press, 2000

Building Functional Techniques into an Object-oriented System

Elena BOLSHAKOVA, Andrey STOLYAROV
Lomonossov's Moscow State University,
dept. of Computational Mathematics and Cybernetics,
Vorobjevy Gory, 119899, Moscow, Russia.

Abstract. A method is proposed how to integrate techniques developed within various programming styles (paradigms) on the basis of object-oriented style, permitting to keep the significant facilities of programming languages to be integrated.

The paper starts with a brief description and comparison of basic programming paradigms (i.e., imperative, functional, logic and object-oriented) and corresponding programming techniques. Then it is argued that integration of different techniques is needed to simplify implementation of large programming projects. The key idea of the integration method proposed is to build into widespread imperative object-oriented language (such as C++ or Ada) useful techniques from another paradigm via creating in the former language a set of special classes of objects and operations. These classes represent a knowledge about syntax and semantics of language constructs to be built into. It is considered important that the source object-oriented program code with the built-in constructions would be compiled in an ordinary manner without any preprocessing, and that there's no syntactic analysis of the code at the runtime.

The paper describes in more details the experimental implementation of the method discussed: functional techniques of the programming language Lisp (including Lisp structures and functionals) were built into the C++ language.

1 Introduction

Modern programming is based on several main styles (paradigms, or models) of programming - imperative, functional, logic and object-oriented styles, which present different modes of thinking about a program and its execution. Various programming techniques (data and control structures, language constructs, etc.) were developed independently within each paradigm during the more than forty-years history of programming, but nowadays the necessity of integration of these techniques is realizable. Though algorithmic languages usually include programming techniques from different styles, they may be classified in accordance with the main style and techniques supported.

The imperative (procedural) style is the oldest and most traditional. It has grown from machine and assembler languages, whose main features reflect the John von Neuman principles of computer architecture. Thus, the imperative program consists of explicit commands (instructions) to be consequently executed carrying out operations on data and modifying the values of program variables and external environment.

The functional style is in fact old style too, since it has arisen from evaluation of algebraic formulae and its elements were used in first imperative algorithmic languages, such as Fortran. The pure functional program is a collection of mutually related (and possibly recursive) functions, each of them represents a certain expression for computing a value. Execution of functional program is simply evaluation of these values.

Within the logic paradigm the program is thought of as a set of logic formulae - axioms (facts), describing properties of certain objects, and a theorem to be proven. Program execution is the logical proving (inference) of the theorem, and successful proving results in construction of the objects with properties described.

The essential difference between these three styles concerns not only the concept of program and its execution, but also the concept of program variable. In contrast with imperative programs, there are neither explicit assignment statements nor side effects in the pure functional and logical programs. The variables in such a program are similar to those in mathematics - they denote actual values of function arguments or objects being constructed during inference. Unlike imperative languages, functional languages (Lisp [6], Refal [8], etc.[2]) are usually recursive and interpretive, most of them are oriented towards symbolic processing, as well as the unique famous logic language Prolog [5].

Programming techniques developed within functional and logic styles include (besides recursion) flexible data structures for representing complex symbolic data (Lisp, Refal, Prolog), pattern matching mechanisms (Refal, Prolog), functionals, or high order functions (Lisp), and mechanisms of partial evaluations (Refal).

In the object-oriented style a program describes the structure and behavior of so called objects and classes of objects. Classes represent sets of objects with the same structure and behavior (operations, or methods). In general case descriptions of classes compose the inheritance hierarchy including polymorphism of operations. Execution of object-oriented program is regarded as exchange of messages between objects modifying their states.

The object-oriented paradigm is the most abstract, its basic ideas can be easily combined with principles and programming techniques of other styles. Really, an object method may be interpreted as a procedure or a function, whereas the sending of message may be interpreted as procedure or function call. Just that way of integration of basic object principles with programming techniques of different styles has led to object-oriented variants of famous languages, for example, C++ [7], Ada95 [4] or Object Prolog.

Each programming style has its own scope of applicability: functional programming is useful for symbolic processing, while logic programming is useful for deductive data bases and expert systems, but both of them are not suitable for interactive tasks. Imperative languages are equally convenient for numeric and symbolic computations, giving up to most of the functional languages (and Prolog) in the power of symbolic processing techniques. The object paradigm is useful for creating large programs (especially interactive) with complicated behavior and with various types of data.

2 The key idea

Nowadays, imperative object-oriented languages C++, Ada and Object Pascal are the most popular for implementation of large program project. But in large projects one or several subproblems often belong to the symbolic processing domain, for which functional languages are more suitable. For example, creating a complicated data base (of a hundred or so various relations) with a natural language interface involves the task of syntax and semantic analysis of natural language queries, including elements of logical inference. Hence, languages such as Lisp or Prolog are preferable for this task. We see that the integration of programming techniques from different programming styles is needed to simplify the implementation of large programming projects.

It seems quite attractive to enhance the power of popular imperative object-oriented languages with special data structures and control mechanisms from non-traditional languages such as Lisp and Prolog. We'll discuss a method how to integrate techniques developed within various programming styles on the bases of object-oriented paradigm. The key idea of the method is to build into imperative object-oriented language useful techniques from another style (language) via creating in the former language a set of special classes of objects and operations. These classes represent a knowledge about syntax and semantics of language constructions being built in, and permit to model these constructs within the object-oriented language. It is assumed that this object-oriented language allows overriding of standard operations for user-defined classes (types), as the language C++ or Ada do.

Such a way of integration makes it possible to use different styles and techniques of programming within the same file (program module) working (in a strict sence) with the object-oriented programming language only. One might call this way as "immediate integration", though built-in techniques and constructions may have modified syntax (but not semantics). It is considered important that the source object-oriented program code with the built-in constructions would be compiled in an ordinary manner without any preprocessing, and that there is no syntactic analysis of the code at the runtime.

3 Experimental implementation overview

An experimental implementation of the integration method discussed has been carried out for building functional techniques of programming language Lisp into C++ language resulting in the InteLib library of C++ classes. This library supports a dialect of Lisp with the following facilities:

- Lisp S-expressions (numberic and string constants, symbols, dot pairs and lists);
- Wide range of built-in functions and special forms, starting with CAR and CDR, ending with MAPCAR, APPLY, EVAL;
- User-defined functions (lexical closures), lambda-expressions;
- User-defined macros (in the sence of Common Lisp [6]) and so called nlambda functions (functions that don't evaluate arguments).

In contrast with most of known dialects, in the dialect supported by InteLib (InteLib Lisp), one can pass to a functional (such as MAPCAR) as its argument not only an ordinary function, but also any functional object such as nlambda functions, special forms and even macros.

Both lexical and dynamic styles of bindings of Lisp variables (symbols) are available as well as supporting constant symbols. InteLib provides DEFVAR and DEFCONST special forms (similar to those in Common Lisp) for this purpose. The library also implements a collection of miscellaneous functions (such as input/output functions, hash table handling functions and so on).

4 Architecture and implementation of the InteLib library

InteLib is based on a hierarchy of polymorphic classes representing various types of S-expressions. The abstract base class LTerm implements the common properties of all these types. LTerm has a method Evaluate intended to evaluate and return the value (in the sence of Lisp) of the given S-expression.

In the discussed version of the library LTerm class has the following child classes:

- LTermNil (represents empty list);

- LTermInteger and LTermFloat (numberic constants);
- LTermString (string constants);
- LTermSymbol (Lisp symbols);
- LDotPair (elements of a list).
- LForm and its child classes corresponding to various functional forms.

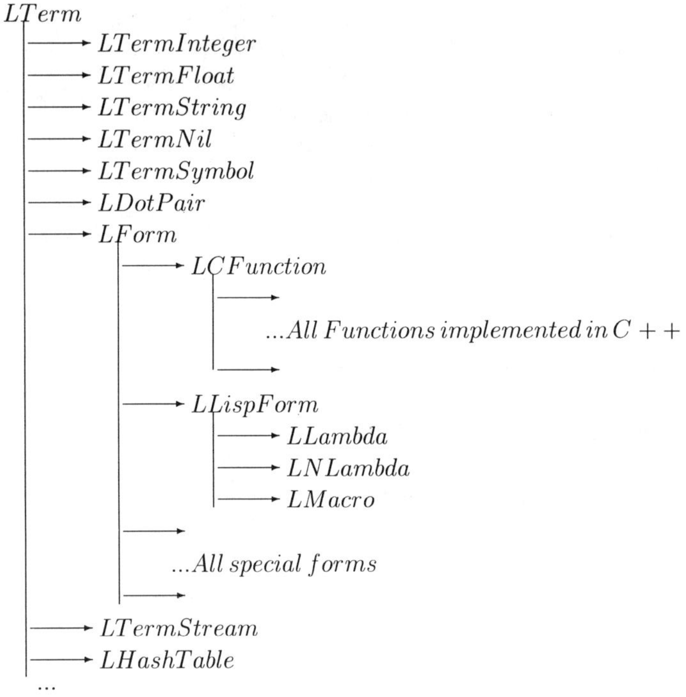

The LTermSymbol class shown at the diagram in fact stores a reference to an object of LSymbol class, which is not a member of the LTerm hierarchy itself. LSymbol class stores global (dynamic) value association, function association, text representation of the symbol and binding scheme (either lexical or dynamic).

To represent functionals as data, LForm subhierarchy has been developed within the LTerm hierarchy. The subhierarchy has LCFunction and LLispForm clases. Lisp special forms are represented with classes also descended directly from LForm.

The LCFunction class represents functions implemented in C++, including all "built-in" functions such as CAR, CDR, CONS etc. To add a new Lisp function to the library, a programmer needs to declare a class descended from LCFunction with only one method (DoCall) overriden.

The LLispForm class is intended to represent forms defined with Lisp constructions (lambda functions, nlambda functions and macros). It has references to the lambda-list (the list of formal parameters), the function body and the lexical context of the form. LLispForm class has child classes corresponding to different kinds of forms:

- LLambda (ordinary Lisp function);
- LMacro (Lisp macro evaluated as in Common Lisp);
- LNLambda (Lisp function that does not evaluate its arguments).

In most cases, the objects of LTerm class hierarchy reside in dynamic memory and are not operated directly (altough it is possible). In order to provide garbage collection, a class LReference has been created. LReference behaves like a pointer to LTerm and notifies the pointed object that a new pointer is created or that an existing pointer is either destroyed or reassigned. Using these notifications, LTerm object counts existing references to itself and deletes itself when there is no more references.

LReference class is designed to be primary API to Lisp objects represented with InteLib: it has about 20 constructors that allow to create various types of Lisp objects. In particular, it is possible to construct a Lisp object from any of standard C numeric or string constant. It is also possible to create an LTerm object explicitly with operator new and let LReference take care about it.

To construct Lisp lists and to specify them within C++ programs, special class LListConstructor has been added to InteLib and a C++ built-in operation "," (comma) has been overriden for LReference class as the left operand. LListConstructor class has no data members and usually has only one instance named L. Here's its complete definition:

```
class LListConstructor { public:
  template <class T> LReference operator |(T t)
    { return LReference(new LDotPair(LReference(t))); }};
```

The only purpose of this class is to turn anything into a Lisp list of one member.

The new version of comma operation assumes its left-hand operand is an LReference object pointing to a list (possibly empty) and appends its right-hand operand to this list. C++ implicit type conversion allows to use any numeric and string constants as a right-hand operand of the comma operation as well as LSymbol class objects.

Besides that, "~" (tilde) operation has been overriden for LReference and LSymbol classes to represent abbreviated form of QUOTE traditional for Lisp.

Using LListConstructor and the two operations with the new semantics, a programmer can represent Lisp lists in C++ code like this:

```
(L| "I am the walrus", 1965)    // ("I am the walrus" 1965)
(L| 1, 2, (L| 3, 4), 5, 6)      // (1 2 (3 4) 5 6)
(L| (L| 1, 2), 3, 4)            // ((1 2) 3 4)
(L| CAR, ~(L| 1, 2))            // (CAR '(1 2))
```

To the right of comment symbol, the represented lists are written in traditional Lisp syntax.

The syntax shown is clear enough for a human programmer to work with, but in case of large fragments of code to be written in Lisp it might be more convenient to code in traditional syntax. The process of translation from traditional Lisp into the corresponding C++ constructions is quite simple and easy to implement. A translator has been created for this purpose.

5 One example

In conclusion we give an example of Lisp function in traditional syntax and its C++ analogue. Function ISOMORPHIC takes two trees as arguments and determines whether they have the same topology (equivalent structures):

```
(defun isomorphic (tree1 tree2)
   (cond ((atom tree1) (atom tree2))
         ((atom tree2) NIL)
         (t (and (isomorphic (car tree1) (car tree2))
```

```
                    (isomorphic (cdr tree1) (cdr tree2))))))
```

The result of translation of this code into C++ language generated by the translator follows:

```
LSymbol ISOMORPHIC("ISOMORPHIC");
LSymbol TREE1("TREE1");
LSymbol TREE2("TREE2");
static void LispInit() {
  (L|DEFUN, ISOMORPHIC, (L|TREE1, TREE2),
    (L|COND,
      (L|(L|ATOM, TREE1), (L|ATOM, TREE2)),
      (L|(L|ATOM, TREE2), NIL),
      (L|T, (L|AND,
        (L|ISOMORPHIC, (L|CAR, TREE1), (L|CAR, TREE2)),
        (L|ISOMORPHIC, (L|CDR, TREE1), (L|CDR, TREE2))))))
  .Evaluate();
}
```

Please note that symbols that correspond to standard Lisp functions used in the example (DEFUN, COND, ATOM, NIL, T, AND, CAR and CDR) are provided by the library so there's no need to define them explicitly.

In order to use this code, the programmer must call the function LispInit which evaluates the only top-level form of the example (DEFUN special form). Then the function ISOMORPHIC can be used in the C++ program.

6 Conclusion

In fact, the idea of translation of Lisp code into an imperative language (primarily into C) is not new (e.g., Gambit-C [1]). The main advantage of the proposed method is that the C++ code that corresponds to a Lisp code remains quite human-readable and human-maintainable after translation. Moreover, the use of translator is not necessary, one can write directly in C++ using Lisp's technique.

Now the ways of further development of the library are investigated. The set of classes representing semantics of Refal language kernel is being created on the bases of InteLib. Also we plan to build some dialect of Prolog into C++ language using this method.

References

[1] Feeley M. Gambit Scheme. http://www.iro.umontreal.ca/~gambit/

[2] Field A., Harrison P. Functional Programming. Adison-Wesley, 1988.

[3] McCarthy J. Recursive functions of symbolic expressions and their computation by machine. Communications of the ACM, 3 (1960), 184-195

[4] Mitchell R. Abstract Data Types and Ada. Prentice Hall, 1996.

[5] Robinson J. Logic programming - past, present and future. New Generation Computing, 1, 1983, p.107-121.

[6] Steele G. L. Common Lisp the Language, 2nd edition. Digital Press, 1990.

[7] Stroustrup B. The C++ Programming Language, 3rd edition. Addison-Wesley. 1997.

[8] Turchin V. REFAL-5, Programming Guide and Reference Manual. New England Publishing Co., Holyoke, 1989.

Knowledge-Based Software Engineering
T. Hruška and M. Hashimoto (Eds.)
IOS Press, 2000

DPFinder: A Tool for Automatic Recognition of Design Patterns

Mária SMOLÁROVÁ, Michal KADLEC
Department of Computer Science and Engineering, Slovak University of Technology, Ilkovičova 3, 812 19 Bratislava, Slovakia
smolarova@dcs.elf.stuba.sk, kadlec@nex.sk

Abstract. Reusing of design patterns (DP) results into pattern instances that are embedded in the code of software system. Our aim has been to support automatic recognition of DP instances in an existing code. We designed and implemented DPFinder, a tool that supports DP instance recognition. In this paper, our main results are presented and evaluated. DPFinder can recognise a wide variety of possible DP instance implementations thanks to its flexibility achieved by various criteria controlling DP recognition. However, a definitive confirmation about the presence of a DP instance is left to a human.

1 Introduction

A design pattern (DP) gives a general solution to particular design problem in such a way that it can be applied in an own specific context [3]. Application of a DP results into pattern instances that are embedded in the code/design of software system. Unfortunately, most of DP instances are neither known nor documented in current software systems. Since DPs help view existing software systems in larger units, a tool that could automatically recognise (some of) DP instances in existing code would make comprehension, maintenance and evolution of software systems significantly easier.

When aiming to support DP recognition, the nature of DP solution must be understood. We stress out that a DP solution is both abstract, i.e. released from concrete details, and general, i.e. application independent, description of required structure and collaboration. Abstraction as well as generalisation, two distinct concepts that are often confused [6], must have been applied when an existing solution was extracted in a form of DP. In order to incorporate a DP solution into the software system (that is to create a particular instance of DP solution) both specialisation and concretisation steps are required [7]. They both may proceed in several different ways. As a result, an actual implementation of DP instance varies according to required software system's functionality, the chosen programming language, the constraints that rise up from overall system's architecture, the individual skills and habits of a programmer, etc.

Besides this, a DP instance is not localised in one place in the design/implementation. Its particular parts are scattered over several places in the design/code.

The variety of possible DP implementations as well as its intertwining with other parts of software system makes DP recognition difficult. More sophisticated approaches than a simple looking for the pre-defined code fragments is necessary. A tool for DP recognition must be able to find a match between the specific and concrete DP instance as actually implemented in the code and the abstract and general DP solution as presented in a pattern description.

We are of course aware of limitations for a fully automated approach to DP recognition: any tool cannot definitely approve the presence of a DP instance in the code. However, we hope a tool could reasonably help in looking for perspective candidates.

The rest of the paper is structured as follows. First, our goals are described. Next, architecture of our tool named DPFinder is given alongside with the core of it: representation of DP and searching algorithm. In Section 3, experiments that have been carried out are described and evaluated. Section 4 relates our work to other systems for DP recognition. We conclude with the suggestions for future work.

2 Overview of Our Approach

DP recognition is in our approach based on referential DPs that represent DP solution at its general and abstract level. An appropriate representation of DP is therefore central. However, the searching algorithm alone should be independent of a particular representation of referential DP. It should not make use of some specific implementation or programming language. The recognition algorithm should perform the same behaviour regardless of which referential DP it is looking for so that a tool can be simply extended by adding new referential DPs. In this sense, our approach is radically different from [1, 2].

Another important goal is to accept distinct criteria for matching DP solutions and their instances. An exact match between referential DP and source code fragments is rare. Therefore, each criterion would allow to make the matching algorithm less strict and rigour in regarding what constructs in the source code still constitute a particular DP instance.

We took a static strategy to DP recognition that is all information about DP instances is obtained from the source code analysis. A dynamic DP recognition will be the subject of our further investigation.

2.1 Architecture of DPFinder

In Figure 1, an overall architecture of our tool named DPFinder is depicted. In the contextual view, DPFinder takes as inputs both the model of source code and the referential DPs. DPFinder accepts currently the source code represented in the textual Petal file format, an intermediate representation of object-oriented systems developed by Rational that is independent of particular programming language. Referential DPs are represented textually in a form that is similar to petal file.

The parser of source code model and the parser of referential DPs transform the input files into DPFinder's internal representation based on graphs. The repository contains source code as well as referential DPs represented in the form of graphs. The recogniser, the heart of DPFinder, looks for particular occurrences of referential DPs in the source code. A graph-based approach allows to reduce the problem of DP recognition to the problem of finding a subgraph in a graph. As distinct criteria for rigorousness in searching are allowed, certain kinds of similarity between graphs are accepted as well. A more detailed description of searching algorithm is given later.

As depicted in Figure 1, DPFinder is centrally controlled. That is, control module activates and synchronises the other parts of system during the run time. Individual modules in the DPFinder are implemented as dll components that can be dynamically loaded during the run time. This approach allows us to alter particular module in case several of them are available. For example, if the format of the source code data changes, it would be possible to dynamically change the type of source code parser according to actual needs.

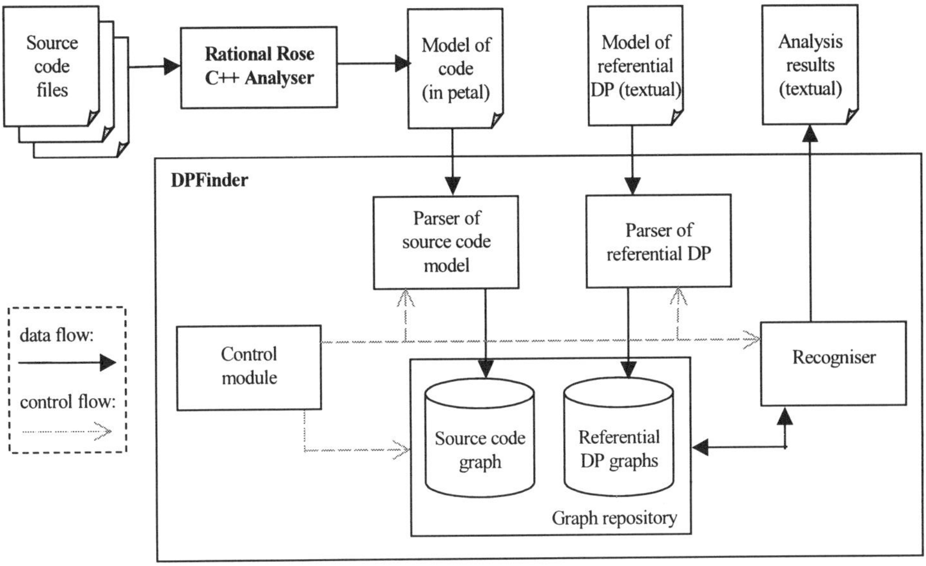

Figure 1. An overall architecture of DPFinder

2.2 Graph Repository and Recogniser

The internal repository of DPFinder stores the structure of both source code and referential DPs in the form of directed labelled graphs. Each graph G = (N, E) consists of a set of nodes N and a set of edges E. Classes, their methods and attributes are represented as nodes N in the graph G, each possibly having some additional values attached, for example whether a class is abstract or concrete. Edges E in G are directed and labelled with the name of the relationship. Besides showing the relationships that are usual in object-oriented development such as inheritance, aggregation and association, edges also connect a class with its methods and attributes.

Though both source code and referential DPs are represented similarly, there are some significant differences between them. First of all, nodes and edges in referential graph are thought as being variables that will be bound when an instance is formed. Also, some nodes may have value multi attached within referential graph which means that they may have multiple occurrences when instantiated.

At each moment, there is one source code and several referential graphs located in the graph repository. The recogniser takes referential DP graphs from the repository one after another and searches for its presence in the source code graph. As already mentioned, it is in fact the problem of finding a subgraph in a graph. However, some important differences must be considered. First, correspondence between names in referential and source code graph must be taken into account. Next, the multiplicity of particular nodes in the referential DP is to be reflected accordingly in the source code graph. Also, various criteria for relaxing the match have to be integrated. Among those we have proposed, the most important ones are:

(1) allowing an additional inheritance: a direct inheritance relationship in the referential graph may become transitive in the source code graph i.e., a child class that is in a referential DP a direct successor, i.e. directly inherits from its parent class, can be in the source code substituted by any class in the inheritance hierarchy that directly or indirectly inherits from a parent class;

```
(pattern Composite
   (abstrclass Component)
   (class Leaf IsSubclassOf Component multi)
   (class Composite IsSubclassOf Component)
   (Composite Aggregates Component through children multi))
```

Figure 2. Textual representation of the COMPOSITE referential DP

(2) disregarding the difference between abstract and concrete: those classes that are declared as abstract in the referential DP do not have to be abstract in the source code; concrete classes can substitute the role of abstract classes;

(3) disregarding the difference between aggregation and association relationships: it is often reasonable not to distinguish between both relationships because an aggregation is often implemented in the same way as an association; when the source code is reverse engineered, no difference between association and aggregation exists;

(4) ignoring multiplicity in relationships: similarly to (3), no distinction between multiple and single relationships can be observed when the source code is parsed because both have often the same implementation.

Because of the space limitations, we do not present the whole pattern-recognition algorithm. Instead, we briefly outline the ideas incorporated in the algorithm by means of an example. In Figure 3, we show two source code graphs that are recognised as correct instances of COMPOSITE DP (as represented in Figure 2). Additional values attached to the node/edge are put into brackets. Equalities describe correspondences between names in referential and source code graphs. In the example 3a, criteria (2) and (4) are to be applied in order to recognise the given graph as an instance of Composite. Figure 3b describes an instance of DP COMPOSITE accepted when criteria (1) and (3) are applied.

3 Empirical Results

DPFinder has been designed and implemented as an experimental tool that allows to run a series of distinct tests each aimed to recognise those source-code structures that correspond to the solution part of a DP. In the next sections, we give an overall view of our experiments and present and evaluate the results we have achieved.

3.1 Overview of Experiments

In order to test DPFinder, a number of experiments with both well-known object-oriented software systems as well as software systems built specially for testing purposes have been accomplished. Several test applications were created with the objective to cover as much variants of correct DP instances as possible. Only one of them named TestAppl is listed in the following tables. The real-life software systems we chose contain several instances of

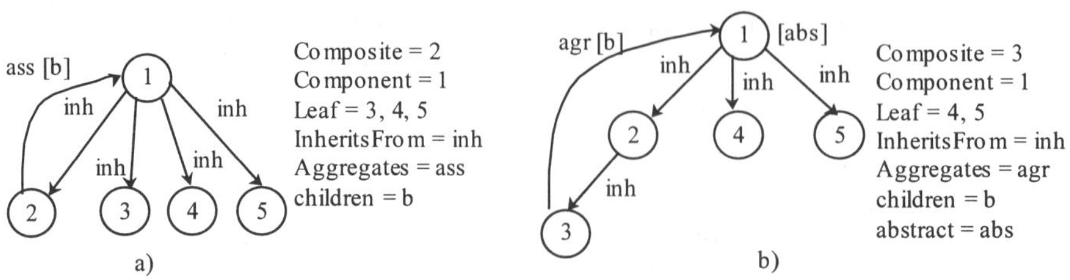

Figure 3. Two examples of correct instances of COMPOSITE DP in the source code graph

DPs and/or allow to compare our work with others. We chose four C++ programs, namely LEDA (a library of the data types and algorithms of combinatorial computing), ET++, InterViews, and UniDraw (frameworks well known from [3]). Unfortunately, we did not have exact descriptions of which classes constitute the DP instances. Therefore, results by testing these systems cannot be straightforwardly validated.

Table 1. The tested systems and their basic characteristics

	size[kB]	# of						
		classes	abstract classes	relations	inheritance	association	aggregation
ET++	2607	373	0	1328	248	609	471
InterViews	2084	415	0	828	197	508	123
LEDA	998	161	0	362	66	116	180
UniDraw	1330	336	0	721	247	272	202
TestAppl	167	32	7	60	31	21	8

The tested programs ranged in size from 32 classes to 415 classes. Their basic characteristics are listed in Table 1. All tested programs had to be transformed from C++ code into Petal files before running tests with DPFinder. The transformation was done externally by using products Rational Rose and Rational Rose C++ Analyser (depicted also in Figure 1).

The recognition algorithm of DPFinder relies on referential DPs. DPFinder accepts referential DPs represented textually in the same way the COMPOSITE DP in Figure 2 was represented. For testing, we selected a set of DPs from [3] comprising the patterns BRIDGE, COMPOSITE, DECORATOR, FLYWEIGHT, PROXY, and COMMAND.

The DPFinder was tested in a series of tests. The characteristics of the most significant ones are summarised in Table 2. For each of nine tests, those of the criteria (1) to (4) that have been applied are marked by an x.

Table 2. Particular characteristics of tests with respect to criteria (1) to (4) described previously

	test #1	test #2	test #3	test #4	test #5	test #6	test #7	test #8	test #9
(1) additional inheritance			x			x	x		x
(2) abstract = concrete		x	x	x	x	x	x	x	x
(3) association = aggregation				x		x		x	x
(4) ignore multiplicity					x		x	x	x

3.2 Test Results and Evaluation

In every test, each of the five above listed software systems was tested in a separate run. For all tests, the same set of referential DPs was provided.

A summary of testing results we obtained is given in Table 3. For each software system, only a total number of recognised instances is indicated. Except for TestAppl, we do not present particular views on the number of detected instances (regarding each of the referential DPs) because the exact number of true DP instances was not known.

As shown in Table 3, the results of test #1 are negative because none of DPs was recognised. The reason is in fact simple: each of the referential DPs chosen for testing contains at least one abstract class. Because ET++, InterViews. LEDA, and UniDraw do not contain abstract classes at all (see Table 1), none of DP instances could be recognised in the exact mode used in test #1. Therefore, the criterion (2) was applied in the rest of our testing (see Table 2).

The rest of results achieved for the real-life applications may be with respect to the number of recognised DP instances grouped into three groups: tests #2, #3, #5, #7, tests #4, #6, and tests #8, #9. Though not obvious from Table 3, the instances were detected correspondingly within each group, that is, when a DP instance was recognised in test #4 for example, the same classes and relationships were involved in the instance detected in test #6.

Surprisingly, additional inheritance (criterion (1)) did not influence the obtained results for ET++, InterViews. LEDA, and UniDraw significantly. The reason is that the inheritance hierarchy is shallow in the analysed applications.

Table 3. The total number of recognised DP instances

	test #1	test #2	test #3	test #4	test #5	test #6	test #7	test #8	test #9
ET++	0	4	4	171	4	171	4	224	225
InterViews	0	3	3	77	3	77	3	78	78
LEDA	0	1	1	11	1	11	1	11	11
UniDraw	0	3	3	76	3	76	3	78	78
TestAppl	9	11	12	20	17	22	19	27	31

On the other hand, applying criterion (3) which disregards differences between aggregation and association (tests #4, #6, #8, #9) changed the number of detected instances radically. The principal growth was observed for BRIDGE and COMMAND DPs but the probability they are real DP instances is low. When the criterion (3) is considered the structure of DPs BRIDGE and COMMAND becomes a frequent one. Our hypothesis about the necessity of human intervention in the recognition process was confirmed: as DPFinder detects the required structures automatically, a definitive confirmation about the presence of a DP instance must be left to a human.

Exact evidence about the number of DP instances and their particular constituents was available only for the TestAppl. We therefore give a more detailed view on this application in a separate table (see Table 4). Here, the number of intentionally created DP instances as well as the testing results is listed for each of the referential DPs. In the test #6, all instances were found successfully. Beside the correct instances, a few more candidates were discovered for the BRIDGE, PROXY and COMMAND DP. After inspecting the source code we realised that these were recognised correctly but such structure occurred incidentally in the TestAppl. We would like to stress again that a human intervention is needed in order to confirm the instance's presence.

Table 4. The number of recognised DP instances in the TestAppl

	#of intentionally created DP instances	#of recognised instances in								
		test #1	test #2	test #3	test #4	test #5	test #6	test #7	test #8	test #9
BRIDGE	2	3	3	3	4	3	4	3	4	4
COMPOSITE	4	1	2	2	3	3	4	4	5	7
DECORATOR	3	1	1	2	2	1	3	2	2	4
FLYWEIGHT	1	1	1	1	1	2	1	2	2	2
PROXY	2	2	2	2	3	3	3	3	4	4
COMMAND	1	1	2	2	7	5	7	5	10	10

In the test #1, only those instances were detected which were implemented exactly in the same way as in the referential DP. In the real-life application, such implementation may not always be possible for several reasons. Therefore, we are convinced, some criteria making the algorithm less strict are necessary in order to obtain reasonable results in the DP recognition. Though structures which are detected when running the test with some criteria being applied may not always be the real instances, we consider our results useful enough as they do give a reasonable number of candidates that should eventually be confirmed (or rejected) by a human.

Judged from the viewpoint of particular DPs, our tests for TestAppl do not give similar results. The significantly worse results for the Command DP have certainly something to do with the static strategy that is less sufficient for behavioural DPs. For structural DPs, the obtained results are satisfactory.

4 Related Work

Detection and identification of DP instances in the source code has been a subject of several studies mostly in the context of reverse engineering and source code visualisation. One of the first systems is KT [2]. Its strength resides in the ability to perform some level of dynamic analysis of the source code. Thanks to Smalltalk that was chosen as a target language, dynamic message flows between objects may be recorded and used for detecting not only structure but also behaviour of a DP. Unfortunately, both structure and behaviour of a selected DP are coded into the algorithm so that KT cannot be flexibly extended.

DP++ [1] is a tool that automates design-pattern detection in C++ programs. As a first step, DP++ does a partial analysis of the source code and stores information about class structure and functionality in internal data structures. The pattern-detection algorithm works on these internal data structures. Unlike DPFinder, referential DPs are not represented independently of DP++ and the algorithm relies on built-in knowledge about DP structure and functionality. This approach makes the extension of DP++ more troublesome.

A Prolog-based approach to DP representation is taken in Pat [5]. Here, each DP is represented as a rule describing all participants and required relationships. As a result of C++ source code parsing, a set of facts representing that code is obtained. When an instance of particular DP is searched for, the advantage of Prolog's backtracking facilities is fully taken. Our recognition algorithm is similar to certain extent because of the systematic way it looks for corresponding nodes in the code graph.

SPOOL [4] is a pattern-based environment for reverse engineering that is capable of matching the structure of DPs with the C++ source code. Similarly to our approach, SPOOL defines the required structure of DPs separately from the tool and places it into a repository. DPs are described in an intermediate format. However, DP detection in the SPOOL environment relies on a set of pre-defined, in the repository stored implementations of DPs (called concrete DPs). Our approach based on various criteria is much more flexible.

A comparative summary of the above mentioned pattern-detection tools and DPFinder is given in Table 5.

Table 5. A summary of pattern-recognition tools

	Recognised DP categories	Pattern-recognition strategy	Accepted DP implementation	DP representation	Programming language dependency
DP++ [1]	Structural	static	one predefined	embodied in the algorithm	yes, C++
KT [2]	Structural, behavioural	both static and dynamic	one predefined	embodied in the algorithm	yes, Smalltalk
Pat [5]	Structural	static	flexible	in Prolog rules	no, C++
SPOOL [4]	Structural	static	several predefined	independently in textual file	no, C++
DPFinder	structural, behavioural	Static	flexible	independently in textual files	no, C++

5 Conclusions and Future Work

In this paper we aimed to present our approach to automatic recognition of DP instances in an existing code. DPFinder, a tool we have proposed and implemented, is flexible with respect to new referential DPs. Thanks to distinct criteria applied in the recognition algorithm, a wide variety of possible DP instance implementations is accepted.

We described a set of experiments with several object-oriented software systems and evaluated the results. Despite of the capability of DPFinder to find candidates for DP instances correctly, a definitive confirmation about the presence of a DP instance is to be left to a human.

In the future, we would like to improve DPFinder in two significant ways. First, DPFinder should run with more detailed information about the source code. Since our internal representation is capable to express any further details in the form of a graph, this aim needs just to change the sort of the input information provided. Thanks to a flexible architecture of DPFinder current Petal file format can be simply replaced by other, richer format. Accordingly, the referential DPs would be enhanced.

Second important thing to do would be to incorporate more criteria for relaxing the recognition algorithm. Similarly to current criteria, they should reflect heuristics gained by observing the real-life implementations of DPs.

Beside these, several other directions can be followed in the future work. Visualisation of obtained results would certainly bring in significant improvements. Also, experimentation with other than C++ programs would be useful. In addition, an extension of DPFinder towards dynamic recognition strategy is still an open question.

Acknowledgements

The work reported here was partially supported by Slovak Science Grant Agency, grant No. G1/7611/20.

References

[1] Bansiya, J.: Automating Design-Pattern Identification, *Dr. Dobb's Journal* **6** (1998) 20-28.

[2] Brown, K.: Design Reverse-Engineering and Automated Design Pattern Detection in Smalltalk. Technical Report TR-96-07, Department of Computer Science, North Carolina State University, 1996.

[3] Gamma, E., Helm, R., Johnson, R., Vlissides, J.: Design Patterns, Elements of Reusable Object-Oriented Software. Addison-Wesley Longman, 1995.

[4] Keller, R. K., Schauer, R., Robitaille, S., and Page, P.: Pattern-based Reverse Engineering of Design Components. In: Proc. of the 21th International Conference on Software Engineering, Los Angeles, IEEE Computer Society Press, 1999, pp. 226-235.

[5] Krämer, Ch., Prechelt, L.: Design Recovery by Automated Search for Structural Design Patterns in Object-Oriented Software. In: Proc. Working Conference on Reverse Engineering, Monterey, IEEE Computer Society Press, 1996, pp. 208-215.

[6] Návrat, P.: A Closer Look at Programming Expertise: Critical Survey of Some Methodological Issues, *Information and Software Technology* **1** (1996) 37-46.

[7] Smolárová, M., Návrat, P., Bieliková, A Technique for Modelling Design Patterns. In: Proc. JCKBSE'98, Knowledge-Based Software Engineering, P. Návrat and H. Ueno (eds.), IOS Press, 1998, pp. 89-97.

Knowledge-Based Software Engineering
T. Hruška and M. Hashimoto (Eds.)
IOS Press, 2000

Model-View Separation Architecture BeaM and its Evaluation

Hironori WASHIZAKI, Junko SHIROGANE, Yoshiaki FUKAZAWA
Waseda University, Ohkubo 3-4-1, Shinjuku-ku, Tokyo 169-8555, Japan

Abstract. GUI application components, which are developed by combining the most basic generic GUI components and appending the required application logic, have been widely utilized. Their target is domain-specific and instance-level software reuse. In traditional methods, the separation between the application logic part and GUI part is incomplete. As a result, sufficient reusability and extensibility of the GUI application components cannot be realized. In this paper, the Model-View separation architecture BeaM (Bean for Model-view separation), which realizes complete independence between the application logic part and GUI part, is proposed. Also the evaluation results are analyzed based on the implementation in Java language.

1 Introduction

In order to realize instance-level reuse, component libraries are supported in some rapid application development tools (RAD tools) or operating systems. Combining generic components such as panels and bottoms in these libraries and adding application-dependent logic, new complex components are often developed. These combined components, called application components, are dependent on the target application domain.

Generic components are classified into visible components (widgets) and nonvisible components. In this paper, application components which contain one or more widgets are called GUI application components.

The objective of developing GUI application components is to use them as a subsystem or service package.

Grouped combined objects developed as subsystems are often called business components [1]. For GUI application components which are mainly utilized as business components are developed and used in the application development process, reusability is not the most important factor, however, flexible extensibility is important for their maintenance in the future. In particular since the design of the GUI structure is changed frequently, the generic GUI component and its reference in the application logic should be easily modified.

In software service packaging with GUI, reusability is the most important factor. For example, the internal application logic part and GUI part must be easily modified or updated. For GUI application components, the lower the dependence between the GUI part and application logic part, the higher the degree of reusability or extensibility can be realized.

For this purpose, the Mode-View separation pattern [2] or Model-View-Controller architecture [3] is widely used. However, the Model-View separation proposed up to now is not sufficient for complete separation, because GUI-related fragments are included in the application logic part.

In this paper, a software architecture BeaM (Bean for Model-View separation) is proposed and evaluated. BeaM can realize complete separation between application logic part and GUI part. Therefore application logic part and GUI part can communicate each other without acknowledging the detail structure of the other part.

2 GUI application components and Model-View separation

2.1 Traditional GUI application components

In some RAD tools and operating systems for supporting GUI, application frameworks to realize "weak" Model-View separation are supplied. AWT/JFC [4] (delegation event model) in Java2SE and MacApp for Macintosh are typical examples. GUI application components supplied by these application frameworks are made up of the GUI part (presentation layer) and application logic parts (model layer) such as in Figure 1. Figure 1 is based on the UML (Unified Modeling Language) [5]. In this paper, the GUI part and application logic part are referred to as GP and ALP, respectively.

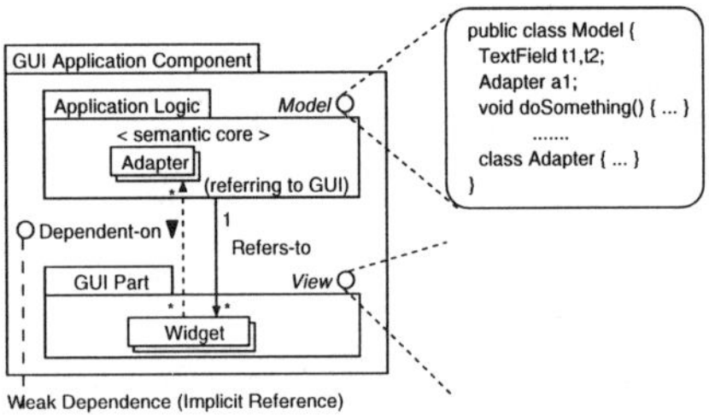

Figure 1: Traditional GUI application component structure

1. GUI part (GP): GP has some GUI components (widgets) supplied from given component libraries. GP should not contain any application logic and it is possible to adjust its representation.
2. Application logic part (ALP) : Some elements of GUI application parts, except for GP, are referred to as ALP. Almost all application frameworks are based on the event-driven architecture where their activity is controlled by the GUI events. Therefore ALP consists of a semantic core and GUI reference. The former contains both the process and data concerning the target application. The latter has the responsibility of accepting and processing the user events from GP.

In many application frameworks, communication between ALP and GP has been realized as follows.

(1) From GP to ALP

In GUI application components, application logic must accept an event notification from a generic GUI component and process it properly. In order to reduce the dependence, one of the following implementations is adopted [6].

1. Based on the Observer pattern, references from GP to ALP are realized via an adapter.
2. Based on the Template Method pattern, hook methods in ALP are prepared to call back.

As an example, communication from GUI to the application logic of the Java2SE delegation event model is shown in Figure 2. Using the adapter, sufficient independence is realized (Figure 2: [Adapter] dependent-on [GUI-part]).

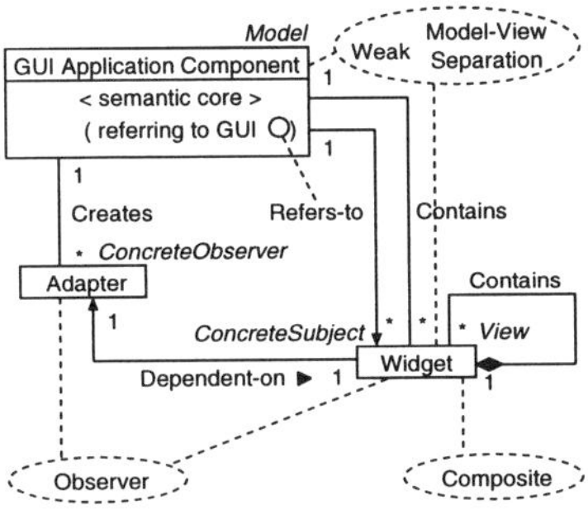

Figure 2: Class diagram of traditional GUI application component

(2) From ALP to GP

Following the behavior of application logic, the state change must be reflected to GUI and its GUI must be updated. In the conventional Model-View separation principle, every generic component is directly referred to and manipulated from ALP (Figure 2: [Model] refers-to [View]). This hard coding is the cause of strong dependence. This dependence is the reason why Model-View separation is "weak" and causes the following serious problems.

1. Decrease of maintainability and extensibility

   When a part of the GUI is changed because of specification modification, it is necessary to change not only corresponding adapters but also the GUI reference part in application logic. Since the GUI reference part is mixed in ALP, it is difficult to detect the lines to be changed. This leads to the decrease of maintainability and extensibility.

2. Difficulty of concurrent development

   In the design and implementation of the GUI application component, GP and ALP cannot be concurrently developed although the GUI designer and application designer are different people.

2.2 Toward complete Model-View separation

There has been some research work performed to exclude the mutual dependence between ALP and GP by introducing some object-oriented design principles such as design patterns [6]. MFC (Document-View) in Win32 [7], Pluggable MVC [3] in Smalltalk and the additive UI framework Jaguar [8] are examples. These approaches are aimed at realizing complete Model-View separation applying the Observation pattern to both directions of communication (Figure 3).

In these approaches, the one-to-one correspondence between a data item in ALP and a property of a generic GUI component means an increase in the number of adapters. This makes the adapters and message flow much more complicated. As a result, some points to be changed are scattered over many adapters. This is a very weak structure for future modification.

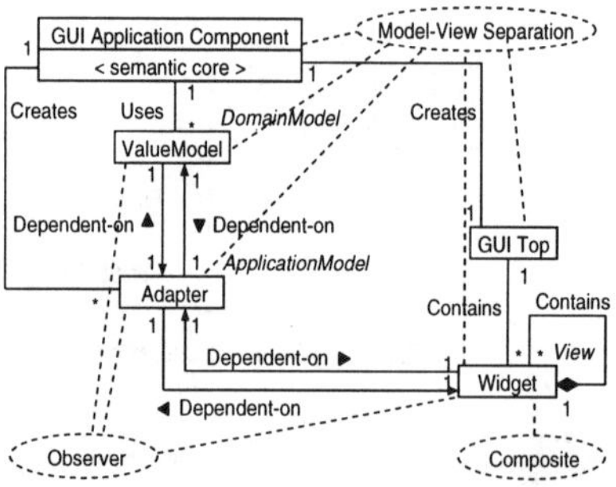

Figure 3: Class diagram of complete Model-View separation

3 BeaM architecture

In order to realize complete separation between ALP and GP in the development of GUI application components, BeaM (Bean for Model-View separation) is proposed. BeaM is the additional architecture for JavaBeans. By the Mediator pattern [6] in BeaM, both mutual independence between ALP and GP and localization of modification points can be realized. Therefore flexible extensibility and high maintainability can be obtained.

BeaM components can be categorized into three kinds of objects: Container, Model and UI (Figure 4).

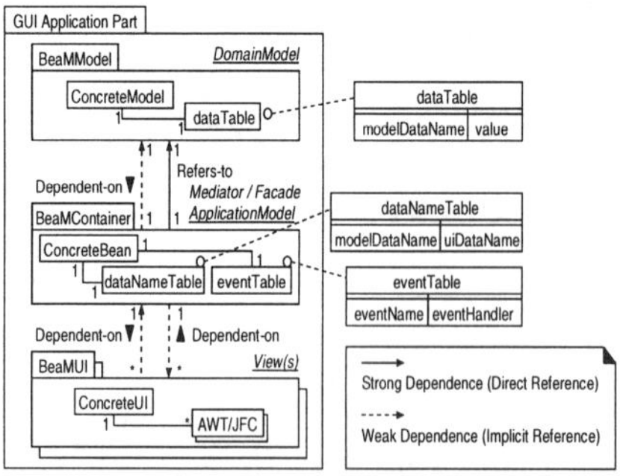

Figure 4: Conceptual model of BeaM architecture

Container object: Container objects generate Model objects and UI objects, and also mediate between data and event notification between them. They are implemented by inheriting the BeaMContainer class. The Container object has a name-table internally.

Model object: Model objects contain data, their operation and references to the Container objects. These objects have the BeaMModel interface.

UI object: UI objects interact with users through GUI and refer to Container objects. These objects have the BeaMUI interface.

3.1 Dependence reducing mechanism

A container object mediates all the communication between Model objects and UI objects in order to maintain the independence of each other (Figure 5).

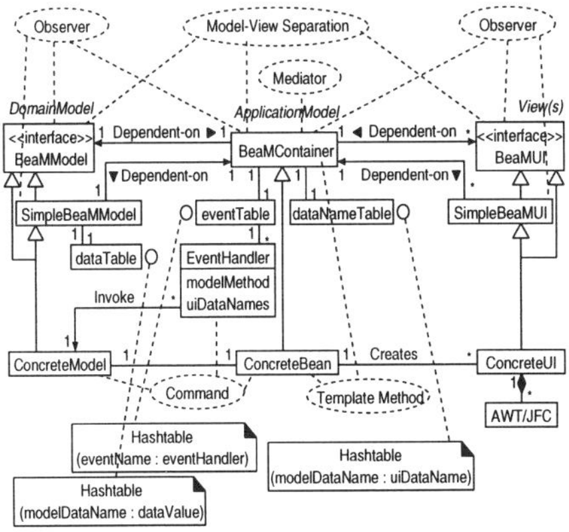

Figure 5: Class diagram of BeaM components

1. **Data sharing :** Application developers determine data in Model objects shared with UI objects in the design phase. BeaM supplies an automatic mechanism for data sharing along with the Observer pattern [6], where a Model object acts as "Observable" and a UI object acts as "Observer". Shared data and their data-names for the Model objects are registered initially in the data-table of the Container objects, and the UI objects are automatically noticed when the value is changed. The UI objects extract the value using the data-name for the UI object from the Container object, and pass it to GUI.
2. **Internal event transaction :** Internal events are transferred from a UI object to a Container object with an identifier (event-name) for the event and data-name on GUI components to be obtained. Our architecture first obtain input data from a GUI component on a UI object using its data-name, and then shared data are updated automatically. After that, required operations for the event-name are performed on a Model object defined previously.

An external behavior for a JavaBeans component is realized as access transfer to properties of a Model object or a UI object from the outside of the component and event notification to the outside via a Container object.

4 Integrated development tool BeaMBuilder

A tool, in which BeaM components can be developed along with BeaM architecture visually, is required because components are generally integrated visually using RAD tools which are based on the WYSIWYG philosophy [4]. BeaMBuilder is a tool for developing BeaM components. ModelBuilder (for Model), UIBuilder (for UI) and Integrator (for Container) in BeaMBuilder give functions for each kind of object.

- ModelBuilder : ModelBuilder helps developers to develop Model objects. Developers determine a data-name for a Model object with shared data in data definition. ModelBuilder generates the necessary program codes for data sharing and stores the information about shared data in ModelInfo objects.
- UIBuilder : UI objects can be designed visually using UIBuilder. Developers declare to keep watch on shared data in Model objects using data-name for UI. UIBuilder generates the necessary program code for data sharing. Internal events are defined after event-names are defined for events from GUI. The information about shared data and internal events is automatically stored in UIInfo objects.
- Integrator : Using this, developers can obtain information about shared data from ModelInfo and UIInfo, link shared data to Model objects and UI objects visually, and describe transactions for identifying an internal event from UI objects. Based on these operations, Integrator generates the codes for Container class (ConcreteBean class in Figure 4) and stores properties and events to show as JavaBeans components, in BeanInfo objects.

5 Example of development and its evaluation

Through an example, we will show the method for developing GUI application components based on the BeaM architecture by BeaMBuilder, and also the advantages for correction and extension against existing methods. We adopted JBuilder2.0 [9] of Inprise Corporation as a comparative target.

LoginFormBean along with the JavaBeans framework is a Bean of which the functions in AuthenticatorBean [10] are simplified. LoginFormBean is used for entering the ID and password. It has id and password as its properties, and its access methods are made public.

5.1 Detailed customization in each component

JTextField for password is changed to JPasswordField, and JtextField for ID to JComboBox. In the existing methods, for such modification, developers must modify access methods for the properties of id and password. These access methods are not modified by changing the design of GUI. As a result, it becomes difficult to customize GUI or ALP in each. When BeaMBuilder is used, developers only determine the data-name in the same manner as before the change by UIBuilder, and they need not modify Model objects for ALP at all. Developers can visually determine data-name for the property of each GUI component by UIBuilder. Therefore it is easier to change GUI application components.

In Table 1, we compared JBuilder2.0 with BeaMBuilder with respect to the number of modified lines in these changes. Based on these results, using BeaMBuilder, developers may need to modify the linking definition in Container objects when changing and modifying one GUI. However, because the linking definition is independent between Model objects and UI Objects, developers need not modify the other objects.

5.2 Coordination of output data

Referring to the above, property "password" must be updated not only for direct input from users to GUI but also for other input from systems in LoginFormBean. If applications are carefully designed for interaction between internal data of components and output to GUI, this problem can be avoided. However, developers need not take care of coordination between

Table 1: Number of modification code lines for GUI customization [lines]

Tool	HC	VE	AC	(LP)	Total
JBuilder	8	0	6	4	14
BeaMBuilder	1	4	6	0	11
(UIBuilder)	1	2	6	0	9
(Integrator)	0	2	0	0	2

HC: HandCoding, VE: VisualEditing, AC: AutoChange,
LP: LogicalPart∈HandCoding

Model objects and UI objects regarding shared data, because UI objects always keep watch over the status of shared data.

5.3 Multiple views for ALP

The existing methods for providing multiple GUIs for ALP in application components are only the following: developers must change the description of transactions for moving data to GUIs in application components, or make GUI and ALP independent and register another components, which move data to multiple GUIs, as an event listener for changed data. For example, in LoginFormBean, developers must add the lines in adding new output to GUI. However, it is necessary to perform modification on receiving the updated results for shared data, thus it is expensive to find program codes to modify and to modify them appropriately.

If those components are BeaM components, a unique Model object is not necessary to recognize the existence of UI objects and automatically notify updated messages. Therefore, developers can define multiple UI objects easily. For example, for LoginFormBean, in the case of adding output to GUI in the similar manner, developers can only develop new UI objects, and change (add) shared data and the linking definition of internal events in LoginFormBean. Addition of new UI objects to existing BeaM components with necessary linking definition can be performed visually and easily using BeaMIntegrator. In Table 2, comparison between JBuilder2.0 and BeaMBuilder regarding the number of modified lines in the above for adding items to GUI is shown. From these results, using BeaMBuilder, the Model object and the UI object are not directly recognize each other and the Model object, only one object in a component, can depend on multiple UI objects via Container objects. Therefore, it is easy to plug GUIs dynamically, or display the same data to multiple GUIs at the same time.

Table 2: Number of modification code lines for GUI addition [lines]

Tool	HC	VE	AC	(LP)	Total
JBuilder	7	1	0	2	8
BeaMBuilder	1	6	0	0	7
(UIBuilder)	0	2	0	0	2
(Integrator)	1	4	0	0	5

HC: HandCoding, VE: VisualEditing, AC: AutoChange,
LP: LogicalPart∈HandCoding

5.4 Runtime Performance

Applying BeaM architecture to GUI applications, the runtime performance becomes lower in exchange for the higher reusability. To evaluate the degradation of the performance, we measured the execution time by automatically repeating the fixed number of sequences of actions, i.e., entering values, firing LoginEvent and clearing the values. The result is shown in Table 3. Referring to this, the difference is comparatively small, so BeaM experiences no performance problem in practical application.

Table 3: Execution time comparison between traditional style and BeaM [ms]

	SingleView		DualView	
Loop[times]	Old	BeaM	Old	BeaM
100	17125	18828	18697	18787
1000	169804	176374	179588	183494
10000	1809102	1937265	2015458	2024081

Sun Java2SEv1.2.2, WindowsNT4.0 Server,
500MHz/PentiumIII, Memory256M

6 Conclusion

As the development method of GUI application components, a new architecture BeaM and corresponding development tool BeaMBuilder are proposed, and their superiority over the conventional method and related research are also shown. The main target of our research is to overcome the difficulty in extension and maintenance.

Now a design method based on the BeaM architecture has been developed. The close connection between the design method and software architecture developed will yield the easy and extensible GUI application components.

References

[1] D. D'Souza and A. Wills, Objects, Components, and Frameworks with UML, Addison-Wesley, 1998.

[2] C. Larman, Applying UML and Patterns, Prentice Hall, 1997.

[3] A. Goldberg, Smalltalk-80, Addison-Wesley, 1986.

[4] G. Hamilton, JavaBeans 1.01 Specification, Sun Microsystems, 1997.

[5] G. Booch et al., The Unified Modeling Language User Guide, Addison-Wesley, 1999.

[6] E. Gamma et al., Design Patterns: Elements of Reusable Object-Oriented Software, Addison-Wesley 1995.

[7] Microsoft, Microsoft Foundation Class Library Reference, Microsoft Press, 1996.

[8] A. Lovejoy and F. Mervine, Jaguar: A UI Framework for Java, OOPSLA'99, 1999.

[9] Inprise, Borland Jbuilder. Available at http://www.borland.com/jbuilder/.

[10] Sun Microsystems, HotJava HTML Component.
Available at http://java.sun.com/products/hotjava/bean/.

Knowledge-Based Software Engineering
T. Hruška and M. Hashimoto (Eds.)
IOS Press, 2000

Specifying Downloadable Properties for Reusing Software Components: A Case Study of Java

Haruhiko KAIYA, Kenji KAIJIRI
Faculty of Engineering, Shinshu University
4-17-1 Wakasato, Nagano City, 380-8553, JAPAN
{kaiya, kaijiri}@cs.shinshu-u.ac.jp
http://www.cs.shinshu-u.ac.jp/~kaiya/

Abstract. In this paper, we propose a specification of software components which can be loaded not only from your local system but also from the other systems over the computer network. Because components from the other system are not always enough reliable or safe to act freely in your own system, you should limit their activities to a certain context. Because some existing systems like Java RMI and an Applet provide a mechanism for such limitation implicitly, users sometimes lose sight of the abilities and limitations of such components. Therefore, they fail to reuse the components in the right way. We provide a way to specify such properties, so that component users can precisely understand the abilities and limitations.

1 Introduction

For reusing software components, we need suitable documents of specification. Unfortunately, as many of such documents tend to be long, incomplete, redundant or vague, component users sometimes can not reuse such components adequately. For example, the specification of RMI[1] consists of about 90 pages of documents and it is hard to read completely. But small manuals in many books are too simple to understand the components. One of the suitable tool for reuse is formal method. Though writing a formal specification of components looks like expensive, we can retrieve the costs for using the components and the specification repeatedly [2]. Several formal or semiformal specification of components are already used, e.g. signatures, pre/post conditions and invariants. But we can not simply specify the mobility of components [3], because each component will change its behaviors along with its birthplace, running place and so on.

In this paper, we propose a way of specification for mobile components, which are not autonomous but downloaded by the other components or systems. We call such kind of mobile components as *downloadable components* in this paper. With our specification, users of downloadable components will be able to use them adequately. Though the specification here is developed through the case study of Java, we do not limit the discussion to Java, but discuss how downloadable components should be designed from the users' point of view.

In section2, we introduce the properties and problems of downloadable components. In section3, we summarize what should be specified in addition for such properties, and we give an example in section4 to show the advantages of the specification. In the last section, we summarize our results and discuss the future works.

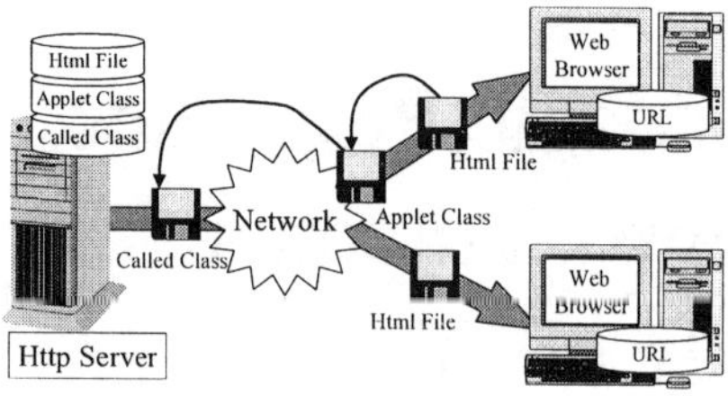

Figure 1: Applet Overview

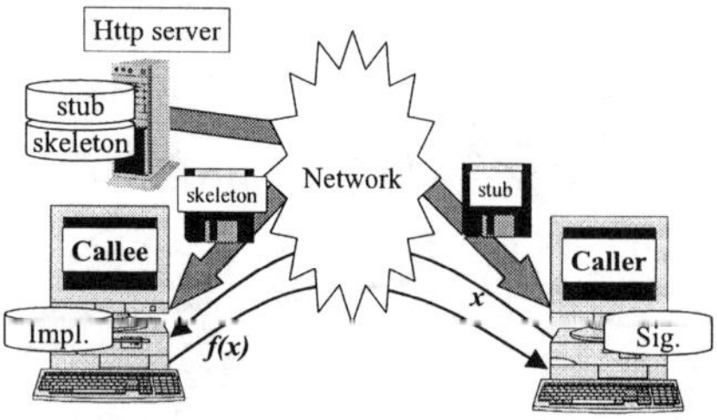

Figure 2: RMI Overview

2 Properties and Problems of Downloadable Components

In this section, we introduce examples, underlying mechanism and problems of downloadable components. Because examples in this section are all about Java system, we regard the term '*class*' in the same light as the term 'component'.

2.1 What is Downloadable Component?

The most famous system using downloadable components is an Applet. In Figure1, we illustrates the typical behavior of an applet. In this paper, the icons of diskette represent downloadable components, and the icons of cylinder represents the components that are deployed in the local system. Web browser running an applet only knows an URL of html file, which is a bootstrap script, where the filename of the applet class is specified. After loading the script, the applet class and other classes called from the applet class are loaded one after another. Therefore, we can use sophisticated reusable class libraries like AWT graphics and Java Beans on any browser. Because the loaded classes are not enough reliable or safe, the classes are not allowed completely to operate system resources, e.g. file system or network connections, among the browser side system.

RMI (Remote Method Invocation) is regarded as object-oriented RPC (Remote Procedure Call) for Java[1]. In Figure2, we illustrates the outline of RMI. For establishing RMI, both a *caller* (or RMI client) program in a machine and a *callee* (or RMI server) program in another machine should be able to use components, *stub* and *skeleton*, for passing the arguments of the procedure and for receiving the results over the network. Because the components are not enough safe to operate the system resources of the caller and callee, their behaviors should be also limited. In RMI system, in contrast with an Applet, programmers should explicitly manage the limitation by the `SecurityManager` in Java. Therefore, you can use the downloadable components without limitation, if you want.

2.2 User-defined Class Loaders

Thanks to *user-defined class loaders* in Java Virtual Machine (JVM) [4], we can use the downloadable components and manage their behaviors in Java. The purpose of class loaders is to support dynamic loading of software components on the Java platform [5]. JVM has two different kind of class loaders, *a system class loader* and user-defined class loaders [6]. Because each user-defined class loader can limit the behaviors of components loaded by the loader respectively, a component can behave differently with respect to its loader.

In Java application, the system class loader is used to load a class, whose `main` method act as a bootstrap, from the local file system. All classes used directly in the class are also

```
import java.net.*;
import java.io.*;

public class DLoader extends ClassLoader{
    // several definitions are omitted .....

    protected Class loadClass(String name, boolean resolve)
    throws ClassNotFoundException{
        Class clazz = null;

        try{ return findSystemClass(name); }
        catch(ClassNotFoundException e1){}
        catch(NoClassDefFoundError e2){}

        clazz=findLoadedClass(name);
        if(clazz != null){ return clazz; }

        clazz=findClass(name);
        if(clazz == null ){ throw new ClassNotFoundException(name); }

        return clazz;
    }

    private synchronized Class findClass(String name){
        // finding byte code from the network resource and define class.
        // .....
            return defineClass(name, data, 0, total);
        // .....
    }

    // several definitions are omitted .....

    public static void main(String args[]){
        try{
            DLoader loader=new DLoader(new URL(args[0]));
            Runnable cmd=(Runnable)loader.loadClass(args[1]).newInstance();
            cmd.run();
        }catch(Throwable e){
            e.printStackTrace();
        }
    }
}
```

Figure 3: Example: Simple User-defined Class Loader

loaded from the loader[1]. An user-defined class loader is implemented as a subclass of `ClassLoader`, and used as shown in Figure3. A class loader `DLoader` defined in this figure is loaded a component `args[0].class`, which is implemented the `interface Runnable`, from the network stream.

We can decide the policy of security in the following steps.

1. Decide whether your class loader takes account of the `SecurityManager` or not. For example, the loader in Figure3 does not, but loaders of RMI and an Applet does.
2. Decide each security policies listed in class `SecurityManager`. The manager class has about 30 numbers of check lists for limiting the operations for the system resources, e.g. file systems and network connections[1]. You can implement your own manager as a subclass of `SecurityManager`. For example, the manager for RMI, i.e. `RMISecurityManager` disallows most of all system operations.

Then, the decision affects the behaviors of loaded classes as follows.

- If a class loader is designed to require its `SecurityManager` but the manager is not given, the class loader itself can not run. As a result, classes loaded by the loader also can not run.
- If a loader is not designed to require its `SecurityManager`, the loader itself and classes loaded by it can run.
- Methods in Java class libraries for operating the system resources are designed to refer the related check lists in the `SecurityManager`, if the manager is defined. Therefore, the activities of each method is limited by the manager.

2.3 The Problems: Loader Selection & Deployment

As mentioned above, Java has flexible but complex mechanism for loading its components. As a result, without deep understanding of class loading and security system, component users tend to lose sight of the abilities and limitations of such components, especially those downloaded from the other system over the network. Here we summarize the problems.

As explained above, a component of Java changes its behaviors along with its class loader. Therefore, component users should know the specification of components with their loaders. But it is not so easy because

- application programmers normally do not care about the class loaders,
- and the *defining loader* is dynamically decided according to both the logic of the *initiating loader*. and the deployment of components.

If a component `C` is the result of `L.loadClass()`, a loader `L` is called initiating loader of C. If a component `C` is the result of `L.definClass()`, a loader `L` is called defining loader of C [5].

The logic of the initiating loader specifies the order for selecting defining loader. For example, `DLoader` in Figure3 uses the following order to select its defining loader; 1. system class loader (line 11-13), 2. cache of this loader (line 15-16), 3. `defineClass` method of this class via the method `findClass` (line 18-19).

As a result, components in the local system, which will be loaded by the system class loader, have the priority in `DLoader`, therefore the security manager sometimes gives no effect to the components. Loaders of RMI and an Applet have similar logic of selection.

3 Additional Specification for such Properties

For specifying the downloadable properties and its problems mentioned in section2. We should describe the following items in the specification of the components.

1. **Security policies for each components**: Because downloadable components are not enough reliable or safe to act freely, we should specify how a component may act and may not.
2. **Birthplace of each component**: Because the birthplace of a component is good indicator for its reliability, it should be also specified.
3. **Location for running the components**: Because relative location of a birthplace from the location where the component will run defines its reliability, we should also specify where the component will run.
4. **Deployment of components in each location(or machine)**: Under the environment connected by the network, the deployment of each component are dynamically changed in every moment. Therefore we should globally specify such deployment.
5. **Logic for selecting defining-loader**: In Java, because users can define the logic for loading components, the users can use flexible and complex mechanism for downloading them. Therefore we should specify such logic.

4 Example

In this section, we introduce an example to show how the specification in section3 is useful for component users to understand the properties of downloadable components. We use Z notation for our specification in this paper because it is widely known in the software engineering field, and because it is fit for object-oriented mechanism.

4.1 Stub with Cracking Code: Counter Example

Suppose we should use the RMI call for our system, even though the call contains cracking codes which will steal our password. For limiting such stealing, we use a `SecurityManager`. Moreover, we carefully deploy current version of stub codes so as to stop the progress of cracking in the codes. Here we check the safety of this situation. Note that we only take account of the item 1 in Section3 in the following specification.

First, we specify the system resources and their security limitation in *SysRes*. As the security limitation can change only at once by `SetSecurityManager` method in Java, we model this method in *SetLimit*.

SysRes

$res : R \nrightarrow Bool;\ limit : \mathbb{P} R$

$limit \subseteq \mathrm{dom}\, res;\ \forall x : limit \bullet (x, \mathrm{false}) \in res$

SetLimit

$\Delta SysRes;\ l? : \mathbb{P} R$

$limit \neq \varnothing \Rightarrow l? = limit'$

R is basic type which represents a set of resources. Schema *SysRes* represents a security level of this machine.

A method itself and the cracking codes can be represented as follows;

$Func \mathrel{\widehat=} [x?, y! : \mathbb{Z} \mid y! = f(x?)]$ $\quad Crack \mathrel{\widehat=} [pas! : R, \Xi SysRes \mid (pas!, \mathrm{true}) \in res]$

All the method will be observed from the component users as follows;

$F \mathrel{\widehat=} (Crack \mathbin{⨾} Func \land \Xi SysRes) \setminus \{pas!\}$

Then we check the following expression,

$SetLimt \mathbin{⨾} Crack \mathbin{⨾} (Func \land \Xi SysRes) \mid pas! \in l?$

This represents that cracking is established even if corresponding operation is protected by the security manager.

This schema is inconsistent because both $(pas!, \mathrm{true}) \in res$ and $(pas!, \mathrm{false}) \in res$ are satisfied at the same time even if *res* is function. Therefore, we can conclude that the cracking is never established and our protection is enough safe.

Unfortunately, the cracking can be established in fact because the policy of security checking is changing along with the birthplace of components. We will resolve this problem in the next.

4.2 Stub with Cracking Code: Resolved

We introduce two additional basic types, *Loc* for location of byte codes, and *ByteCode* for realizing a class and an instance in run time. Then we define the deployment of byte codes over the network (the item 4 in Section3) as follows;

$deploy : Loc \nrightarrow \mathbb{P}\, ByteCode$

We extend *SysRes* schema with the location where the components are running (the item 3 in Section3), and introduce *Class* schema for representing the birthplace, byte code and the logic for selecting the birthplace of the class (the item 2 & 5 in Section3).

SysRes

$res : R \nrightarrow Bool;\ limit : \mathbb{P} R;\ here : Loc$

$limit \subseteq \mathrm{dom}\, res$
$\forall x : limit \bullet (x, \mathrm{false}) \in res$
$here \in \mathrm{dom}\, deploy$

Class

$birth : Loc;\ byte : ByteCode$
$lslctr : \mathrm{seq}\, Loc$

$birth \in \mathrm{ran}\, lslctr$
$birth \in \mathrm{dom}\, deploy$

Then the attribute *birth* in schema *Class* is defined the following schema.

SetLoader

$sl?;\ \mathrm{seq}\, Loc;\ \Delta Class$

$lslctr' = sl?$

$\forall x, y : \mathbb{N} \bullet byte \in deploy\ lslctr'\ x \wedge x \in \mathrm{dom}\, lslctr' \wedge lslctr'\ y = birth' \Rightarrow y \leq x$

The second line of predicate part (the item 5 in Section3) is slightly complex, but it simply says that the first location which involves *byte* in *lslctr* is its *birth*.

The schema *Crack* is modified as follows for representing the effect of birthplace.

$Crack \mathrel{\widehat{=}} [pas! : R;\ \Xi SysRes;\ \Xi Class \mid here \neq birth \Rightarrow (pas!, \mathrm{true}) \in res\ ]$

Then the following expression becomes consistent,

$SetLimit \fatsemi (SetLoader \wedge \Xi SysRes \fatsemi Crack \fatsemi Func \wedge \Xi Class \wedge \Xi SysRes) \setminus Class$
$\mid pas! \in l? \wedge sl? = \langle here, there \rangle$

under the situation of $deploy = \{(here, \{byte, \cdots\}), (there, \{byte, \cdots\}) \cdots\}$. In Figure2, *here* corresponds to 'Call', *there* to 'Http server', and *byte* to 'stub'. As a result, cracking can be established even if corresponding operation is protected by the security manager under this situation. So if you want to stop the cracking, you should change *sl?* or *deploy*.

5 Discussion

In this paper, we discuss and propose how to specify downloadable properties of software components for suitable reuse, through the case study of Java. Though the style of specification here is not different from the style of traditional specification, we can clarify how and what kind of items should be described. Formalization for JVM is already proposed [7] and the security issue of Java is also reported [8], but these researches are not intended to encourage the reuse of components.

From our case study, we can discuss how downloadable components should be designed from the viewpoint of users. For example, in a system where each component can have different security policy, we can develop more flexible but complex system. Also the reliability of each component can be decided not only by its birthplace but also its frequency of use. Now we have no metrics for measuring the trade-off between the flexibility of the system and the requirements of users, we can not rationally select the suitable language system for developing a system for the users. Formal description of components may also contribute to make such metrics.

References

[1] Sun Microsystems, Inc. *Java Remote Method Invocation Specification*, Feb. 1997. Revision 1.4, JDK1.1 FCS.

[2] Bertrand Meyer. The Next Software Breakthrough. *COMPUTER*, 30(7):113–114, Jul. 1997.

[3] Tommy Thorn. Programming languages for mobile code. *ACM Computing Surveys*, 29(3):213–239, Sep. 1997.

[4] Tim Lindholm and Frank Yellin. *The Java Virtual Machine Specification*. Addison Wesley Longman, second edition, Apr. 1999.

[5] Sheng Liang and Gilad Bracha. Dynamic class loading in the Java virtual machine. In *Proc. of OOPSLA*, pages 36–44, Oct. 1998.

[6] Jon Meyer and Troy Downing. *Java Virtual Machine*. O'Reilly, first edition, Mar. 1997.

[7] T. Jensen, D. Le Metayer, and T. Thorn. Security and Dynamic Class Loading in Java: A Formalization. In *Proc. of Int. Conference on Computer Languages*, pages 4–15, May 1998.

[8] Drew Dean, Edward W. Felten, and Dan S. Wallach. Java Security: From HotJava to Netscape and Beyond. In *Proc. of IEEE Symposium on Security and Privacy*, pages 190–200, May 1996.

Knowledge-Based Software Engineering
T. Hruška and M. Hashimoto (Eds.)
IOS Press, 2000

Database Reuse as a Support for Conceptual Database Modeling

Tatjana WELZER[1], Ivan ROZMAN[1], Marjan DRUŽOVEC[2]
[1]*UM FERI Maribor, Smetanova 17, SI-2000 Maribor, Slovenia*
[2]*UM FS Maribor, Smetanova 17, SI-2000 Maribor, Slovenia*

Abstract. The rapid growth and increasing demand for more and more complex applications built upon databases has stimulated the need for higher-level concepts, tools and techniques for a database design and development. One of the possible concepts applies reuse to the database design. However, the reuse in database environment seems not to have received enough attention, because until now the most of the research had been done only on the software reuse. In the paper the influence of database reusability on the conceptual modeling will be shortly presented.

1 Introduction

Database is the main building block of any modern information system. As an essential component, the database must be very carefully designed to contain all the information required by the user. To achieve greater efficiency the database is designed in a progressive process decomposed into conceptual, logical and physical design. The aim of the conceptual design, which results in a conceptual model, is to describe the information content of the database on an abstract and general way, independent from a particular logical model or DBMS. For that reasons the conceptual model is an essential, important component that is in principle used only once, i.e. within a single database design. This seems to be at least very time consuming. The design process for each of different databases requires a lot of time. Numberless conceptual models were designed and never used again, not even parts of them [8]. Why? Is each database really so unique that no common and hence reusable data components of conceptual models are to be found?

In software engineering reusable components have been well known and practiced almost since the first programs were written. Reuse has been considered as a way for overcoming the software crisis. Although it was never restricted only to the programs [6] it was also applied to results of different phases of development as well as to human resources. However, reuse means to use previously acquired concepts and objects in a new situation.

2 Reuse

Reuse or reusability is not a specific, algorithmic, heuristic or only a simple set of guidelines. It is also not achieved by a particular language, data organization, management technique, library or operating system [4]. Considering these facts we should ask ourselves: "What reuse actually is?"

In general, the term reuse is familiar with reusable containers, recycling various resources (aluminum, paper, newsprint, and glass) as well as reusing an evaluation procedure that worked previously in a similar situation [4]. Actually in the reuse field there is no single accepted definition for most of the terms connected with this field, as well as the field of databases. According to C. Brown [1] and T. Welzer [8] we will try to give detailed explanation about terms "database reuse" and "reusable database components":

- Database reuse is a process of using existing database conceptual models or parts of them rather than building them from the scratch. Typically, reuse involves abstraction, selection, specialization and integration of reusable parts, although different techniques (when they will be defined) may emphasize or de-emphasize some of them.
- The primary motivation to reuse database components (conceptual models or parts of them) is to reduce the time and efforts required when building a conceptual model, actually a database. Because the quality of software systems is enhanced by reusing quality software artifacts, which also reduces the time and efforts required to maintain software, (similarly) reusable database components can, first of all, influence logical and physical database design and (not at last) also the database maintenance.

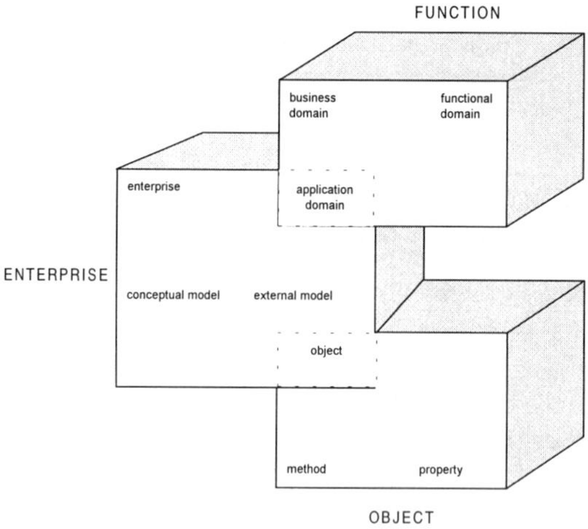

Figure 1. Concept of the MetaBase

3 MetaBase

Our approach to apply reuse concepts to the database design is based on an object oriented meta data model. We have decided for object oriented paradigm with a purpose to take the advantages of its concepts (reuse, inheritance, methods) to represent our meta data model. The MetaBase *(Figure 1)* model is introduced as a three-level model distinguishing the object level, the enterprise level and the functional level.

Enterprise level. It is the central level in the MetaBase model and contains the conceptual models and external models (submodels) that describe the particular enterprise. This central block presents a connection to a functional level across application domain and enterprise. On the other hand it is also related with a subordinated object level across objects. The application domain is a very important part of our structure because reuse of conceptual models (database components) is more promising if their application domains are the same or similar [3].

Functional level. Each application domain is characterized by classification in two dimensions: the business domain (e.g. health care, banking, tourism, and airline) and the functional domain (e.g. accounting, order processing, etc.). In our meta data model both business domain and functional domains are organized in a generalization hierarchy, the functional domain, furthermore, in an aggregation (part-of) hierarchy.

Object level. The object level contains the representation of semantic objects, which constitute the conceptual and external models. The structure we are discussing here *(Figure 1)* is designed according to the object oriented data model. The key reason for this decision was to include operations (methods) to make the structure more active and to open possibilities to integrate reuse of software and re-use of database design [2].

4 Conceptual Database Design Supported by Database Reuse

For the "classical" conceptual database design different authors have introduced different steps of conceptual database design. Observations of different conceptual design methodologies [7] lead us to the following statements:

- The input and output of the database conceptual design are the same in all approaches. Independent of the database as well as conceptual model approach all the methodologies start with user's documents, needs, wishes and requirements.
- Different steps in presenting methodologies can be grouped into two general: requirements analysis and building of the conceptual model.

4.1 Steps of Conceptual Database Design Supported by Database Reuse

By designing the conceptual model according to the database reuse paradigms two approaches are possible. In the first which is called *shopping approach* [8] the major tasks are collecting and analyzing requirements, searching for similar conceptual models, modification of appropriate conceptual model and integration of a conceptual model into a new one. In the second approach, called *tailor approach* similar tasks for successful conceptual database design are identified:

1. Requirements analysis
   - collecting user's needs, wishes and requirements
   - formulating and analyzing requirements
   - searching for similar "objects" in the MetaBase structure
2. Building of the conceptual model
   - modifying a similar "object" with respect to requirements analysis
   - integrating a conceptual model in a new one
   - iterating the first two steps if needed by using intermediate results

The most important difference between both approaches is in the meaning of "object". In the shopping approach the "objects" are conceptual models and their parts and in the tailor approach the "objects" are parts of different conceptual models. Some of the tasks will be described in detail.

Collecting and analyzing requirements. In this step user's needs and wishes are collected as well as organized for further use and relationships among potential similar objects are identified and structured.

Searching for similar conceptual models. MetaBase is an object-oriented repository in which conceptual models are saved. They are organized according to the business and the functional domain that identify an application domain. Within the set of objects of an application domain the user has the following choices when searching for similar objects [7]:

- User can restrict the search by specifying an ontological classification.
- Starting from a single object (or a group of objects) the system can determine similar objects. The user directs this search by specifying the length of the path to a common ancestor to be considered.
- The system can search for objects with similar properties as the given object.
- The user can choose a set of conceptual models or external models and restrict the search to the objects contained in the selected models.
- The user can browse through the whole MetaBase, looking for all the properties of an object, for objects that are contained in an external or conceptual model, in which models an object is contained, in which objects a certain property is referenced, and so on.

Modification. The results of previous step are conceptual models appropriate for further design. According to the user requirements it is possible that some changes are needed. The results of this step are changed conceptual models prepared for the last step.

Integration. Modified models are joined into a new conceptual model considering some extra requirements, which are not a subject of reused conceptual models.

5 Conclusion

Conceptual models of different databases are not right or wrong [5]. They are more or less useful. The useful part presents a starting point for new design. Actually this are reusable database components from the MetaBase repository, that are presented as a starting point for conceptual database design supported by database reuse and of course according to the MetaBase view they are more or less reusable.

Normally MetaBase provides a structure for archiving database components of several applications. All components are classified according to the business domain and the functional domain of their application domains. The structure allows not only storing database components of several applications but also to classify and compare them from different applications. A powerful search strategy aid the database designer to efficiently use the MetaBase for retrieving database components, which may be used directly or adopted in a new design.

References

[1] C.L.Brown, Reuse: In J.J. Marciniak (Ed.) Encyclopedia of Software Engineering, John Wiley & Sons, 1994, pp. 1055-1069.

[2] J. Eder, W.Rossak: An Archive of Semantic Data Models as Basis for Software Re-use, In Proc. 8th International Symposium on Applied Informatics, Innsbruck, Austria, February 1990, pp. 284-287.

[3] P. Freeman: Reusable Software Engineering Concepts and Research Directions, In P. Freeman (Ed.) IEEE Tutorial Software Reusability, 1987, pp. 10-25.

[4] P. Freeman: A Perspective on Reusability, In P. Freeman (Ed.) IEEE Tutorial Software Reusability, 1987, 2-8.

[5] M. Fowler: Analysis Patterns: Reusable Object Models, Addison Wesley, 1997.

[6] C. W. Krueger: Software Reuse, ACM Computing Surveys, Vol. 24, No. 2, 1992, pp. 131-184.

[7] T. Welzer: Model of the database system with explicit built in expert knowledge, Doctor of Science Thesis, 1995.

[8] T. Welzer: Database reuse a new way to the conceptual database design, In: K. Kuchcinski (Ed.) Short Notes Proceedings of the 22nd Euromicro Conference, Prague, Czech Republic, IEEE Computer Society Press, 1997.

Knowledge-Based Software Engineering
T. Hruška and M. Hashimoto (Eds.)
IOS Press, 2000

A Knowledge Based Approach to Design with Patterns

Ahmet SIKICI, N. Yasemin TOPALOGLU
Ege University, Computer Engineering Department
Bornova, Izmir-Turkey
E-mail: ahmets@egenet.com.tr, yasemin@bornova.ege.edu.tr

Abstract. In this paper, we introduce an approach to pattern formalization based on a fully generalized and purely symbolic interpretation of the patterns which simply focuses on the representation of knowledge. Our model does not deal with the semantic content of the patterns directly but it can provide a base for higher order models that support a specific type of the patterns.

1 Introduction

In this paper the necessity of the formalization of design patterns is discussed and a knowledge based pattern model is introduced as a solution to the vagueness in the common approach.

A pattern is a set of abstract descriptions that provide a ready solution to a common problem. We agree that a pattern is a solution idea sometimes even beyond the scope of a literal expression [1]. However we further believe that patterns can be handled analytically, just as ideas can be. In our work, an artificial intelligence point of view has been chosen for the representation of patterns and we believe that our point of view is suitable to enlighten the frontier where vague nature of most patterns can meet a safer and better automated incremental reuse that a suitable formalism can provide.

2 Previous Work

Software engineering community never came to a consensus on what a pattern really was. Some developers stuck to Alexander's approach and used informal definitions extensively [2]. Most of them narrowed down the domain to class diagrams or architectural diagrams. Some of these also managed to reach physical formalism up to some degree, in the expense of loosing a little more of the generality [3].

If a vague pattern model is assumed, having no automation in mind, the attempts are normally towards formalizing the *developer behavior* instead of the *pattern behavior*. A format which consists of 13 fields, 7 of which are descriptions in natural language is defined in [2] as a standard format that should be used by the developers.

Eden et al. [4] defines the creation of new patterns as discovery or invention and explains the fact that, the design pattern practice can be an art, in the sense that scientific discovery is an art in accordance with the old-fashioned philosophical concept of the context of discovery.

A high level declarative language called LePUS, which has been introduced by Eden et al. [3] employs symbolic logic to produce a meta description to guide the specialization process of patterns, which is called refinement.

In section 3, a knowledge based approach to design pattern formalisation is introduced which is based on a general tool for expressing and using patterns. We also aim reusing the design patterns effectively for building new patterns

3 A New Approach to Pattern Formalization

3.1 Pattern Lifecycle

Most of the terminology about the patterns is vague and it is difficult to describe the common conception about the life cycle of a pattern. We also doubt that the life of a pattern is usually cyclic. The usual misconception that considers the patterns as immortal atomic solutions, seems to have led to preventing them from being modified or updated to fulfil the possible upcoming needs. Some patterns are always considered to be good enough hence they require no modification at all.

It has been stated that the application and description of the design patterns are good candidates for automation while the production activities require techniques that appear to belong to the realm of artificial intelligence or knowledge based reasoning [4].

It is our opinion that, automating the application and the description phases of the life cycle and plugging some artificial intelligence to the discovery and invention phases, is not the most structured way of formalizing the process. In order to reach the desired reuse performance in terms of accuracy, safety, scale and speed, the life cycle needs to be considered as a whole.

The upper row of the lifecycle diagram in Figure 1 represents the application line of the patterns. The two extensions to the state of the art lifecycle can be considered to be the presence of the pattern authoring and the pattern processing phases. The evolution from invention to authoring is due to the pattern reuse facility that enables the *author* to build new patterns with the aid of ready building blocks that can be manipulated by operations as straightforward as cut and paste.

The upper row of the lifecycle diagram in Figure 1 represents the application line of the patterns. The two extensions to the state of the art lifecycle can be considered to be the presence of the pattern authoring and the pattern processing phases.

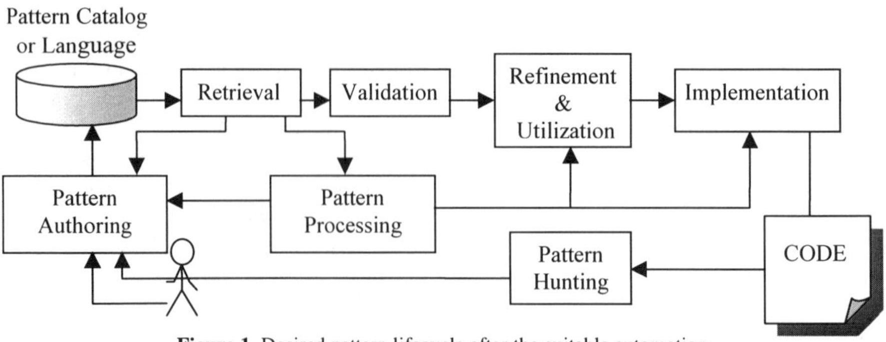

Figure 1. Desired pattern lifecycle after the suitable automation.

The evolution from invention to authoring is due to the pattern reuse facility that enables the *author* to build new patterns with the aid of ready building blocks that can be manipulated by operations as straightforward as cut and paste.

Pattern processing is the phase that patterns are transformed automatically and momentarily by a pattern based language's compiler or a pattern based component system. The transformations are defined by a set of production rules which altogether constitute a system called the *pattern arithmetic* as defined in [5]. The aim of processing the patterns is to produce a suitable pattern for the context imposed by the software design problem.

3.2 Pattern Reuse

In our opinion, a differentiation between reusing the patterns, and reusing with or by the patterns is required. In this study, pattern reuse represents the reuse of known patterns, in order to build new patterns. However, our view of the patterns does not impose any degree of abstraction, so the resultant pattern can resemble a refined design or an implementation. For this purpose, pattern arithmetic [5] can be employed as an alternative to traditional methods of design pattern creation.

It is believed that the production of new patterns would improve in terms of quality and quantity if older patterns could be reused in fabricating the new ones.

3.3 The Proposed Approach

At present, without suitable formalism, design patterns are described partly using class diagrams, partly using object diagrams, and partly using source code text. Since none of these tools is complete with reference to design patterns, the general form is mainly described by natural language prose [4].

In our definition a knowledge representation point of view is adopted and all the graphical notation styles are considered to be special purpose semantic networks. It must be stressed here that our pattern model is purely symbolic. The meaning that can be attributed to the elements in our model is only related to the pattern concept in general and the model itself does not imply any pattern type or programming style. From this point of view our work can be described as a knowledge representation tool that has been fine tuned for the description of patterns.

The model we propose [5] is a graph composed of four types of elements, each having a name and a set of attributes. The most important of these attributes is a Boolean value that indicates whether the node or the link is a hot or a cold element. (The word "element" is used as a common name for nodes and links.) Figure 2 defines the four types of elements. Elements can be interpreted as objects since they have a fixed number of attributes.

A hot element is an element that can be replaced by a whole pattern. This way a pattern can be nested inside the other through the hot element. The pattern type specified as one of the attributes of the hot element imposes a restriction upon the alternatives that can take its place.

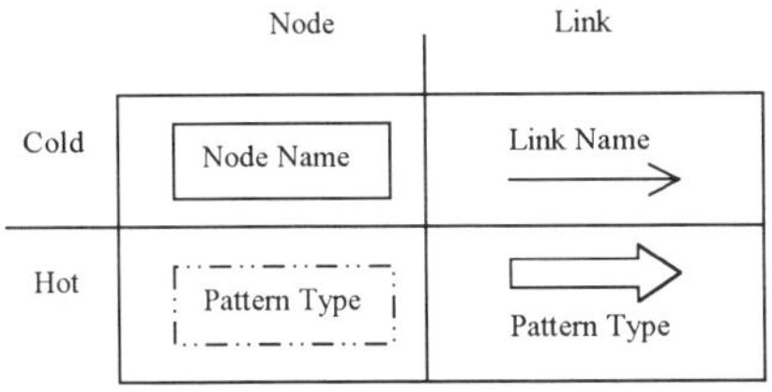

Figure 2. Four types of Elements of the Pattern Model

Using the operations of the *pattern arithmetic* [5], we can refine patterns, generalize them into more abstract forms, nest them inside one another, add or remove nodes or links and we can superpose two patterns to make a new pattern that captures both of their meanings. It is also possible to browse the patterns with various algorithms or perform queries about certain aspects of the pattern. All of these operations are related solely to *pattern morphology* and within the model there is no direct implication about software or reuse. Aspects related to specific reuse strategies and reuse of certain types of design are implemented in a higher layer as *pattern frameworks*[5]. In these frameworks pattern arithmetic can be employed to implement the rules related to the structures like meta patterns or architectural patterns. This point makes our work appear as a knowledge based approach to pattern formalization.

Within this context, the model involves a compatibility check operation on patterns. Compatibility check for a software construct can be defined as the detection of its ability to take part in certain operations, by investigating the safety and the meaning of the operation. Therefore the ability to cooperate with other constructs can be determined by a compatibility check. The compatibility check for the objects is firmly integrated with the type checking mechanism of the host language. A type checking on an object can query all the structural knowledge enclosed within that object in one step.

The compatibility check issue on patterns can be considered as an ill structured problem from a pure mathematical point of view. The distributed nature of the patterns makes it problematic to perform a compatibility check. It is difficult to reach all the structural knowledge that effects the pattern's behaviour. A distant node can remain untouched in the checking operation but still be crucial in the pattern's functionality.

In our work artificial intelligence techniques are used to overcome the problems related to the chaotic nature of the patterns. For compatibility check the patterns are browsed using a standard query interface to check whether the two patterns are isomorphic or not.

4 Conclusions

In this work, an general approach to pattern formalization based on a minimalist pattern model is introduced. The difference of this approach from the previous approaches is its generality resulting from its knowledge-based nature. Our model provides a general framework for a new interpretation of pattern reuse. The point of view that has been adopted in this approach enhances the pattern production by processing and reusing existing patterns.

This work is a part of a project that aims the development of a pattern based advanced component system or a pattern based language.

References

[1] Alexander, C., "The Timeless Way of Building", Oxford University Press, New York, 1979.

[2] Gamma, E., Helm, R., Johnson, R. and Vlissides, J. "Design Patterns, Elements of Reusable Object Oriented Software.", Addison Wesley, 1994.

[3] Eden, A. et al., "Towards a Mathematical Foundation for Design Patterns", OOPSLA 1998.

[4] Eden, A. et al., "Automating the Application of Design Patterns", Journal of Object Oriented Programming, 10:(2), May, 1997, pp 44-46.

[5] Sıkıcı, A. and Topaloglu, Y., "Design Patterns as Building Blocks in Reusable Software Design", Proceedings of The Fourteenth International Symposium on Computer and Information Sciences (ISCIS XIV), Ege University Press, Turkey, 1999, pp 247 - 256.

Knowledge-Based Software Engineering
T. Hruška and M. Hashimoto (Eds.)
IOS Press, 2000

Program Understanding by the Use of Case-Based Reasoning

Haruo KAWASAKI

Kokushikan University, 4-28-1 Setagaya, Setagaya-ku, Tokyo, Japan

Abstract. In program understanding systems, it is impossible to understand programs without presupposed knowledge in general. However, we concentrate our attention on systems' outputs, if there is no presupposed knowledge of programs. We propose a new program understanding system based on case-based reasoning. Even if our program understanding system has no knowledge of a program, our system may give an idiomatic explanation text of the program by using knowledge of similar programs. A similarity of programs is introduced by using the computational purpose network. Our system generates idiomatic explanation texts by using modification of similar idiomatic texts, that is, by the use of the paraphrase.

1 Introduction

Several studies have ever tried to program understanding [1], [2], [3]. Program understanding systems have effects on programming education. We have been continuing our research in an intelligent programming environment that consists of a program understanding system for novice programmers and a novice program evaluation support system for teachers.

In general, it is required for program understanding systems to have a large amount of presupposed knowledge on model solution programs and buggy programs. Although, it is not easy to obtain the full knowledge required for understanding programs. Program understanding systems, of course, can not understand programs without the corresponding knowledge as a rule. In this case, the question now arises: program understanding systems come up with any answer other than "I can not understand". On the other hand, homework programs presented by students tend to be similar in many cases. This tendency is, in fact, the key to solve this question.

The aim of this paper is to propose a new program understanding system by the use of knowledge on similar programs, that is, by the use of case-based reasoning [4] and to provide the answer to the question mentioned above. To answer this question, only few attempts have been made so far. Generally, program understanding systems give users' explanation texts (or sentences) for explaining purposes of the programs after receiving input programs [1], [3]. Thus, program understanding systems may be regarded as explanation texts generating systems [5], in some sense, that use knowledge of programs.

In our system, even if the system does not have direct knowledge of a program, the system may generates explanation texts of the program by the use of knowledge of similar programs, that is to say, by the modification of similar explanation texts. Strictly speaking, our system does not understand programs on this occasion. If the system is able to generate idiomatic explanation texts of programs, however, we may intend to regard this condition as successful understanding of programs.

We have to conduct a research into similarities of programs in order to apply case-based reasoning. There are a few researchers that have ever tried to investigate similarities of programs by using non-statistical methods. Dershowitz [6] applies templates to deal with this subject. However, there are many programs that differ from a model solution in programming education. On this occasion, this method does not work well. Thus, we adopt the computational purpose network [7] for introducing a similarity of programs. This network gives us information on top-down decomposition of programs as a result of inferring programmers' intention without presupposed knowledge.

Also, we have to conduct a research on generating idiomatic explanation texts of programs. We realize the generation by modification of similar idiomatic explanation texts. We may regard the process of this generation as that of idiomatic explanation texts by using paraphrase [8], [9] in the natural language processing. We construct a prototype system using Common LISP and ZERO [10] on the SUN workstation.

2 Overview of Our System

Fig. 1 shows the processing flow of our system. Cases of programs are characterized by the computational purpose networks. Also, every program in the case base has an idiomatic explanation text that is regarded as knowledge represented by a natural language. When our system does not have presupposed knowledge of a program, the explanation text of the program is obtained by using modification of the similar explanation text.

3 Similarity of Programs

COSMO [7], inferring programmers' intention system, selects effective slicing criteria automatically and obtains the computational purpose networks with information on top-down decomposition of problems. We introduce a similarity of programs by using the networks. For example, four programs are given in Fig. 2. Fig. 3 shows the computational purpose network of the model mean value program. Fig. 4 shows that of the student program-1. Student program-2 has the same computational purpose network as the model program has. Also, student program-3 has the same network as student program-1 has. Our system introduces a similarity of programs by using this sameness of the networks and applies it to case-based reasoning.

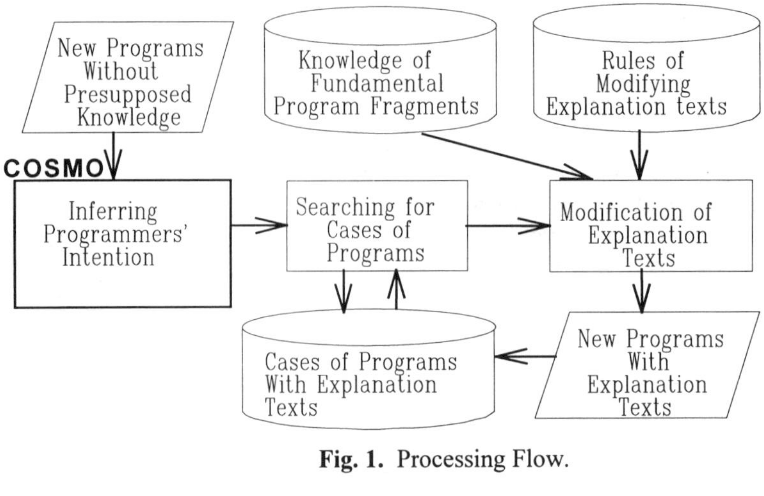

Fig. 1. Processing Flow.

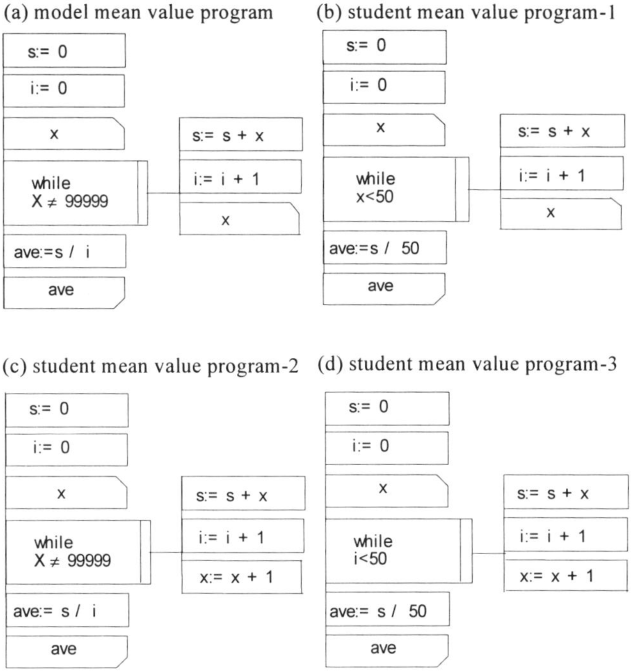

Fig. 2. Model Mean Value Program and Students' Mean Value Programs.

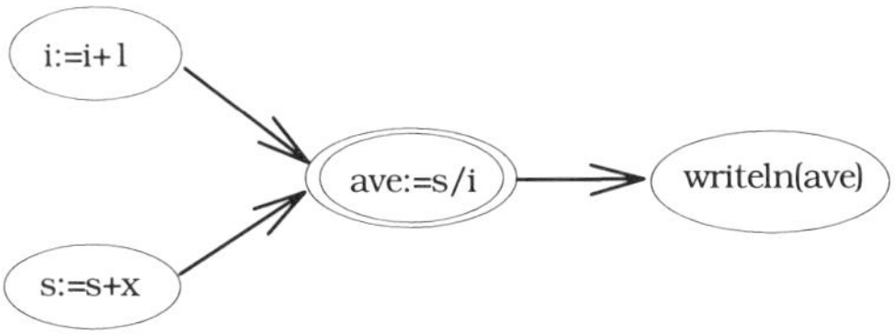

Fig. 3. The Computational Purpose Network of Model Mean Value Program.

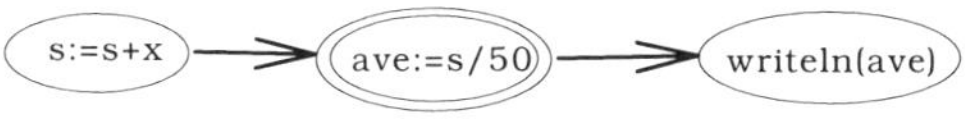

Fig. 4. The Computational Purpose Network of Student Program-1.

4 Paraphrase by Using Case-Based Reasoning

Fig. 5 shows the generating process of explanation texts of programs without presupposed knowledge. For the model mean value program, explanation texts of the idiomatic representation level and that of the direct representation level are presupposed to our system. Also, for the student mean value program-2, the direct level representation is obtained automatically by using knowledge of fundamental program fragments. We regard the process of generating idiomatic explanation texts as that of the paraphrase [8] in natural

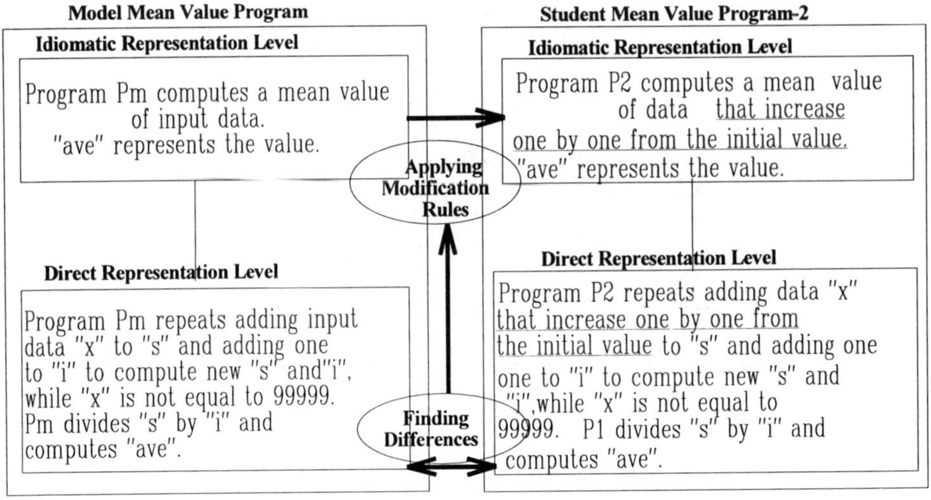

Fig. 5. Generating Idiomatic Explanation Texts of Programs.

language processing. Thus, we realize the paraphrase by the use of case-based reasoning. The upper underlined part of program-2 in Fig. 5 is added by applying modification rules. To keep modified idiomatic explanation texts be idiomatic, we now deal with programs that have computational purpose networks in common (e.g. (a) and (c) in Fig. 2).

5 Discussion and Conclusion

We propose a new program understanding system by using case-based reasoning and carry on more investigation into the modification rules of texts and the paraphrase.

References

[1] W. E. Johnson, and E. Soloway, PROUST: Knowledge-Based Program Understanding, IEEE Trans. on Soft. Eng., Vol. SE-11, No. 3, pp. 11-19, 1985.

[2] K. Kaijiri, Novice Program Recognition/Diagnosis System Based on Goal/Plan Concepts, IEICE Trans. D, pp. 321-332, 1995.

[3] H. Ueno, INTELLITUTOR: A Knowledge Based Intelligent Programming Environment for Novice Programmers, Proc. COMPCN 89 Spring, pp. 390-395, 1989.

[4] J. Kolodner, and C. Riesbeck , Case-Based Reasoning, IJCAI-89 Tutorial-MA-2, 1989.

[5] H. Ueno, Knowledge Based Intelligent Programming Environment, J. IPS Japan, pp. 1280-1296, 1987.

[6] N. Dershowitz, The Evolution of Programs, Birkhäuser, 1983.

[7] H. Kawasaki, Inferring Programmers' Intention by the Use of Context Structure Model of Programs, IEICE Trans. on Inf. & Syst., pp. 835-844, 2000.

[8] M. Dras, Reluctant Paraphrase: Textual Restructuring Under an Optimization Model, Proc. of Pacling97, pp. 48-55, 1997.

[9] J. Robin and K. McKeown, Empirically Designing and Evaluating a New Revision-Based Model for Summary Generation, Artificial Intelligence, Vol. 85, No. 1-2, pp. 135-179, 1996.

[10] H. Ito and H. Ueno, „ZERO: Frame + Prolog", Logic Programming '85, LNCS221, pp.10-17, 1986.

Knowledge-Based Software Engineering
T. Hruška and M. Hashimoto (Eds.)
IOS Press, 2000

An XML Approach to Knowledge Discovery in Databases

Petr KOTÁSEK, Jaroslav ZENDULKA

Brno University of Technology, Department of Computer Science and Engineering, Božetěchova 2, 612 66 Brno, Czech Republic, {kotasekp, zendulka}@dcse.fee.vutbr.cz

Abstract: In recent years, the XML language has been receiving much interest among IT community. It has many nice properties that make it a great candidate for representation of different kinds of data. In this paper we will propose an XML framework for the domain of knowledge discovery in databases. This is not a specification document; this article tries to be a compendium of ideas and remarks concerning the broad area of knowledge discovery in databases. It tries to outline one of the many possible solutions - the usage of XML.

1 Introduction

There are huge amounts of data stored in various repositories (databases) and it is behind human capabilities to reasonably process it. It is no longer possible for us to look at the database, see any useful *patterns* in the data and consequently derive some potentially useful *knowledge* from our observation.

There are several areas in which one comes across the term *knowledge*:

- Knowledge discovery in databases (KDD)
- Data archaeology
- Knowledge management and representation systems

Knowledge discovery in databases refers to a process mentioned in the first paragraph: we want to find some useful and interesting patterns in the database. The key point to mention here is that we know what pattern we are looking for *in advance*. For example, if we decide to search for association rules, we pick algorithms that find association rules in databases and run them against the data.

Data archeology, on the other hand, refers to a process of browsing the data without actually knowing what we are looking for. The data analyst incrementally browses through the data, refines his knowledge and redefines his goals. The process is highly skilled.

In knowledge management and representation systems, the term knowledge is broad and refers to any piece and kind of information stored in the system. These systems use different formats to store the knowledge, based on different formalisms (e.g., description logic). Main goals of knowledge representation and management systems are to help humans understand and map the specific domain of interest, support the decision process etc.

There exists The Knowledge-Sharing Effort (KSE) Consortium [4] which is defining standards to cover various aspects of knowledge representation and sharing:

- Common formal language for expressing the content of knowledge bases (the Knowledge Interchange Format - KIF).
- Common constructs for representation languages (Description Logic - DL).
- Sharable ontologies for particular topic areas (described in KIF).
- Language for communication between software agents (the Knowledge Query Manipulation Language - KQML).

The reason why we mention the KSE here is to show the parallel between knowledge management and knowledge discovery. The main effort in knowledge discovery has so far been devoted to development of efficient mining algorithms, but there are not many contributions to the complex solution of the problem. There is no set of techniques and methodologies to support the entire process. We believe that it is worth trying to propose a framework for a systematic approach to KDD similar to that developed by the KSE for knowledge management and representation systems. As the knowledge discovery is a wide, open and evolving topic, the methodologies designed for it must reflect its needs; they have to be open and extensible, too.

The remainder of this paper is organized as follows: In Section 2, we describe briefly the XML language. Readers familiar with XML can skip this section. Section 3 presents ideas how XML could be used in the knowledge discovery process. We conclude and outline the future work in Section 4.

2 The XML language

2.1 Brief History of XML

The Extensible Markup Language (XML) is a simplified subset of the Standard Generalized Markup Language (SGML). The main goal of SGML is to provide mechanism for platform-independent representation of structured data. Unfortunately, SGML is very complex and therefore the cost of its implementation is high. The Hypertext Markup Language (HTML), on the other hand, has very poor representation capability. Actually, it is only oriented towards presentation and as such it is becoming insufficient for growing demands of the World Wide Web. Therefore an initiative was started by The World Wide Web Consortium (W3C) to build XML. It is much simpler than SGML (and therefore easy to implement) but still very powerful to represent structured data. It has been recognized by many researchers as a promising solution to their problems.

2.2 Brief Description of the XML Concept

XML is a method for putting data in a text file. Actually, it has evolved into a whole family of technologies.

It is not meant to be read by humans but it is very easy to read. So if you are an expert or a programmer debugging applications, you can use simple text editors to look at XML files or even repair them.

XML looks very much like HTML but has nothing to do with it. HTML only marks up the data for a browser to visualize it, whereas XML purely represents the logical structure of the document regardless of its possible future presentation form. Tags in HTML are predefined and users can do nothing about it – in other words, HTML is an application of SGML. In XML, users can define their own tags and attributes (the grammar of an XML document) – in other words, XML is a subset of SGML.

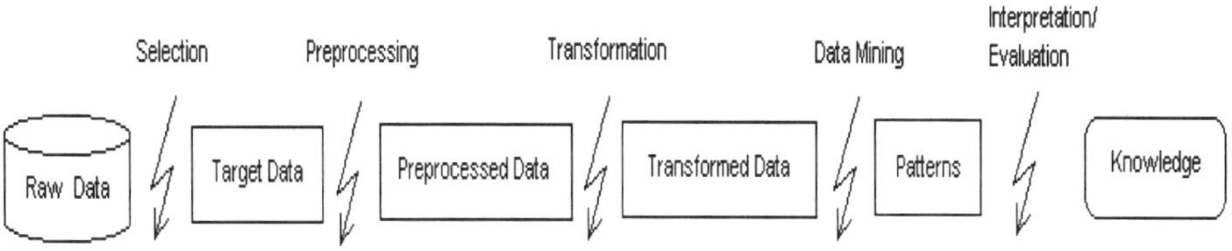

Figure 1 The Knowledge Discovery Process

2.3 Advantages of XML

XML users will find many advantages depending on their field of interest, but there are some more general advantages that become obvious in every application domain.

- **Platform Independence**
  XML is a text format that can be displayed or processed on any device. The device will need to know the Document Type Definition (DTD) of the given XML document. DTD represents the definition of the grammar – the XML document has to comply with its grammar. If the DTD is publicly available (e.g., through WWW), device can withdraw it, parse the document and transform it in any possible way.
- **Robustness**
  XML documents have to be well-formed, meaning each starting tag must have a corresponding closing tag, there must be only one root element, and so on. As the format is textual, it is more resistant to transport errors.
- **Extensibility**
  This is another important feature, together with platform independence. Via DTDs, the XML technology serves as a metalanguage for definitions of other languages. Moreover, one of XML technologies called Extensible Stylesheet Language (XSL) provides means for transforming XML documents. A part of XSL called XSL Transformations (XSLT) is an XML vocabulary for doing such transformations. Then it is not a problem to take an XML tree and convert it to another completely different one.

3 Using XML in the Knowledge Discovery Process

Let us describe the potential of XML in the domain of knowledge discovery and data mining. The process of knowledge discovery in databases has several steps that are shown in Figure 1. Its goal is to retrieve some potentially useful and usable information (knowledge) from large amounts of data, and to use this knowledge for decision support, marketing, etc.

It would be very nice if we could run the data mining algorithm against the raw data from the database. Unfortunately, many steps have to be taken prior to actual mining can take place:

1. Relevant data have to be selected; this is a joint work for the data mining expert and the domain expert. At this point we assume that we have already decided which type of knowledge we want to discover and what particular data mining algorithm we will use.

Different knowledge types need different algorithms and different algorithms require different data. If we ran data mining algorithm against data which is irrelevant, we could receive useless results (which is the better case) or even results that are confusing and therefore potentially harmful, if applied in real world (this is the worse case).

2. Once the relevant data are known, they have to be preprocessed and transformed into the shape that will be understood by the data mining algorithm. Typical preprocessing activity is the elimination of the erroneous data (data cleaning). In the vast majority of experiments, transformation involves extracting data from the database source and saving it in plain text files. This is the task for the data mining expert and without a doubt it is the most time-consuming part of the whole process, as the format of these files is proprietary to given mining algorithms.
3. Now we can run the data mining algorithm against the data. It produces results (in some proprietary format again) that have to be visualized somehow and interpreted by domain experts.

Actually, the three steps mentioned above under 1. and 2. (selection, preprocessing and transformation) overlap each other in real process. Selection can be understood as identification of relevant data without actually touching it. Preprocessing and transformation are activities that deal with physical data.

Most researchers in this field concentrate on developing new data mining techniques, which is only one step along the long path. To our knowledge, little attention has been paid to formats of data being processed.

3.1 An XML Framework Proposal for Data Interfaces

During the discovery process, data travels through many stages that all have well-defined functionality. It would be convenient to define input data formats (we will refer to these as **data interfaces**) for these stages using some platform-independent, robust, extensible and human-readable technology. What a task for XML! If we decide to use XML, we can define XML data interfaces for respective knowledge discovery steps. Then the overall architecture might look like this (please refer to Figure 1):

Data Selection. The target data have to be extracted from the database system and stored in XML format. We will call this data interface XML-TargetData. There are basically two ways to do this. In first scenario, application has to be written that accesses the database, retrieves data through the standard interface provided by the DBMS (typically, SQL) and converts the data into XML. This attitude requires additional coding. Fortunately, major database system vendors are beginning to realize the importance of XML and start to incorporate XML interface into their database engines. So extraction of data in an XML format should be a straightforward process in near future.

Data Preprocessing. The data preprocessing phase receives data in XML-TargetData format. The data is checked, cleaned, whatever possible processing is performed, and the output is created in XML-PreprocessedData format. This interface contains data for mining that is semantically ready to be used by the data mining algorithm, but its syntactic structure might be different from the syntax understood by the algorithm.

Transformation. In the original architecture from Figure 1 the transformation phase was a single, highly specialized procedure. Imagine this scenario: Preprocessed data are in text format. It is quite understandable because preprocessing deals with data checking and

cleaning so it is desirable that the data mining expert can read the format easily. Unfortunately, the data mining algorithm is ready to receive data in his own proprietary binary format. So someone has to sit down and code a program to convert the human-readable text format into algorithm-friendly binary format.
With XML, the transformation step is just a simple conversion from XML-PreprocessedData to XML-TransformedData – the input interface for the data mining algorithm. XML technology provides instruments for simple transformation of XML documents among each other (please recall the XSLT from Section 1.3). Actually, with XML, there is no unique transformation step in the discovery process any more. Rather, many local transformations can be performed easily and effectively on each data interface using simple and straightforward XSLT transformations.

Data Mining. The data mining algorithm takes the data in the XML-TransformedData format and mines the data for knowledge. The output of this step is the XML-Patterns data format.

Interpretation/Evaluation. This step demonstrates the strength of XML in its full range. We receive data from the XML-Patterns interface and want to visualize it in human-friendly fashion. Using XSLT (or any other transformation tool or program), data can be transformed into any data format and displayed by different programs. Nowadays, all the end-user programs use their own proprietary formats (.doc, .xsl, .jpg, ...). If we manage to create widely accepted and respected XML vocabulary for a specific domain, we will only be left with the task of defining transformations from/to these proprietary formats. Some steps are being taken by W3C in this field (e.g., Precision Graphics Markup Language – PGML, Vector Markup Language – VML, Document Definition Markup Language – DDML, Mathematical Markup Language – MathML). Consequently, it is desirable to create a markup language for data representation on all the data interfaces of the knowledge discovery process.

Another good thing to mention here is knowledge transformation. It is often necessary to transform one knowledge representation to another, e.g. classification tree to association rules. Again, no problem with XML and its transformation capabilities.

In previous paragraphs, we have assumed that data would be extracted from the database and stored in XML formats between successive steps. We have accepted this assumption to emphasize the individualistic character of respective KDD steps. In real world applications, this attitude would result in an unacceptable waste of space. Why should we store the same (or almost same) data twice? Rather, the data will be transformed into XML on the fly while being read from a database. Actually, only the final product of the whole process, the XML-Patterns data, is expected to be stored permanently for future use.

Figure 2 shows the KDD process again, but now with corresponding XML data interfaces. Here is the summary of benefits resulting from XML usage in the knowledge discovery process:

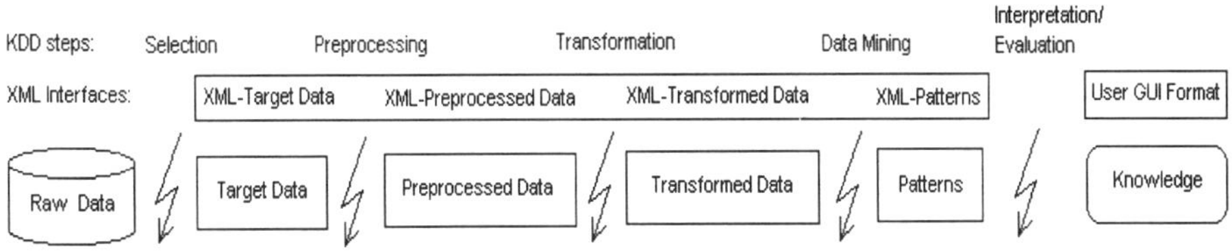

Figure 2 The Knowledge Discovery Process with XML Data Interfaces

1. Each step in the process has its input and output XML data interfaces. If the input and output interfaces of two consequent steps do not match, data can be transformed easily using XSLT transformations.
2. Consequently, it is possible to combine different discovery components to perform the whole process. This feature becomes most appreciated in the data mining step for testing purposes. Now it is easy to compare different mining algorithms against each other. All that has to be done is transformation from the XML-TransformedData interface into the proprietary format (which can but does not necessarily have to be XML) of the data mining algorithm.

3.2 An Example: XML-Patterns Interface

There are different types of knowledge patterns that can be discovered in data: data generalization, summarization, characterization, association rules, classification trees, clustering analysis, regression analysis, time series, web mining, path traversal patterns (mining for user access patterns in interactive systems), etc. We will give a demonstration for association rules.

An association rule is an expression of the form $X \Rightarrow Y$, where X and Y are sets of items. Intuitive meaning of such a rule is that sets of items that contain X as their subset tend to contain also Y. Association rules are being mined for in relational databases.

The typical application is in analysis of sales data; databases contain huge amount of transactions typically consisting of the transaction date and items bought in the transaction. One of the well known examples is this association rule: nappies $\Rightarrow$ beer. The idea behind this strange rule is that fathers who were sent out by their wives to buy nappies decided to reward themselves for their heroic performance by buying beer. When a good market specialist sees this rule, he or she immediately moves beer together with crackers closer to nappies to satisfy the thirsty husbands' temptation.

A fraction of an XML document representing this situation, and the DTD to which this document conforms, might look like the one in Table 1. It is a very idealized and non-realistic example. It only says that the association rule exists, nothing more. In real world applications, there are other data associated with rules; typically, some metrics that measure the value of the rule. Moreover, association rules can have different forms: quantitative, generalized, fuzzy etc. The XML document would have to be able to accommodate all these variants.

Table 1 An XML and DTD Example for the XML-Patterns Interface

XML Document	DTD
<Knowledge>	<!ELEMENT Knowledge (AssociationRule+)>
<AssociationRule ruleid="1">	<!ELEMENT AssociationRule (Antecedent,Consequent)>
<Ascendent>	<!ATTLIST AssociationRule ruleid CDATA #REQUIRED>
<AscendentItem>	<!ELEMENT Antecedent (AntecedentItem+)>
<Name>nappies</Name>	<!ELEMENT AntecedentItem (Name)>
</AscendentItem>	<!ELEMENT Consequent (ConsequentItem+)>
</Ascendent>	<!ELEMENT ConsequentItem (Name)>
<Consequent>	<!ELEMENT Name (#PCDATA)>
<ConsequentItem>	<!--Knowledge is a root element. It can include one or more
<Name>beer</Name>	AssociationRule elements. Each AssociationRule element has a unique
</ConsequentItem>	identifier ruleid. AssociationRule consists of one Antecedent and one
</Consequent>	Consequent. Each Antecedent and Consequent must have one or more
</AssociationRule>	AntecedentItem and ConsequentItem elements. Each AntecedentItem
</Knowledge>	and ConsequentItem has one name, which is a string. -->

```
<DataMiningAgent>
  <Name>AprioriItemset</Name>
  <Description>
  This is a data mining algorithm used for mining association rules among sets of items.
  </Description>
  <BaseUrl url="http://www.fee.vutbr.cz/Mining/Algorithms/AprioriItemset.cgi" method="post"/>
  <InputDataInterfaces>
    <InputDataInterface url="http://www.fee.vutbr.cz/Mining/DTDs/AprioriItemsetInput1.dtd">
      <Description>DTD for one of input data interfaces accepted by AprioriItemset</Description>
    </InputDataInterface>
  </InputDataInterfaces>
  <OutputDataInterfaces>
    <OutputDataInterface url="http://www.fee.vutbr.cz/Mining/DTDs/AprioriItemsetOutput1.dtd">
      <Description>DTD for one of output data interfaces produced by AprioriItemset</Description>
    </OutputDataInterface>
  </OutputDataInterfaces>
  <InputParameters>
    <InputParam name="input_dtd_url"/>
    <InputParam name="input_xml_url"/>
    <InputParam name="output_dtd_url"/>
  </InputParameters>
</DataMiningAgent>
```

Figure 3 An Example of Communication Interface of the Data Mining Agent

3.3 An XML Framework Proposal for Communication Interfaces

So far we have used XML to define data interfaces, i.e. the formats of input/output data for given discovery steps. The usage of XML in this context is implicit as XML is designed for data representation.

XML can also be very well used to define **communication interfaces**. We can assume that respective KDD steps are performed by *agents*. By agent, we mean a software application which is able to communicate with other applications (agents).

A computing environment is becoming more and more parallel and distributed and this holds true for knowledge discovery as well. Therefore, it makes sense to think of various KDD steps as tasks being performed by specialized agents that expose their functionality to the rest of the world through an XML-defined communication interface. Typically, the data mining algorithm will reside on a computer and will define its communication interface through the XML document shown in Figure 3.

The interface in Figure 3 says that there is a data mining agent called AprioriItemset located at BaseUrl. It can accept documents conforming to the DTD stored in the file named AprioriItemsetInput1.dtd. The output of the agent conforms to the DTD stored in the file named AprioriItemsetOutput1.dtd. The AprioriItemset agent accepts several input parameters: URL of DTD to which the input XML data conforms, URL of the XML input data, and URL of DTD for output data. This example assumes that the communication between agents is built on top of the http transport protocol. Again, this is a very simplified view of the problem to show how XML could be utilized.

4 Conclusion and Future Work

We tried to show the potential of XML and related technologies in the domain of knowledge discovery in databases. There is no 'one and only' solution for this problem. In our approach, software applications (agents) are used to perform successive knowledge discovery steps. These agents have to define their communication and data interfaces. As these interfaces are defined using XML, the environment is open and easily extensible. It is easy to build new components and it should also be easy to accommodate the existing ones. Of course, we could use another vocabulary or define a vocabulary of our own, but XML is already here and is ready to be used.

We have shown how XML might be used for knowledge discovery in databases. This is a very young idea that will need a deeper investigation. Please notice that XML is only suitable as an implementation solution; a complex methodology can hardly be built only on XML. With respect to this, there are several question (and other will arise during future research) that have to be addressed:

1. Will it be necessary to design a more sophisticated communication language? In an example in Figure 3, the AprioriItemset agent can accept only one request that is defined implicitly by its input parameters – the request to mine patterns in input data. But agent should understand many more language primitives; e.g. the request to return an XML document specifying his communication interface will be essential. Thus, the definition of a communication language is a must.
2. As amounts of data are huge, should it not be rather an agent who will travel? It will depend strongly on the size of data whether it is better to send the data to the agent or vice versa.
3. How open should the methodology be? Will it serve only the KDD problem or should it try to integrate data archaeology and knowledge management as well? Or should we try to build a much more general model for agent communication and data (knowledge) interchange and sharing? How far can we go with such a generalization?

As you can see, we started with a simple idea of defining data and communication interfaces of knowledge discovery agents using XML, and we ended up with thoughts about agent interoperability and data exchange. Thus, the future work will lie in definition of an unifying approach that would embrace the KDD process as much as possible, using XML as one of the supporting implementation technologies. As the knowledge discovery in databases is a data-centered process, it seems relevant to start with the definition of ontologies that would describe semantic properties of data involved in the process. The solution for the communication-related portion of the work will come next (and we believe it will be possible to use some existing approach; communication is addressed by many researchers and solutions exist that can be utilized). Before we want to communicate, we have to agree on a common conceptualization of the world we want to talk about; this conceptualization will have the form of ontologies for KDD. Then these ontologies will serve as a formal description of the data part of the domain, on top of which a common platform for data processing and interchange can be build. The Knowledge Interchange Format (KIF) is an example of a convenient formalism to describe these ontologies, and XML can serve as an implementation technology in the way similar to that outlined briefly in this paper.

References

[1] World Wide Web Consortium XML page, http://www.w3.org/XML

[2] G. J. John, Enhancements to the Data Mining Process, dissertation, Stanford University, 1997.

[3] U. M. Fayyad, G. Piatetsky-Shapiro, P. Smyth, R. Uthurusamy, eds., Advances in Knowledge Discovery and Data Mining, AAAI Press/The MIT Press, 1996.

[4] The Knowledge-Sharing Effort Consortium, http://www.cs.umbc.edu/kse

Knowledge-Based Software Engineering
T. Hruška and M. Hashimoto (Eds.)
IOS Press, 2000

A Chaotic Effect in the VSF Network

Yoshitsugu KAKEMOTO[1], Shinichi NAKASUKA[2]
[1]*The Japan Research Institute, 16 Ichbancyo Chiyodaku, TOKYO, Japan*
[2]*The University of Tokyo, 7–3–1 Hongo Bunkyouku, TOKYO, Japan*

Abstract. In this paper, it is described the influence of a chaotic factor by the VSF network in additional pattern learning tasks. At first it is described the relation between situation and articulation of information of autonomous system. In the next section, an experiment result about additional learning of pattern by the VSF network in an obstacle avoidance task of a rover and considerations about it are made after brief description of VSF network are shown.

1 Situation and articulation

It needs to articulate incoming information and to re-construct information when system to intend acquiring knowledge. Information articulation is an action to extract only necessary part of information based on experience. New part within information interacts with acquired information and a new internal representation will be constructed.

1.1 Representation of Concept

If we will implement information extraction system with neural network, we need to extract composite concept that was acquired by preceding experiences. It is thought that composite concepts corresponding to an output are encoded in a hidden layer in hierarchical neural network.

Since the early days of neural network study, theories and models about information encoded in hidden layer of hierarchical neural network have been proposed [4]. However, it was concluded that both internal structure extraction acquired by network and processing on the basis of internal structure were difficult.

A source of this difficulty is that the most of neural network models were based on the Hebb type assembly model. For this issue, a model based on a dynamical coding that yields a time series pattern firing of neuron group is suggested [1]. If extracted information are encoded in a hidden layer, it is valid to consider simultaneously working neuron group. Basic requests for the neuron group are following each point.

1. A concept consists of forms that concepts connect to other concept according to situation, and to can be put together by other concept. In other words a concept consists of its subordinate concept, and they must be encoded to take its output according to situation.
2. As for neuron which are related mutually and encode feature, they should constitute a neuron assembly.
3. If a pattern changed, status of neuron changes quickly and must form new aggregation.

1.2 Formation of articulated information

Articulation of external information depends on an output based on the knowledge that system has acquired currently and a difference with feedback for it. If network acquires knowledge a difference between output value of network and teacher signal for network describe recognition ability of network and its present difference. If an output of a network is near to action formed by current knowledge, neural net articulate current knowledge in order to improve discrimination. On the other hand neural network investigates other solution if difference of result is large. Neural network constitutes other basin which are different from basin deciding current solution in order to change output. Strengthen current basin for solution more if the difference is small in other word do with basin deciding with current solution deeply. When more than one pattern is input into in learning or recognizing phase, patterns will be encoded simultaneously. When encoded pattern in recognize phase is shown simultaneously, neural network can recognize the both patterns. In addition, neural network can recognize the pattern also when the pattern that neural network can recognize to be one part of learned pattern was shown.

2 VSF network

We designed the VSF (Vibrate Synchronous Feature) network as network to articulate the external information which satisfied the following requirement [2].

- By dynamic link of concept that system have learned, system recognize patterns.
- By difference between teacher signal and output from neural network, it change its learning method.

An overview of the VSF network is shown in the figure 1. The VSF network is hierarchical neural network to learn with back propagation. It is a hybrid model neural network that consisted of feedback layer to tie both back propagation module (it called BP module as follows) and local feature detection module to learn of self-organization type map (it called LF module as follows).

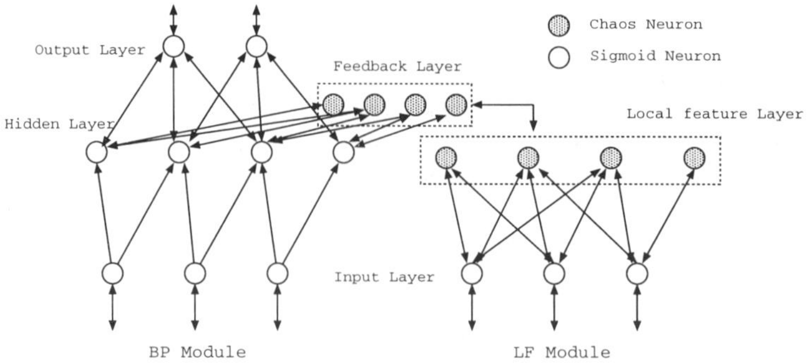

Figure 1: Processing flow on VSF network

By the VSF network, we express it with lattice cluster formed subordinal concept to constitute a higher concept by interaction between chaotic vibration lattice on the basis of the CML (Coupled Mapping Lattice) model [3].

Situated coding of the external information is the process that this lattice cluster namely neuron groups at hidden layer is formed in our model.

Vibration on the VSF network depends on following two factors.

1. A chaotic vibration lattice is realized by the feedback layer of VSF network.
2. Mixture of the BP module and the LF module.

Input value of the feedback layer is a firing value of the hidden layer of the BP module and firing value of the feature detection layer of the LF module. Learning done with the BP module is a kind of back propagation and learning done with the LF module is a kind of learning without teacher. Knowledge acquired by the BP module is the knowledge that is suitable for one action purpose. Knowledge acquired by the LF module is the knowledge which neural network watched original pattern. For knowledge acquired by the BP module, knowledge acquired by the LF module is a vibration factor to investigate new knowledge.

Neuron group is constituted by doing behavior of the weak chaos that they are accompanied with self-feedback in the feedback layer. Knowledge acquired by precedence learning is used as initial value of associative weight between each layer of VSF network. Neurons that are showed near firing value at first time will show more same firing value by vibration at the feedback layer. Neurons that are different in firing value come to catch more different firing value. Furthermore, based on changed firing value, weights between each layer of the BP module are changed.

3 Recognition and avoidance of an obstacle

We applied it in an obstacle avoidance action acquisition of a rover and confirmed performance of the VSF network. We designed tasks to examine concept addition and subtraction in order to evaluate articulational ability of the VSF network learning ability.

3.1 Task Setting

As task environment of rover, we set up an experimental space which is shown in the figure 2. We made a distance sensor value of rover put in arbitrary places in experiment space with input and judgment with output whether the rover can turn at a direction in order to arrive at goal. However, we eliminate the impossible place physically.

3.2 Procedure

We set a single obstacle, a T character road, a compound obstacle condition as a pattern of the obstacle which rover meet with between turning action.

1. A single obstacle:
   There is an obstacle in progress direction front of rover. This configuration is shown in the figure (1) of 2.
2. A T character road:
   Rover moves by a course surrounded right and left by an obstacle. This configuration is shown in the figure (2) of 2.
3. A compound obstacle:
   Single obstacle condition and T character road condition are mixed. This configuration is shown in the figure (3) of 2.

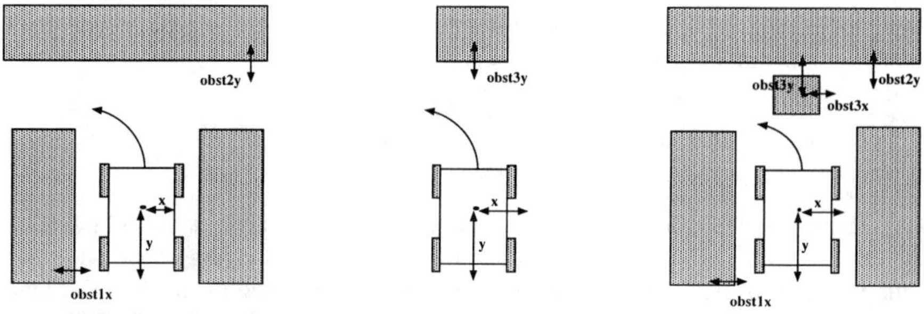

Figure 2: Task set for pattern addition

Training data and recognizing data is generated depending on following variables.

- Road width of a course.
- Road width of penetration road.
- Starting position of turn.

Experiment consist of the following 3 phases and we provide the data set which is different every each phase. We select a pattern from generated patterns at random and provide it to the rover.

- Precedence learning phase :
  A phase to learn the precedence knowledge. Using hierarchical neural network trained by general back propagation method. In addition, network learned by the Kohonen-Map using the same training data in order to do it with precedence learning data of the VSF network in re-learning phase.
- Re-learning phase :
  We apply other task with the VSF network and other hierarchical network for comparison.
- Recognition phase :
  Re-set weight between each layer obtained in the re-learning phase to hierarchical neural network and recognize with other task set.

Among the patterns that network learned with the precedence learning and re-learning phase, we provide the pattern that each pattern appears with additional condition with recognition phase. We train network with a series of task showed in the figure 2 and let network recognize. We mix the T character road task showed in the figure (1) of 2 in precedence learning phase and provide network and learn network reconfiguration using weights that so were acquired. We give a single obstacle task showed in the figure (2) of 2 as a training set in the re-learning phase. For verification of pattern acquired through both phase, we give a compound obstacle mixture problem showed in the figure (3) of 2 as a recognition task and examine performance of network. With a 1-3-1 series, a 1-3-2 series and a 1-3-3 series, we give task 1 (a T character road task) by initial learning and give task 3 (a simple obstacle task) as a re-learning task next and problem 1 or 2 (a compound obstacle task) 3 as recognition task last.

4 Results and Discussion

4.1 A change of recognition rate

Even if re-learning for recognition of a compound obstacle task2 progresses in hierarchical network, the recognition rate of it does not change. Compared with it, recognition of compound task will improve with re-learning by the VSF network.

Besides, with a series of 1-3-1, recognition rate of a T character road task becomes worse with progress of re-learning with the VSF and hierarchical network. It was showed that additional learning is difficult in neural network. However, we compare it when a task is re-learned by hierarchical network again, there is a little degradation of knowledge of T character road task in VSF network performance.

With a series of 1-3-3, recognition rate of single obstacle task is improved with proceed of re-learning with the VSF and hierarchical network each. However, learning capability of efficiency is high when it is re-learn by the VSF network.

4.2 Learning factors

Learning capability of VSF network is controlled by the following factors that give affect to action of the CML in the feedback layer. It is the night in coefficient of chaos function in action phase of the CML at the feedback layer and diffusion coefficient with whether the value to be near or a value lefts all values.

- Chaos strength coefficient of firing function of the feedback layer.
- Interaction coefficient between cells of the feedback layer.
- Mixing rate of the BP module output and the LF module output.

We examined the affect that these factors give to learning of the VSF network. Each factor gives large affect to archiving facility of the knowledge that is acquired by precedence learning.

In weak chaos status ($1.44 \leq$ and ≤ 1.5), it shows good performance than non-chaos status (≤ 1.43), as showed in the figure 3. When firing of the feedback layer is weak chaos status, its performance improved as degree of chaos becomes large. However, when chaos coefficient sounds than 1.6, a value shows emission while vibration is repeated in the feedback layer, and neuron becoming unsettled value afterward begins to occur it, and in particular performance by a compound task is worsen. From this reason, strong chaos status (≥ 1.5) is not an appropriate value.

Interaction coefficient factor between CML cells give affect to free movement of each neuron. A fellow neuron which has small interaction coefficient shows a behavior each separate from and fellow neurons which have large interaction coefficient is going to each put behavior of a partner together with behavior of oneself. Interaction coefficient and chaos coefficient restrains each other's effect in relational. When interaction coefficient is small (< 0.05), there is the case that firing value of neuron emits even if it is weak chaos status. On the other hand the affect that is hanged down by (> 0.3), affect of chaos function is denied almost and the VSF network shows "chaos rigidity".

As described in the previous section, knowledge acquired with the LF module is a shaken to investigate new knowledge for knowledge acquired with the BP module. If the value of the BP module is given priority to value of the LF module, knowledge acquired by it is precedence. On the other hand knowledge acquired by the LF module is precedence if the value of the LF module is given priority to value of the BP module,

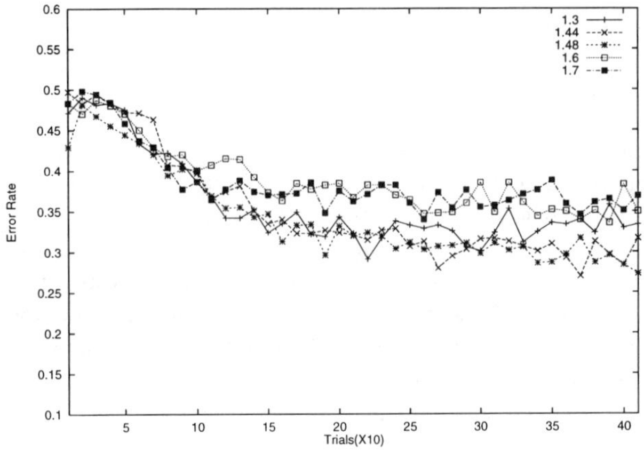

Figure 3: Effects of chaotic strength

When the affect of the BP module is small (< 0.3), recognition rate of final patters become worse. On the other hand the affect of the BP module is large (< 0.8), recognition rate of final patters also become worse.

5 Conclusion

In this paper, we examined the following factors to give to acquisition of addition of concept in the VSF network.

- Chaos strength coefficient of firing function of the feedback layer.
- Interaction coefficient between cells of the feedback layer.
- Mixing rate of a BP module output and a LF module output.

Through an application of the VSF network to an obstacle avoidance task of rover, each factor identified that it affects the acquisition the addition of concept.

References

[1] Von der Malsburg. Am I Thinking Assemblies? In *Brain Theory (eds G.Palm and A.Aertsen.* Springer–Verlag (Berlin), 1986.

[2] Y. Kakemoto and S. Nakasuka. A situated information articulation neural network: Vsf network. In *Proceedings of Third Pacific–Asia Conference, PAKDD–99*, pages 252–257. Springer Verlag., 1999.

[3] K. Kaneko. Period-coupling of kink-antikink patterns, quasi-periodicity in antiferrolike structure and spatial intermmittency in coupled map lattice. – toward a prelude to a field theory of chaos –. *Prog. Theor. Phys*, 72, 1984.

[4] D. E. Rumelhart, J. L. MaClelland, and PDP Research Group. *The Generalized Delta Rule, The Encoding Problem.*, volume 8, chapter Parallel Distributed Processing, Exploration in the Microstructure of Cognition. MIT Press, 1986.

Knowledge-Based Software Engineering
T. Hruška and M. Hashimoto (Eds.)
IOS Press, 2000

Exploiting Real-World Knowledge to Enhance the Intelligence of Knowledge-Based Database Design Tools: A Validation

Shahrul Azman NOAH[1], Michael WILLIAMS[2]

[1]*Faculty of Information Science & Technology, National University of Malaysia, 43600 UKM Bangi, Selangor, Malaysia*

[2]*Department of Computing & Mathematics, Manchester Metropolitan University John Dalton Building, Chester Street, Manchester M1 5GD, UK*

Abstract. Knowledge-based (KB) database design tools have the capability of providing intelligent support to humans during the process of database analysis and design. However, the capacity of such tools to simulate the intelligent behaviour of human designers when performing a design task by making use of their knowledge of the real-world remains a question. Therefore, in recent years there have been a number of attempts to develop tools that are capable of exploiting such knowledge. It has been claimed that the use of such knowledge has the potential to increase the appearance of intelligence of the tools. However, to date, little if any formal validation of this claim has taken place. This paper presents a testing and validation on three approaches proposed to facilitate the system-storage and exploitation of real-world knowledge: the thesaurus, dictionary and knowledge reconciliation approaches. Results obtained have revealed that certain aspects of intelligence were portrayed when exploiting such representations of real-world knowledge.

1 Introduction

Knowledge-based (KB) database design tools have the capability of providing intelligent support to human designers during the process of database analysis and design. However, the capacity of these tools simulate the intelligent behaviour of human designers when performing a design task such as suggestions of missing design elements and detection of inconsistencies by making use of their knowledge of the real-world remains a question. The use and exploitation of such knowledge was, therefore, found to be an important requirement of the currently existing KB database design tools in order for such tools to be realistic alternatives to human designers [1,2]. A number of approaches to representing and exploiting real-world knowledge have been proposed including the dictionary [3], thesaurus [2,4] and knowledge reconciliation [5,6] approaches. Although, claim [1,2] has been placed that such use of knowledge capable of increasing the appearance of intelligence of the tool, little if any formal validation of this claim has taken place. This paper presents a testing and validation of the aforementioned approaches, the intention being to initiate the gathering of evidence to support or otherwise the claim previously stated.

2 Brief Overview of Existing Approaches to Representing Real-World Knowledge

The following provides a brief overview of the methods of knowledge representation employed by the dictionary, thesaurus and knowledge reconciliation approaches. Those interested in detailed discussions of each approach, along with the claimed benefits associated with their use, are referred to the relevant source literature [2-6].

The dictionary approach to representing and exploiting real-world knowledge by an intelligent database design tool is illustrated by the Intelligent Interview System (I^2S) of Kawaguchi et al. [3]. The I^2S approach organises the encapsulated real-world knowledge into a series of domain specific dictionaries, each dictionary comprising of verb information with both past and present forms of each verb being presented. During a design session, I^2S attempts to make use of the dictionary in an attempt to "interview", extracting a series of simple queries that the eventual database will be expected to satisfy. These queries are analysed by the system and used in the generation of a logical structure representing the target database.

The thesaurus approach is illustrated by the Object Design Assistant (ODA) system of Lloyd-Williams [7]. Knowledge is represented within the thesaurus structure by making use of series of concepts and associated synonyms, linked together via abstraction mechanisms, categorised according to those recognised by the system (aggregation, association and generalisation). During a design session, the ODA system attempts to make use of the thesaurus in order to obviate the need to ask what may be viewed as being trivial questions of the user.

The knowledge reconciliation approach is illustrated by the Common Sense Business Reasoner (CSBR) system of Storey et al. [5,6]. The approach is similar to the thesaurus in that it organises domain knowledge into a collection of domain specific concepts and relationships between these concepts. Synonyms, however, are not represented by this approach. During a design session the system attempts to reason with this knowledge in order to reconcile it with the user-specified application domain, the intention being to provide the user with meaningful suggestions of concepts and relationships missing from the evolving database design, and to augment the contents of the domain knowledge after the completion of each design session.

3 Empirical Testing and Validation Strategies

In order to validate the intelligence of KB database design tools when using and exploiting real-world knowledge, a validation framework has been proposed consisting of the following steps.

- Develop a prototype intelligent database design tool which acts as a research vehicle to this validation experiment. Integrate and implement the thesaurus, dictionary and knowledge reconciliation approaches into the prototype tool.
- Establish a set of performance-related criteria used to validate the intelligence of KB database design tool.
- Generate a representative set of test cases. Execute the test cases on the tool with and without the use of real-world knowledge.
- Results obtained from the execution of test cases when exploiting the information provided by the thesaurus, dictionary and knowledge reconciliation approaches are compared with the results obtained when no such knowledge is in use.

A discussion of the above steps follows below.

3.1 Development of a Prototype KB Database Design Tool

A prototype KB database design tool, called the Intelligent Object Analyser (IOA) [8] was used as a research vehicle to this study. As a result, the tool was designed to operate in four different modes; either using real-world knowledge provided by the thesaurus, dictionary or knowledge reconciliation approaches (this paper refers them as the thesaurus mode, dictionary mode and knowledge reconciliation mode respectively) or without the use of real-world knowledge (basic mode).

When processing in the basic mode, IOA follows a two-step procedure:

- The first step involves creating an initial representation of the application domain (known as the problem domain model) and the subsequent refinement of this model.
- The second step involves the refinement of the problem domain model by detecting and resolving any inconsistencies that may exist, and the transformation of the model into object-oriented form.

At various stages during this mode of processing, the IOA conducts a dialogue with the user in order to confirm its understanding of the application domain or to obtain additional information. When making use of real-world knowledge provided by the thesaurus and dictionary approaches (processing in the dictionary mode and thesaurus mode respectively), the tool refers to this knowledge wherever possible, only resorting to questioning the user if the real-world knowledge cannot provide the required information. This procedure is also followed by when making use of real-world knowledge provided by the knowledge reconciliation approach. However, in addition to this procedure, IOA also attempts to conduct a process of *reconciliation of knowledge*, where the description of the application domain submitted by the user is compared and matched with the system-held real-world knowledge in order for IOA to construct an understanding of the contents of the application domain. The understanding gained by the tool from this activity, is used and exploited throughout the design processes wherever possible

3.2 Establishing Criteria

The establishment of criteria of which the performance of KB database design tool can be validated was found to be central in the testing and validation activities. The set of criteria established within the scope of this work focuses on the aspects of appearances of system's intelligence, which were mainly derived from the following opinions and suggestions.

The justification of the appearance of tool intelligence can be judged from the extent to which a tool is capable of simulating the approach taken by a human designer when performing a design task, such as making helpful suggestions and inferences, identifying potential errors and inconsistencies, and forwarding questions to the user only when necessary [1,6]. The elements such as the number of user/tool interactions, the number of errors capable of being detected and resolved by the tool, and suggestion of missing design elements were, therefore, seen as suitable for validating this claim. Fewer user/tool interactions indicate the capability of the tool to internally understand and confirmed certain aspects of the domain description submitted by the user. The capability of the tool to identify potential inconsistencies and to provide intelligent inferences and suggestions are reflected from the number of errors detected and resolved, and the number of suggested (required) missing design elements respectively.

Based upon these, the following criteria have been established.

- *User/tool interaction*. User/tool interaction refers to the number of interactions required between the tool and the user, in order for the tool to confirm its understanding of some aspects of the application domain or to acquire additional information should it be required.

- *Detected and resolved errors.* This criterion refers to the number of errors (previously synthesised and used to generate a range of test-cases) that have been successfully detected and resolved by the tool. The errors included synonymous class(es), synonymous relationship(s) and combination of both.
- *Suggestions of missing design elements.* This criterion measures as whether the elements (within the generated design) are based entirely upon user-provided information, or are included as a direct result of the system consulting its real-world knowledge.

3.3 Generation and Execution of Test-Cases

The set of test-cases used during the testing were generated from a set of design problems which were primarily extracted from the available literature. The advantage is that the accompanying solution could be used as a benchmark and compared with the IOA-suggested solution in order to confirm the appropriateness or otherwise of the designs produced [9]. The synthesisation of multiple test-cases from existing design problems instead of using the real-world test-cases which are not easily available has been previously proposed by O'Keefe and O'Leary [10] and implemented in [11] and [12].

To validate the claim made regarding the use and exploitation of real-world knowledge to the intelligence of KB database design tools based upon the criteria previously established; two types of test have been designed. The first test (Test A) involved the generation and execution of a set of test-cases with varying degrees of complexity, and the second test (Test B) involved the generation and execution of a set of test-cases with a different number and combination of types of errors. This was to ensure that the two aspects of processing; design synthesis and design diagnosis proposed by Oxman and Gero [13], are being considered in this study. Design synthesis is where the tool has the capability of generating design output, whereas, design diagnosis is where the tool detects any inconsistencies or redundancies and suggests corrections in design.

In performing Test A, each of the example of design problems was systematically altered by dividing them into multiple test-cases with varying degrees of complexities [9]. Within the scope of the testing, the complexity of a design test-case is defined as the number of concepts, and the relationships between the concepts [14,15].

However, in the second test (Test B), each of the example design problems was systematically embedded with a series of intentionally-synthesised errors to generate a number of test-cases [16]. Each of these generated test-cases contains a combination of different types and numbers of synthesised errors, including synonymous concept(s), synonymous relationship(s) and combinations of both.

The test-cases were then executed in all four modes of processing. Thus, for each test-case, four sets of results were obtained and compared, following an approach recommended by O'Keefe & Preece [17].

3.4 Method of Analysis of Results

Since all the selected criteria are quantifiable, the quantitative method of analysis was employed. In this study the results observed from the execution of test-cases using the dictionary, thesaurus and knowledge reconciliation modes of processing were subsequently compared with the results observed from the execution of test-cases in basic mode.

A statistical *hypothesis test* was then conducted to assess the significant differences between these observed results at the 5% of significance level.

Although there are several recommended statistical methods available to test such hypotheses, the paired t-test method is highly appropriate in such circumstance as those prevailing in this study [10,18]. The paired t-test method is a form of *repeated measures design*, where the same variable (observed criterion) is measured on several occasions (processing modes) for each subject (test-case).

4 Results and Findings

The results presented here emanate from a series of tests performed on library domain problems found in the general literature. A total of 20 and 49 test-cases were generated for Test A and Test B respectively. The real-world knowledge (thesaurus, dictionary and knowledge reconciliation) used was constructed as the result of a series of interviews with researchers, the results of the interviews being integrated in order to form a single representative of the domain. It is not claimed that these representations portray the definitive knowledge of the library domain, but it does provide an illustration of the way in which such knowledge may be stored and exploited by a KB database design tool.

A discussion of the analysis of the observed results for each type of tests follows.

4.1 Test A

The objective of Test-A was to validate the intelligence of the IOA tool when using and exploiting real-world knowledge (represented as the thesaurus, dictionary and knowledge reconciliation approaches) within the scope of design synthesis. Therefore, the hypothesis of this test was that the use and exploitation of real-world knowledge (thesaurus, dictionary and knowledge reconciliation) increases the appearance of intelligence of the IOA tool by reducing the number of user/tool interactions required per complexity and increasing the number of missing design elements suggested.

Based upon the paired t-test results presented in Table 1, it is apparent that only the thesaurus approach significantly reduced the number of user/tool interactions required per complexity (based upon the significance level and the negative t-Value) and only the knowledge reconciliation approach significantly increased the number of missing design elements suggested (based upon the significance level and the positive t-Value). Accordingly, aspects of appearance of tool's intelligence have been achieved from the exploitation of both approaches respectively. Using and exploiting the dictionary approach, however, did not influence either aspects of tool's intelligence.

Table 1. Paired t-test results - Test A (Design Synthesis)

Criteria	**Thesaurus**		**Dictionary**		**Knowledge Reconciliation**	
	t-Value	***P***	***t-Value***	***P***	***t-Value***	***P***
Interactions per complexity	-3.26	0.00	N/A	N/A	2.36	0.03
Suggestions of missing design elements						

4.2 Test B

The objective of Test B is similar to Test A, however, the testing is directed towards the IOA approach to design diagnosis. As a result the criteria under observation were the number of user/tool interactions and the number of errors resolved per test. The hypothesis for this test, therefore, was that the use and exploitation of real-world knowledge increase the appearance of intelligence of the IOA tool by reducing the number of user/tool interactions required per error detected and increasing the number of errors detected and resolved per test.

As illustrated in Table 2, when processing using the thesaurus and dictionary approaches, the appearance of tool's intelligence has been significantly increased, as evidenced by the significant reduction in the number of user/tool interactions required to detect and resolved errors and the significant increased in the number of errors detected and resolved per test. Processing using the knowledge reconciliation approach although capable of increasing the number of errors detected and resolved, but also resulted in an increase of the required number of user/tool interactions to detect such errors.

Table 2. Paired t-test results - Test B (Design Diagnosis)

Criteria	**Thesaurus**		**Dictionary**		**Knowledge Reconciliation**	
	t-Value	***P***	***t-Value***	***P***	***t-Value***	***P***
Interaction per error	-5.94	0.00	-1.71	0.04	5.66	0.00
No. of errors resolved per test	4.39	0.00	2.35	0.02	2.43	0.01

5 Discussions and Conclusions

Table 3 and 4 present a summary of analysis for Test A and Test B respectively, and Table 5 illustrates the conclusions reached for the thesaurus, dictionary and knowledge reconciliation approaches in both approaches to design.

Table 3: Summary of results for Test A

Observed Criteria	**Approaches***		
	Thes.	**Dict.**	**K-R**
Increases the no. of user/tool interactions	Yes	No	No
Increases the no. of suggested missing design elements	No	No	Yes

Table 4: Summary of results for Test B

Observed Criteria	**Approaches***		
	Thes.	**Dict.**	**K-R**
Reduces the no. of user/tool interactions	Yes	Yes	No
Increases the no. of errors resolved	Yes	Yes	Yes

* *Thes. = Thesaurus, Dict.. = Dictionary; K-R = Knowledge Reconciliation*

Table 5. Increase the appearance of tool's intelligence - conclusions

Representation Approaches	**Approach to Design**	
	Design Synthesis	**Design Diagnosis**
Thesaurus	Unjustifiable	Yes
Dictionary	No	Yes
Knowledge Reconciliation	Unjustifiable	Unjustifiable

Within the context of design synthesis, the claim for an increase in the appearance of tool intelligence largely remains unresolved. When processing in the thesaurus mode, although, significantly reduced the number of user/tool interactions required, was augmented by a corresponding non-significant increase in the suggestions made regarding possible missing design elements within the evolving design. The knowledge reconciliation approach on the other hand, although significantly increased the number of suggestions made for missing design elements, was found incapable to significantly reduce the number of user/tool interactions required. The dictionary approach however did not support this claim.

A more encouraging results, however, were obtained from Test B. When performing the tasks of design diagnosis, exploiting the thesaurus and dictionary approaches increases the appearance of intelligence of the IOA tool. Synonyms which are explicitly represented by the thesaurus approach enhance the capability of the IOA tool to detect and remove redundant elements (errors) as well as simplifies the process of detecting and resolving such elements. As for the dictionary approach, exploitation of the verbs-related information, has facilitated IOA to detect and remove redundant relationships (represented by different tenses of the same verb); as well as capable of removing certain aspects of confirmation and augmentation with the user, which subsequently results in the reduction of the number of user/tool interactions required per error. The claim of increasing the appearance of tool's intelligence when using real-world knowledge represented as the knowledge reconciliation approach, however, remains unresolved. The reconciliation of knowledge process which results in the "understanding" of the user's specification, although, capable of increasing the number of errors detected and resolved per test, was also found to result in the increased in the number of user/tool interactions required per error detected.

Although encouraging results have been obtained from the testing and evaluation work, it is recognised that consideration must be given to a number of practical issues. The effectiveness of the tool depends greatly on the accuracy and completeness of the system-held real-world knowledge, and the results obtained from the tests may be influenced to certain extent by the variety and coverage of the generated test-cases.

6 Summary and Future Work

This paper has presented the findings of an assessment of the thesaurus, dictionary and knowledge reconciliation approaches to representing and exploiting real-world knowledge by a KB database design tool (IOA) within the context of design synthesis and design diagnosis. The aim of the investigation was to ascertain whether the use of such real-world knowledge capable of increasing the appearance of intelligence of the tool. Results obtained have demonstrated that certain aspects of tool's intelligence have been achieved.

Although, there are a number of methodologies proposed for the performance testing and validation of KB system [10,18], there are only a handful of papers that describe actual experiences related to the testing and performance validation of operational system. This paper has presented a framework and methodology for performing such a task.

Ongoing work includes assessing the implication of exploiting such knowledge to the performance of the tool within both approaches to design (design synthesis and design diagnosis) synchronously. Therefore, the test-cases generated should varies in terms of the complexities as well as the number of errors synthesised. This type of test-cases is believed to be a more natural representative of the domain description submitted by any users (varies in complexity and types of errors).

References

[1] V.C. Storey, Real world knowledge for databases, *Journal of Database Administration*, 3(1) (1992) 1-19.

[2] M. Lloyd-Williams, Knowledge-based CASE tools: improving performance using domain specific knowledge, *Software Engineering Journal*, 9(4) (1994) 167-173

[3] A. Kawaguchi et al., An intelligent interview system for conceptual design of database, in: *ECAI '86: The 7th European Conference on Artificial Intelligence*, Conference Services Ltd., London, 1986, pp. 1-7

[4] M. Lloyd-Williams, Exploiting domain knowledge during the automated design of object-oriented databases, in: D. Embley and R. C. Goldstein, (eds.), *Proceedings of the 16th International Conference on Conceptual Modeling*, Spinger-Verlag, Berlin, 1997, pp. 16-29

[5] V. C. Storey et al., Knowledge reconciliation for common sense reasoning, in: P. De and C. Woo (eds.), *Proceeding of the 4th Annual Workshop on Information Technologies and Systems*. Univ. British Columbia, Vancouver, 1994, pp. 87-96

[6] V. C. Storey et al., Database design with common sense reasoning and learning, *ACM Transactions on Database System*, 22(4) (1997) 471-512.

[7] M. Lloyd-Williams, Expert system support for object-oriented database design, *International Journal of Applied Expert Systems*, 1(3) (1993) 197-212.

[8] S. A. Noah, Knowledge-based CASE Tool for Object-Oriented Database Design. In: *Malaysian Science & Technology Congress 1999*, Johor Bahru, Malaysia.

[9] S. A. Noah and M. Lloyd-Williams, "An Evaluation of Two Approaches to Exploiting Real-World Knowledge by Intelligent Database Design Tools", in: *Proceedings of the 17th International Conference on Conceptual Modelling, Singapore*, Springer-Verlag, 1998, pp.197-210.

[10] R. M. O'Keefe and D. E. O'Leary, "Expert System Verification and Validation: A Survey and Tutorial", *Artificial Intelligence Review*, 7(1) (1993) 3-40.

[11] A. J. Gonzalez et al., Performance Evaluation of a Large Diagnostic Expert System Using a Heuristic Test Case Generator, *Engineering Application of Artificial Intelligence*, 9(3) (1996) 275-284

[12] L. A. Miller, Dynamic Testing of Knowledge-Bases Using the Heuristic Testing Approach, *Expert Systems with Applications*, 1(3) 1990 249-269.

[13] R. Oxman, R. and J. S. Gero, Using an Expert System for Design Diagnosis and Synthesis, *Expert Systems: The International Journal of Knowledge Engineering*, 4(1) (1987) 4-14.

[14] S. Kesh, Evaluating the Quality of Entity Relationship Models, *Information and Software Technology*, 37(12) 1995 681-689.

[15] N. Pippenger, Complexity Theory, *Scientific American*, 238(6) (1978) 90-102.

[16] S. A. Noah and M. Lloyd-Williams, Exploitation of Domain Knowledge by Knowledge-Based Database Design Tools: The Dictionary Approach. In: P. Navrat and H. Ueno (eds.), *Proceedings of the 3rd Joint Conference on Knowledge-Based Software Engineering, Smolenice, Slovakia.* Amsterdam: IOS Press, 1998, pp. 250-257.

[17] R. M. O'Keefe and A. D. Preece, The Development, Validation and Implementation of Knowledge-Based Systems, *European Journal of Operational Research*, 92(3) (1996) 458-473

[18] R. M. O'Keefe et al., Validating Expert System Performance, *IEEE Expert*, 2(4) (1987) 81-90.

Knowledge-Based Software Engineering
T. Hruška and M. Hashimoto (Eds.)
IOS Press, 2000

Using Local Search to Validate Knowledge-Based Systems

Éric GRÉGOIRE

CRIL, Université d'Artois, F-62307 Lens Cedex France

Abstract. In this paper, a new method for detecting conflicting information in first-order clausal knowledge-based systems (*KB*s) is proposed. It is based on a progressive instantiation schema and on a non-standard use of local search algorithms.

1 Introduction

A serious but difficult knowledge engineering task consists in checking that knowledge-based systems (*KB*s) are logically consistent, i.e. that they do not contain pieces of conflicting information. On the one hand, this problem is a computationally-hard one as even the basic propositional case is NP-complete, meaning that any algorithm to solve it is exponential in the worst case (unless P=NP) [3]. Dealing with a knowledge representation language that exhibits the expressive power of first-order logic is an even harder task. On the other hand, this problem should be solved when query-answering from a *KB* involves deduction, since anything (and its contrary) can be deduced from any set of conflicting information.

This last decade, some really impressive progress has been obtained w.r.t. *propositional* consistency checking thanks to the use of local search techniques [9, 10, 13, 15-18]. It has even been shown that these techniques can often be used as efficient "oracles" to find inconsistent knowledge, as well [1,13]. A current hot topic of research consists in extending these results to finite *first-order* clausal (i.e. conjunctive normal form) *KB*s by instantiating these latter *KB*s into some ground (i.e. variable-free) counterparts without giving rise to a space-complexity blow-up [18]. In this respect, an interesting progressive instantiation schema has been proposed recently in [2]. It has been used to ensure the consistency of *KB*s that are built in an incremental way. To this end, an efficient technique based on local search that ensures that no inconsistency can be derived using less than a given number of reasoning steps has been developed [2]. In this paper, this technique is improved, exploiting the duality between consistency and inconsistency in a systematic manner. It is shown that is well-suited and powerful to handle forms of negation by failure, too.

The paper is organized as follows. First, some background about local search techniques to prove consistency and inconsistency in the propositional setting is provided. Then a progressive instantiation schema from [2] and its companion algorithms are revisited. Then, it is shown how the duality between consistency and inconsistency can be further exploited to improve the algorithms in the general case. It is explained why this technique is well-suited and powerful to handle forms of negation as failure. Before we conclude, some experimental illustrations of the approach are provided.

2 Local search for detecting inconsistent information

These last years, really impressive progress has been obtained w.r.t. propositional consistency and search, allowing large propositional *KB*s to be checked for consistency, using local search algorithms [9, 10, 13, 15-18]. Most of these algorithms perform a greedy local search for a satisfying assignment (i.e. a model) of a set of propositional clauses. Actually, it is assumed here that *KB*s are in clausal normal form, i.e. are sets of clauses, which are finite disjunctions of positive or negated atomic propositions (resp. function-free predicates, in the first-order setting). The algorithms generally start with a randomly generated truth assignment of the atomic propositions (i.e. with an interpretation that assigns *true* or *false* to each atomic propositions). Most of them then change („ flips “) the assignment of the proposition that leads to the largest increase in the total number of satisfied clauses. Such flips are repeated until either a model is found or a preset maximum number of flips is reached. This process is repeated as needed up to a preset maximum of times. To escape from local extrema, local search algorithms are provided with additional (e.g. random) moves. In the following, a variant procedure called TSAT is used [10, 14]. It makes use of a tabu list forbidding recurrent flips and appears competitive in most situations.

Although local search techniques prove efficient in showing the consistency of many hard propositional *KBs*, they are clearly logically incomplete in the sense that they do not cover the whole search space of interpretations and cannot thus directly prove that a *KB* is inconsistent, i.e. that no interpretation is a model of *KB*. Recently, it has been discovered that the trace of local search algorithms can allow one to discover sets of conflicting information very often when they fail to prove consistency within a preset amount of computing time [1, 11, 13]. More precisely, for each clause, taking each flip as a step of time, the number of times during which this clause is falsified is updated. A similar trace is also recorded for each literal occurring in *KB*, counting the number of times it has appeared in the falsified clauses. When the local search technique fails to prove consistency, it appears extremely often that the most often falsified clauses conflict one another when *KB* is actually inconsistent. In other words, the trace of a failed local search can often be a good oracle to find where the inconsistent information is. This heuristic often applies when realistic *KB*s are considered [12, 13].

3 A progressive instantiation schema

As described above, local search techniques apply to propositional *KB*s, only. In order to tackle finite function-free first-order clausal *KB*s, one straightforward manner would require a full instantiation of the *KB* into its Herbrand counterpart, namely all possible instantiations using the constants occurring in *KB*. Obviously enough, this cannot be done in the general case without a combinatorial space blow-up. To avoid this drawback as much as possible, some compromises have to be made. Here, we adopt two restrictions. On the one hand, we just consider the restricted problem of incrementally building a consistent *KB*. More precisely, *KB* is assumed consistent and a clause *f* is to be introduced into *KB*. We want to show that $KB' = KB \cup \{f\}$ is itself consistent or find the involved conflicting information. On the other hand, we make do with a progressive instantiation of *KB'* inside a propositional setting that ensures that (in)consistency cannot occur using less than a given number *i* of reasoning steps. From a practical point of view, this policy can be justified by the following assumptions about practical situations; on the one hand, inconsistency is often due to a limited number of rules and facts, limiting the reasoning steps that are necessary to prove it. On the other hand, if the available time-resources are limited, we can make do with a guarantee that inconsistency will not occur within a preset limited depth in the reasoning steps. Let us revisit the instantiation schema that was initially proposed in [2].

Assume that *KB* is a consistent finite set of function-free clauses and that *KB* contains at least one constant. Assume that *f* is a clause. Let $KB' = KB \cup \{f\}$. As *KB* is consistent, any inconsistency is due in part from information (constants and/or predicates) from *f*. Accordingly, we shall expand the information from *f* inside *KB* and check for inconsistency step by step.

More formally, let **T** be the (non-empty) set of constants occurring in *KB*'. Actually, a form of multi-sorted logic is required here to avoid a direct combinatorial blow up; namely any constant must be given its exhaustive list of predicate arguments that it can instantiate. For clarity of presentation, this is left implicit in the following. However, let us stress that this is a really important requirement since it will avoid exhaustive instantiations using the whole list **T**. Let $\mathbf{C_0}$ be the singleton $\{f\}$. Let KB_0 contain all ground clauses that can be obtained by instantiating clauses from $\mathbf{C_0}$ using **T**. From these starting points, we shall augment KB_0 to mimic the possible information links between *f* and the contents of *KB*, translating reasoning steps starting from *f* and using information from *KB*.

Let us stress that this approach differs from [2] in the sense that we do not put in KB_0 all the ground clauses from *KB*', since they might not directly take part in the inconsistency when this latter one exists w.r.t. *KB*'.

Let us note *Ground*(**C**) the set of ground clauses obtained by instantiating clauses in **C** using **T** as instantiation domain.

Depth-i consistency/inconsistency is defined in the following way

Definition 1.
Let $\mathbf{C_i}$ be the set of clauses from *KB'* containing at least one predicate from $\mathbf{C_{i-1}}$.
Let $KB_i =_{def} KB_{i-1} \cup \{Ground(\mathbf{C_i})\}$. We say that:
KB is depth-*i* consistent (resp. inconsistent) iff KB_i is consistent (resp. inconsistent)

This concept converges on the standard definitions of consistency and inconsistency.

Proposition 1.
$\exists\, n$ *s.t.* KB_n is *stable*, i.e. $KB_n = KB_{n+1}$. (Such a fixed-point KB_n is noted KB_{end}).

Proposition 2.
KB' is consistent (resp. inconsistent) iff KB_{end} is consistent (resp. inconsistent).

Since $KB_i \subseteq KB_{end}$ for any *i*, we know that whenever KB_i is inconsistent then KB_{end} is inconsistent. Accordingly, at each instantiation step, when an inconsistency is encountered, it can be reported to the knowledge engineer as no further instantiation step will allow consistency to be recovered. On the contrary, no definitive proof of consistency is obtained until KB_{end} is shown consistent.

4 Using the duality between consistency and inconsistency in a better way

The above instantiation schema mimics reasoning steps starting from *f* and linking information from *KB*. However, it should be noted that it diverges from implementing the standard logical resolution principle in an important way. Each time we include a clause in KB_i because it contains a predicate that also belongs to KB_{i-1}, we do not require that these two occurrences of the same predicate are of opposite signs, as it would be a basic requirement for the resolution principle to apply. This last feature can be exploited in order to exploit the duality between consistency and inconsistency in a better way, and which was not taken into account in [2], nor in [6]. Let us explain this in more details.

In the previous section, we have seen that whenever a ground KB_i is shown inconsistent then *KB*' is itself inconsistent. On the other hand, we can only be sure that *KB*' is consistent when KB_{end} is reached, which can often be out of reach. But consider the following dual problems. Let *KB* be a consistent set of clauses, $\neg$ stand for the logical negation connective and f be a clause.

1. Is $KB' = KB \cup \{f\}$ consistent ?
2. Is $KB'' = KB \cup \{\neg f\}$ consistent ?

Actually, the above expansion schema yields propositional subsets KB_i and KB''_i for both problems that differ only on either instantiations of f or instantiations of $\neg f$ are included. Accordingly, we can define a double check policy. At each instantiation level, we test KB_i and KB''_i for consistency. Whenever one of these checks yields inconsistency, we know that we have got a definitive answer about the consistency of *KB*'. In particular, when KB''_i is inconsistent, that means that *KB*" is inconsistent and thus that *KB*' is consistent.

Accordingly, this is a significant way to soften the requirement asserting that no definitive consistency result can be established about *KB*' until KB_{end} is reached. On the other hand, from a logical point of view, showing that *KB*" is inconsistent amounts to proving that f is an actual logical consequence of *KB*. Accordingly, when such a situation is encountered, it is worth telling the user that the additional information f to be introduced in *KB* is redundant w.r.t. *KB*, at least from a logical point of view.

Let us also stress that switching from KB_i to KB_{i+1} can take advantage of previous computations. Mainly, the initial interpretation selected by the local search algorithm to find a model of KB_{i+1} is not obtained randomly but should be the previously found model of KB_i.

5 Handling nonmonotonic *KB*s

In many applications, the representation formalism of the *KB* allows negation by failure or limited forms of default reasoning to be represented. Our local-based search technique is very well-suited to handle forms of negation by failure operators. Imagine that we want to represent the rule asserting that any resident must pay taxes (except ambassadors). This can be represented by $resident(\mathrm{x}) \wedge \mathrm{not}(ambassador(\mathrm{x})) \Rightarrow taxes(\mathrm{x})$, or in clausal form by $\neg resident(\mathrm{x}) \vee \neg \mathrm{not}(ambassador(\mathrm{x})) \vee taxes(\mathrm{x})$, where $\wedge$, $\vee$ and $\Rightarrow$ represent the standard conjunctive, disjunctive and material implication connectives while "not" represents the negation as failure operator. In intuitive terms, if we can assume consistently that an individual a is not ambassador then $\mathrm{not}(ambassador(a))$ is set to *true*.

We can take advantage of our heuristics about the trace of local search when it fails to find a model, to handle this form of non-monotonic reasoning efficiently, at least very often. The idea is as follows. First, assume that all ground literals that are prefixed by the "not" operator in KB_i are *false*. Accordingly, their truth value is fixed and is not allowed to change during the local search. If this latter search leads to a model, then we were obviously right in ensuring this truth value. Assume now that it fails to give us a model and also that a further complete logically search also fails to find one. Now, we may look at the clauses with the highest scores that contain one atom prefixed by the "not" operator and force the truth value of this atom to *true*. In this way, we satisfy this clause. Very often, running a local search or a complete search on this new *KB* leads to a model. This approach is discussed more formally and in a variety of nonmonotonic frameworks in [8, 11]. The main idea is that we can start assuming *false* all that is *normally false*; if this fails to deliver a model then the trace of the local search provides us with a good oracle of the assumptions that are wrong, most probably.

6 Some experimental illustrations

As the adequacy and the good performance of the instantiation schema has been discussed elsewhere [2], we shall not repeat it here. Simply, the current size of the instantiated KB_i should not currently overpass 100 000 clauses on standard Pentium computers, which allows many applications to be handled. On the other hand, the depth of reasoning leading to inconsistency should not require an instantiation that leads to a larger number of clauses. Let us thus simply illustrate the extensive tests that we have conducted and of the results that we have obtained by means of a typical example in the nonmonotonic case. More results are given in the full version of the paper. All tests were conducted on a 450 Mhz Pentium II, under Linux, using a straightforward (i.e. non optimized) implementation of a Davis, Logemann and Loveland procedure [4] and TSAT [10, 14]. In order to simulate realistic *KBs* that are difficult w.r.t. consistency checking, we have built new benchmarks starting from DIMACS standard Boolean consistency ones [5]. For instance, we have mixed consistent ii16 problems with the so-called aim-50-1_6-yes and with an inconsistent Dubois16, all from [5]. These benchmarks have been rewritten using a shared set of Boolean variables. The generated instances are made of more than 19 000 clauses using more than 1500 Boolean variables and are clearly inconsistent. Then, we have introduced additional atomic propositions in the clauses in a random fashion, with at most one marker per clause and a (#markers/ (#other Boolean variables)) ratio being 1/3. These additional atoms are assumed to be interpreted *false* by default. The introduction of these propositions was however operated in such a way that new instances were consistent, which was easily established using TSAT [10, 14]. Setting these additional propositions to *false*, we let TSAT run during a 30 sec. No model could be found (indeed, such simplified instances are inconsistent). We then assigned the truth value *true* to the additional propositions occurring in the clause with the highest score. TSAT exhibited a model in less than 8 sec. on average.

7 Conclusions

This approach to check the consistency of large knowledge bases that are built in an incremental way exhibits several salient features. First of all, it should be noted that the representation language is full (function-free) first-order clausal logic. In this respect, disjunctive information and non-Horn clauses are handled without additional difficulties. On the other hand, for the instantiation schema to avoid a combinatorial blow up, it is necessary to consider a form of multi-sorted logic. But it is a natural requirement that any constant cannot match any variable in a *KB* and that constants should be associated with a restricted list of predicate arguments, only. Also, the way successive partially instantiated *KB*s are generated allows us to exploit the duality between consistency and inconsistency in a systematic way, improving our previous works in that domain. Let us stress that it is also a straightforward task to extend this work to take non-constant function-symbols into account, at least as far as the finite case is still considered.

Acknowledgements

This work was supported in part by the Région Nord/Pas-de-Calais. Many thanks to the whole SAT group at CRIL for fruitful discussions about this paper, especially D. Ansart, L. Brisoux, P. Marquis, B. Mazure and L. Saïs.

References

[1] Bessant, B., Grégoire, É., Marquis P. and Saïs, L., "Combining nonmonotonic reasoning and belief revision: a practical approach", In: *Proc. 8th Int. Conf. on Art. Int. Methodology, Systems and Applications (AIMSA'98)*, F. Giunchiglia (ed.), Sozopol, Bulgaria, LNCS 1480, Springer, pp. 115-128,1998.

[2] Brisoux, L., Saïs, L. and Grégoire, É., "Validation of knowledge-based systems by means of stochastic search", In: *Proc. DEXA workshop on verification, validation and integrity issues in expert and databases systems*, R.R. Wagner (ed.), Vienna, IEEE Computer Press, pp. 41-46, 1998. Extended version to appear in *Int. Journ. of Intelligent Systems.*

[3] Cook, S.A., "The complexity of theorem-proving procedures", In: *Proc. of the 3rd Annual ACM Symposium on Theory of Computing*, pp. 151-158, 1971.

[4] Davis, M., Logemann, G. and Loveland D., "A Machine Program for Theorem Proving", *JACM*, **5**, pp. 394-397, 1962.

[5] DIMACS, Second Challenge on Satisfiability Testing organized in 1993 by the Center for Discrete Mathematics and Computer Science of Rutgers University. http://dimacs.rutgers.edu/Challenges/

[6] Grégoire, É., "Progressive Instantiation for the logical validation of nonmonotonic KBs", in: A. Vermesan and F. Coenen (eds), Validation and Verification of Knowledge Based Systems, Kluwer, pp. 37-52, 1999.

[7] Grégoire, É., „Handling inconsistency efficiently in the incremental construction of stratified belief bases", *Proc. of the Fifth European Conf. on Symbolic and Quantitative Approaches to Reasoning and Uncertainty (ECSQARU'99)*, in A. Hunter and S. Parsons (eds.), London, LNCS 1638, Springer, pp. 168-178, 1999.

[8] Grégoire, É., „Overcoming the Christmas Tree Syndrome ", *Proc. of the Eleventh IEEE Int. Conf. on Tools with Artificial Intelligence (ICTAI'99)*, Chicago, IEEE Computer Press, pp. 425-430, 1999.

[9] Hansen, P. and Jaumard, "Algorithms for the maximum satisfiability problem", *Journ. of Computing*, **22**, pp. 279-303, 1990.

[10] Mazure, B., Saïs, L., Grégoire, É., „Tabu Search for SAT ", In: *Proc. of the 14th Nat. Conf. on Artificial Intelligence (AAAI-97)*, Rhode Island, pp. 281-285, 1997.

[11] Mazure, B., Saïs, L. and Grégoire, É., „Checking several forms of consistency in non-monotonic knowledge-bases", In: *Proc. ECSQARU-FAPR97*, LNCS 1244, Springer, pp. 122-130, 1997.

[12] Mazure, B., Saïs, L. and Grégoire, É., „An Efficient Technique to Ensure the Logical Consistency of Cooperative Agents ", *Int. Journ. of Cooperative Information Systems*, World Scientific, **6**(1), pp. 27-36, 1997.

[13] Mazure, B., Saïs, L. and Grégoire, É., „Boosting Complete Technique Thanks to Local Search Methods ", *Ann. of Math. and Artificial Intelligence*, 22, pp. 319-322, 1998.

[14] Mazure, B., Saïs, L. and Grégoire, É., „System Description: CRIL Platform for SAT", In: *Proc. of the 15th Int. Conf. on Automated Deduction (CADE'15)*, LNCS 1421, Kirchner C. and Kirchner H. (eds.), Springer, pp. 124-128, 1998.

[15] McAllester, D., Selman, B. and Kautz, H., "Evidence for Invariants in Local Search", In: *Proc. of the 14th Nat. Conf. on Artificial Intelligence (AAAI-97)*, pp. 321-326, 1997.

[16] Selman, B., Levesque, H. and Mitchell. D., „A New Method for Solving Hard Satisfiability Problems ", In: *Proc. of the 14th Nat. Conf. on Artificial Intelligence (AAAI-97)*, pp. 440-446, 1992.

[17] Selman, B., Kautz, H. A. and Cohen, B., „Local Search Strategies for Satisfiability Testing ", In: *Proc. 1993 DIMACS Workshop on Maximum Clique, Graph Coloring, and Satisfiability*, 1993.

[18] Selman, B., Kautz, H. and McAllester, D., "Computational Challenges in Propositional Reasoning and Search", In: *Proc. of the 15th Int. Joint Conf. on Artificial Intelligence (IJCAI-97)*, Nagoya, Japan, pp. 50-54, 1997.

Knowledge-Based Software Engineering
T. Hruška and M. Hashimoto (Eds.)
IOS Press, 2000

A Tool for Automatic Execution of Hierarchical-Incremental Testing

Toyohiko HIROTA, Masayuki ITO, Kouji ADACHI, Masaaki HASHIMOTO
Kyushu Institute of Technology, Iizuka, 820-8502 Japan

Abstract. As object-oriented software development becomes common, and programs become more complex, program reuse becomes more encouraged. Therefore program testing becomes more important and higher level of testing is required. However object-oriented program testing technique is not advocated, and most of people use existing program testing techniques. This paper describes a tool for automatic execution of hierarchical incremental testing.

1 Introduction

To increase the productivity and the reliability of software, reuse is an important means. However if the reliability of the component to be reused is not sufficient, its reuse will cause the decline in the productivity and the reliability of the whole system.

To prevent such a decline, we should apply exhaustive unit testing to a reusable component by preparing test drivers and test stubs. To prepare all necessary drivers and stubs for the component under test, however, requires much efforts.

We have developed a support tool for unit testing to automate statement coverage and branch coverage [1]. The tool automatically generate a test driver and test stubs from the signatures of the entries (functions) of the component under test and those of other components and libraries which are called from the component. The generated test driver and test stubs read test script from a file and automatically execute testing according to the script.

Recently, testing of object-oriented programs becomes a serious problem. It seems that conventional statement coverage or branch coverage is insufficient. Shel Siegel has proposed a hierarchical approach as a comprehensive test approach for object-oriented programs. The hierarchical approach uses five kinds of test suites, that is, hierarchical-incremental test suite, conditional test suite, integration test suite, system test suite, and regression test suite. Among them, the hierarchical test suite and the conditional test suite apply to an individual component.

In this research, we have studied our support tool to support the hierarchical-incremental test suite. As a result, it proved that our tool can support to test four test models, that is, control-flow test model, data-flow test model, state-transition test model, and transaction-flow test model, among five test models required for the hierarchical-incremental test suite. The excepted test model is only exception test model.

2 Testing System

Central components of the test system are test suite, test model, test object, and test script [2]. The relation among them are shown in Figure 1.

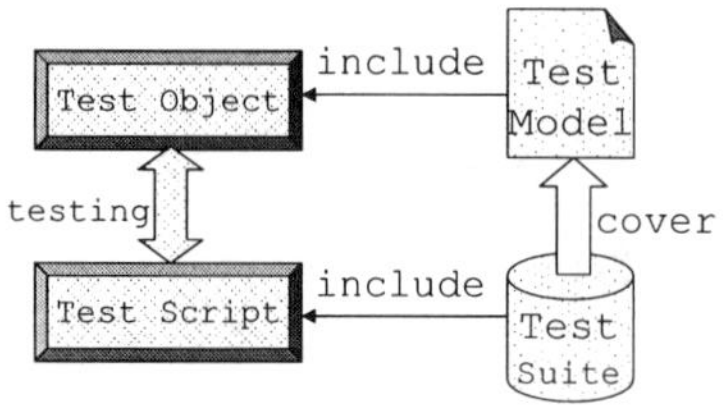

Figure 1: Central components of the test system

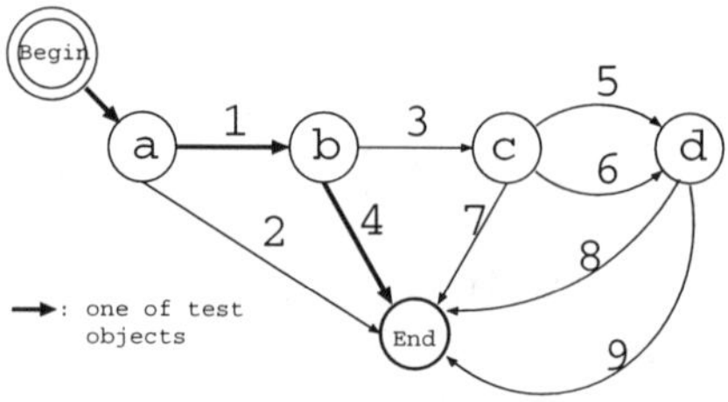

Figure 2: Example of control-flow test model

The test suite is a collection of test scripts, and it covers one or several test models. Any set of test scripts can be a test suite, but we usually make a set based on the type of test model or test script. The hierarchical-incremental test suite which is supported by our tool is focused on class-object testing.

The test model models a technical component from the tester's perspective. Because using source code as a model for testing causes several problems, we use other kinds of test models. The hierarchical-incremental test suite covers five test models, control-flow test model, data-flow test model, state-transition test model, transaction-flow test model, and exception test model, which we will explain in Section 3.

The test object represents an instance of a test model. We can derive as many test models from a test model as we want. Test coverage can be computed as the ratio of the covered test objects to the derived ones. However to derive too many test objects will require too much cost for testing.

The test script is the executable form of the test object that actually implements the test. When using our tool, test script consists of parameter descriptions which are read in a test driver and test stubs.

3 Hierarchical Incremental Test Suite

The hierarchical-incremental test suite [2] is a set of test scripts that test objects as instances of classes and as part of a system of interrelated systems. Our study aims to cover all the test models except exception test model which are covered by the suite.

3.1 Control-Flow Test Model

The control-flow test model models a class method as a sequence of nodes and edge (a graph). This control-flow graph represents the control structure of the method and hence is a structural model of the class. Figure 2 shows a sample flow graph.

A control-flow test object is a path through the control-flow diagram that goes from the method entry to the method exit. In Figure 2, the sequence of thick lines shows one of the test objects. Because the control-flow model allows loops, it might have an infinite number of paths. The hierarchical-incremental test suite relies on branch coverage for test object generation.

3.2 Data-Flow Test Model

The data-flow test model is a kind of control-flow test model annotated with data elements that shows what happened to those data as you move through a method execution. Figure 3 shows an example of data-flow test model.

A data-flow test object is the same kind of path as a control-flow test object. In Figure 3, the sequence of thick lines shows one of the test objects. We add some paths to the set of control-flow test objects to satisfy a certain coverage.

The hierarchical-incremental test suite adopts the coverage to test all the paths through the graph from a definition of a variable to a use of that variable with no intervening definition.

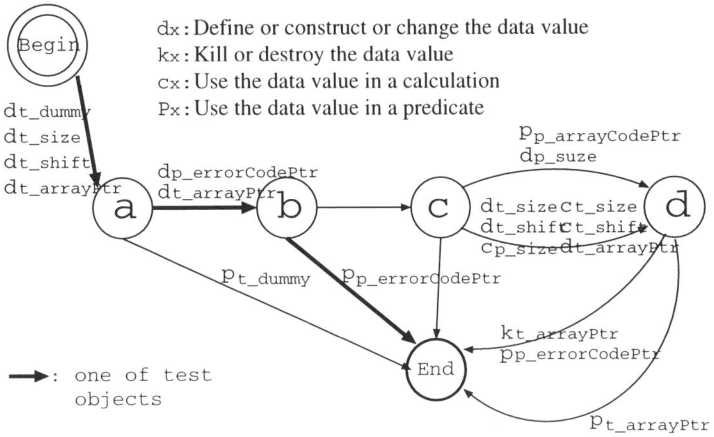

Figure 3: Example of data-flow test model

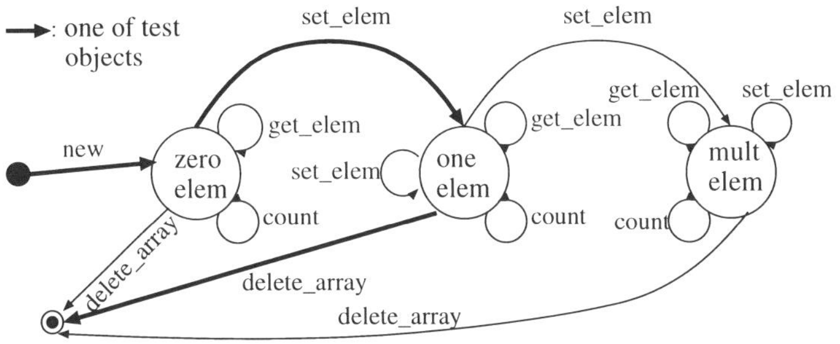

Figure 4: Example of state-transition test model

3.3 State-Transition Test Model

Transitioning from testing individual methods to classes introduces the concept of class behavior. Many different object-oriented design methods use the state-transition model to represent the behavior of a class.

Figure 4 shows an example of state-transition test model. The edges in the graph are the transitions; the labels on these consist of the events and the actions that occur in the transition from state to state. The actions correspond to class method names, while the events are simply named user interface or other events in the system such as conditions or messages.

A state-transition test object is a transition path from the construction of the object to the destruction of the object. In Figure 4, the sequence of thick lines shows one of the test objects. For the hierarchical-incremental test suite, we pick a set of paths through the state-transition model that exercises each transition at least once.

3.4 Transaction-Flow Test Model

A transaction-flow test model is a kind of control-flow test model that applies to the class as a whole rather than to just a method of the class. Using the same structures and approaches as the control-flow model, the transaction-flow model scales the control logic up to deal with the object life cycles rather than with method life cycles.

Figure 5 shows an example of transaction-flow test model. The flow graph that models the transaction begins with the construction of the object. In this case, the "new" method creates an object. The flows then model how the object responds to its environment by calling its methods. The nodes reflect the public attributes and methods of the class.

A transaction-flow test object is a path through the transaction-flow model. In Figure 5, the sequence of thick lines shows one of the test objects. We must derive the individual transaction-flow paths that exercise each edge at least once. However the minimal covering tests for a transaction-flow test model seems insufficient to yield many failures. We should try to find particularly long and involved tests that reflect situations the designers did not consider, or that reflect missing requirements.

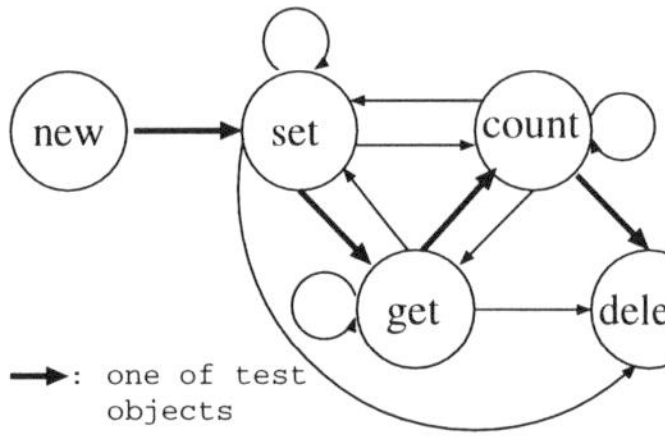

Figure 5: Example of transaction-flow test model

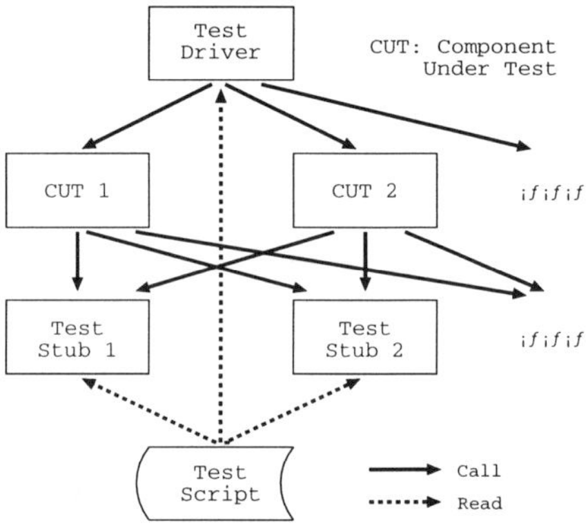

Figure 6: Program configuration for component testing

4 A Tool for Automatic Execution of Testing

We have developed a support tool for unit testing to automate statement coverage and branch coverage. The tool automatically generate a test driver and test stubs from the signatures of the entries (functions) of the component under test and those of other components and libraries which are called from the component. The generated test driver and test stubs read test script from a file and automatically execute testing according to the script.

4.1 Automatic Execution of Testing

A testing program is configured as shown in Figure 6. The test driver and the test stubs are automatically generated by our support tool. The test script must be manually written by a tester. If a suitable test script is prepared, the testing is automatically executed by initiating the testing program.

4.2 Test Script

A test script for our tool consists of independent lines which define parameter values read by the test driver or test stubs. Figure 7 shows a part of a test script.

```
0 set_test_case 1
1 next_call 1
1 set_parm_new 0 0
1 error_error
1 eval_result_new
1 next_call 0
1 set_test_case 2
2 next_call 1
2 set_parm_new 0 1
2 malloc -1
2 error_error
2 eval_result_new
        ...
```

Figure 7: A partial test script

4.3 Application to Hierarchical Incremental Test Suite

We have proved that our support tool can apply to the hierarchical incremental test suite through an experiment.

In the experiment, we used a sample program component named "array.c." It manages elements with integer indexes in a tree structure. Its language is C, but it is deigned as an object model. It has a constructor, a destructor, and three methods, `setElem`, `getElem` and `getElemCount`.

We derived test objects for each test model, and convert them into the test scripts. They are summarized in Table 1. The test objects of data-flow test model were the same as control-flow test model.

Table 1: Summary of test objects and test scripts

method	lines	control		state		trans.	
		O	S	O	S	O	S
new	42	4	33				
getElem	37	9	56				
setElem	57	9	47	15	387	14	330
getElemCount	21	4	22				
delete	39	4	27				

Legend
control: control-flow test model
state: state-transition test model
trans: transaction-flow test model
O: number of test objects
S: number of test script lines

5 Discussion

We developed our tool to support structural testing such as all-statement testing of all-branch testing, but the experiment proved that our tool can apply to functional testing which is included in the hierarchical test suite. The primary policy of the tool is to control the test driver by a test script and to specify parameters to the component under test through a test script. We consider this policy effective for program testing. To write a test driver and test stubs which interpret a test script is tiresome and long-time work, but our tool can automatically generate them to avoid such work.

For the state-transition test, we needed to modify the test driver manually. To automate this modification, we must define the states of the component under test. It will be a difficult problem especially when there is no single variable which represents the state of the component, or when there are no methods to observe the internal state.

It depends on each test model to assure if a test object is covered. About the control-flow test model and the data-flow test model, the coverage is automatically measured by some monitoring tools [1]. Because a test object of the transaction-flow test model is a sequence of the methods, the testing is judged successful if all the test scripts are processed by the testing program.

About the state-transition test model, we must assure the component under test is in a specific state at a certain time during the execution. In general, we will need an extra method to get the internal state of the component. However, we did not need such extra method because the example "array.c" has the method `getElemCount`. Therefore, some code to get and display the internal state of the component after each state transition was added to the test driver. We manually checked the sequence of displayed states.

This research excluded the exception test model in the hierarchical test suite, but it is an easy task to implement it. The exception test model is to test the raising of exceptions, then we have only to add some code to catch the designated exceptions, and the automatic generation of such code is not difficult.

6 Conclusion

In this research, we have shown that our support tool for component testing can apply to the hierarchical-incremental test suite which has been proposed for object-oriented software testing. The hierarchical-incremental test suite includes control-flow test model and data-flow test model as structural models applicable to each method, and also includes state-transition test model and transaction-flow test model as functional models applicable to the whole class. This means that our support tool can apply to various test models.

Hereafter, we will study the problems discussed in Section 5, and also try to combine the tool with a configuration management tool.

References

[1] T. Hirota and M. Hashimoto. Integrated testing environment for C++. In *Proceedings of Japan-CIS Symposium on Knowledge Based Software Engineering '94*, pages 120–125, May 1994.

[2] Shel Siegel. *Object–Oriented Software Testing: A Hierarchical Approach.* John Wiley & Sons, 1996.

Knowledge-Based Software Engineering
T. Hruška and M. Hashimoto (Eds.)
IOS Press, 2000

A Method for Implementing a System to Guide Interview-driven Software Requirements Elicitation

Seiichi KOMIYA[1], Junzo KATO[2], Morio NAGATA[3], Shuichiro YAMAMOTO[4], Motoshi SAEKI[5], Atsushi OHNISHI[6], Hisayuki HORAI[7]

[1]*Software Technology Center, Information-Technology Promotion Agency, Japan (IPA)*
16th floor, Center office Bldg, Bunkyo Green court,
2-28-8, Honkomagome, Bunkyo-ku, Tokyo 113-6591, Japan,
e-mail: komiya@ipa.go.jp

[2]*Comnic -Soken Corp., e-mail: kato@foresee.or.jp*

[3]*Keio University, e-mail: nagata@ae.keio.ac.jp*

[4]*Nippon Telegraph and Telephone Corp., e-mail: yamamoto.shuichiro@lab.ntt.co.jp*

[5]*Tokyo Institute of Technology, e-mail: saeki@cs.titech.ac.jp*

[6]*Ritsumeikan University, e-mail: ohnishi@cs.ritsumei.ac.jp*

[7]*Fujitsu Lab. Ltd., e-mail: horai@iias.flab.fujitsu.co.jp*

Abstract. A system that provides guidance in the work of eliciting software requirements by interviews with clients conducted over the WWW is being developed. This paper describes the method for implementing a system to guide interview-driven software requirements elicitation.

1 Introduction

Software is developed on the basis of a requirements specification document, which defines the client's requirements for the software that is to be developed. Therefore, if the client's requirements are not correctly and completely reflected in the specifications document, the serious development delay and cost increases that may accompany the necessary corrections can strike a fatal blow to the development project. This fact makes it essential to elicit the client's complete and accurate requirements for the software. That is not an easy task, however, no matter how experienced the software engineers are. We were therefore motivated to develop technology that would allow even relatively inexperienced software engineers to elicit correct and complete requirements. The process of analyzing software requirements involves three phases: 1) eliciting client requirements, 2) writing the requirements specifications, and 3) analyzing the requirements specifications for deficiencies. Research and development on technology based on formal requirements specifications description is in progress to support phases 2) and 3), but research on phase processes in phases 2) and 3) are not possible until phase 1) is accomplished, research on the requirements analysis process requires particular attention to the requirements elicitation process. The requirements analysis processes in previous research and in our research are compared in Table 1.

Order	Previous Research (Differs from the work-site process)	Work-site Process	Our Research (Same as the work-site process)
1	(Omits requirements elicitation process)	Elicit requirements from many persons (informal description of results).	Expert guidance by computer so that anyone can elicit software requirements.
2		Check for redundancy and conflicts in the requirements.	
3		Decide on the specifications by group consensus	
4	Describe the requirements by using a formal specification description language.	A requirements specification document (informal description) is written by many persons.	The requirements specification document (informal description is generated automatically.
5	The requirements specifications are analyzed for deficiencies on the basis of the formal description.		
6	(The design process begins here.)	(The design process begins here.)	(The design process begins here.)
7	The program is generated automatically on the basis of the formal description.	Design specification documents, etc. are written on the basis of the requirements specification document. This work is divided up among many persons.	Computer support by the GroupWork Manager for design proposals and their corresponding group discussions.

Table 1. Comparison of Software Requirements Analysis Processes

Software requirements analysis has so far been a matter of software engineers (SEs) eliciting the requests of clients through person-to-person interviews and document exchanges, followed by the writing of a requirements specification document based on the knowledge and experience of an expert software engineer. It is desirable to make it possible for an SE that does not have that expert knowledge to elicit requirements from the client and to produce the requirements specification document. Recognizing that the software requirements elicitation process is an interview process, we are doing research and development on a system for guiding that interview process on the basis of expert SE knowledge.

To achieve this research objective, we have adopted the following approach. First, create a tool that has the minimum functions that are required for the task of extracting software requirements by means of interviews. Next, test that tool in the process of extracting software requirements by means of interviews. Then, improve the tool according to the test results and again test the improved tool in the process. The research proceeds by repeating this cycle until acceptable results are obtained.

To maintain generality, the tool is developed under the assumption that an interview may involve multiple persons on the client side and multiple SEs. It is also assumed that this tool will be used under the direction of an SE leader (Fig. 1). For effective interviewing, it is desirable to be able to display a list of past questions and answers on the screen. For that reason, we chose to conduct the interviews, which had previously been done face-to-face in person, on the WWW.

We are also implementing functions for maintaining security so that the Web can be used so as to allow engineers who work in different locations to participate in the discussions without leaving their own workplaces. Using the Web has the added value of making it possible for the engineers to accomplish the software requirements elicitation task without having to make frequent visits to the client.

This paper is organized as follows. Section 2 explains a method for guiding the requirements elicitation work. Section 4 is the summary and conclusion.

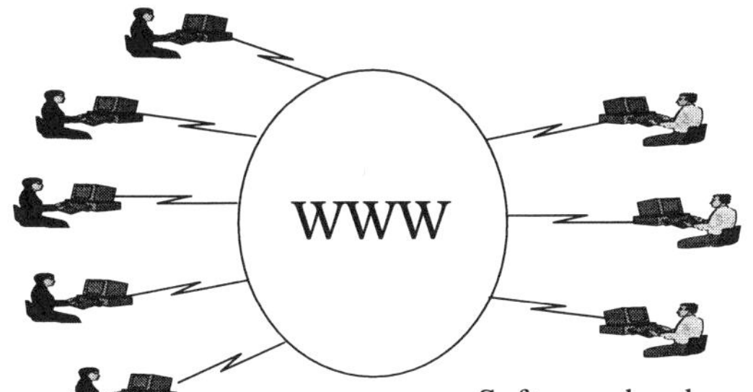

Figure 1. Software Requirements Elicitation over WWW

2 Method for Guiding the Requirements Elicitation Work

2.1 Support by means of scenarios

In order to guide the interview process in which software engineers elicit the client's requirements for the software specifications, it is necessary to clarify what needs to be discussed in the first place. For that purpose, we conducted experiments in which hypothetical interviews were used to elicit requirements (S. Komiya,.1997). As an example of software development, we selected "a system for accepting applications for packages travel tours over the Internet and processing them by computer." The test subjects were five persons divided into three groups of one person each and one group of two persons. An example of the data obtained from that experiment is listed in Table 2, along with the analysis results.

Speaker	Category	Utterance	Utterance type
SE	Schedule	Concerning application support functions for a package tour, about how soon would you like to implement it ?	Question
Client	Schedule	If it is sure to be able to implement it, we would like to implement it as soon as possible.	Answer
Client	Examples	In such cases, how long does it usually take to implement it?	Question

Table 2. Example of hypothetical interview experiment data and analysis

The analysis reveals that the subjects that should be discussed in eliciting the requirements can be classified into the nine categories (sets of topics) listed below.

What: The functions of the software to be developed.
Examples: Examples that show what kinds of things are possible
Why: The reasons for the development and the background situation
Budget: The financial constraints on development
Schedule: The development period
Current System: Questions about the current system

Conditions: Design conditions, etc.
Constraints: Constraints on development
Policies: The development Policies

Moreover, the efficiency of the elicitation process seems to depend on the order in which the issues are raised. Therefore, there is a need to control the flow of the interview by ordering the categories into preset sequences, called scenarios, that are registered in the system.

Here we describe our approach to the construction of the scenarios that should be provided by the system. For efficient elicitation of requirements, the first thing the SE should do in the interview is to clarify the overall image of the system. An effective way to do that is to begin the interview with a discussion of the functions of the system to be developed. Thus, the first set of issues that should be raised in the interview is the *What* category. In attempting to correctly understand the desired system functions, the discussion most often proceeds smoothly if specific examples are brought up at this time. These examples belong to the *Examples* category. Next, to correctly determine whether or not the functions that satisfy the client's requirements are truly necessary, it is necessary to understand the background situation that affects the system development and the reasons for the development. Issues related to that fall under the category of *Why*. To be able to decide on the functions of the system to be developed, it is necessary to discuss the client's current system. These issues belong to the category *Current System*. Accordingly, the topics that belong to these categories should be discussed together at the same time. For the reasons presented above, the topics that belong to the category *What* should be taken up first in the SE's interview with the client to elicit requirements, and topics that belong to the categories *Examples*, *Why*, and *Current System* are needed to resolve the issues of the category *What*.

The discussion up to this point, has concerned the system functions. The next subject to be discussed is the design conditions, which are the premises for the implementation of the functions. The discussion of this subject involves topics that belong to the *Conditions*, *Constraints*, and *Policies* categories. The final subject of discussion includes the development budget, time frame and other such factors that affect the execution of the development. The reason for discussing these factors at this point is to determine whether or not it is possible to implement all of the functions that have been discussed so far, given the restrictions of budget and development time. These issues belong to the categories of *Budget* and *Schedule*.

An example of a scenario constructed according to the approach described above is shown in Table 3.

Category	Order	Type	Category	Order	Type
What	1st	P	*Examples*	1st	P
Why	1st	P	*Current System*	1st	P
Constraints	2nd	S	*Policies*	2nd	S
Conditions	2nd	S			
Budget	3rd	P	*Schedule*	3rd	P

Table 3 Scenario Provided by the System

The order shown in Table 3 indicates the order in which the sets of issues are to be taken up in the interview for eliciting requirements. For example, for the three groups (the 1st group, *What*, *Examples*, *Why*, and *Current System*; the 2nd group, *Conditions*, *Constraints*, and *Policies*, and the 3rd group, *Budget* and *Schedule*) the order in which the topics that belong to the respective groups is the same within a group, but differs between groups. This indicates that the issues that belong to the 1st group should be taken up first, followed by those of the 2nd group and then, finally, those of the 3rd group.

The P type and S type that are seen in Table 3 indicate differences in the method for transition between topics within a group. For the topics in the 1st group, for example, topics from the category *Examples*, *Why*, or *Current System* may be taken up before all of the topics for the category *What* have been dealt with, but the discussion cannot move on to the topics of the 2nd group until all of the topics of the 1st group have been completed. That is to say, until all of the topics of a given group (set of categories) have been finished, the discussion cannot move on to any topic of a category that does not belong to that group. This is referred to as the P (parallel) type topic transition method. For the topics that belong to the second group, on the other hand, while the discussion can begin with a topic from any of the categories in this group, once a topic is taken up, all of the topics of that category must be completed before any topic from another category is taken up. For example, if all of the topics of the category *Policies* have not been completed, it is not permitted to take up any of the topics from the category *Constraints*. This is referred to as the S (sequential) type topic transition method.

The group that consists of the categories *Conditions*, *Constraints* and *Policies* in Table 3 is regarded as type S and is registered as such, but another approach would be to make these P type categories. Yet another approach would be to reverse the order of the 2nd group and 3rd group. Therefore, these different possible combinations are provided by the system as four different scenarios. Moreover, as there are various approaches to creating scenarios, a function for creating, registering, modifying and deleting scenarios is also provided to allow the SE to freely create and register scenarios.

2.2 Progress control support by means of a table

In requirements elicitation by interview, it should be possible to control the progress of the elicitation work if the items that must be discussed are classified into nine categories and the transitions between topics to be taken up in the interview are defined by scenarios. That is to say, it is possible to control how far along in the scenario the interview proceeds if the interview proceeds according to a scenario and the progress is controlled category by category. Therefore, the progress control table shown in Table 4 is provided for the purpose of controlling the progress of requirements elicitation by interview. Table 4 adds a column labeled Progress Status to Table 3. For. each category listed in Table 3, this column contains a number that indicates whether the discussion for that category has not yet started (0), is currently in progress (1), has been completed (2), or is not required (3). In this example, the progress status of all of the 1st group categories is 2, which indicates that the discussion of the topics of those categories has been completed. Looking at the Progress Status column for the 2nd group categories, we see that *Conditions*, *Constraints* and *Policies*, respectively have status values of 2, 1 and 0, indicating that discussion of the *Conditions* topics has been completed and discussion of the subsequent *Constraints* topics is in progress. The progress status for each category is determined by the SE leader, who then sets the corresponding values in the progress control table. Thus, by using a progress control table such as the one presented in Table 4, *it is possible to control the progress of requirements elicitation work at the level of the information to be communicated*. A technology that takes a similar approach is the overlay model that is used in intelligent CAI. In that model, the knowledge that the learner is to acquire is considered as a subset of the knowledge of the creator of the teaching materials in determining the extent of the learner's progress. Thus, the progress control table described above can be considered an extension of the overlay model.

Category	Order	Type	Progress Status	Category	Order	Type	Progress Status
What	1st	P	2	*Examples*	1st	P	2
Why	1st	P	2	*Current System*	1st	P	2
Constraints	2nd	S	2	*Policies*	2nd	S	1
Conditions	2nd	S	0				
Budget	3rd	P	0	*Schedule*	3rd	P	0

[Status] 0: Not started 1: Being discussed
2: Discussion completed 3: Discussion not required

Table 4. Progress Control Table

2.3 Method for generating navigation messages

To make it possible for even inexperienced persons to elicit client's requirements correctly, completely, and efficiently, a function is required for generating navigation messages that indicate what is to be done next.

The approach we are taking to the provision of navigation messages by the system is illustrated by the following examples.

(1) Guidance for beginning the interview

"In one word, what will the system do?"

The above question is the first question that the software engineer should ask at the beginning of the interview. Conversely, the interview cannot begin without this one word. That is because when eliciting requirements by interview, it is best to begin with a rough understanding of the overall function of the system that is to be developed. It cannot be said, however, that the interview must always begin with this question. In the case where the client has already conveyed an overview of the system to be developed before the interview, for example, the interview cannot begin with a question such as the above. In that case, the interview should begin by expressing the client's system overview with one word in a request for a more detailed description, such as ***"I understand that you want to develop a system that ..., but could you please explain what the system is to do in more detail?"*** Which question is appropriate depends on the situation at the time of the interview, so this cannot be decided by the navigation system. Nevertheless, always placing the responsibility for deciding which question to use on the interviewer may put an excessive burden on some interviewers. Therefore, in order to give the navigation system the ability to decide which question is appropriate, a checklist of the information needed to judge the situation is prepared in advance and given to the interviewer to fill out. Then, the system generates a navigation message on the basis of the filled-out checklist. This is not to say that we have adopted a method in which the system understands the context of the interview and generates a message that tells the user what to do next. Rather, the understanding of the interview context is left to the human interviewer, who marks the checklist on the basis of his or her own understanding, and that information is then used by the system to generate the required message.

(2) Message generation based on a progress management table

Because the topic transition method differs according to whether a category is a P type category or an S type category, the timing of the message output also differs. In the case of P type categories, a message for stimulating the discussion for that group is output only at the time of a transition to a new group. In the example shown in Table 4, there are two such occasions, one upon entering the 1st group and one at the transition from the 2nd group to the 3rd group. The message to be output at the time of entering the 1st group was explained in item (1) above, 'Guidance for beginning the interview'. For the transition from the 2nd group to the 3rd group, the message ***'Please let me hear your thoughts concerning the software development budget and schedule.'*** is output, because the categories of the 3rd group are *Budget* and *Schedule*.

In the case of S type categories, on the other hand, a message for stimulating the discussion for a category is output only at the time of a transition to a new category. For example, at the time of the transition to the category *Conditions*, the message ***'Now I would like to discuss the design conditions. We have prepared some examples of design conditions for you to consider. Please look at these.'*** is output.

(3) Message generation based on the type of utterance.

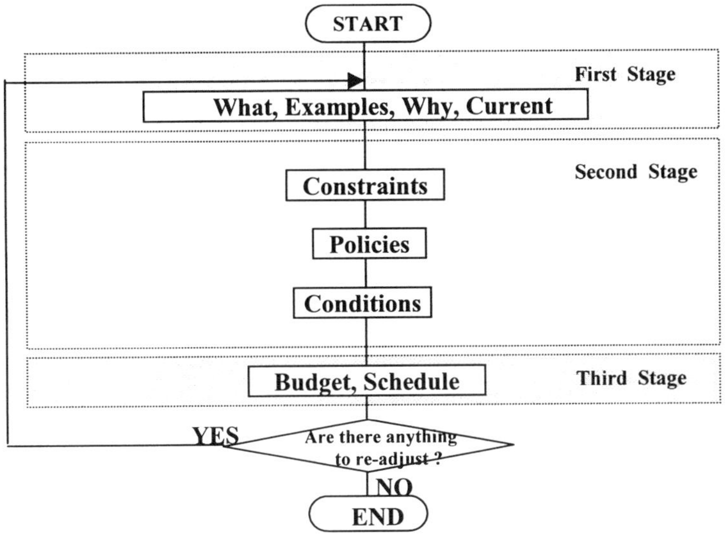

Figure 2. A Flowchart of the Interview-Based on a Scenario Provided by the System

The utterances of the client and the SE during the course of an interview can be classified into *utterance types* according to their role in the interview. There are 15 utterance types: questions, answers, confirmations, suggestions, supplements, corrections, provision of materials, requests for materials, references, proposals, evaluations, decisions, work requests, commitments, and others.

A message that guides the next utterance is generated according to the utterance type only when the utterance type is one that shows a transition to the next topic.

When the SE or the client makes an utterance he or she decides the type of his or her own utterance and selects that utterance type from a menu to issue the utterance. (An input field is placed on the screen so as to display a single utterance type.) While some might feel that requiring the client to perform this kind of operation places a burden on the client, having the client and the SE select their own utterance type has the effect of making each utterance simple.

A flowchart of the interview based on a scenario provided by this system shown in Fig. 2.

2.4 Category-specific support functions

The guidance method that has been described up to now is one that outputs messages for eliciting client utterances and eagerly awaits the client's proposals. With this, the interview will not last long. The reason is that for persons who have not developed and used similar software before, it is difficult to correctly and completely formulate their own requirements for the specifications of the software that is to be developed. It is known, however, that accurate decisions can be obtained even from such clients if the SE presents specific suggestions while at the same time providing the client with the explanation and data required to decide whether or not to accept the suggestion and acting so as to elicit the client's decision. The above type of behavior on the part of the SE is widely known as the proposal type SE behavior. To support the proposal type SE behavior, it is necessary to provide support functions for each topic category.

(1) For the 1st group

The interview objective of the 1st group is to list the functions that are required for the software that is to be developed, and examined them one by one. There are two effective methods for enumerating the functions. The first is to ask the client what is not satisfactory about the current system, obtain information about the current system and analyze that information, and then make specific suggestions about how to improve the current system. For this purpose, a function for guiding the inquiry for determining the customer's points of dissatisfaction with the current system is needed. The other effective method is store functions that are believed to be necessary in each software application domain in a database, and present them to the client for selection during the interview. Implementing this kind of support in the system proposed in this paper requires a function that makes it possible to store those examples in the form of a requirements specification document that can be searched during the interview process.

(2) For the 2nd group

A function is provided for explaining the differences of *Conditions*, *Constraints* and *Policies*, as well as presenting examples of them to the client so that the client can choose what is required.

(3) For the 3rd group

Data to serve as criteria in considering the software development budget and schedule are presented to the SE so that they are available for reference during the interview process.

3 Conclusion

We have described a system for guiding software engineers in the task of eliciting client software requirements by means of interviews conducted over the WWW.

References

[1] IEEE Std 830-1993, "IEEE Recommended Practice for Software Requirements Specifications."

[2] Julio Cesar Sampaio Do Prado Leite and Ana Paula Pinho Gilvaz, "Requirements Elicitation Driven by Interviews: The Use of Viewpoints," Proceedings of Eighteenth International Workshop on Software Specification and Design (IWSSDD-8), pp. 85 – 94, 1996.

[3] S. Komiya, "An Interview-based Software Requirements Analysis Process and a Support Environment for it Constructed on the WWW," Proceedings of the 16th Technical Conference of the Information-Technology Promotion Agency Japan, pp.19-26, 1997

[4] R. Lecoeuche, C. Mellish, D. Robertson, "A Framework for Requirements Elicitation through Mixed-Initiative Dialogue," Proc. of 4th International Conference on Requirements Engineering, pp. 190-196, 1998. C. Potts, K. Takahashi, and A. Anton, "Inquiry-Based requirements analysis," IEEE Software, Vol. 11, No. 2, pp. 21-32, March 1994.

[5] C. Rolland and N. Parakash, "Guiding the Requirementsw Engineering Process", Proc. of APEC94, pp. 82-91, 1994.

Knowledge-Based Software Engineering
T. Hruška and M. Hashimoto (Eds.)
IOS Press, 2000

Co-operative Abstract Data Types: A Stack Example

P. CHAMPAGNOUX, L. DUCHIEN, D. ENSELME, G. FLORIN,
Laboratoire CEDRIC - CNAM
292 rue St Martin, Fr 75141 Paris Cedex 03
{champag,duchien,enselme,florin}@cnam.fr

Abstract. This paper presents co-operative types designed to specify the co-operation between distributed objects. Our aim is to introduce environment hypothesis in Abstract Data Type (ADT) to express concurrency and distribution properties. These co-operative properties must be introduced in ADT in order to define precisely a co-operative behaviour. To illustrate the CADT approach, we give the example of a co-operative stack used in the *crankback* algorithm for ATM virtual circuits construction.

1 Introduction

Abstract Data Types (ADT) [5] provide a mathematical tool to formally specify a problem. They strictly separate specification and implementation aspects. Complete specifications with ADT are useful in software engineering, software reuse, and software proof domains. In classical ADT, operation semantics disregards execution environment hypothesis. They give a mathematical definition of result values in accordance with input values. For example, a pure mathematical vision of ADT cannot catch concurrency and distribution aspects of co-operative environments.

The specification must be independent of any computation technique. In an abstract type **Stack** that defines operations *push, pop* or *top* for members of *Element* type, we can find functional axioms like:

$$\forall e \in Element, \forall s \in Stack, top(push(s,e)) = e$$

A pure mathematical point of view of the ADT does not exclude assumptions specifying the environment of the defined type. If these assumptions are formally expressed they can condition the results. For example, one can define a type in a temporal context and make so that the operation results depend on past or on concurrent operations.

In this paper, we study a new definition of ADT called Co-operative Abstract Data Type (CADT) where assumptions on a co-operative environment are introduced. Indeed, the main differences come from the existence of groups that are the principal feature of the co-operative environment. We consider groups of servers that carry out the type, groups of clients that use the type, and groups of data handled by the type. We think that generally a classical ADT specification is insufficient to precisely define the semantics of co-operative operations. More details need to be precised with regards to the communication between the builders of a co-operative type and the users.

We consider two formalisms to express the co-operative assumptions: First, epistemic logic [3] [8] modelizes data distributed over group members. A knowledge approach is also particularly useful when exists a significant indeterminism on the data used in the environment of the different participants. In the concerned sets of information (client, server, and data), knowledge modalities describe knowledge levels. Second, temporal logic [1] [7] [2] specifies the operation result in a concurrency context.

Environment hypothesis introduction takes place in approaches such as *aspect programming* or *open implementation* [6]. In this way other environment features could be introduced as security, performance, or fault-tolerance domains. The security assumptions can be expressed by deontic logic. Performance can be defined by determined or stochastic timing assumptions. Finally, fault-tolerance assumptions can be expressed by quantitative hypothesis with random variables and processes.

As far we know, other works deal with concurrent object typing [11] based on π-calcul developed by Milner [9] to describe concurrency. They develop a system of deductive rules to define conditions that must be satisfied by the language in a particular environment. They only focus their approach on concurrency aspects.

The major benefits of CADT are to provide a way to specify concurrency and distribution aspects, and to complete a more global process of specification methodology [10] composed of distributed behavior patterns and an associated specification language.

The outline of the paper follows. Section 2 presents the general concepts of CADT. Section 3 describes the various aspects of CADT by a co-operative stack example used in the framework of virtual circuit establishment protocol [4]. We define the semantics of one operation with temporal and epistemic logics. Finally, we conclude and present some future works.

2 CADT general concepts

2.1 Groups associated with co-operative types

The principal feature of a co-operative environment is to introduce groups that exchange information to provide a service. A group is a set of members that cooperate to define a service. In CADT definition, three main groups are defined. We distinguish the group of clients, the group of servers and the group of data.

- **Group of servers**: CADT must define the precise specification of the semantics carried out by a set of operations whatever the way these operations are implemented either in a centralized way, or in a co-operative one. The most general case is a co-operative realization of a CADT by a group of servers. The main problem of CADT definition is to specify the temporal and epistemic constraints of the group of servers that carries out the type.
- **Group of clients**: They are the group of values of co-operative types allowed to emit requests to the specified CADT.
- **Group of data**: A co-operative type is designed to handle data. For the typing point of view, the data are input or output parameters of co-operative operations.

2.2 Notations of CADT specifications in temporal and epistemic logics

2.2.1 Temporal logic of action

Modalities of temporal logic

In this paper we use a linear time temporal logic. Let us recall in few words the meaning of the different temporal logic operators ($\mathcal{G}, \mathcal{F}, \mathcal{X}, \mathcal{U}$). The predicate $\mathcal{G}f$ expresses that the property f is always true. The predicate $\mathcal{F}f$ means that the property f is eventually true. The predicate $\mathcal{X}f$ means that f is true in the next state. The predicate $f\mathcal{U}g$ means that f is true until g becomes true. Classically $\forall f$ means that for all paths f is true and $\exists f$ that it exists a path in which f is true.

Logic of actions

We use TLA notations [7] to introduce the temporal evolution according to an operation execution. For a variable used in an operation (for example $f(x) : x := x + 1$) we denote x the value of the variable before the operation (at the logical moment i) and x' the value of the variable after the operation (at the logical moment $i + 1$) (for example $f(x) : x' := x + 1$).

Classical ADT definition considers a set of operations with values of different types as parameters and a value as result. In the example $f(s, e) : push(s, e)$, s is a stack, e an element and the function result f a stack. Considering active objects, operations semantics depend on actions processed in the past and/or in concurrency

Co-operative action notation

The notation $(s', e') = c.push(s, e)$ reflects the three main aspects associated with an action:

- the values of input s, e and output s', e' parameters: s and s' represent the successive values of the stack before and after the operation $push$. The pushed element e has also a result value because e has an additional knowledge denoted e' after the operation $push$.
- the value of the client type (the operation requester client) represented by a dotted notation $c.$.
- the nature of the operation itself characterizes one operation of a service, e.g. $push$. Like in TLA, an action predicate is associated with the operation ($push$). It becomes true at logical time when the corresponding action is enabled.

Finally the predicate $(s', e') = c.push(s, e)$ is true, if the action $push(s, e)$ is carried out at the logical time by the request of client c. Its result is the pair (s', e').

2.2.2 Epistemic logic

Modalities of epistemic logic

The epistemic logic allows to model group environment, knowledge levels and group behaviours. Halpern and al [3] argue that the right way to understand distributed computing is to consider how messages modify knowledge of sites. Knowledge is defined by a hierarchy of knowledge operators. Distributed knowledge is the weakest level. The highest level is the common knowledge. The exchange between processes increases the level of knowledge. In this paper, we only use two levels.

The distributed knowledge of ϕ is denoted $\mathcal{D}_G\phi$. No process of a group G knows ϕ, but the group can deduce ϕ from its current knowledge. A simple example is a process i that knows ψ and another process j can deduce ϕ from ψ. Another important operator is $\mathcal{S}_G\phi$. It means that somebody has the knowledge of a given fact ϕ for the groupe G.

Co-operative knowledge notation

In comparison with Halpern and al.'s work, we introduce the notion of knowledge level when an action is enabled. For example, for a type value s, Gs denotes the group of servers that realizes s. We use the following notations $\mathcal{D}^A_{Gs}$ where A is an action. $\mathcal{D}^A_{Gs}(\psi)$ means that ψ is a distributed knowledge for the group Gs when the action A is enabled. In fact we restrict the definition $\mathcal{D}^A_{Gs}(\psi)$ to ψ is true in all possible worlds in which A is enabled. In the same way $\mathcal{S}^B_{Ge}(\psi)$ (somebody knows) means that ψ is an instanciated knowledge (ψ is known by some member) in the group Ge when B is enabled.

To express the operation semantics by knowledge levels, we must define a set of basic predicates. For exemple $[top\_of(s, A) = e]$ is a predicate that defines the top of the stack s when the action A is enabled. This predicate is not to be mixed up with the action predicate $[e = c.top(s)]$ that is true when the action top is enabled. top belongs to the set of the type $Stack$ operations. top_of is used to express the knowledge levels of the different participants. It summarizes a temporal logic formula to express the top of the stack.

Finally, $\mathcal{D}^A_{Gs}(top\_of(s, A) = e)$ characterizes one of the semantics aspect of our stack. It means that the current value of the top of the stack s is the value e when A is enabled.

3 CADT stack example

The following example of a stack illustrates the various concepts that we introduce in the CADT definition. This example considers a unusual semantics with regards to the well known stack ADT. The operation semantics corresponds to co-operative behaviour needed for the virtual path opening algorithm in the ATM network scope[4].

This algorithm used in the PNNI (Private Network Node Interface) signaling protocol processes as following. When from a host request, a switch wants to open a new virtual path, it refers to its view of the global topology of the network and determines the optimal path. Nevertheless knowledge used at the beginning to compute the route can be obsolete when opening the path because of switch or link allocation policy or failures. Then the PNNI protocol suggests a method called *crankback*. To implement it, we manage a partial route of a graph (the graph of the network topology). We use a stack to store each new visited node to reach the addressee by pushing the node. This operation allows to know from which previous site we must back track when a route becomes intractable (with an operation *pop*).

First, we explain the different elements of the CADT stack. Second, we give some features of the CADT stack semantics. Then we only comment in details predicates of the operation $push$.

3.1 General description

3.1.1 Declaration of the type

The beginning of the description gives some general information about the CADT **Stack**. The specification is split in three main sections that define data, clients and servers. The structure of these sections is similar (Figure 1).

Line 1 gives the type name after the keyword **type**, i.e. Stack. With line 2, we declare parameter types used in the specification after the keyword **type parameter**. In this example, **Entity** represents any type. This definition is classical in ADT. We define here the

```
1:  type Stack;
2:      type parameter Entity
3:  data
4:      input type parameter Entity
5:      output type parameter Entity, Boolean
6:  client
7:      client type Entity
8:  server
9:      operations
10:         top : Stack → Entity
11:         pop : Stack → Stack * Entity
12:         push : Stack*Entity → Stack * Entity
13:         isempty : Stack → Boolean
14:         new : → Stack
15:     server semantics
16:     knowledge
17:         before(A,B) : Boolean
18:         between(A,B,C) : Boolean
19:         [top_of(s,A)=e ]: Boolean
20:         [members(s,A) = Se ]: Boolean // Se is a set of entity
21:         empty_stack(s,A) : Boolean
22:         [builder(s,A) = e ]: Boolean
```

Figure 1: Header of CADT stack

data type that must be organized in the abstract structure (for example in a stack). In line 3, the paragraph **data** defines data constraints used by the abstract type. In the example, we mainly mention information about type declarations as in classical ADT. Lines 4 and 5 specify the data types for the input and output parameters of operations carried out by the stack operations. The line 6 describes the paragraph **client** that defines the global features of the co-operative environment of the client. With the line 7 the keyword **client type** mentions the list of group of objects that can be clients of this type.

3.1.2 Server group

The server group paragraph is described as follows in Figure 1. At line 8, the paragraph **server** defines the features of type semantics that we specify. **operations** paragraph specifies the signatures of the primitives that define the **Stack** CADT service. This stack interface is very usual. From the point of view of temporal logic, a predicate is associated to each action. This predicate has the same name than the operation. The predicate is true when the action is carried out at the current moment. In line 15, the paragraph **server semantics** defines the stack semantics. We split in two parts the semantis defintion. First, with lines 16-22, we define knowledge predicates. Second, from line 23 (Figure 3), we define co-operative axioms.

The different knowledge predicates used in the operation semantics definition are first defined according to this **Stack** type. This knowledge is used in the axiom specifications to define the level of knowledge of the different groups according to the specified co-operative data structure. The knowledge level exclusively focuses on predicates. We use logic expres-

$$\forall e \in Elements \wedge s \in Stack$$
$$A1 : top(push(s,e)) = e$$
$$A2 : pop(push(s,e)) = s$$
$$A3 : is\_empty(new)$$
$$A4 : \neg is\_empty(push)$$

Figure 2: Axioms of ADT stack

sion as $top\_of(s, A) = e$ to apply epistemic predicates as $\mathcal{D}^{A}_{Gs}(top\_of(s, A) = e)$.

Knowledge predicates summarize the execution history at a given moment. Consequences of past actions are considered through pre-conditions for operation executions. The operation semantics specifies transformations between pre- and post-conditions and between levels of knowledge.

With the lines 17-18, predicates correspond to order relations between actions. *before* defines the order between two actions and *between* the order between three actions. Line 19 defines the value of top of the stack s in any state when an action A is enabled. Line 20 gives a predicate that defines the set of pushed entities in a stack s when an action A is enabled. Line 21 defines a predicate that provides the information about the stack state that is empty or not. Line 22 defines the value of the stack builder entity.

3.2 Co-operative stack semantics

For a usual stack the algebraic abstract type is defined by the set of axioms defined in Figure 2. We wish that the semantics of our co-operative stack preserves this functional axiomatic but we also want to add properties related to the co-operative environment. Our logical specifications of the co-operation with epistemic and temporal logics must infer these preceding properties. We also wish that the semantics of our co-operative stack preserves this functional axiomatic but we also want to add properties related to the co-operative environment. Our logical specifications of the co-operation with epistemic and temporal logics must infer these preceding properties.

In a general way we use a classical approach with pre- and post-conditions to specify a CADT operation. Alternative styles based on functional equations system or on inductive definition can also be used.

3.3 Epistemic and temporal specifications of the operation *push*

This specification only defines the epistemic aspects of the operation *push*. Because we introduce the axioms $A1, A2$ and $A4$ in the definition of operations *pop*, *top* and *is_empty*, we must also give their specification to complete the specification *push*, but due to the lack of space, we only comment the operation *push* (Figure 3).

Two cases are defined in the specification: an empty stack and a partially full stack. The result is the same in both cases. A full stack that does not authorize an operation *push* is not defined.

3.3.1 Case of a partially full stack

$$\forall \mathcal{G}[(\mathcal{F}A \wedge (B = \mathcal{X}A)) \wedge (\mathcal{D}^{A}_{Gs}(top\_of(s, A) = c) \wedge \mathcal{D}^{A}_{Gs}(e \in Entity - members(s, A)))]$$

co-operative axioms
$A \widehat{=} (s', e') = c.push(s, e)$
$\forall \mathcal{G}((\mathcal{F}A \wedge (B = \mathcal{X}A))$
$\wedge((\mathcal{D}^A_{Gs}(top\_of(s, A) = c) \wedge \mathcal{D}^A_{Gs}(e \in Entity - members(s, A)))$
$\vee(\mathcal{D}^A_{Gs}(empty\_stack(s, A)) \wedge \mathcal{D}^A_{Gs}(newer(s, A) = e \wedge (c = e)))))$
$\Rightarrow \mathcal{D}^B_{Gs'}(top\_of(s', B) = e')$
$\wedge \mathcal{D}^B_{Ge'}(top\_of(s', B) = e') \wedge \mathcal{S}^B_{Gc}(top\_of(s', B) = e')$

Figure 3: Semantics of $push$

$$\Rightarrow \mathcal{D}^B_{Gs'}(top\_of(s', B) = e') \wedge \mathcal{D}^B_{Ge'}(top\_of(s', B) = e') \wedge \mathcal{S}^B_{Gc}(top\_of(s', B) = e')$$

An important co-operative aspect that we force in the type definition $Stack$ is that at a given moment, only the entity at the top of the stack can perform the operation $push$. $\mathcal{D}^A_{Gs}(top\_of(s, A) = c)$ expresses that the request for the operation $push$ called A comes from the client c that is at the top of the stack s. Moreover, only one entity that is not already member of the stack can be pushed as defined by the predicate $\mathcal{D}^A_{Gs}(e \in Entity - members(s, A))$.

Finally, we define the resulting knowledge that is the knowledge level before the next operation B that will be enabled. In this state, the server group (Gs) of the stack must know the new top as a distributed knowledge. Moreover, the pushed entity must know that itself (Gc) is the new top of the stack. It is the result forced by data specification defined by input paramaters and result parameters. Finally, the client group (Ge') also knows the new top of the stack.

3.3.2 Case of an empty stack

The constraint defined in the following specification corresponds to an empty stack. Only the builder of the stack has the right to push itself, i.e. its own value.

$$\forall \mathcal{G}[(\mathcal{F}A \wedge (B = \mathcal{X}A)) \wedge (\mathcal{D}^A_{Gs}(empty\_stack(s, A)) \wedge \mathcal{D}^A_{Gs}(newer(s, A) = e \wedge (c = e)))]$$

$$\Rightarrow \mathcal{D}^B_{Gs'}(top\_of(s', B) = e') \wedge \mathcal{D}^B_{Ge'}(top\_of(s', B) = e') \wedge \mathcal{S}^B_{Gc}(top\_of(s', B) = e')$$

In this formula, the pre-condition states that the stack is empty, the stack builder is e and the group of clients is reduced to the only possiblity $c = e$. The result is the same as previously.

The case of a full stack is not defined. Pratically for a finite memory environment, this last case forbids to push a new element. Moreover, in a co-operative stack, we consider that a full stack looses its meaning and the specification of the case is not significant.

4 Conclusion and future works

In the previous specification, we introduce co-operative environment constraints on the abstract types. Adding complementary assumptions defines some refinement in usual specifications. Because this approach associates functional semantics aspects and co-operative semantics aspects, these semantics are difficult to express and to modularize.

On the opposite, we have tried to systematize the concurrency and distributed aspects of the specification in a global approach of a co-operative type semantics. This need allows us to point out the differences between ADT and CADT. We essentially do it by the use of groups (clients, data and servers) and the introduction of epistemic and temporal predicates.

Because we did not find an ideal model, we have used a multi-formalism to represent a CADT. We have introduced temporal and epistemic logics to represent dynamic constraints in the behavior semantics. As all formal approaches, this one is long and fine even if the multi-formalism approach simplifies the work. Let us remark that both formalisms are modal logics used to specify analogous problems as communication protocols.

Some possible enhancements are possible. First, we haved underlined limits of current works about the joint using of the temporal and epistemic logics. This problem only started on [3]. Nevertheless it is defined in a general way, in particular without reference to a precise temporal logic. Thus a theorical work on the foundation of these joint used logics has to be done. Second, we have chosen the temporal logic of actions (TLA) [7] because we are in a universe of actions (operation execution on types). This logic is widely spread. Moreover, we have seen that this logic is convenient for our example. However, we only modelize sequential executions in the stack example. It is consistant with the design choice of TLA where only one action exists at a given moment. This assumption could become very restrictive with other more concurrent examples. Finally, we also must introduce more precisely the different notions according to the co-operative type, e.g. sub-type, inheritance. For example, we think that sub-typing in co-operative types should allow to give a more formal framework to define the refinement approach.

Acknowledgements

Thanks to Jean-Franois Peyre (CNAM, Laboratoire CEDRIC) and Denis Poitrenaud (University Paris 6, Laboratoire LIP6) for helpful discussions on temporal logic predicates.

References

[1] E. Audureau, P. Enjalbert, and L. F. D. Cerro. *Logique Temporelle : semantique et validation de programmes paralleles.* Masson, 1990.

[2] E. Emerson. *Temporal and Modal Logic.* Elsevier Science Publishers, 1990.

[3] R. Fagin, J. Halpern, Y. Moses, and M. Vardi. *Reasoning about knowledge.* MIT press, 1995.

[4] A. T. M. Forum. Private network-network interface, specification version 1.0, Mar. 1996.

[5] M. Gaudel. *Algebraic Specifications.* Chapter 22 in Software Engineer's Reference Book, John Mc Dermid, Butterworth, 1991.

[6] G. Kiczales, J. Lamping, C. V. Lopes, C. Maeda, A. Mendhekar, and G. Murphy. Open implementation design guidelinesg. In *ACM*, 1997.

[7] L. Lamport. The temporal logic of actions. *ACM Transactions on Programming Languages and Systems*, May 1994.

[8] J. Meyer and W. van der Hoek. *Epistemic Logic for AI and Computer Science.* Cambridge University Press, 1995.

[9] R. Milner, J. Parrow, and D. Walker. A calculus of mobile processes (part i and ii). *Information and Computation*, 100, 1992.

[10] L. Seinturier, L. Duchien, and G. Florin. A meta-object protocol for distributed oo applications. In *TOOLS-USA'97*, pages 306–317, Santa Barbara, Californie, July 1997. IEEE Computer Society.

[11] V. Vasconcelos. *A process-calculus approach to typed concurrent objects.* PhD thesis, Keio University, 1994.

Knowledge-Based Software Engineering
T. Hruška and M. Hashimoto (Eds.)
IOS Press, 2000

Visual Software Requirements Specification Based on Communication Model

Atsushi OHNISHI
Department of Computer Science, Ritsumeikan University, 525-8577, Japan
e-mail: ohnishi@cs.ritsumei.ac.jp

Abstract. A communication model and a computer assisted communication method are introduced. With this model incorrect communications between humans are explained and then a method to lead successful communications with computer is illustrated. This method improves qualities of communications and can be applied to co-operative works. On the basis of the communication method, we have been developing a co-operative visual software requirements definition method via network with a visual requirements language named VRDL. Our method will improve quality of software requirements specification (SRS).

1 Introduction

Progress in network technologies strongly promotes co-operative works via network. In a communication, a symbol is correctly transferred from a sender to a receiver if both the sender and the receiver know the meaning of the symbol and use the same expression of the symbol. However it is difficult to communicate (1) a symbol which the receiver does not know, (2) a symbol whose expressions are different between the sender and the receiver, and (3) a symbol whose expression has different meanings between the sender and the receiver. Successful communication even in such cases causes effective co-operative works.

First a communication model and incorrect communications are explained in this paper. Second a computer assisted communication method is introduced. This method enables to lead incorrect communications to successful communications. Next, a visual software requirements language and method are described. The author proposes a co-operative visual requirements definition method via network based on the communication method.

2 Communication Process

2.1 Basic Communication Model

Communication is a process that a sender expresses his concept and transfers it through some communication medium, and then a receiver reads the expression and interprets it. This process includes (1) *perception*, (2) *conceptualization*, (3) *identification with verbal symbols*, (4) *expression*, (5) *transmission*, (6) *audio-visualization*, (7) *decoding*, (8) *comprehension*, (9) *reaction* [4].

In communication, several symbols are used. Each symbol has its meaning. We introduce a set of symbol expressions and their meanings as follows.

$$E \ : \ a\ set\ of\ symbol\ expressions \tag{1}$$

$$M \ : \ a\ set\ of\ symbol\ meanings \tag{2}$$

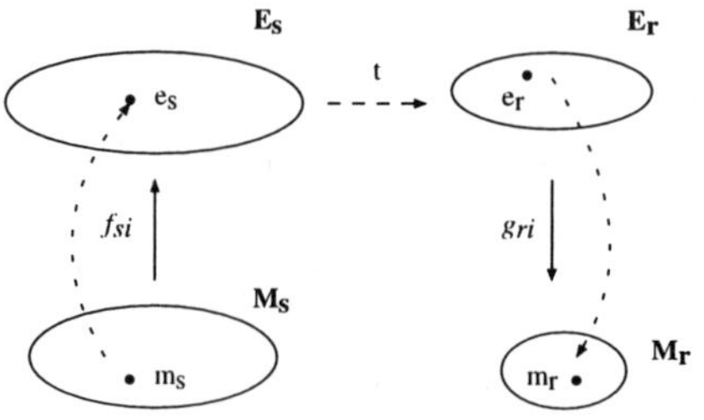

Figure 1: Simple Communication model

As for a sender, he has a set of symbol expressions: E_s and a set of symbol meanings: M_s where subscription *s* means "*sender.*" A receiver has E_r and M_r where *r* means "*receiver.*"

A function of conceptualization: f_s is defined as follows.

$$f_s \ : \ M_s \rightarrow E_s \tag{3}$$

f_s should be *total*, since every element in M_s has at least one its symbol expression in E_s. Generally a sender can use different symbol expressions each of which corresponds to the same meaning. It means the sender has a set of the f_s. We assume that under a certain *context* he selects one of the functions and that the function is *one to one.* We express this function as f_{si} where i means "*under a context* i." Since f_{si} is *total* and *one to one*, there exists an inverse function [6] as follows.

$$f_{si}^{-1} \ : \ Im(f_{si}(M_s)) \rightarrow M_s \tag{4}$$

A function of interpretation under the context i: g_{ri} and a function of transmission: t are introduces as follows.

$$g_{ri} \ : \ E_r \rightarrow M_r \tag{5}$$

$$t \ : \ E_s \rightarrow E_r \tag{6}$$

Fig.1 shows a communication process. e_s, e_r, m_s, m_r are elements of E_s, E_r, M_s, M_r respectively.

$$e_s = f_{si}(m_s) \tag{7}$$

$$e_r = t(e_s) \tag{8}$$

$$m_r = g_{ri}(e_r) \tag{9}$$

The formula labeled (7) shows that a sender expresses his concept m_s as e_s. e_s is passed to a receiver as e_r as shown in (8). The formula (9) shows that the receiver decodes the e_r and comprehends it as m_r.

The formula (7) corresponds to the processes of identification with verbal symbols and expression. The formula (8) corresponds to the process of transmission. The formula (9) corresponds to the processes of audio-visualization, decoding, and comprehension. We define a *correct communication* if and only if e_r is equal to e_s and m_r is equal to m_s. The author assumes that there are no errors in the transmission. It means that the transmission function t becomes the *identity* function and that e_r is always equal to e_s.

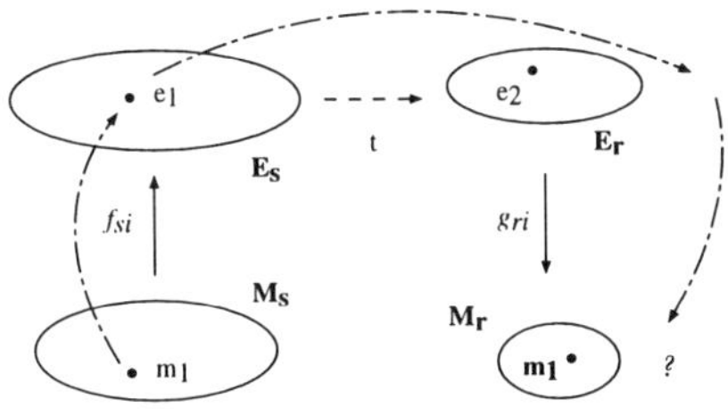

Figure 2: Incorrect communication

If

(1) E_r is equivalent to the E_s,

(2) M_r is equivalent to the M_s, and

(3) g_{ri} is equivalent to f_{si}^{-1},

then the receiver can decode the transmitted symbol expressions and can comprehend the sender's concept correctly. It is a quite simple and actually rare case of communication, because the above three conditions; (1), (2) and (3) seldom hold.

2.2 Incorrect Communications

Generally M_s is not equivalent to M_r and E_s is not equivalent to E_r. Sender's function of conceptualization, f_{si} becomes different from receiver's f_{ri} and sender's function of interpretation g_{si} is different from receiver's g_{ri}. These situations cause incorrect communications. We show three cases of incorrect communications.

(case 1) receiver has neither the symbol expression nor its meaning

(case 2) receiver has the symbol meaning but doesn't have the symbol expression

(case 3) receiver has the symbol expression but g_{ri} is not equivalent to f_{si}^{-1}

In case 1, sender has m_s, e_s, f_{si} such that $e_s = f_{si}(m_s)$, but $e_s \notin E_r$ and $m_s \notin M_r$.

In case 2, $m_s \in M_r$ but $e_s \notin E_r$. This situation leads to receiver's misunderstandings as shown in Fig.2. Formally, there exists $m_1 \in M_s$ such that $e_1 = f_{si}(m_1)$ and $e_1 \notin E_r$. In this case, if the sender adopts another function of conceptualization, f_{sj} such that

$$\mathrm{m}_1 = g_{rj}(\mathrm{e}_2), \quad \mathrm{e}_2 = f_{sj}(\mathrm{m}_1), \quad \mathrm{e}_2 \in E_r, \quad \mathrm{e}_2 \in E_s$$

communication will be correct as shown in Fig.3(left). In this figure, the sender expresses his concept m_1 as e_2 instead of e_1. e_2 is included in E_r and the following formulae hold.

$$\begin{aligned} e_2 &= f_{sj}(m_1) \\ m_1 &= g_{rj}(e_2) \end{aligned}$$

Even if e_1 is a more natural expression than e_2, we often use e_2 to correctly communicate with a computer. For example, we use formal specification languages and programming languages, although they are not natural. If e_2 is not in E_s, the sender must learn f_{sj} and e_2. In other words we may use restricted expressions or may learn formal languages. This is one of the reasons why it may be difficult to read/write/understand a software with a formal language.

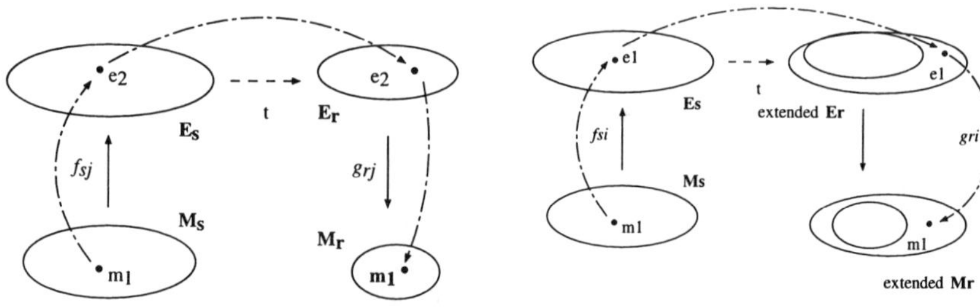

Figure 3: Correct communications

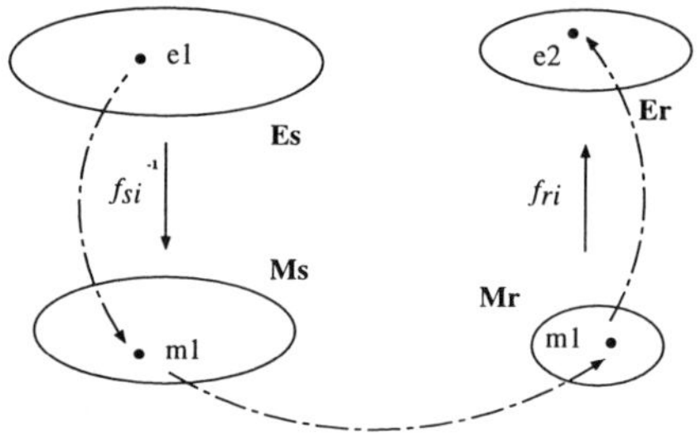

Figure 4: Another correct communication for case 2 & 3

3 Computer Assisted Communication

In the previous three cases, computer assistance enables correct communications. We assume that (1) communication between humans with a computer language, and that (2) computer grasps E_s, E_r, M_s, M_r, f_{si}, f_{ri}, f_{si}^{-1}, f_{ri}^{-1}, g_{si}, and g_{ri}.

In case 1, under the assumption (2) the computer knows that receiver does not have e_s and m_s. So, the computer shows $e_r (=e_s)$, $m_r (=m_s)$, and g_{ri}: $(m_r = g_{ri}(e_r))$ and makes the receiver acquire them. After the acquirement the receiver correctly gets the symbol expression and its meaning. This is illustrated in Fig.3(right).

In case 2, if the sender uses e_1 and if e_2 such that $e_2 = f_{ri}(f_{si}^{-1}(e_1))$ will be transferred to the receiver instead of e_1, the receiver correctly understands the symbol e_2 and its meaning m_1. This is illustrated in Fig.4.

This process explains a machine translation. For example, a Japanese sentence (sender's expression) is once transformed into a conceptual form (its meaning) and then transformed into a English sentence (receiver's understandable expression). In this solution the sender need not know receiver's E_r and M_r. This solution can be also applied to solve the case 3.

In Chapter 4, the author introduces a visual requirements language. One of the features of this language is that two or more users can share a visual SRS via network. Each developer may want to use different icons for a certain object. In such a case we provide a successful communication based on the Fig.4.

Table 1: Icons definition

Icon	semantics (label, type)		Icon	semantics (label, type)	
	customer	human		order DB	file
	secretary	human		order form	data
	clerk	human		liquor	data
	warehouse	function		fax	device
	liquor shop	function		track	device

4 Visual requirements definition method/environment

4.1 Visual requirements language: VRDL

We have been developing a visual requirements definition language named VRDL to specify flow requirements [7, 8]. The features of VRDL are

1. Requirements describer can define icons
2. He can specify data/control flow requirements with icons and arrows
3. Visual SRS can be executed by giving icons' movement descriptions
4. Via network multiple describers share a visual SRS

4.2 Icon definition

Several visual requirements languages have been developed. Most of them are based on the DFD (Data Flow Diagram) [3]. These languages provide icons whose syntax and semantics are predefined. A describer cannot use other icons such as flow chart symbols instead. If he uses icons that faithfully reflect his original image, he can write down requirements more easily.

VRDL user can define both the shape and semantics of icons. This feature enables the user to easily write his original image as a visual SRS. Table 1 shows examples of icon definition.

A describer can define the shape of icons as color pixmap data with existing tools, such as a "pixmap" editor. He can also define an icon of image data (GIF format). After the definition of the shape of icons (syntax), the describer defines their types and labels as the semantics of the icons and stored them in an icon dictionary. Each describer can have his own icon dictionary. A shared standard icon dictionary is also provided to eliminate to define all the icons separately.

The shape of icon corresponds to symbol expression and the semantics of icon corresponds to symbol meaning. With the icon dictionaries computer can grasp a VRDL user's E, M, f and g. If a symbol meaning (label and type) of a describer's icon is same as a symbol meaning of another describer's icon, computer judges that these symbols are same.

4.3 Writing a visual SRS

The describer places the icons on a sheet provided by the VRDL editor. First he selects an icon of human or function types listed in the palette of icons window as the source case object by pointing the selected icon with a mouse. Then he specifies the location of the icon with the mouse. Then he specifies the goal case object in a similar way. Next he selects the arrow command, one of the pop-up menu commands, by pointing the EDIT button in the upper side

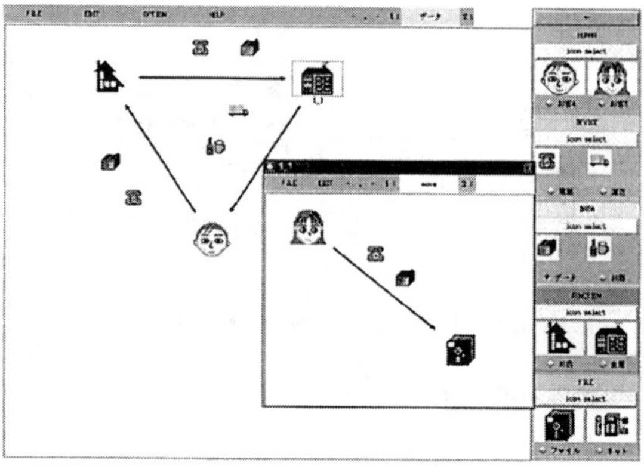

Figure 5: VRDL example

of the window and sets the starting point and the ending point of the arrow. Then he specifies a device type icon and a data type icon.

Fig.5 shows a data flow requirements of an inventory control system of liquor stock. The upside data flow sentence means *"A liquor shop sends an order form to a warehouse via fax,"* if icons in the sentence are defined as shown in Table 1.

In order to define a complicated requirements, an SRS can be written structurally just like DFD. In this figure, the icon "warehouse" is detailed into another window labeled 1_1 to specify data flow requirements in the warehouse.

VRDL supports both data flow and control flow, since flow requirements are easily and naturally visualized. We assume that requirements about the other concepts including data structures, functional structures, and file manipulations are written with the text-base requirements language.

4.4 Co-operative visual requirements definition

For a large software requirements definition, several developers needs to make an SRS. We provide a co-operative SRS definition method. Under a TCP/IP network environment, different users can share a visual SRS. The features are as follows.

- a visual SRS can be shared by two or more users
- A user's editing SRS will reflect others' SRSs
- Each SRS is transformed with a user's icon dictionary

Visual requirements may be defined by several developers. The first and the second features enable to co-operative requirements definition. Each developer adopts different icons for a certain object. For example, one developer uses  as a reception clerk. Another developer uses  as a reception clerk. In such a case, the third feature enables that each user can see an SRS with his own icons. In other words, when an *describer A*'s icon which represents an object is different from *describer B*'s icon which represents the same object, a visual SRS with *A*'s icon can be transformed into a visual SRS with *B*'s icon.

This mechanism is illustrated in Fig.6. The icon in describer A's SRS will be transformed into its meaning with A's icon dictionary, then expressed as the shape of B's icon with B's icon dictionary. Describer A need not know what icons other describers use. The Fig.6 reflects the Fig.4. In this way, the synonym problem (different icons and same meanings) can

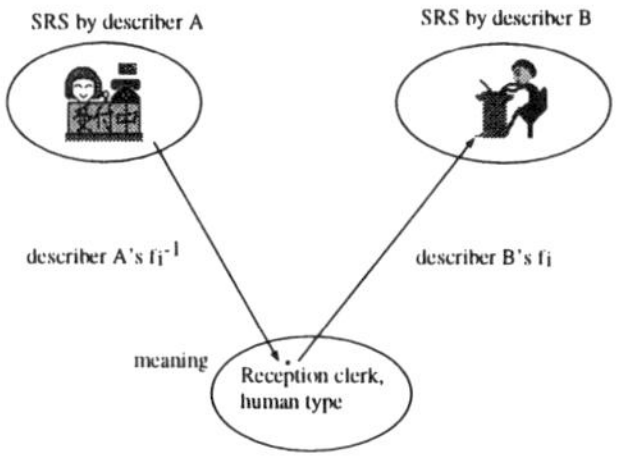

Figure 6: Icon transformation

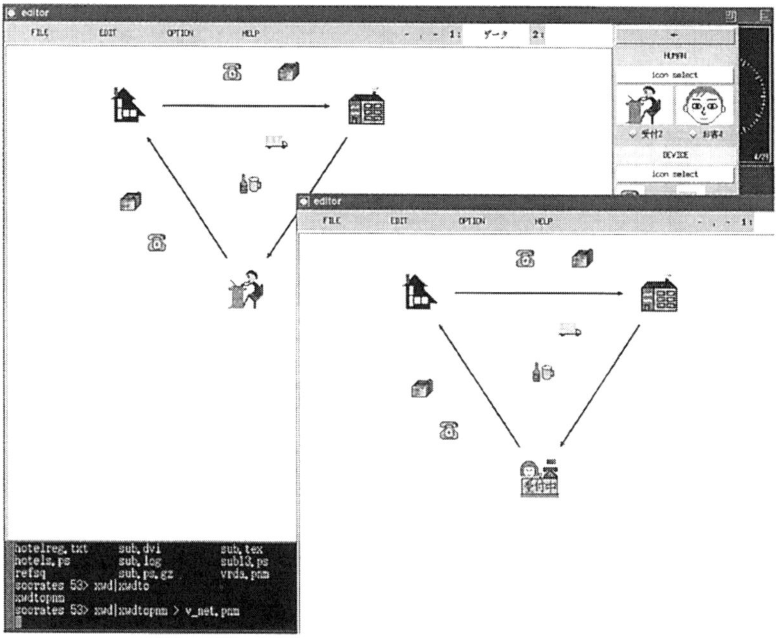

Figure 7: Shared SRS via network.

be solved. As for the homonym problem (same icons and the meaning of A's icon is different from the meaning of B's icon), under the assumption that each developer has standard icons for some objects in SRS and his own icons and their meanings for the other objects in SRSs, it can be solved.

We have been developing a visual SRS server/client program. The server first checks the difference between server's icon dictionary and each client's icon dictionaries, and then sends different part of icon's definition and an SRS internal code to clients. So each user can see visual SRSs with his own defining icons in a local icon dictionary and with standard icons of the server icon dictionary. In Fig.7 an icon corresponding to reception clerk in a SRS is different from the icon in the other SRS as discussed in the previous subsection. If one of the VRDA users changes the SRS, the modified codes will be sent to other users via communication server. Every client and the communication server has their own icon dictionaries, icon files and a visual SRS which is shared by the server and the clients.

5 Discussion

Several researches have been addressed communication and collaboration in requirements definition. [5] provides a representation of a Universe of Discourse based on speech act theory and models a communication as sequences of events with discourses. [9] gives a technique to structure utterance records of the meeting for requirements elicitation based on speech act theory. [10] gives a method to support collaboration in requirements analysis with hypermedia.

We divided a communication into several processes, such as identification with verbal symbols and expression, transmission, audio-visualization, decoding, and comprehension. Our communication model well describes these processes, however communication model in [5] do not explain them.

We also proposed an SRS definition method based on the communication model. If a computer grasps both sender's and receiver's symbols, symbols meaning, and functions between symbols and symbols meaning, it can assist correct communications between sender and receiver. When multiple developers co-operatively define software requirements, correct communications are indispensable. Our method guarantees correct communications among the developers.

6 Conclusion

In this paper, we proposed a communication model and describe an SRS definition method based on the model. If a computer grasps both sender's and receiver's symbols, symbols meaning, and functions between symbols and symbols meaning, it can assist correct communications between sender and receiver. We described a visual requirements method on the basis of the above method.

We have been applying our method to specify several small problems, such as library system, stock management system, program chairman's assistance, and so on. The evaluation of our visual requirements definition method/environment is left as a future work.

References

[1] Davis, A.M.: *Software Requirements, Objects, Functions, & States,* Prentice-Hall, Inc., NJ, 1993.

[2] Eco, U: A Theory of Semiotics, Indian Univ. Press, 1976.

[3] Fisher, A.S.: *CASE Using Software Development Tools*, John Wiley Inc., 1988.

[4] Hirai, M.: "Encyclopedia of words (in Japanese)," San-sei-do Co., 1982.

[5] Johannesson P.: "Representation and Communication - A Speech Act Based Approach to Information Systems Design," *Information Systems,* Vol.20, No.4, pp.291-303, 1995.

[6] Lew, A.: "Computer Science: A Mathematical Introduction," Prentice-Hall, 1985(pp.65).

[7] Ohnishi, A.: "A Visual Software Requirements Definition Method," *Proc. IEEE ICRE'94*, 1994, pp.194-201.

[8] Ohnishi, A.: "VRDL: A Visual Software Requirements Language," Trans. of the *Society for Design and Process Science,* Vol.3, No.3, pp.43-52 (1999).

[9] Saeki M., Matsumura K., Shimoda J., Kaiya H.: "Structuring Utterance Records of Requirements Elicitation Meeting Based on Speech Act Theory," *Proc. IEEE ICRE'96*, 1996, pp.21-30.

[10] Takahashi, K.,Potts, C., Kumar V., Ota K., Smith J.D.: "Hypermedia Support for Collaboration in Requirements Analysis," *Proc. IEEE ICRE'96*, 1996, pp.31-40.

[11] Thayer, R., Dorfman, M.: *System and Software Requirements Engineering*, IEEE Computer Society Press Tutorial, 1990.

Knowledge-Based Software Engineering
T. Hruška and M. Hashimoto (Eds.)
IOS Press, 2000

A Software Package for Rapid Prototyping of Repetitive Distributed Control

Jarosław STAŃCZYK, Zbigniew A. BANASZAK
Technical University of Zielona Góra, ul. Podgórna 50, 65-246 Zielona Góra, Poland

Abstract. This paper addresses the problem of designing the steady-state behavior of a system composed of a set of repetitive processes competing for access to shared resources. Its objective is to provide a tool allowing to prototype a robust distributed control policy as a function of the characteristics of the component processes and dispatching rules involved. The proposed logistics-oriented methodology integrates production routes design, buffers capacity assignment, and allocation of the dispatching rules that control the work-flow as well as allows one to evaluate system's behavior including its steady state and transient state.

1 Introduction

The integration of resource allocation over time (production planning) and inventory/transportation policy making (logistic planning) is receiving increasing attention. The aim is to develop a scheduling strategy that can simultaneously reduce an impact of both logistic and manufacturing costs, while maintaining high levels of customer service. So, the question is how to achieve a well-synchronized behaviour of the dynamically interacting components, where the right quantity of the right material is provided in the right place, and at the right time. In order to meet this objective many different assumptions regarding, for instance, the capacity of available AGVs and/or local buffers, allocation of working cells and warehouses, production routings and guidepaths, etc. have to be taken into account [2].

The optimal solution (if any) can be obtained, however, for a special combination of those constraints. Therefore, the solution can be obtained either through searching of a space of all possible variants (each variant has to be examined either it is feasible one or not) or through a synthesis of an admissible, e.g., guaranteeing the presumed qualitative and quantitative system behaviour.

Some conditions for designing the control procedures that allow achieving the required performance of the system composed of a set of repetitive processes competing for access to common resources, while preserving some of its qualitative constraints have been already presented [4]. A dispatching strategy that results from a set of dispatching rules allocated to the common resources (it is assumed that each dispatching rule specifies an order the competing process can access a shared resource) is possessing a self-synchronized property, i.e. encompasses a work-flow robust control. Such a self-synchronized system is capable of returning to a unique steady state from any state it was forced into as a result of an accidental disturbance, i.e., each time a disturbance (e.g., caused by operation time change, and delivery time delay) disappear a system results in the same, nominal, cyclic steady state behaviour. Application of such design method [2], [4] supporting evaluation of system time behaviour is limited, however, to an algebraic structure (i.e. determining a coupling operation) which in turn depends on dispatching policy actually employed. In order to overcome this disadvantage an event driven simulator implemented in Java language has been developed [5].

This paper summarizes our previous work [3], [4] and presents a modeling framework that provides a logistics-oriented methodology for rapid prototyping of a robust control policy. The methodology proposed integrate production routes design, buffers capacity assignment, and allocation of the dispatching rules that control the work-flow as well as allows one to evaluate system's behavior including its steady state and transient state.

2 Software Package

The idea was to combine the modern and attractive capabilities of Java language for platform-independent and distributed work-flow control with an analytical approach to synthesis of distributed discrete dynamic systems that incorporate concurrently interacting repetitive processes [1], [4]. Thus, both Java and algebraic structure supporting evaluation of system time behaviour would complement each other, compensating each others disadvantages: a Java based software would incorporate mathematically proven formulas and algebraic structure based designing method would increase its flexibility. Properly compound they would act as a mean for rapid prototyping of a distributed control policy. Consequently, similar complement would not only allow to proof-test the work-flows control policy, but also would present an inexpensive mean for investigation, illustration and even advertisement of cyclic scheduling strategies.

The main objective of this work is to demonstrate ability of the software package for discovering the relationship existing between the behaviour of a system composed of a set of cyclic processes and the structural as well as functional parameters of its components. In this context, the problem is to find, for a given class of systems, the conditions that will guarantee the required quality of concurrently executed work-flows.

3 Implementation

Consider the Distributed Control Rapid Prototyping System (CRP for short) which is decision support tool [5] aimed at modelling and performance evaluation of concurrently interacting processes. Its design enables one to specify (including operation times, capacity constraints and dispatching rules), and then to simulate repetitive processes interacting via a set of shared resources.

In order to illustrate its application, let us examine a repetitive processes system. As shown in Fig 1a, the system consists of the three resources and three processes. Access to resources is realised in mutual exclusion mode. To ensure proper system's functionality (cyclic realisation), at least one resource has to have capacity equal two.

In graphic specification of system from Fig. 1a (see Fig. 1b) the following notation is used: instead of arrows the small dots are used (so in the case of the process P_1 instead of the circle composed of two arcs the edge, ended both sides with dotes, is used. The arcs occurring in Fig. 1a are labelled in CRP specification (see Fig. 1b).

Let $DR_i = (P_{i1}, P_{i2}, ..., P_{in})$ denotes the dispatching rule determining the order the process $P_{i1}, P_{i2}, ..., P_{in}$ can access to the the i-th resource. It assures that after the n-th access (i.e., of the P_{in} process) the next one is P_{i1}, and then P_{i2}, and so on. Assuming the following dispatching rules: $DR_2 = (P_1, P_1, P_2)$, $DR_3 = (P_2, P_3)$, $DR_1 = (P_3|\{P_1, P_3\}, P_1)$, and the following initial processes allocation: the process P_1 is allocated to the resource R_2, the process P_2 to R_3, and P_3 to R_1.

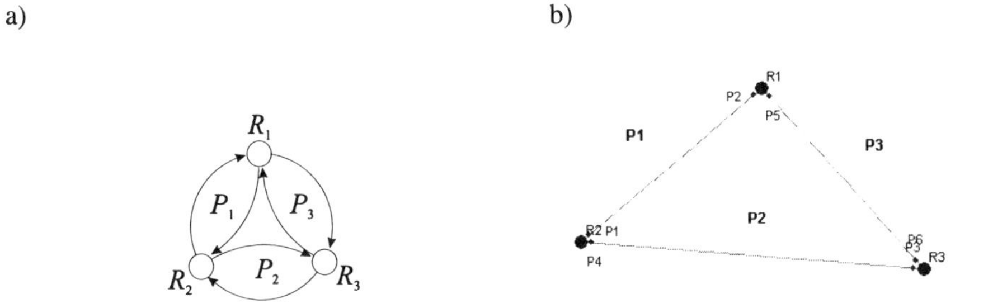

Figure 1: Graphic representation of repetitive processes system (a) and their representation in CRP (b).

The task at hand is to determine the shortest cycle time T and the performance index η of the system considered determined by the following formula:

$$\eta = \frac{nT - \sum_{i=1}^{n} t_{is}}{nT} \tag{1}$$

where: n is the number of all the component processes, T is the cycle time of the system, and t_{is} is the time of the i-th process is suspended.

Besides of quantitative features, the qualitative ones can be evaluated (see Fig. 2).

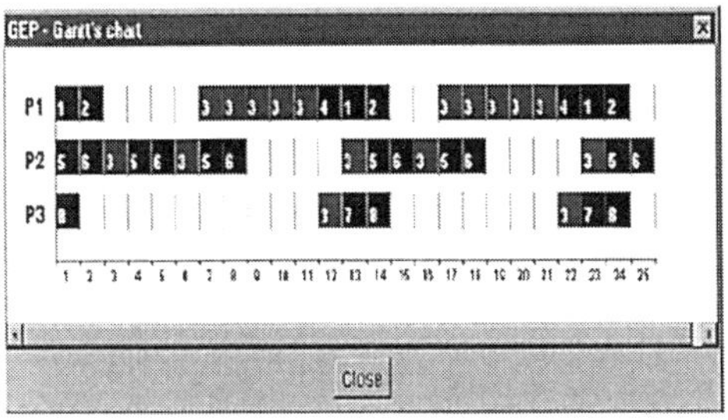

Figure 2: Exemplary Gantt's chart.

3.1 Computer experiment

Let the operation times for the processes considered are as follows: for the process P_1: $t_{R_1} = 1$, $t_{R_2} = 1$, and for P_2: $t_{R_2} = 1$, $t_{R_3} = 2$, and for P_3: $t_{R_1} = 3$, $t_{R_3} = 1$.

Example 1. The three possible additional capacity allocations are considered, assuming that the given dispatching rules and initial state are constant. The initial allocation of processes: the process P_1 is allocated to the resource R_2, the process P_2 to R_3, and P_3 to R_1. The dispatching rules allocated to resources are: $DR_1 = (P_3|\{P_1, P_3\}, P_1)$, $DR_2 = (P_1|\{P_1, P_2\}, P_1|\{P_1, P_2\}, P_2|\{P_1, P_2\}|P_1)$, $DR_3 = (P_2, P_3)$. In variant I resources capacity are: $R_1 - 2$, $R_2 - 1$, and $R_3 - 1$. In variant II additional capacity is allocated on resource R_2, it means, that capacity R_1 is 1, capacity R_2 is 2, and capacity R_3 is 1. In variant III additional capacity is allocated on resource R_3: that is, capacity R_1 is 1, capacity R_2 is 1, and capacity R_3 is 2.

Table 1: Variants of the additional capacity allocations.

Additional capacity on	R_1	R_2	R_3
Variant	I	II	III
T	4	4	6
η	0.917	0.75	0.75

Example 2. An exemplary application of various distributed control procedures represented by the local dispatching rules. In particular cases, the following initial state and capacity allocation are assumed. Initial state: the process P_1 is allocated to the resource R_2, P_2 to R_3, and P_3 to R_1. Capacity for R_1 is 2, for R_2 and R_3 is 1.

Table 2: Variants of the dispatching rules allocation.

Dispatching rules	T	η
$DR_1 = (P_3 \| \{P_1, P_3\}, P_1)$, $DR_2 = (P_1, P_1, P_2)$, $DR_3 = (P_2, P_3)$	4	0.917
$DR_1 = (P_3 \| \{P_1, P_3\})$, $DR_2 = (P_1, P_2, P_2)$, $DR_3 = (P_2, P_3)$	8	0.667
$DR_1 = (P_3, P_1, P_1)$, $DR_2 = (P_1, P_2, P_2)$, $DR_3 = (P_2, P_3)$	1	deadlock

The examples presented show that for a given topology of processes it is possible to determine a pair: an initial state (processes allocation) and a set of dispatching rules that guarantee deadlock-free and starvation-free processes execution. A still open problem is how to determine a relevant pair guaranteeing systems optimality, e.g., in the sense of h performance index. Another remaining problem is how to refine operators that could support an algebraic approach to a system synthesis from a given set of presumed components (processes).

4 Conclusion

This paper presents a new approach to the problem of designing of a steady-state behaviour of a system composed of a set of repetitive processes that share a set of reusable resources.

The approach presented is relevant to and can be of significant interest for evaluation and synthesis of a variety of distributed discrete dynamic systems that incorporate concurrently interacting repetitive processes, and whose evaluation in time depends on complex interactions of various parameters and constraints. Besides of the manufacturing systems the computer/communication networks are the most representatives ones.

References

[1] F.G. Baccelli, et al., *Synchronization and Linearity, An Algebra for Discrete Event Systems*, John Wiley & Sons, Chichester, 1992.

[2] Z.A. Banaszak, et al., Logistics Approach to Repetitive Workflows Modelling. In: J. Jedrzejewski (ed.), Innovative and Integrated Manufacturing, Wroclaw University of Technology, 1999, pp. 45–51.

[3] S. Kłos, B. Skołud and J. Stańczyk, Computer Aided Scheduling of Repetitive Production. In: P. Navrat and H. Ueno (ed.), Knowledge-Based Software Engineering, IOS Press, Amsterdam, 1998, pp. 317–320.

[4] M.B. Zaremba, K.J. Jedrzejek and Z.A. Banaszak, Design of Steady-State Behaviour of Concurrent Repetitive Processes: An Algebraic Approach. *IEEE Trans. on Systems, Man, and Cybernetics*, Vol. 28, **2**, 1998, pp. 199–212.

[5] The WWW presentation of the Distributed Control Rapid Prototyping System, URL `http://www.iiz.pz.zgora.pl/ppt/iiz/crp/`, 1999.

Knowledge-Based Software Engineering
T. Hruška and M. Hashimoto (Eds.)
IOS Press, 2000

Structure Clash Detection Method in Architectural CAD System Generation

Efendy LUKMAN, Masaaki HASHIMOTO, Toyohiko HIROTA
Faculty of Computer Science and Systems Engineering
Kyushu Institute of Technology
Kawazu 680-4, Iizuka 820-0067 Japan
e-mail: lukman@minnie.ai.kyutech.ac.jp
hasimoto,hirota@ai.kyutech.ac.jp

Abstract. As indicated by Jackson, in order to create an automatic design for an efficient program structure which uses data flow for its computations, we should detect and solve the problem of the clash of input-output data structures. This paper proposes a general framework to characterize the problem of structure clash. This framework employs a method using relational inference to detect and solve an ordering clash as one of the struture clash. At the same time the solution designs a basic structure of generated procedural program. Moreover, the paper describes an application of this method for CAD system generation, directed particularly at solving the problem of recursive program and the hierarchical input and output data in the domain of architecture.

1 Introduction

The improvement of software productivity and reliability is one of the main concerns in software engineering. In order to develop reuse technology for program specifications as one of measures considered[1], we have already defined *domain-specific* BDL (Building Design Language) for architecture experts to describe modelers of architectural structure in CAD systems by themselves[2]. Moreover, we have proposed *a CAD system generation method* and its prototype implementation[3]. The method transforms the model into a specifications of domain-free specification language (DFSL) based on the ER (Entity-Relationship) model which can describe specification free from domain knowledge to avoid the necessity of creating various CAD system generators for differing domain-specific languages. However, the generated prototype stores all data not on disk file but on memory. When the amount of data becomes large, the data should be stored in an object-oriented database and *data flow* should be adopted for the program computations.

To automatically design an efficient program structure which adopts data flow for its computations, we should detect and solve the *structure clash* [6][7], especially the *ordering clash* of unsorted input and output data[8]. This paper describes a general framework for a method of detecting and solving the ordering clash using the concept of relation. The data flow is expressed in a directed graph which is analyzed to reveal the ordering clash. The solution for detected clashes is achieved by providing lists for storing data in order to wait for the other data to be computed synchronously, while variables are provided for non-clash data. A program structure design is then generated based on this clash-free directed graph.

Moreover, this paper describes an application of this method for generating an architectural CAD system, explains the characteristic of the domain problem, and solves the recursive

```
INFORMATION
E beam
  A number K NUM
  A weight NUM
R plugSocket
  C .column
  C .beam
 E column
  A number K NUM
  A weight NUM
  A load NUM = weight + (beam..weight * 1/2)
DATA
I beamData
    IX beamId
    G beamRecord ON EndOfFile(beamData)
  O beamRecord = beam
    %8d beamNumber = beam.number
    %8d beamWeight = beam.weight
I columnData
    IX columnId
    G columnRecord ON EndOfFile(columnData)
  O columnRecord
      = plugSocket..beam
      = plugSocket..column
    %8d beamNumber = beam.number
    %8d columnNumber = column.number
    %8d columnWeight = column.weight
    %8d columnWeight = column.weight
ACCESS
D beamFile INPUT 16 beamData
D columnFile INPUT 24 columnData
```

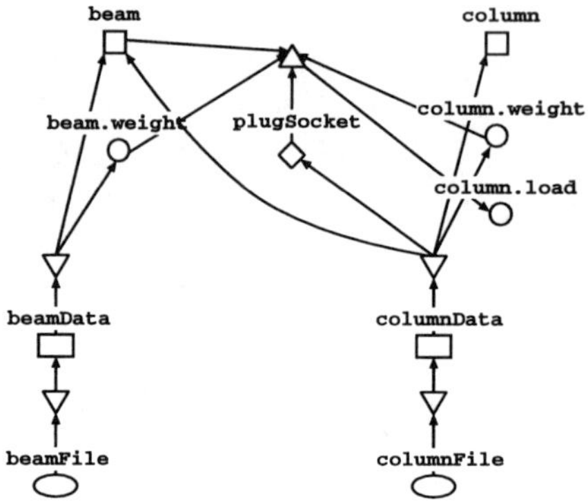

Figure 1: Example of program specification and directed graph containing the ordering clash

program and the hierarchical input and output data problem on this domain. Section 2 describes our research background. Section 3 defines general framework for the structure clash detection method. Section 4 explains the method's application to architectural CAD system generation. Section 5 concludes our work.

2 Research Background

The aim of our research is to develop a methodology for system generation using domain knowledge which is applied to the generation of an integrated CAD system based on the object model in the domain of architecture.

2.1 System Generation

Program specification sescription language (PSDL) as a domain-free specification language is defined using the ER model as its conceptual model. program specifications of PSDL is then transformed into a procedural program such as C++[5]. Moreover, when a programmer of a procedural language describes a program containing the ordering clash, the programmer must detect and solve it by coding the program using lists in order to wait for the arrival of the other data to be processed synchronously.

However, structure clash is a program implementation rather than a program specification issue. Furthermore, it must be accurately detected and solved in order to produce an efficient program. Therefore, we should develop an important non-procedural language class in which a programmer need not be concerned about the issue of structure clash, and which would allow a compiler to accurately detect and solve it.

2.2 Structure Clash

Since the PSDL uses data flow for its computations, by assuming the input data is unsorted, the ordering clash as one of the structure clash will occur. An example of a program specification and its directed graph containing the ordering clash are shown in Figure 1. The directed graph expresses program execution in which an arc and a triangle express data flow and computation constraint, respectively. A square, a circle, a diamond, and a rectangular express data storage, while an oval indicates data access.

The above simple program specifications contains beam and column input files. Beam records include a beam number and weight. Column records contain a column number and weight, and a beam number to which the column is connected. After inputting these records, the program computes a column load by adding the column weight and half of the beam weight.

To compute each column load, both the beam and column weight in the beam record and column record which contain the same beam number must be referred to. However, since the beam and column records are unsorted their records which contain the same beam number cannot be synchronously entered. In other words, a beam record which is now flowing has not determined the correct partner of a column record which is also flowing. Thus, an example of ordering clash is detected in this program.

3 General Framework for Structure Clash Detection Method

We first describe a general framework for the ordering clash detection method and then apply the framework to our specific domain. The general framework is meant to provide an insight on how the approach might be applied to other related problem domains[10].

3.1 Principal Idea of General Framework

The ER model adopted by the PSDL is based on mathematical set and relationship concepts[4]. Moreover, the data flow presents arcs in the directed graph which are obtained from the PSDL. We define a synchronousness concept based on the *relation* concept in order to detect the ordering clash. We can classify relation between data which flow in adjacent arcs into well-ordered relation and ill-ordered relation. Furthermore, inference regarding the relation can also be determined in order to obtain synchronicity in certain areas of the directed graph. The directed graph and the definition of synchronicity used in its analysis are described in the next subsection.

In this paper, the method for detecting structure clash is described under the following restrictions:

1. The input and output files are all sequentially accessed, and the input records are assumed to be unsorted.
2. Each of the files contains only one file record data type. The I statements are restricted to the record iteration.
3. Each record represents, at most, one entity and one relationship in the same type.

3.2 Problem Formulation

(1) Directed graph

A directed graph G obtained from a program specification, consists of vertex set V and arc set A[9]. The set V is divided into a set of structure vertices V_s and constraint vertices

V_c. Moreover, V_s is divided into a set of entity type vertex $V_{\mathcal{E}}$, non-primary key attribute vertex $V_{\mathcal{A}}$, relationship type vertex $V_{\mathcal{R}}$, data type vertex $V_{\mathcal{D}}$, and dataset type vertex $V_{\mathcal{S}}$. V_c is divided into a set of attribute value dependency constraint vertex V_{AD}, relationship existence dependency constraint vertex V_{RD}, entity existence dependency constraint vertex V_{ED}, Information and Data layers association constraint vertex V_{ID}, and Data and Access layers association constraint vertex V_{DA}. Vertices, structure vertices and constraint vertices are expressed by v_i, v_{s_j} and v_{c_k}, $(1 \leq i, j, k \leq |V|, |V| = |V_s| + |V_c|)$, respectively.

Arc a_{ij} stretches between two vertices v_i to v_j. The arc direction flows out from vertex v_i, if its data are referred to. Or it flows into the vertex if the data goes to the vertex. Structure vertices are assumed to hold data due to be referred to, while constraint vertices are assumed to calculate dependency constraints.

(2) Data flow Synchronousness

Formalization assumes that a generated program processes data in the following way: Consider an arc. One of the end points of the arc is structure vertex v_s, while another end point is constraint vertex v_c. A type of data corresponds to the structure vertex. Data of that type flows in sequence along the arc such as denoted in Figure 2. After one of the data which has flowed on the arc is stored to the end structure vertex, or consumed by calculation of the another end constraint vertex, the next data can flow on the arc. Thus, data of the same type is processed by the same method one by one.

A totally-ordered set S_{ij} is data elements o_{ijm}, $(m = 1, 2, ..., n)$, each of which sequentially flows on arc a_{ij}. In a program, there can be a collation process between data which is expressed as arcs which flow from several arcs into the same structure vertex. Furthermore, the same data can be referred to several times. For these reasons, the order of data in each totally-ordered set is different from one another. This difference causes the ordering clash. Therefore, it is important to define a relations R_{ijk} between two totally-ordered sets S_{ij} and S_{jk}, which connects the elements of S_{ij} and S_{jk}. If the relations satisfies the following condition, it is called *well-ordered relation*; if not, it is called *ill-ordered relation*:

$$\forall m, m', l, l' (o_{ijm} R_{ijk} o_{jkl} \wedge o_{ijm'} R_{ijk} o_{jkl'} \Longrightarrow \\ ((o_{ijm} \neq o_{ijm'} \Rightarrow o_{jkl} \neq o_{jkl'}) \wedge (m < m' \Rightarrow l < l'))).$$

Notice that $o_{ijm} \in S_{ij}$, $o_{jkm'} \in S_{jk}$, $i \neq j \neq k$, and m, m', l, $l' \neq 0$. Intrinsically, we assume that computations performed in a constraint vertex have no side-effects. Thus, the relations between data sets flowing into and out of it must be well-ordered.

3.3 Basic Detection

The previous section indicated that detecting the ordering clash is synonymous with determining ill-ordered relation. Based on the part of the analyzed directed graph, ordering clash detection can be classified into local and global clash detection.

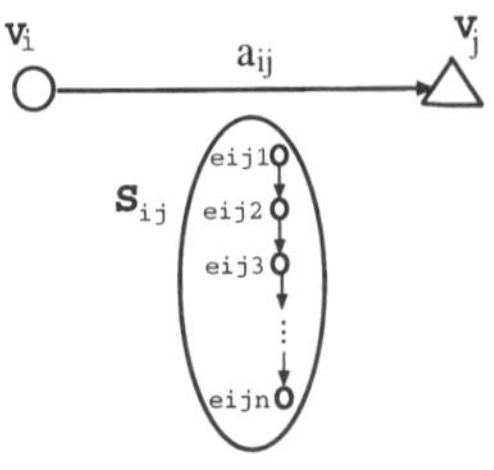

Figure 2: Totally-ordered set.

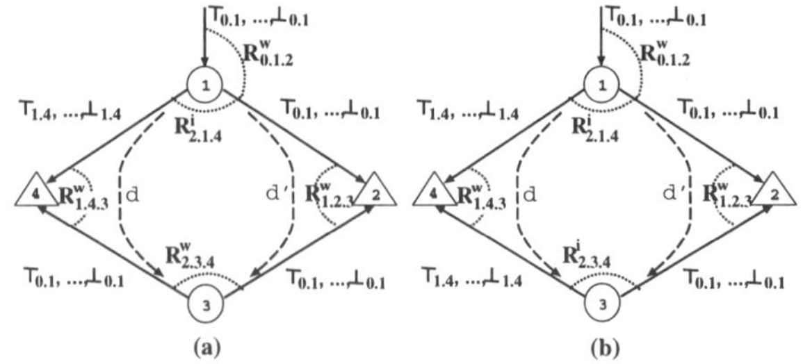

Figure 3: Contradiction and solution in a 2-way circuit.

(1) Local clash detection

Local clash detection is directed at all relations of the pair of totally-ordered sets obtained from the adjacent arcs connected by a structure vertex. Two cases determine whether a relations will be ill-ordered. First, if the constraint vertex performs a calculation which needs two or more input data from different structure vertices, data collation will be performed in one of those vertices. This is indicated by two or more arcs $a_{j_h i}, (h = 1, 2, \cdots, n)(n > 1)$ flowing into an entity type vertex $v_{\mathcal{E}_i}$ or a relationship type vertex $v_{\mathcal{R}_i}$. Consequently, each relation between their totally-ordered sets is ill-ordered.

$$\forall\, i, j\, \exists\, h, h'(a_{j_h i} \wedge a_{j_{h'} i} \in A \Longrightarrow R^i_{j_h i j_{h'}}),$$

where, $1 \leq i,\ j \leq |V|,\ i \neq j,\ h = 1, 2, ..., n,$ and $n > 1$. Secondly, if the relations of data calculation is not in 1 to 1 correspondence. It will not appear on a directed graph. However, we can detect which structure vertex has not 1 to 1 relation by looking at the program specification. Consequently, the relations between two totally-ordered sets of two adjacent arcs a_{ij} and a_{jk} connected by the vertex is ill-ordered.

$$\forall\, i, j, k\, \exists\, m, l, l'(o_{ijm} R_{ijk} o_{ijl} \wedge o_{ijm} R_{ijk} o_{ijl'}) \Longrightarrow R^i_{ijk},$$

where, $1 \leq i, j, k \leq |V|,\ i \neq j \neq k,\ 1 \leq m \leq |S_{ij}|$, and $1 \leq l, l' \leq |S_{jk}|$.

(2) Global clash detection

Global clash detection aims at detecting a contradiction in a directed graph. The contradiction means that an executable program cannot be generated from the graph. This contradiction exists in a 2-way circuit which is a subset of a directed graph which forms a circuit and includes arcs of different directions d and d', as denoted in Figure 3(a). To detect this contradiction, we need to define an ordering number for each element of a totally-ordered set S_{ij}, where $\top_{ij}$ specifies the first element and $\bot_{ij}$ the last element number of the set.

$$S_{ij} = \{o_{ijm} | (m = \top_{ij}, \cdots, \bot_{ij}, \top_{ij} \overset{t}{<} \bot_{ij}),$$

where, $\top_{ij} \overset{t}{<} \bot_{ij}$ means that the data with element number $\top_{ij}$ flows before data with element number $\bot_{ij}$. Actually, we need to know only the first and the last of the ordering numbers of the set in order to determine the sequence of two totally-ordered sets. Between two totally-ordered sets S_i and S_j obtained from adjacent arcs whose an ill-ordered relations, $\bot_i \overset{t}{<} \top_j$ is imposed, otherwise, $\bot_i \overset{t}{=} \top_j$ is available.

We can then set the ordering number for each arc in the 2-way circuit in order to detect whether there is a contradiction, as illustrated in Figure 3(a). Obviously, a contradiction exists for well-ordered relation where $\bot_{0.1} \overset{t}{<} \top_{1.4}$. It can be solved by changing the relations $R^w_{2.3.4}$ into $R^i_{2.3.4}$, as shown in Figure 3(b).

4 Architectural CAD System Generation

The specifications described in the BDL by the domain experts should be transformed automatically into the programs in order to ensure development efficiency and software reliability. We represent the domain-specific abstract structure such as *binary* plug and socket relation into the specifications of DFSL by a compiler. This allows the integration of the specifications of different domains. Moreover, if we develop a program code generator only for the domain-free language, we do not need ones for domain-specific languages.

4.1 Domain Problem

Using local and global clash detection, we can detect and solve the ordering clash in the directed graph. However, these basic detections are not powerful enough to both detect an

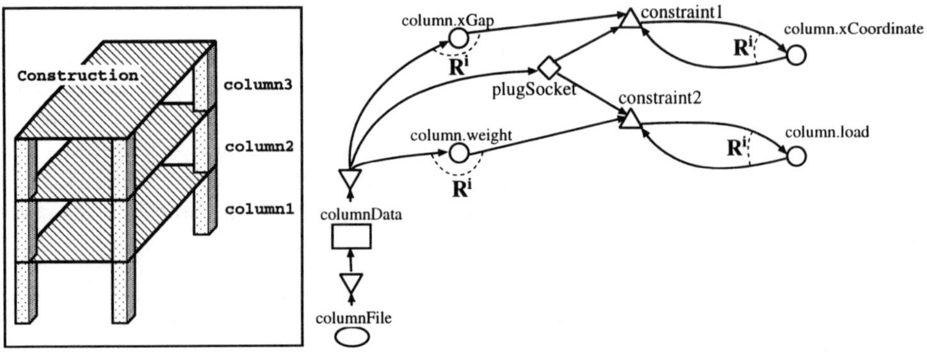

Figure 4: Directed graph for column load and coordinates calculation.

ordering clash and optimize an allocating memory for its solution. An extension of the basic detection method suited to the domain problem is needed to generate an efficient program. In the domain of architectural CAD system generation, we complete our method by applying several extension methods in order to completely solve the ordering clash problem and to enhance the efficiency of the memory allocation. Recursive program and complicated input-output data are two problems faced in this domain.

4.2 Recursive Program Solution

A recursive program is one which applies the same computation to itself. Therefore, it is expressed as a 1-way circuit in the directed graph. A method to analyze the 1-way circuit has not yet been established within the general framework. A solution for this problem is needed because it arises not only in the architectural domain but also in many other domains. However, it usually appears as a problem characteristic to a particular domain. Therefore, we do not solve this problem in terms of general domains, but focus on efficient and domain-specific solutions.

Generally, recursive function can be expressed as:

$$F(x_n) = F(x_{n-1}, \cdots, x_0).$$

The relation of this expression which is not considered as 1 to 1 correspondence; therefore, its general solution should be achieved by assuming the relation on the 1-way circuit as ill-ordered relations. Consequently, we should provide lists as long as the number of data to the all vertices of the circuit. However, this solution is only suitable for a few cases in several domains. The other domains have specific recursive problems for which the solution can be optimized, such as the following example in the architectural domain.

A 1-way circuit appears in the calculation of column load and column coordinates as shown in Figure 4. A column load is obtained by adding its weight and the upper column load. In contrast, its coordinates are obtained by referring to the lower column and its gap. Obviously, before the calculation can be performed in 1-way circuit, data must be stored in "column.xGap" and "column.weight", respectively. Moreover, because the next data is not certainly a correct partner of the previous data, both of the circuits have ill-ordered relations. However, we do not allocate lists as long as the number of data, but perform the calculation as follows: as an initialization, an arbitrary data flows into each circuit. Then, according to the "plugSocket" relationship, the previous partner can be found and stored. This process

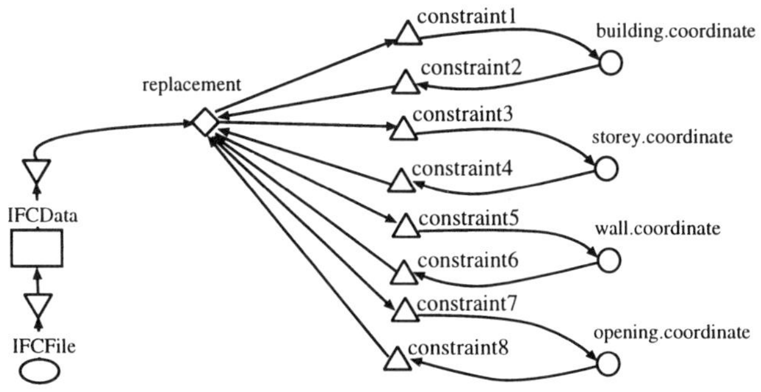

Figure 5: Directed graph of IFC to BDL coordinates transformation.

is repeated until the first data for both calculations are obtained and can be calculated. This procedure can cut the number of lists to be averaged in half, and can perform both of calculations in the same loop. The other computations such as a convergent power of column and so on can be transformed to the resemble procedure.

4.3 Complicated Input-output Data Solution

In the architecture industry, the IAI (International Alliance for Interoperability) has been defining the IFC (Industry Foundation Classes) as a set of standard data specifications to be exchanged among CAD systems[11]. The IFC require wide applicability throughout the architecture life cycle. Therefore, the specifications are defined using the relational model-based EXPRESS language which is general enough to be applied to various domains.

In an experiment conducted by the Japanese chapter of the IAI in 1998, we successfully implemented a data conversion tool between BDL and the IFC[12]. The relational model belongs to the generation of data models previous to that of the object model, and lacks the concept of association in the object model. In the experiment, this problem is one of the primary challenges in our implementation of a tool for converting data from the IFC to the BDL. Moreover, the differences of the coordinates system force us to recalculate the coordinates from the relative to the absolute coordinates system in order to allow objects to be displayed.

The directed graph intended to deal with this large amount of physical data is shown in Figure 5. A data record includes building, story, wall, and opening coordinates in which all of these entity types are connected by only "replacement" relationship type. Hierarchically, the story coordinates depend on the building coordinates, the wall's depend on the story's and so on. Therefore, the data transformation should be achieved hierarchically by providing a stack for each entity type. Thus, wall data coordinates are held until all opening coordinates at the wall have been calculated. Similarly, story's are held until all wall coordinates in the story have been calculated. The data which is not needed then removed. In this case, because between the same entity type in the IFC's physical file has no relation, the procedure need to provide lists only as much as the number of circuits. Moreover, the lists provided for "replacement" can be optimized by directly executing the calculation of the entity type which has the largest amount when the data arrived. This procedure only need one variable for that entity type data.

5 Conclusion

This paper proposed a general framework to characterize the problem of structure clash, particularly the ordering clash detection method. This framework employs the concept of relation to detect ordering clash and at the same time apply the relational inference to obtain certainly synchronic area as a basic part of program structure. Moreover, the paper described an implementation of the method in CAD system generation, especially in regard to solving the recursive program and the hierarchical input and output data problems in the domain of architecture. This method constitutes an extension of the basic detection method defined in the general framework in order to enhance the efficiency of the memory allocation for obtained procedural program.

References

[1] R.G. Lanergan and C. A. Grasso, Software Engineering with Reusable Design and Code, *IEEE Trans. Softw. Eng.*, Vol. SE-10, No.5, (1984)498-501.

[2] K. Okamoto and M. Hashimoto, Visual Programming with Reusable Specification Described by a Conceptual Data Model- and Constraint-Based Language. *Proc. Int. Conf. Human-Computer Interaction*, (1991)587-591.

[3] E. Lukman, M. Hashimoto, K. Katamine and T. Hirota, A Reference Model of CAD System Generation from Various Object Model-Based Specification Description Language Specific to Individual Domains, *IEICE Trans. on Inf. and Sys.*, Vol. E83-D, No. 4, (2000)713-721.

[4] P.P. Chen, The Entity-Relationship Model Toward a Unified View on Data, *ACM Trans. Database Syst*, Vol. 1, No. 1, (1976)9-36.

[5] N. S. Prywes and A. Pneuli, Compilation of Nonprocedural Specifications into Computer Programs, *IEEE Trans. Softw. Eng.*, Vol. SE-9, No. 3, (1993)267-279.

[6] M.A. Jackson, *Principles of Program Design*, Academic Press, London, 1975.

[7] B. Michel, A 'Division' Transformation for Program and Data Structures and the Structure Clash Problem, *Sci. of Comp. Prog.*, 10 (1988)247-280.

[8] M. Hashimoto and K. Okamoto, A Set and Mapping-based Detection and Solution Method for Structure Clash Between Program Input and Output Data, *Proc. of IEEE International Computer Software and Application Conference*, (1990)629-638.

[9] R.J. Wilson, Introduction to Graph Theory, *Longman Group Limited*, London, 1985.

[10] S. Bhansali and T.J. Hoar, Automated Software Synthesis: An Application in Mechanical CAD, *IEEE Trans. on Soft. Eng.*, Vol. 24, No. 10, 1998.

[11] International Alliance for Interoperability, *Industry foundation classes - release 1.5 model reference documentation final version*, 1996 - 1997.

[12] T. Nakasima, K. Katamine, M. Hashimoto, and T. Hirota, A report on Implementation Experiment of Architectural CALS, , *Technical Report of IEICE*, KBSE98-43, 1999.

Knowledge-Based Software Engineering
T. Hruška and M. Hashimoto (Eds.)
IOS Press, 2000

Cost-Benefit Analysis Using CVM for IT Investments

Shigeo KANEDA[1], Shigeki ISHITANI[2]

[1] *Graduate School of Policy and Management, Doshisha University, 602-8580, Japan*
E-mail: skaneda@mail.doshisha.ac.jp

[2] *Sekisui Chemical Co., Ltd., Japan*

Abstract. One of the major problems in IT (Information Technology) investments is the difficulty in making a cost-benefit analysis of the investments. Conventional man-hour cost accounting methods often report cost demerits for successful IT investments. A new cost-benefit analysis approach is needed in this era of competitive strategies. To satisfy this need, this paper proposes a cost-benefit analysis method using CVM (Contingent Valuation Method), which is used widely in environment assessment research. By using CVM, we can numerically evaluate the cost merit of customer satisfaction (CS) and the resulting economic damage when a competitor deploys a new service/product. The proposed CVM approach is suitable for CGI (Common Gateway Interface). We also experimentally demonstrate a new dynamic CVM method that makes the most of CGI capabilities.

1 Introduction

Currently, IT (Information Technology) systems cover a wide range of businesses, and the area is expanding rapidly with the advances in computer and network technologies. Previously, the goal of IT systems was to improve productivity in business, such as man-hour reduction, cost retrenchment, or space consolidation. In the present situation, however, the business target is quality improvement, such as customer satisfaction (CS), quick response (QR), and gaining advantage over competitors.

This change in purpose has brought about a new and difficult task: making a cost-benefit analysis of the IT investment. For example, CS is one of the current major targets. However, CS is a sensory assessment item: the degree of it depends on the competitor's strategy. It is very difficult to analyze cost-benefit aspects of CS. Conventional estimation methods, such as the man-hour method or functional point method[6], are not suitable. If the target of an IT system is CS, only the customers can evaluate the value of the IT investment. Accordingly, we have to estimate a customer's degree of satisfaction.

On the other hand, the total amount of IT investment is generally estimated to reach a few percent of the total sales of an enterprise. An inappropriate IT investment causes a severe financial burden for the enterprise. Therefore, accurate cost-benefit analysis of IT investments is indispensable for enterprise management.

This paper proposes a new method to make cost-benefits analysis by using CVM (Contingent Valuation Method). CVM is widely used to estimate the value of a natural environment. The proposed method numerically evaluates the customer's degree of satisfaction.

Section 2 describes a judgement procedure for IT investment in Japan. Section 3 explains CVM. Section 4 proposes an application of CVM to evaluate IT investments.

Section 5 evaluates CVM experimentally and proposes a new CVM approach suitable for CGI (Common Gateway Interface). Section 6 concludes the paper.

2 IT Investment in Japan

2.1 Programmer's Grief

The Japanese cost accounting researcher M. Yamamoto[1] has shown that few Japanese enterprises put emphasis on cost-benefit analysis in their decision making for IT investments. It is conjectured that IT investments are decided by emotional motivations: "A competitor has already adopted the plan." "The president prefers the plan." or "The parent company has employed the plan." The actual decision process for IT investments is as follows in many Japanese companies.

Decision Making Process for IT Investment
(STEP I) A system development section makes an IT investment proposal. The executives of the enterprise ask, "How much will total sales increase?" However, the system development section cannot answer this question. The section is obliged to draw beautiful graphs using a tabular format tool. The graphs reveal a "bright future," even if the graphs have no grounding in actual facts.
(STEP II) Usually the IT system succeeds in decreasing business errors, reducing response time, or increasing the quality of products. However, the section cannot accurately calculate the cost-benefit picture. As a result, their explanations become emotional and not quantitative: "Customers will be amply satisfied with the quality improvement," or "Decreased errors will make a favorable impression of our enterprise."
(STEP III) The system development section repeats the above presentation using the "ill-grounded beautiful graphs" until the executives say, "We agree with the plan." Even if the investment is approved, the members of the system development section are tired by the presentation work and lose their energy to implement the actual application system.

2.2 IT System for Competitive Strategy

Porter describes in his book[2] that competitive ascendancy arises from a value that an enterprise creates for its customers. The value is expressed in a term of money that the customers pay in exchange for the product/service. This scheme is also applicable to IT system investments.

The above discussion shows that IT benefits should be evaluated from the customer's viewpoint. This customer's value must be numerically expressed in the price. However, customer satisfaction is emotional and depends on the competitor's strategy. The conventional man-hour cost accounting method is inadequate to evaluate the service/product provided by the IT investment. Only customers can evaluate the value of the IT investment. The value of the IT system should be evaluated by a questionnaire. We focus on the CVM (Contingent Valuation Method) questionnaire method to resolve this problem.

3 CVM: Contingent Valuation Method

3.1 CVM

CVM (Contingent Valuation Method) infers individuals' payable price for natural environmental amenities from their choices involving money quantities[3][4]. CVM asks for a "Yes" or "No" answer to the question, "Would you be willing to pay $X...? to keep this amenity?" This $X is each individual's response and reveals only an upper bound (for a

"No") or a lower bound (for a "Yes"). The printed \$X value should be changed on each version of the questionnaire sheet. CVM follows the three steps below.

(Q1) The following photos show the current status of Karasuma River. If the planed dam is constructed, the amenity will be changed into the condition shown in the right-hand side photos.

We can adopt an alternative approach instead of the dam. In this case, the Karasuma River amenity has no change. However, you have to pay 20 dollars more tax per year. Can you accept this tax?

(If your answer is "Yes," please go to Q2; otherwise, please go to Q3.)

(Q2) If the tax increase is 40 dollars, can you accept this tax value?

(Q3) If the tax increase is 10 dollars, can you accept this tax value?

Figure 1. Example CVM Questionnaire

(STEP I) Display Photos/Figures

The questionnaire presents different photos or figures of a natural environment: one is an original natural setting and the other is an image of destruction. For example, photos of pretty birds, a beautiful valley, or a large lake are displayed for the evaluation of a natural environment. Figure 1 shows an example of a CVM questionnaire sheet but is shortened for simplification. The left-hand side photos reveal the current state. The right-hand side photos represent the envisioned degraded future state.

(STEP II) Determine Whether the Sample Value can be Accepted or Not

The purpose of the questionnaire is to get an individual's "willing to pay" (called ***WTP*** in this paper) as tax or an entrance fee to keep the natural amenity. Each individual has an acceptable maximum tax/fee value. However, we cannot know this individual's WTP value directly. Thus, it is assumed that individual WTP values have a statistical distribution. The questionnaire system should be able to estimate the mean or median of this distribution.

Each questionnaire sheet has concrete prices[1] as shown in Fig. 1. Each concrete value is selected from the candidates of sample values. The range of these candidate values should cover the range of the statistical distribution of WTP values.

[1] A simple hypothetical question is to ask people what value they place on a specified change in an environmental amenity or the maximum amount they would be willing to pay as tax. However, questions posed by this simple method are very hard to answer. It is well known that many individuals cannot fill in the blanks. Also, we can let an individual select one value from a list of acceptable values. This method has a strong *bias* statistically. Thus, the statistical results are not reliable.

(STEP III) Estimate WTP Statistically
The mean or median of the WTP distribution is statistically estimated from the many "Yes" or "No" answers collected from the individuals. The statistical methods used here are equivalent to those used for estimating average life span in the life insurance field. To calculate the mean value, the Kaplan-Meire Method and Actuarial Method are well known in environment CVM surveys[3]. A non-parametric method can also be applied. The details of statistical methods are omitted in this paper.

The design of the questionnaire is called "Survey Design" and is one of the most essential processes of CVM. The reliability of the questionnaire depends on survey design, especially on the selection of the candidate sample values. The purpose of the questionnaire is to get WTP distribution. However, the WTP distribution should be roughly known in advance to design the CVM, which poses a difficult contradiction. Thus, the estimation has two processes. First, an outline of the distribution is estimated from the initial survey, and then a detailed distribution is calculated from the final survey.

3.2 Single- and Double-bounded Questions

The CVM has two types of questions.
(Single-bounded Question) Each individual is asked only one time. The answer is "Yes" or "No." The accuracy of a single bounded question is lower than that of a double-bounded question.

(Double-bounded Question) Each individual is asked twice. If the first answer is "Yes," one additional, more expensive sample value is presented. On the other hand, if the first answer is "No," one additional, smaller sample value is presented again. Figure 1 is an example of a double-bounded question. Table 1 shows an example of the candidate sample value set for the double-bounded scheme. Each questionnaire sheet has one of these "versions."

Version	T1	TU	TL
A	$10	$30	$5
B	$30	$60	$10
C	$60	$120	$30
D	$120	$250	$60

T1 Fisrt Exhibited Value
TU If the first anwer is "Yes", this value is invoked.
TL If the first anwer is "No", this value is invoked.

Table 1. Sample Values

4 Benefit Estimation using CVM for IT System Investments

4.1 A New Approach to Evaluate IT Investments

The above CVM is introduced into an evaluation of IT system investments. This process is equivalent to the CVM of natural environment evaluations.

(STEP I) Display Figures of the planed IT System
The questionnaire presents figures: one is a current business model, and the other is a future business model that uses the planned IT system.
(STEP II) Ask Individuals "Acceptable" or "Not"
A sample value is shown to the user/customer. She/he answers "Yes" or "No" in regards to acceptability. The exhibited value is one version of the candidate sample values.
(STEP III) Estimate WTP Value Statistically
Finally, the WTP value is statistically estimated from all of the questionnaire results.

The CVM is suitable for CGI (Common Gateway Interface) implementation. This is because (1) HTML is suitable for photos/figures, (2) computer systems can easily change the exhibited sample value, (3) a change in the question sequence is very easy for computer systems, (4) digitally formatted data require no data entry task, and (5) the users/customers of IT systems are very familiar with computer systems.

4.2 CVM Decision Making

The estimated WTP value is the mean/median of the statistical distribution. A straightforward application of the proposed CVM is shown in the following cost merit strategy.

CVM Decision Making under Cost Merit Strategy
The total benefit of the planed IT system is

Benefit = WTP * N (N: number of the customers).

If the benefit exceeds the total amount of the IT investment, the investment is acceptable:

WTP*N > the total amount of the IT investment.

The benefit of the IT investment depends on the competitor's strategy. If the enterprise has a competitor, the competitor's service/product should be considered in designing the CVM questionnaire. Thus, this paper next proposes another type of CVM that is not known in natural environment research fields.

CVM Decision Making under Competitive Strategy
The mean of WTP is not an upper bound but has another meaning for what a strategic investment offers as an advantage over the competitors in the real business world. First, let's consider the following example.

- There are two competitive enterprises: Company A and Company B.
- Company A supplies product Pa, and Company B supplies product Pb.
- Pa and Pb have the same specifications and price of $100.
- The total production of Pa is 10,000 units. The total production of Pb is also 10,000 units.

Therefore, the total sales of Pa is 10,000*$100=$1,000,000. The total sales of Pb is also $1,000.000.

Next, assume that Company A develops a new technology to realize an attractive feature of Product Pa, and that a $200,000 investment is required to manufacture the new product. Another type of CVM becomes available.

"Thank you for your buying our product Pa! The current price of Pa is $100. Also, our competitor supplies product Pb whose price and function are equal to our Pa. Now, let's assume that our competitor developed a new Pb having a new feature. The price of the new Pb is $120. Would you buy the competitor's new Pb instead of our Pa?"

Let's assume that the estimated mean of WTP is $110. If the new featured Pb is on the market, the sales increase is $10*10,000=$100,000 for Company B. This investment has cost demerit because $100,000 < $200,000. However, Company B should decide to adopt the investment.

If Company A supplies the same new feature-added Pa at price $110, Company B loses 50% of the customers. Thus, the total sales of Company B decreases to 5,000*$100=$500,000. The loss reaches $1,000,000-$500,000=$500,000. On the other hand, the total sales of Company A reaches 15,000*$110 = $1,650,000. The gain is $650,000. This major gain cancels the cost demerit of the IT investment.

Strassmann reported that there is no correlation between IT system investments and price-earnings ratio[5]. Many research efforts in econometrics have reported that IT system investments do not always increase an enterprise's productivity, especially in the service industries. IT investments often result in cost increases. However, the investing enterprise gets substantial increases in total sales under the competitive strategy policy. This gain cancels the cost demerit of the IT investment. On the other hand, the defeated enterprise loses a huge percentage of its sales. It is very hard for the defeated company to adopt the same IT system investment because the IT investment never increases productivity.

This analysis shows that the IT investment should be made even if the investment exceeds the WTP * N. All competitive investments should be decided as soon as possible. Only the first decision-maker can get the benefit of the investment. The others suffer from the huge IT investment under a drastic retrenchment of total sales.

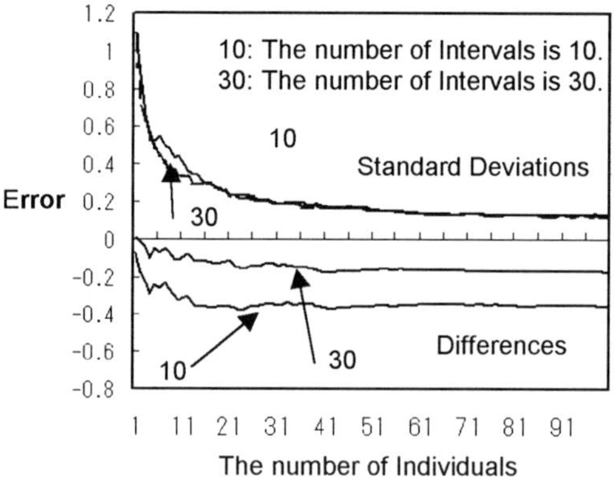

Figure 2. Error between Estimated and True Values

5 Experimental Evaluation of Proposed CVM

5.1 Experimental Evaluation

A Monte Carlo simulation was executed to evaluate the ability of CVM. The experimental conditions are as follows:

- Double-bounded question
- The WTP distribution has the Weibull Distribution between 0 to 10. The average is three[2]. The number of individuals is 100. The trials are repeated 50 times. The total number of individuals is 100*50 = 5,000.
- The interval [0,10] is divided equally. The exhibited sample values of CVM are selected from the boundary values. The first stage sample value has two kinds of distributions: (1) normal distribution having mean = 3 and standard deviation = 2, and (2) normal distribution having mean = 8 and standard deviation = 2. The former distribution corresponds to a good survey design. The later corresponds to an illegal survey design.
- A non-parametric method is employed to estimate the mean of WTP for simplification.

[2] This value is a target of the proposed CVM questionnaire.

Figure 2 shows the error between the estimated WTP and the true mean value (= 3). The numbers of intervals are 10 and 30. The range is from 0 to 10. The candidate sample values are 1, 2, 3, 4, 5, 6, 7, 8, and 9 for 10 Intervals. The horizontal axis is the number of individuals. The CVM experiment starts from the left-most end and stops at the right-most end. The vertical axis is the calculated error. The upper half of Fig. 2 is standard deviation of the error. The lower half is the average of the error.

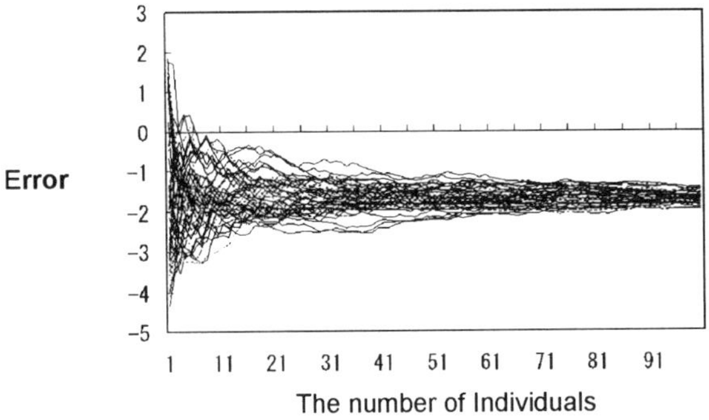

Figure 3. Illegal Sample Value Distribution

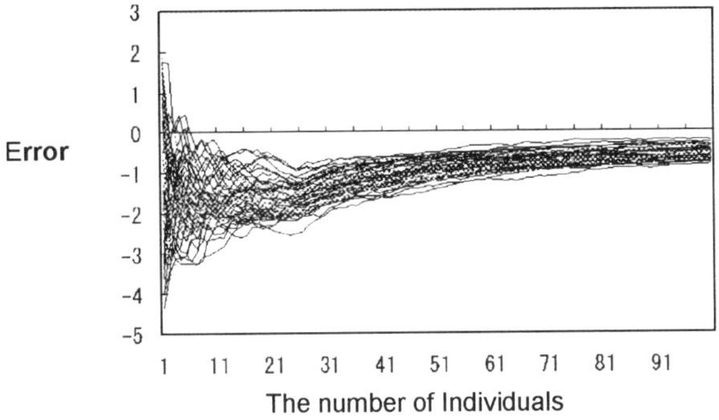

Figure 4. Dynamic CVM

The error converges at a constant value when the number of individuals is about 30; the standard deviation is about 0.2. This is a good result because the interval of the exhibited sample values is one. The double-bounded question scheme is very effective and accurate.

However, the CVM is not effective if the initial survey design is not successful. Figure 3 shows an experimental result where the exhibited sample values are selected from the normal distribution with mean = 8. The vertical axis shows error between the estimated value and the true mean (= 3). The results for 50 trials are shown. The estimated WTP value converges, and the remaining error is very large. The exhibited sample values are usually too expensive for the individuals. Most answers are "No & No." Consequently, it is very difficult to estimate the WTP. The Japanese CVM researcher Kuriyama[4] has emphasized that survey design is essential. This large error is one of the reasons why an initial questionnaire is often recommended.

5.2 A New Approach: Dynamic CVM

The mean of WTP values should be estimated roughly before the CVM questionnaire is given. However, this is somewhat of a contradiction[3]: if the survey designer knows the mean value, there's no need to use the CVM questionnaire. To resolve this problem, this paper proposes a new approach where the exhibited sample value is sifted when most of the answer are "Yes & yes" or "No & No." The proposed method proceeds as follows:

(STEP I) Prepare Three Sets of Sample Values
The programmer prepares three sets of candidate sample values. For instance, we consider mean = 3, 8, 16. The CVM program starts from the mean = 8 distribution
(STEP II) Change the Candidate Sample Values Set
The CVM questionnaire is repeated until the number of individuals reaches a pre-defined number of individuals, such as 25. If most of the answers are "Yes & Yes" or "No & No," the candidate sample values are not adequate. If the answer is "Yes & Yes," mean = 16 is invoked. If the answer is "No & No," mean = 3 is invoked.

Figure 4 shows an experimental result when the dynamic distribution change is employed. In this case, the mean = 8 normal distribution is changed to the mean = 3 normal distribution. This result shows that the dynamic CVM is effective.

6 Conclusions

An investment evaluation method using CVM is demonstrated in this paper. We can get a concrete value of "willing to pay" (WTP) from the customers. The product of the estimated WTP value and the number of users/customers is the benefit of the planed IT system. If the evaluated benefit doesn't exceed the amount of IT system investment, the plan should be canceled.

The estimated WTP value is mean value of the acceptable price given by the customers/users. This indicates that if the competitor employs the new product or service at the WTP price, the competitor takes 50% of the users/customers. This reduction directly affects the total sales of the enterprise, bringing about a severe situation. Even if the estimated benefit doesn't exceed the IT investment amount, the enterprise should decide to make the investment to prevent the competitor from making it.

This paper also clarified that Common Gateway Interface (CGI) is suitable for this CVM questionnaire method to evaluate the benefit of an IT system investment. However, CVM is not perfect. One of its major defects is that rough estimation of WTP should be made before giving the CVM questionnaire, although this is a kind of contradiction. This paper proposes a new dynamic change approach to solving the problem. The proposed dynamic change can also be implemented in a CGI environment.

References

[1] M. Yamamoto, "Management of Strategic Investments" (in Japanese), Bunshin-do, Tokyo, 1998.

[2] M. Porter, "Competitive Strategy", Macmillan Publishing Co., Inc., New York, 1980.

[3] A. Freeman III, "The Measurement of Environmental and Resource Values", Resources for the Future, Washington, D.C., 1993.

[4] K. Kuriyama, "Contingent Valuation Method: Theory and Practice" (in Japanese), Kikuchi-shokan, Tokyo, 1997.

[5] P. Strassmann, "The Business Value of Computers", The Information Economics Press, 1990.

[6] J. Caper, "Programming Productivity", McGraw-Hill, Inc., New York, 1994.

---

[3] Many questionnaire sheets require calculation of the confidence intervals. Even if the mean value is roughly estimated, the CVM questionnaire is essential for practical estimation.

Knowledge-Based Software Engineering
T. Hruška and M. Hashimoto (Eds.)
IOS Press, 2000

A Support Mechanism for Modifying a Class Hierarchy in Software Evolution

Hiroyuki YAMADA

Dept. of Computer Science, Faculty of Engineering, Ehime University,
3, Bunkyo-cho, Matsuyama, Ehime, 790-8577, Japan
yamada@cs.ehime-u.ac.jp

Abstract. In a process of evolution of object-oriented software, a class hierarchy is often reconstructed, when the software is modified due to changes and improvement of the specification. It costs much time to modify software because of side effects caused by the modification. This paper supposes that the side effect caused by the modification of the object-oriented software is based on the relationship (we call it functional relation) that must exist between objects in order to realize some problem solving functions. So, this paper presents how to assist a user in dealing with the side effects using a functional relation model. This model represents functional relation between objects with a kind of network representation. A node in this model has information of when the impact occurs and how to deal with it.

1 Introduction

In a process of evolution of object-oriented software, a class hierarchy is often reconstructed, when the software is modified due to changes and improvement of the specification. However, modifying software will often introduce unexpected side effects into other parts of it. As a result, it is necessary to investigate various classes in the class hierarchy in order to detect the points affected by the side effects caused by the modifications. However, because of features of object-oriented software, such as method inheritance, overriding, polymorphism and so on, behavior of the software becomes unstable by the modification of the software, and the understanding of the software may be made difficult [1,2].

Moreover, the side effects caused by the modifications do not disappear perfectly in modifying a class hierarchy because of some kinds of dependencies among objects. That is, because the problem solving functions have been realized by utilizing the functions defined in other object, objects usually depend on others to solve a problem by communication with each other. Such communication often composes a chain of message invocations. As a result, impact analysis may require tracing such a chain through several objects. It is not easy to detect affected points (such as methods in classes) in the class hierarchy, because of trace of such a chain.

In this paper, the side effect caused by the modification of the object-oriented software is based on the relationship that must exist between objects in order to realize some problem solving functions. So, when an object *A* essentially uses a function defined in an object *B* to solve the problem, the object *A* is functionally related with the object *B*. We call this kind of relation functional relation. The side effect may occur in the object *A* (*B*) in modifying the object *B* (*A*) when the functional relation is not established between them because of the modification.

So we consider a methodology of finding out and deal with the side effects in order to assist a user in modifying software. This paper proposes a framework called a functional relation model, which can describe the functional relationship between objects explicitly, in order to assist to find out and deal with the side effects.

2 A Functional Relation Model

A functional relation model consists of nodes and labeled links between nodes, corresponding to objects (classes) and functional relations between them, respectively. The label given to the link means the functional relation between nodes. This model means that if modifying a class breaks off a functional relation, impact may occur to the class opposite to the modified class. Therefore, the localization of the influence point is possible.

An object oriented software is usually organized in hierarchy of generalization: fundamental classes and their subclasses (application classes), which define fundamental procedures commonly used for solving problems similar to a given problem and specific procedures for solving the given problem, respectively. The model is also organized in a hierarchy of generalization similarly to that of the target software. Then, we call nodes corresponding to the former fundamental nodes, and, nodes corresponding to the latter application nodes. The fundamental node has general information of functional relation. This information is commonly used for their application nodes. While the application one has the more specific information. Moreover, they can inherit functional relation information from their super nodes, if necessary.

In the model, there are two kinds of links: necessary links and optional links. The former means that the functional relation corresponding to the link always holds. The latter means that the functional relation corresponding to the link holds if necessary.

To assist a developer (user) in modifying a target program, a node has the functional relation information, which consists of the following information: (1) the impact detection information, and (2) the modification information. The former is conditional information about when and which functional link becomes broken off in modifying the class definition corresponding to the node, and the latter is modification information about where and how to modify the affected point to deal with impact. He modifies the point so that the functional relation may be established again based on the modification information.

Figure 1 shows a functional relation model of a ferry simulation. In this figure, rectangles and ellipses stand for fundamental and application nodes, respectively. Solid lines and dotted lines between nodes stand for functional relations and hierarchical relations between the corresponding objects, respectively. The figure shows that if a class definition corresponding to the application node *Ferry* is modified, the impact may occur to classes corresponding to nodes linked to the node *Ferry*, that is, the object *FerrySimulation*, the object Island, and/or the object *Mainland*.

Our model-based support is as follows. Firstly, by using the impact detection information in the node *Ferry* and its super node *SimulationObject*, the system can find out which functional links become broken off by the modification. Then, by using the modification information in the opposite node and its super nodes, the user can be given advice on where and how to modify. He modifies the affected point based on the modification information. The more detailed discussion about our model-based support has been presented in [4].

An example of a node representation is shown in Figure 2. This is a part of the node representation of the node *SimulationObject* in Figure 1. This Figure shows that this node is a fundamental node of which the super node is the *Object*. Moreover, the link representation in the node shows that the link 'Scheduling' is a necessary link between this node and the node *Simulation*. The 'Cond' slot shows that if a sub class *#self* of the class *SimulationObject* is defined newly and the class *#self* has an instance method 'tasks', then this link may be broken off. The 'Ir' slot shows that if this link is broken off, a sub class *#param1*, which has an instance method 'tasks', of the class *SimulationObject* should be defined. In Figure 2, a sharp sign followed by a symbol means a variable. Moreover, to refer to the value of the variable #x, an italic font: *#x* is used.

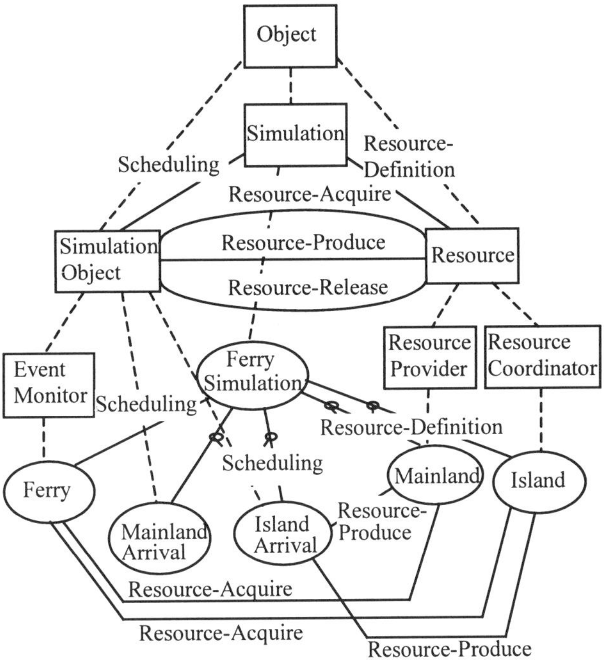

Figure 1. A functional Model of a ferry simulation program.

```
Name:       SimulationObject
Super:      Object
Type:       fundamental
Links: (
  (LinkName: Scheduling
   To:        Simulation
   LinkType:  necessary
   Cond:      defClsAsSubCls(#self #x1) &
              subCls(#x1 'SimulationObject') &
              defIMtd(#self 'tasks')
   Ir:        defClsAsSubCls(#param1 #x1) &
              subCls(#x1 'SimulationObject') &
              defIMtd(#param1 'tasks') ) )
```

Figure 2. A part of a node representation.

3 Modification Support for Modifying Software

A modification support system has been implemented in Visual Works version 2.5J. This system can point out affected positions and suggest how to modify them in modifying the software. This system consists of four modules: the side effect detector module, the use interface module, the functional relation model manager module and the software modification module. Moreover, it has three files: the object level software file, the functional relation model file and the domain theory file.

The domain theory [5,6] in the domain theory file consists of domain independent knowledge and domain dependent knowledge. The former consists of general rules in the object-oriented programming, for example rules of method inheritance and rules of super-subclass relation. The latter consists of facts and rules of the object-level software. It consists of facts of super-subclass relation, facts of methods in each class, facts of categories of methods and rules of functional relations between classes.

The object-level software file has an event-driven queueing simulation software, which has implemented according to [3]. This simulation is executed by event driven style. An event is defined as an occurrence to move the internal state of simulated system. The functional relation model file has node descriptions of the functional relation model of the object-level software.

4 Conclusion

The features of our approach are shown as follows.

We assume that the side effect caused by modification occurs due to functional relation between objects. So, we proposed a functional relation model to represent the functional relations explicitly. Therefore, our approach will be applicable to other application program written in the object oriented programming style.

To build up the domain theory of the object-level software, the information is explicitly represented the functional relation model we proposed. The information in a node is described with high level primitives corresponding to concepts relevant to the application domain.

The system based on this functional relation model assists programmers by localizing the side effect. As a result, following the system's direction can efficiently carry out modifying software. Moreover, since the system has information about the side effect, the user has been released from the need to remember many details and to keep track of the many relations among these details.

References

[1] Wilde, N. and Huitt, R., Maintenance Support for Object-Oriented Programs, IEEE Trans. on SE, Vol. 18, No. 12, pp. 1038-1044, 1992.

[2] Wild, C. and Maly, K., Towards a Software Maintenance Support Environment, Proc. of CSM-88, pp. 80-85, 1988.

[3] Goldberg, A. and Robinson, D., Smalltalk-80 The Language and Its Implementation, Addison-Wesley, 1983.

[4] Yamada, H. and Tezuka, Y., Knowledge-Based Supporting System for Software Modification, Proc. of Third International IFIP Conference on Computer Applications in Production and Engineering CAPE'89, pp. 231-238, 1989.

[5] DeJong, G. and Mooney, R., Explanation-Based Learning: An Alternative View, Machine Learning, Vol. 1, No. 2, pp. 145-175, 1986.

[6] Mooney, R., A General Explanation-Based Learning Mechanism and its Application to Narrative Understanding, Morgan Kaufmann, 166 p., 1990

Knowledge-Based Software Engineering
T. Hruška and M. Hashimoto (Eds.)
IOS Press, 2000

A Digital Enterprise and its Research Project

Morio NAGATA
Dept. of Administration Engineering, Faculty of Science and Technology
Keio University
3-14-1 Hiyoshi, Yokohama, 223-8522, Japan
e-mail: nagata@ae.keio.ac.jp

Abstract. The modern world and business have been changed with information technology in recent years. This technology has improved existing business processes of many companies. However, a present business environment urges us to evolve their business models. This paper proposes a concept of a "digital enterprise" as an enterprise in the near future. Consumers drive the activities of the digital enterprise directly for acquiring materials, services and information. The digital enterprise requires new software systems management methods, and social systems. We are planning to study the technological, managerial and social aspects of the digital enterprise. This paper also discusses research issues on the digital enterprise modeling and business models of the digital enterprise.

1 Introduction

A global and competitive business environment has forced the enterprises to act agilely. Information Technology (IT) is a powerful weapon for those enterprises. IT has improved business processes of many companies. For example, documents for exchanging information have been replaced by e-mails or electronic files on the internet within or without the enterprises. Moreover, IT has been utilized for improving the processes of many enterprises, e.g. supply chains and material flows. As a result, those activities within or between enterprises called Business to Business (abbreviated to "B-to-B") become efficient and the costs are reduced.

Furthermore, the internet has enabled the enterprises to sell goods and services directly to the consumers in recent years. Prices of goods and services via the internet are often cheaper than those of ordinary shopping. We call such activities Business to Consumers (abbreviated to "B-to-C").

Considering above phenomena, we are able to consider that consumers can obtain goods, services and information by driving several functional organizations directly via the digital devices and network facilities. These activities are considered as Consumers to Business ("C-to-B"). We call an enterprise to do business including "B-to-B", "B-to-C" and "C-to-B" as a "Digital Enterprise" [1]. Of course, "C-to-C" is included in the activities. This paper shows a concept, features and research issues of a digital enterprise from the technological, managerial and social aspects.

Recent business models show signs of the digital enterprise. As some examples of the models, we can find on-demand publishing, the apparel industry manufacturing goods designed by the consumers. However, there have been little research papers on the problems of the digital enterprise. When we consider these problems, IT and management issues are closely related to each other [2]. In addition to managerial and technological aspects, we must pay attention to legal issues and social aspects concerning the digital enterprise. Thus we organize researchers on IT, management science, laws and sociology as a research project on the digital enterprise. This paper will discuss research issues of this project.

2 Recent Directions on Business and Information Technology

This chapter describes directions on both business and IT since the mid-1990s. These directions show that the leading part playing in the market is moving from the supplier to the consumer. The consumers will place at the center in our digital enterprise.

2.1 Directions on business using information technology

Business results of many companies using IT, especially the internet, have become well since the mid-1990s. We classify those companies into three levels according to the ways to use the internet.

Level 1: Documents for exchanging information are replaced by e-mails of electronic files on the internet within or without the enterprises.
A lot of business processes are sped up by replacing papers with the electronic devices. Moreover, this replacement often reduces costs, time, and human resources. When BPR (Business Process Reengineering) of a company is completed, it will become this level.

Level 2: Order or selling is processed via the internet.
Many companies, including “Amazon.com”, “Compaq” etc., of this type have succeeded in business. This business model is often called “Internet Business”. The web technology and logistics are key points to the companies at this level. In order to achieve this level, Level 1 is prerequisite to the company.

Level 3: Members of the company share common and enough information for management, innovation, production, sales and customer satisfaction.
If an enterprise at Level 2 gathers enough information and use it effectively, then the company is at this level. In addition to technical aspects, the enterprise at this level has to provide some processes to share information and to make decisions for satisfying customers’ needs by using information. The managerial issues are most important for the companies at this level.

2.2 Directions on enterprise information systems

Recent software systems for enterprises are often implemented by using software packages to support Levels 1 and 2. These packages are called ERP (Enterprise Resource Planning) [3] or SCM (Supply Chain Management). CRM (Customer Relationship Management), SFA (Sales Force Automation) [4] or CTI (Computer Telephony Integration) supports to realize Levels 2 and 3. These packages have been implemented from the information systems of the basic functions of the enterprise to the consumers (Figure 1).

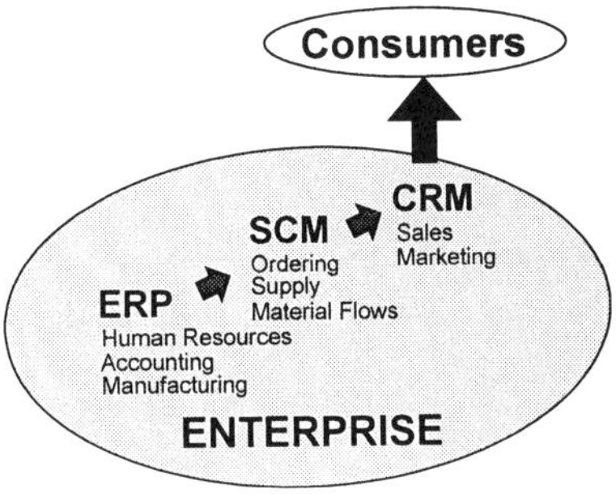

Figure 1. Recent software packages for enterprises

Since above packages support the internet and the WWW (World Wide Web), we can construct the infrastructures easily for Levels 1 and 2 now. Moreover, we can use frameworks and commercial off-the-shelf (COTS) software components for implementing the systems.

2.3 Towards a digital enterprise

It is necessary for any modern enterprise to achieve at Level 3. For satisfying consumers needs, we must use recent information on the consumers and their environments. In general, the enterprise has plenty of information on customers and market. Thus information of the enterprise at Level 3 has to be managed by using IT. If there are some enterprises at Level 3 and the software systems mediating between the consumers and the enterprises are provided, then a consumer can satisfy his/her needs by integrating functional units of the enterprises on the internet. We propose a digital enterprise as the next step of the enterprise at Level 3 (Figure 2).

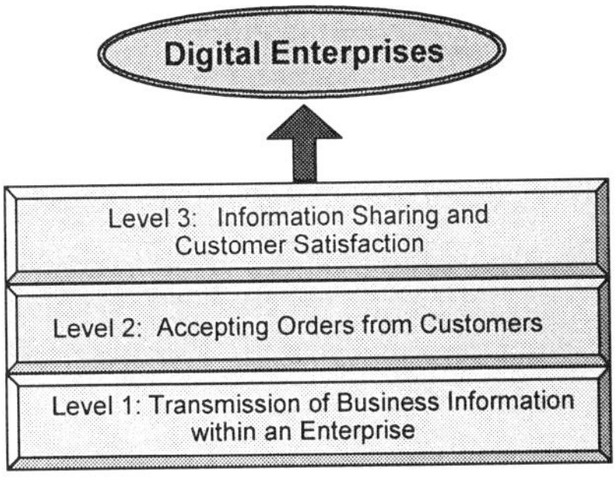

Figure 2. Levels of using information technology for business

3 A Concept of a "Digital Enterprise"

This paper shows an outline of a concept of a "Digital Enterprise". Its concrete version will be framed through our research project.

3.1 A digital enterprise

We assume that the enterprise are at Level 3. Furthermore, there exist software agents for consumers and functional organizations. A consumer can buy goods, services and information by ordering via the internet. He or she can not obtain only existing ones but also order something satisfying his or her needs to a group of functional organizations. We call an enterprise operated in such a situation a "digital enterprise". Figure 3 shows an image of the digital enterprise.

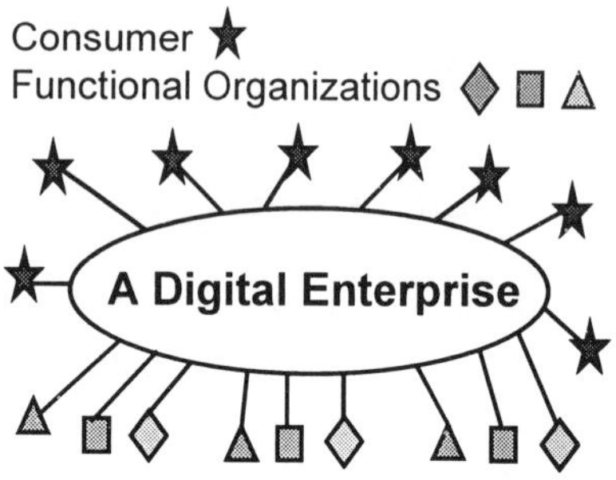

Figure 3. A concept of the digital enterprise

In recent days, we can find some pioneers of such enterprises in U.S.A. or Japan. The examples are on-demand publishing by writers, the apparel industry produced by the consumer's design, and reverse-auctions for the airlines tickets.

In this situation, the consumers' needs organize several functional units virtually as a digital enterprise. It is considered that the organization of the enterprise changes dynamically in accordance with the needs. We will find many digital enterprises in the near future.

On the other hand, the roles of consumers in business have increased in recent years. Researching the history of business concerned with consumption have placed either markets or gender at the center [5]. However, notice that all enterprises will not be the digital enterprises. Needless to say, another type of the enterprise of the digital enterprise will be valuable in a certain kind of business.

3.2 Information technology, management and society of digital enterprises

It is expected that the digital enterprise satisfies the consumers' diverse needs quickly. On the other hand, there will be many problems including the technology, management, legal and social issues. Considering electronic commerce, we must pay attention not only to the security algorithms but also to legal and social issues. Thus we are planning to start a research project on the digital enterprise by combining technological, managerial and social fields. Figure 4 shows an organization of this project.

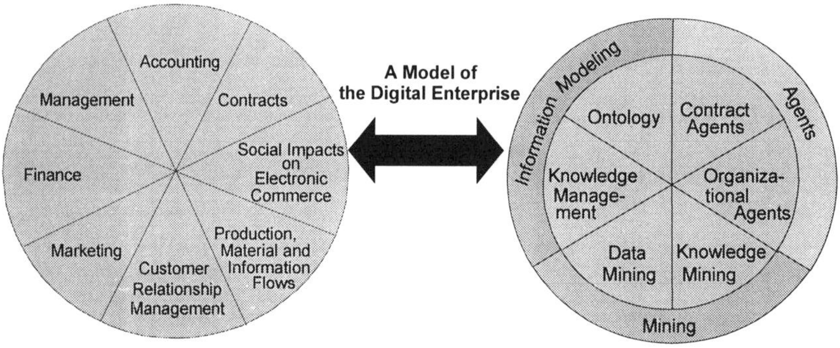

Figure 4. A structure of our research project

Management scientists analyze the modern enterprise from several functional roles. Moreover, they will frame a concrete model of a digital enterprise. Researchers on information technology develop software systems to implement the digital enterprise. Social systems for the digital enterprise are investigated by sociologists and researchers on laws in our project.

4 Managerial Aspects of the Digital Enterprise

Since the activities of the digital enterprise are quite different from those of existing one, the enterprise requires a new structure, functions, and management. Considering the properties of the digital enterprise, we focus on accounting, finance, production, logistics, marketing, and customer relationship management.

4.1 Management, accounting and finance

Our project will propose a new structure of management for the digital enterprise. Especially, we study a relationship between the decision making and the infrastructure for information processing.

It is important for the digital enterprise to balance many elements of customers, functional units, other enterprises and so on. Thus we will propose a concept of a "Dynamic Balance" of accounting. Moreover, we will develop a financial engineering method for the enterprises that change dynamically.

4.2 Production and material flows

Since every material is handled with attached information, this project will propose "an information model of production and material flows". This model represents roles, production processes, and material flows visually. We are planning to apply this model to production and logistics of the digital enterprise.

4.3 Marketing and customer relationship management

One-to-one marketing for each customer is one of the most important research issues in recent years. The marketing activities on the digital enterprise are considered as ultimate one-to-one marketing. Thus advanced research on one-to-one marketing will be applied to the activities of our digital enterprise.

Moreover, now we are entering the customer era that is characterized by seeing customers as valuable asset. Thus the methodology and tools for CRM (Customer Relationship Management) should be introduced by the modern companies. Since the main objectives of CRM for the digital enterprise are different from these of existing CRM packages, this project will provide a new tool of CRM.

5 Technological Aspects of the Digital Enterprise

The most basic technological infrastructures of the digital enterprise are networking, securities and distributed object technology. We consider that the studies on these subjects will be completed within a few years. Thus our project studies IT concerning the contents of the enterprise activities, that is, "information modeling", "mining" and "agents".

5.1 Information modeling

Our digital enterprises will have to process plenty of data. Therefore, this project studies "ontology" of business data and "knowledge management" of the digital enterprise as basic research of information modeling. We will propose a new method of domain ontology of the digital enterprise. Furthermore, this project will show a management model of the digital enterprise.

5.2 Mining

We must use a huge data warehouse for operating and managing the digital enterprise effectively. Thus, our project studies methods for mining business data. Especially, we will study "a method for mining business patterns from a huge data warehouse" and "Knowledge discovery of trends of the enterprise."

5.3 Agents

Since the activities on the digital enterprises are too complex to be handled by consumers and managers, we need software agents for them. This project will propose "contract agents" for customers and "organizational agents" for the digital enterprise.

6 Social Aspects of the Digital Enterprise

When the digital enterprise is realized, some problems besides technological and managerial issues may appear. Among those problems, this project studies legal and social issues on electronic commerce concerning the digital enterprise.

6.1 Legal issues on contracts

In contracting via contract agents or electronic commerce, we must consider the legal issues for protection of individual information, reliability of each enterprise and establishment of contract rules. In order to realize the digital enterprise, it is necessary to propose a mechanism to prevent consumers from troubles.

6.2 Electronic commerce and society

The digital enterprise always uses electronic commerce around the world. Since this situation will force us to restructuring our business across borders, we have to examine social issues on electronic commerce. This project will propose a method for reaching a social consensus to accept the digital enterprise.

7 Discussions

In addition to research problems described above, we must consider the other research issues to complete our project. Some examples will be shown and discussed in this chapter.

7.1 Enterprise models

In order to integrate above research results as a digital enterprise, we need an enterprise model. Recently, many models have been proposes for integrating management with IT [6]. For example, A. –W. Scheer proposes an ARIS (Architecture of Integrated Information System) model that integrates business processes and organizations into an information system [7]. This model assumes that business processes, strategy and organizations were already fixed. However, business processes and organizations of our digital enterprise change dynamically. C. Marshall shows another enterprise model combining a purpose, business processes, entities and management (Figure 5) [8]. Similar to the ARIS model, Marshall's model assumes that those elements were fixed.

Figure 5. Strategic hierarchy of Marshall's model

7.2 Business processes and business flows

Existing models tend to focus on the business processes or business flows. When we use these models, we must describe concrete business processes and flows [9] at first. Next, they have to be integrated and abstracted as a model. Finally, the model is refined by information technology.

The model is usually constructed by the bottom-up approach. An autonomous and network-based model will be required for the digital enterprise. Furthermore, consumers must drive the enterprise in the model.

7.3 Business models

Many patents on the business models have been applied in U.S.A. and Japan. A business model is considered as a part of the enterprise model. Both a way to do business and its support software system are applied as patents. Examples are:

- web shopping carts of Open Market, Inc.,
- on line frequent buyer programs of Netcentives, and
- reverse auctions of Price Line Inc.

This project is planning to take out some patents on the business model for the digital enterprise.

8 Concluding Remarks

This paper shows a concept of the digital enterprise for a type of future business. Comparing with the similar concepts [10], we emphasize importance of the roles of consumers in business of the digital enterprise. Therefore, we would like to study software systems for "C-to-B" and "C-to-C" concerning the digital enterprise in our research project.

Research issues on the digital enterprise were also discussed in this paper. We think that the research subjects on software are information modeling mining and agents. Moreover, our project plans to propose new management methods for the digital enterprise. We assume that consumers' devices of the digital enterprise will not be always personal computers. They may be digital electric household appliances, terminals of video games, or PDA.

We must investigate not only technological aspects but also social and legal issues. Concerning similar problems tackled by our project, some books have been published and research projects have started [11,12] in recent years. Furthermore, the activities of the digital enterprises are across the borders. Thus this issue should be studied internationally.

Acknowledgements

The author would like to thank Prof. Takahira Yamaguchi and Prof. Yoshitaka Kobayashi for their contributions to organize this research project. Comments from the members of this project are valuable for writing this paper. Many managers, consultants and engineers encouraged me to frame a digital enterprise concept. The author also thanks Miss Kumiko Ito for her assistance to complete this paper.

References

[1] M. Nagata, Management and Information Technology for Future Digital Enterprises (Invited Paper), Technical Report of IEICE, KBSE99-46, 2000, pp. 23-30 (in Japanese)

[2] R. B. Walford Business Process Implementation for IT Professionals and Managers, Artech House, Inc., 1999

[3] A. Teshima, T. Negoro and A. Sugino, ERP and Business Innovation, Nikka-Giren Pub. Co., 1998 (in Japanese)

[4] M. Nagata, SFA: An Information System for Customer Satisfaction, IPSJ Magazine, Vol. 40, No.5, 1999, pp. 528-531 (in Japanese)

[5] R. Church, New Perspectives on the History of Products, Firms, Marketing, and Consumers in Britain and the United States since the Mid-Nineteenth Century, Economic History Review, Vol. 52, No. 3, 1999, pp. 405-435

[6] D. A. Taylor, Business Engineering with Object Technology, John Wiley & Sons, Inc., 1995

[7] A. -W. Scheer, ARIS – Business Process Frameworks, Springer-Verlag, 1998

[8] C. Marshall, Enterprise Modeling with UML, Addison Wesley Longman, Inc., 1999

[9] M. Kuroki, and M. Nagata, A Business Flow Diagram for Acquiring Users' Requirements of Object Oriented Software, IEICE Trans. on Infor. & Sys., Vol. E83-D, No. 4, 2000 (in Printing)

[10] W. H. Davidow and M. S. Malone., The Virtual Corporation, Harper Collins Publishers, Inc., 1992

[11] The Project of the JSPS Research for the Future Program, Information Technology and the Market http://www.e.u-tokyo.ac.jp/itme/

[12] S. Nishio, et al., Mutual Understanding, Iwanami Shoten Publishers, 1999 (in Japanese)

Knowledge-Based Software Engineering
T. Hruška and M. Hashimoto (Eds.)
IOS Press, 2000

An XML-based Business Scenario Engine for Networked Enterprises

Takashi NAITO, Keisuke HATA, Shuichiro YAMAMOTO
NTT Information Sharing Platform Laboratories
3-9-11 Midori-cho Musashino-shi, Tokyo 180-8585 Japan
E-mail: {naito.gack, hata.keisuke, yamamoto.shuichiro}@lab.ntt.co.jp

Abstract. We describe a collaborative business scenario description language that is based on XML. This language can be used to describe scenarios for the virtual integration of services over the Internet and intranets. Thus, it enables the business modeling for integrated e-business services to be separated from the software development. This promises to improve the productivity of e-business services, because business managers can easily develop business models using an XML-based scenario without being concerned with application development. The scenario engine executes and controls transactions related to services available from different sites. A preliminary evaluation of the scenario engine has demonstrated its potential usefulness.

1 Introduction

Many enterprise applications have recently been developed on the Internet and virtual private networks. There is, however, a need for enterprise application integration (EAI) tools to cut the cost of developing these applications. Current EAI tools have only a simple message transformation mechanism that supports data transfer among the different applications. These EAI tools do not provide cross-enterprise integration, robust application switching for application faults, or flexible application integration with human activities. Although many workflow management tools make it easier to control the execution of a sequence of applications as specified by a business model encoded by the specific workflow design language, integrating enterprise applications at different sites is still difficult.

To solve these problems, we have developed an XML-based [1] business scenario engine for networked enterprises. The starting point of our approach is as follows.

Enterprise applications are distributed at different sites. These cross-enterprise applications need to be integrated. Human activities are also integrated into business scenarios. If we could integrate and reuse e-services available through networks, the development of e-services would be greatly facilitated; it would be much easier to develop, use, and change services.

If users who are not familiar with enterprise application development could develop business processes using scenarios, they would find it much easier to specify business models and share scenarios among enterprises.

We therefore need to develop scenario-based integration technology to better support the integration of enterprise applications. This technology should also enable the network-wide integration of applications and human activities.

We have developed a scenario-based application invocation mechanism that facilitates the integration of networked applications and user activities. The scenario description language is based on XML because it is flexible, easy to understand, and reusable.

In Section 2 we explain our scenario-based e-service development approach. In Section 3 we describe the architecture of the scenario engine. This engine will help users develop e-services by describing business scenarios using XML and make it easier to integrate enterprise applications at different sites. Section 4 describes the collaboration-oriented scenario markup language (CSML). In Section 5, we discuss the applicability of the proposed method and the effectiveness of CSML.

2 Scenario-based e-service development approach

The e-service development approach (Fig. 1) has two steps. The first step is scenario analysis. In the scenario analysis, the XML-based CMSL – a collaborative business-scenario description language – is used to describe and reuse business processes. A scenario consists of a flow of activities that represent applications and human activities. Using a scenario, the user defines the virtual integration of services in terms of a sequence of activities at Internet and intranet sites. During scenario analysis the user is not necessarily concerned with application details such as GUI presentation, the business logic of applications, or database processing. This enables separation between the business process modeling and the application development for integrated e-services. Productivity in developing and launching e-services is thus improved because business managers without any knowledge of application development can easily develop business models using XML-based scenarios.

The second step is activity development, which includes data integration design and application development. Communication data must be defined for all applications in the same scenario. Each application includes code for the GUI presentation, business logic, database processing, and data integration.

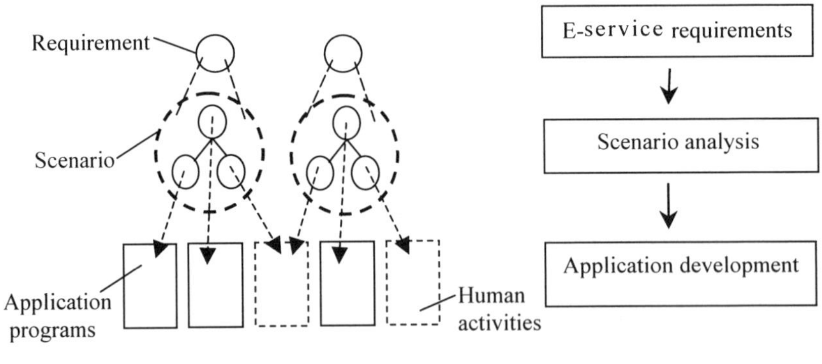

Figure 1. Scenario based e-service development approach

Traditional e-service development cannot separate the business process from the application coding. Therefore, it is often difficult for the end user to integrate the business processes of applications. In contrast, scenario development by the end user makes it much easier to elicit application integration requirements. Because the scenario engine executes scenarios and controls applications, process integration code is developed in the scenario analysis step and requires no further development. Therefore, the development of e-services is strongly supported by the scenario-based e-service development approach.

3 Architecture of the scenario engine

The scenario engine consists of the scenario interpreter, the activity directory, the communication data manager, and the scenario manager (Fig. 2). The scenario interpreter is made up of the scenario parser, the scenario context manager, and the scenario executer. The scenario parser loads a scenario from the scenario manager and transforms it into an intermediate form. The instance generated for a scenario is called a scenario instance, and the context of a scenario instance is controlled by the context manager . The scenario executer initiates activities according to the sequence of scenario statements. The activity directory is used to define the physical position of the activities. For example, the directory describes URLs for services on the Internet and e-mail addresses for human activities. The scenario executer asks the directory about the access method for each activity to be executed. After an access method is specified by the directory, the executer initiates the corresponding activity through this method. For human activities, a mail application can be used to send service requests to the persons responsible for the task specified by human activities. Human activities are defined in the directory with the addresses of the person and the mail application. This mechanism increases the flexibility of the integration between human activities and application programs. Since the directory manages the correspondence between activity names in a scenario and the physical definitions of activities, no scenario modification is needed to change the physical positions of applications for the activities.

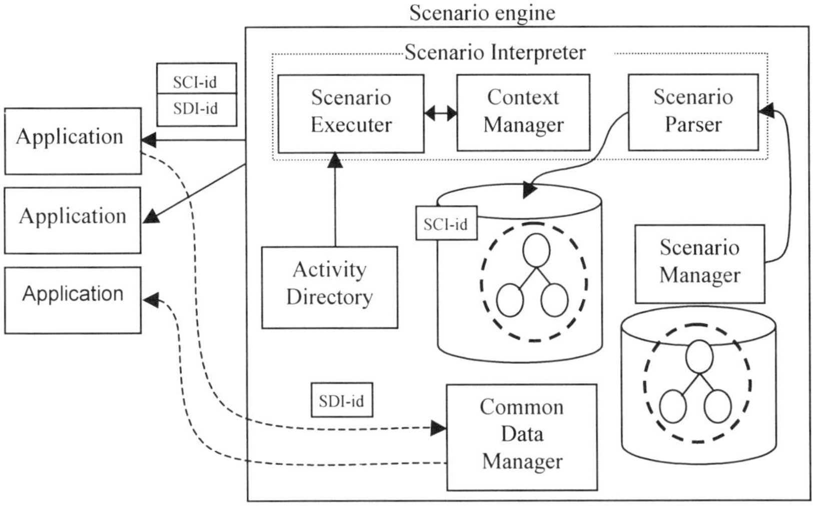

Figure 2. Architecture of scenario engine

The communication data shared among activities are stored with a shared data instance identifier (SDI-id) that distinguishes it from other communication data. Activities of the same scenario instance can easily exchange data through the communication data manager by using an SDI-id and a scenario instance identifier (SCI-id) that specifies the current scenario. Activities include an SDI-id and an SCI-id (an instance identifier pair) when sending communication data to the communication data manager. The receiver activities that use the data can get it from the communication data manager by using the instance identifier pair. The mechanism encapsulates data communication codes from the business process, so an end user can easily construct a business process without any tedious data handling by simply using a scenario.

4 Collaboration-oriented Scenario Markup Language (CSML)

4.1 CSML specification

In CSML, an application that interacts with the operator is called an activity. The scenario defines a processing flow using scenario statements. The scenario definition consists of a scenario header, a declaration part, a body part, and an exception part. The scenario header includes the scenario name and version.

```
<Scenario Name="scenario name" [Ver="version number"]>
   [Declaration part]
    Body part
   [Exception part]
</Scenario>
```

The declaration part contains the scenario description and event description. The event description explains the events used in the scenario.

```
<DeclarationPart>
   [<Description> Scenario description </Description>]
   {<Event Name="event name"> Event description </Event>}*
</DeclarationPart>
```

The scenario statements describe the body part, which contains five kinds of scenario statements:

(1) Activity statement: Execute an activity.

```
<Activity Name="activity name">
  <Event Name="event name" />*
</Activity>
```

Each activity may have a sequence of events. Only one of the events should occur after the execution of the activity.

(2) Concatenation statement: Concatenate two or more scenario statements. Scenario statements are executed in sequence without any pause between them.

```
<Seq>
  Scenario statements+
</Seq>
```

(3) Parallel statements: A parallel AND statement executes two or more processes at the same time, and the system waits until all activities have ended. A parallel OR statement executes two or more processes at the same time, and the system waits until any activity has ended.

```
<Par [Join="AND#|OR"]>
  Scenario statement*
</Par>
```

(4) Switch statement: Input events are compared against specified conditions, and processing that matches the conditions is executed.

```
<Switch>
   { <Case Event="event name">
       Scenario statement +
     </Case>}+
    { <Other>
       Scenario statement +
     </Other>}*
</Switch>
```

(5) Raise Exception statement: Processing is shifted to the exception part when an exception event occurs.

<Raise Event="event name" />

The exception part describes the exception-handling statement by a scenario statement. If another exception occurs while an exception statement is being executed, the execution is stopped and the second exception is executed.

<Exception Event="event name">
Scenario statement+
</Exception>

The end of the exception statement is described by the terminate statement. The default terminate statement is Exit.

<Terminate command="Resume|Exit#|Finish|Abort" />

The termination of an exception is handled in one of four ways.

- Resume: Returns to body part. Processing restarts.
- Exit: Returns to the next upper level of the exception statement. At the top level of the exception, processing returns to the body part.
- Finish: Returns to the next upper level of the exception statement. At the top of the exception, processing ends.
- Abort: Ends processing.

4.2 Example CSML Scenario

The following is an example of a CSML scenario for a travel agency.

```
<? xml version="1.0" encoding= "EUC-JP" ?>
<Scenario Name="travel">
<DeclarationPart>
  <Event Name="cancel"> Reservation cancellation </Event>
</DeclarationPart>
<BodyPart>
  <Activity Name="Airline reservation" />
  <Activity Name="Hotel reservation" />
  <Activity Name="Input personal information" />
</BodyPart>
<ExceptionPart>
  <Exception Event="cancel">
  <Terminate command="Abort" />
  </Exception>
</ExceptionPart>
</Scenario>
```

The hotel and airline reservation applications and the customer administration application operate cooperatively in this scenario.

5 Discussion

5.1 Applicability

We have implemented the scenario engine described above using Java and applied it to an e-mall development project. The project included four different enterprises. Each enterprise developed one e-service using the scenario engine through the Internet. The e-services developed were three digital-content retail sites and a content-contribution site. The digital-content retail sites were to sell photographs, music, and foreign-language-learning content. The content-contribution site was to gather digital content from contributors that would be edited by the site's editors. Each e-service reused the same payment service and account management application. The services included 28 scenarios and 97 activities. The mean number of e-service WWW pages was 62. The success of this project demonstrates the applicability of the scenario engine for e-services.

The numbers of scenarios differed greatly between sites. For example, the contribution site had 17 scenarios, but the photograph site had only one. This difference was due to the scenario development process. The contribution site's designers developed a flow of WWW pages, then defined scenarios. The photograph site's designers defined one logical scenario, then developed applications for each scenario activity. The approach taken for the contribution site probably increased the number of scenarios because scenarios were extracted from each sequence of WWW pages. This demonstrates the importance of the order of steps taken in the scenario-based e-service development approach described in Section 2. Further experiments to precisely determine the impact of various scenario development methods are needed.

5.2 Effectiveness of CSML

The use of CSML has three positive effects.

(1) Business processes to be reused.

- With existing tools, we must define a business process by describing a mixture of processing flows and service-specific information. This makes it difficult to reuse the business process in other services. CSML describes service-specific information and processing flows separately, so a processing flow can be reused in other services.
- With existing tools, we must define business processes with names representing actual physical objects and locations. Such defined business processes cannot be easily used in other services because the physical names differ from service to service. In a CSML scenario, though, application names are described by logical names that are converted to the corresponding physical names upon execution. CSML thus enables the reuse of scenarios in other services with the corresponding physical information provided upon execution.

(2) Business processes are easy to change.

- With existing tools, we must describe application data in the business process (e.g., 'if price>'target value' then execute P1 else P2', where the value (e.g., '$100') given for 'target value' is application data.). In such cases, the business process and the application are closely related, so changing the business process means the application data must be checked and possibly modified. Thus, the business process cannot be changed quickly or easily. With CSML, the scenario does not include application data. The business process is simply defined by describing the processing flow and the execution conditions for the applications.

(3) CSML can be widely applied.

- With existing tools, we must describe business processes using the tools' own notations, but a CSML scenario can be described in the standardized XML notation.
- With existing tools, exception handling cannot be described using programming languages, but can be so described in a CSML scenario.

5.3 Descriptive capabilities of CSML

We compared the description capabilities of CSML to those of Workflow Process Definition Language (WPDL), a similar description language that can also be used to describe a workflow. (WPDL is being developed by the Workflow Management Coalition [2].) The travel agency scenario from above was used for this comparison. We found that:

- CSML, unlike WPDL, can effectively describe exception handling.
- Physical information is included in WPDL scenarios, but excluded from CSML scenarios. In a typical WPDL scenario, about 30% of the lines of code were used to describe the physical information, and about 70% of the lines were used to describe the same logical information as with CSML. Reusing this WPDL scenario for other travel agencies would be difficult, but CSML can reuse all the logical information lines for other travel agencies. Thus, CSML enables scenario reuse.

Also, WPDL uses its own notation, but CSML is based on XML and thus has wider applicability.

5.4 Related work

Applications must be able to cooperate and share their information in order to use information effectively for business [2]. Workflow tools [3], GroupWare tools, and EAI tools have been developed to enable application integration and cooperation between existing applications. In some cases, SWAP [4] also enables these tools to cooperate. These tools, however, still have certain limitations.

- The described business processes cannot be reused by other tools, because the form for describing business processes differs from tool to tool.
- A tool is usually unable to cooperate with another tool.
- These tools cannot describe exception handling for the business process.

Hewlett-Packard has developed an e-speak platform that provides a hierarchical e-service architecture including service, solution, component, and core layers [5]. The service layer provides corporate applications over the Internet. The solution layer is a kind of virtual community service and provides brokerage functions for e-services. The component layer provides basic e-service functions, such as identification, billing, customer management, and preference matching. The e-speak core is a Java-based e-service development environment, and consists of a Java-based e-service API and an e-service engine. The e-service engine manages the messaging, mediation, naming, and monitoring functions. The e-speak API is used by the Java applications of the upper e-speak layers. The metadata which stored on the e-speak core is able to search dynamically among e-services. The e-speak core allows brokering through attribute matching between information requesters and providers. But although the e-speak core provides these useful integration functions, Java applications must still be developed to integrate e-service components. The core provides neither scenario-based higher-level scripting language, nor an application data sharing mechanism.

Although Gruhn and Wellen proposed a process-oriented approach to develop electronic commerce applications [6] their emphasis was on the formal specification of communication interfaces. Their process model is defined by the tuple of the object type, the object states, a set of activities, and the flows between activities and states. Therefore, it is difficult for end users to describe and understand the business processes of EC applications using their specifications.

6 Conclusion

We have described a scenario-based e-service development approach, the XML-based CSML, and the scenario engine. We have also discussed a preliminary evaluation of the scenario engine. The main purpose of the scenario description is to separate the business process from the application coding. This enables end users not familiar with application programming to design business logic. As a consequence, it will encourage the evolution of e-services on the Internet.

CSML is a markup language for describing a business process.

- It enables business processes to be reused.
- It enables applications to cooperate.
- It can describe exception handling for the business process.

Our evaluation of CSML showed that it allows greater reuse and wider applicability than existing tools. We have also described some practical applications of the implemented scenario engine to e-services provided through the Internet, and have explained the importance of the scenario development process.

Future study should include refinement of the scenario specification language, an evaluation of productivity when using the scenario-based e-service development approach, and an evaluation of the scenario engine's performance. We are also designing a scenario editor that allows the user to drag-and-drop icons from a menu of scenario statements to generate CSML business scenarios. Such a visual-scenario interface will greatly promote e-service development as well as the reuse of existing e-services.

Acknowledgements

We thank Takafumi Saito and the members of the scenario engine development team for their comments on this paper.

References

[1] Extensible Markup Language (XML) 1.0 (W3C Recommendation), http://www.w3c.org/TR/REC-xml.

[2] Yuan LI, Zhiping Fan, and Xuan Zhao, An Integrated Framework of Supply Chain Management System, APSEC99, 1999, pp. 196- 199.

[3] Workflow Management Coalition (WfMC), http://www.aiim.org/wfmc

[4] Gregory Alan Bolcer: SWAP Leveraging the Web To Manage Workflow, IEEE Internet Computing, Jan.-Feb. 1999, pp. 85-88.

[5] e-speak, http://www.e-speak.hp.com/

[6] Volker Gruhn and Ursula Wellen, Software Support for Distributed Business Processes, APSEC 99, 1999, pp. 200- 205.

Knowledge-Based Software Engineering
T. Hruška and M. Hashimoto (Eds.)
IOS Press, 2000

Agent-Oriented Workflow with Decision Support

Mirjana IVANOVIĆ, Zoran BUDIMAC, Dragoslav PEŠOVIĆ

Institute of Mathematics, Faculty of Science
Trg D. Obradovića 4, 21000 Novi Sad, Yugoslavia
e-mail: {mira, zjb, dragoslav}@unsim.ns.ac.yu

Abstract. In this paper a proposition of Agent-oriented workflow framework, which merges information flows and maintenance with process of decision making, is presented. The proposed framework represents union of the two different approaches and it can be applied in different institutions. An application in agriculture domain is suggested. The amalgamation of agent and workflow technologies is made in order to increase efficiency and to improve decision-making process.

1 Introduction

The making of a decision is a very important process in different business steps and situations. It is, usually, followed by an analysis of the problem, a search for alternatives to solve the problem, and finally by the application of the selected alternative to solve the problem.

The every step in the decision process needs or requires appropriate information and/or knowledge, based on which the next step is taken. The better information, the better decision is made. Therefore, it is very important for the successful management that the relevant information in the appropriate moment will be delivered as required by the management.

Executive Information Systems (EIS) are special kind of information systems, which have been modeled to support management process in information retrieving and maintaining. The advantages of EIS in management processes are the following [13]:

- it is designed to meet information needs,
- it retrieves information as required,
- it possesses tools for data analysis and further processing of data,
- it reduces the information overflow,
- it retrieves additional information through on-line information access,
- it produces task and work specific reports.

An essential part of an EIS is the information flow, and the main idea is that every user gets only information in accordance with his needs. The information flow defines the distribution of any information and it determines what can be accessed, when, and by whom through an EIS.

In order to increase efficiency in agriculture management processes, we analyzed couple of different institutions (big laboratories, production companies, and farm management) and proposed an Agent-Oriented Workflow Framework (AOWF) applicable, with more or less changes and modifications, in different systems where workflow and decision functions are needed. Agent-Oriented Workflow Framework supports basic functions of an EIS but, also, gains a new approach and improves information flows and processes of decision making based on appropriate and recent information and knowledge.

Agent-Oriented Workflow Framework presents a way for automation of work and decision processes which increases efficiency in information and documents flows between separate wide range users (domain experts, software engineers, managers, end-users...).

2 Agent-Oriented Workflow Framework

Process of designing Agent-Oriented Workflow Framework involved two modern, very attractive and promising fields in computer science:

1. *Software agents* with the attributes they possess: autonomy, social ability, responsiveness, proactiveness are fundamentally new paradigm in comparison with related disciplines of information technology [13]. They are good intelligent elements capable to fulfill functions of decision making. Using the workflow management system is a modern trend in modelling and implementation of information flow and business processes in a company [5]. Well organised and fully implemented, a workflow can replace a large part of a classical information system of a company.
2. *Workflow* [3, 4, 14] is concerned with automation of procedures where documents, information or tasks are passed between participants according to a defined set of rules to achieve or contribute an overall business goal. Also, two distinguishing characteristics are very important and make agents more promising for application in different areas like: personal information management, electronic commerce, business process management:
   - high-level tasks can be delegated to agents who will autonomously carry them out,
   - agents are situated in an environment which can dynamically affect their problem solving behaviour and strategy.

The main idea of designing Agent-Oriented Workflow Framework was to integrate EIS and decision-support capabilities in a unique environment. The Agent-Oriented Workflow Framework with decision-making capabilities has to support following requirements:

- Data and knowledge representation,
- User-friendly interface,
- Expert system shell and decision support model.

Based on these requirements, it seems that centralized workflow architecture [1] is more appropriate. Standard centralized workflow architecture [6] is modified and extended to fulfill processes of decision making [8].

Centralized workflow architecture consists of central workflow engine with appropriate application agents. Apart from that, there are components for definition and modelling, as well as for human-computer interaction (interface).

Proposed framework architecture consists of (Figure 1):

1. *Central workflow unit (CWFU)*,
2. *Workflow definition unit (WFDU)*,
3. *Human-interaction unit (HIU)*,
4. *Decision support unit (DSU)*.

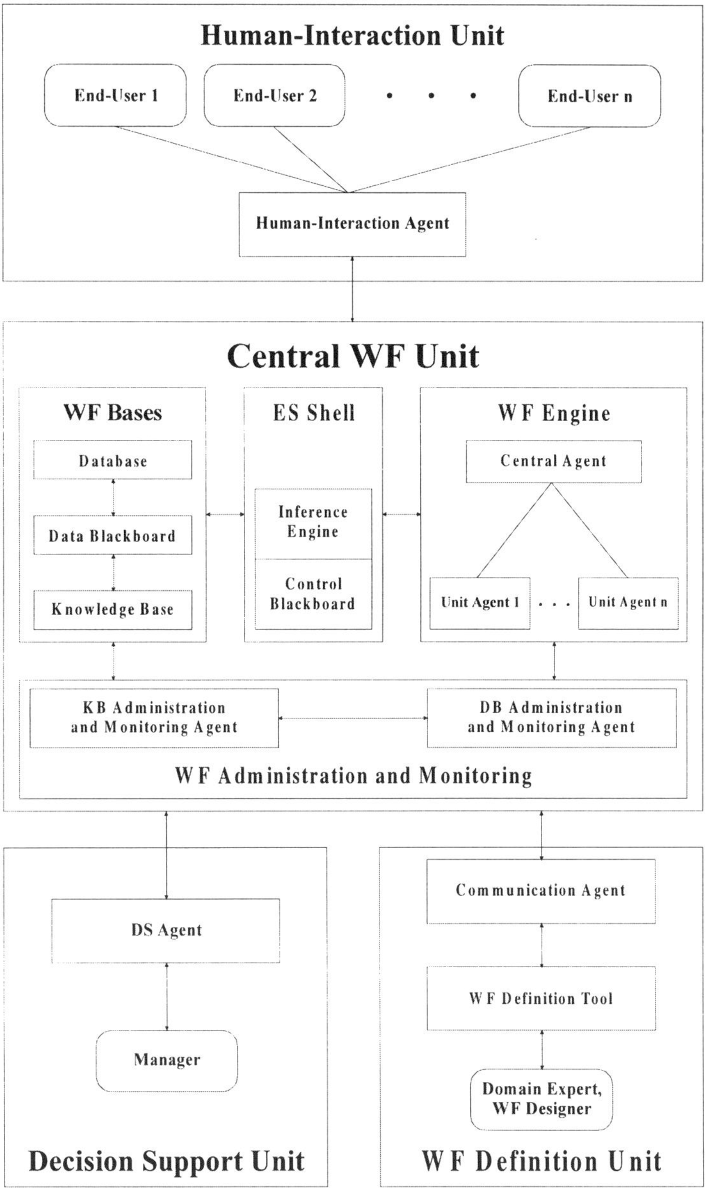

Figure 1 Agent-oriented workflow with decision support

The basic activity of this model is to support flow of wide range of documents carrying different information and knowledge important for management of company and capability to draw out, select and memorize important information based on which appropriate decision will be made. This approach facilitates the construction and manipulation of the knowledge bases, as well as the interchange between the knowledge bases and the databases of the system.

2.1 Central Workflow Unit

The *central workflow unit* consists mainly of:

- *Workflow engine* with central agent and unit (application) agents,
- *Workflow bases* (with database (DB) and knowledge base (KB)),
- *Workflow administration and monitoring* unit with separate DB and KB administration and monitoring agents.
- *Expert system (*ES*) shell.*

The *WF engine* communicates with the workflow database to store and update workflow state data. A workflow scheme (workflow definition) is created by a workflow designer.

Central agent of a workflow engine is responsible for managing all the instances of all schemes by communicating with other workflow engine agents. A workflow scheme is essentially a directed graph with nodes representing the steps to be performed. The arcs connecting the steps are of two types: data and control. The data arc denotes the flow of data between steps while a control arc specifies the ordering sequence between the two steps.

Also, they have a condition associated with it to indicate that the succeeding step is to be executed only if the condition evolves to true.

The engine maintains information about the workflow and steps in various tables in a workflow database, and it selects (according to knowledge-base administration and monitoring) appropriate data and stores them into the knowledge-base.

The central agent is responsible for managing all activities and steps, i.e. it has to schedule the steps of the other agents when they are eligible for execution. It maintains internal control data.

A particular unit agent is responsible for executing the step and communicating back the results of the step to the central agent. Every particular agent has its own instance of a workflow scheme that represents a directed graph specific for the department or the organizational unit that the agent maintains.

WF bases are database (DB) and knowledge-base (KB). A workflow DB serves for storing and updating workflow state data (representing all necessary data for the concrete company, flows of documents and information, and other data responsible for efficient and prompt business management).

The data needed by decision support part of Agent-Oriented Workflow Framework, to carry out decisions, are organized in KB manner.

The *WF administration and monitoring* unit consists of DB and KB administration and monitoring agents. They are responsible for different changes in data, schemes, routing, conditions, and they always keep tracks of all the activities.

They are also capable of tracing a history of a particular process instance, to form history and different statistical reports, useful for business process improvements.

In building knowledge-base of the system, an expert system shell is needed, with special capabilities of getting its knowledge-base from database tables.

Other requirements concern the cooperation and extracting of appropriate data and knowledge with a WF engine and the interchange and (possible) improvements of data between them.

Once an ES shell obtained data and passed it to a WF engine, WF engine agents and DS agents negotiate in order to obtain several logical and most acceptable decisions and offer them to the manager to make the final decision.

The blackboard component is used to coordinate an ES that cooperates to solve a common problem or to integrate an ES with conventional problem solving techniques.

The general problem usually requires a variety of input data and needs to integrate diverse information. Apart from that, it requires many independent or semi-independent pieces of knowledge to cooperate. Multiple knowledge representation and reasoning techniques are often required, which are well suited for the blackboard type solution.

2.2 Workflow Definition Unit

To establish the central workflow unit, it is necessary to organize a workflow definition tool. A workflow designer and a domain expert use it to create the process description based on a formal definition language.

Inputs are appropriate actions in textual and/or graphical form. It also has to support dynamic changes and modifications. To fulfill these activities, a workflow definition tool communicates with a communication agent.

2.3 Human-Interaction Unit and Decision Support Unit

Two kinds of users are eligible to use the proposed Agent-Oriented Workflow Framework:

- *managers* - responsible for making decisions and successful business (they mainly use knowledge aspect of the framework),
- *end-users* - other employees in the company, who are essential elements in flows of information and documents and maintain them in order to promptly fulfill requirements which a Workflow scheme and business policy determines.

The users interact with the system through specially designed unified interfaces (decision support (DS) agent and human-interaction agent), which assimilate the peculiarities of the various components. They provide a user-friendly, and comfortable environment in which person works and communicates with the central workflow unit.

The main idea in realization is that a DS agent has to be realized as an intelligent agent whose intelligence and process of making decisions will be based on fuzzy logic.

To realize intelligent agents, we are going to use the specialized package for agent implementation [1]. Such agents would be able to select actions based on the explicit, logical representation of the current state and the effects of actions.

3 Possible Applications of Proposed Framework

The proposed Agent-Oriented Workflow Framework can be applied in different institutions and organizations with more or less changes and modifications.

The main idea in developing this model was to integrate information flows with decision support functions in the same environment. We tried to unify two separate approaches [2, 5] into one common useful model.

To solve these problems, we employed two emerging fields in the computer science, Agent-oriented programming and workflow management system. This amalgamation is made in order to increase efficiency in information and document flows between separate users and to improve decision-making process based on the big amount of wide range information and knowledge.

3.1 Agent-Oriented Workflow Management System

In the first approach [5], we presented implementation of a general workflow management system using software agents. An agent architecture for workflow management is implemented for medium enterprise (computing section of a corporation for production and distribution of electrical power). The architecture serves to integrate the common work of separate departments of the enterprise. This model is however general enough and it can be easily employed in many other companies as well.

The architecture is user-oriented and independent on other parts of enterprise's information system. It supports basic workflow functions and it is possible to create workflow instance in two ways:

- end-user can define basic workflow structure, routes and conditions
- programmer can create the workflow instance using basic set of classes and the inference mechanism.

The architecture consists of three parts:

1. *Agent-oriented workflow model.* Agents are autonomous, i.e. they have contracts over:
   - the tasks that they may perform
   - the resources available to them
   - coordinating their activities with other agents.

   Therefore the only way in which agents may cooperate in solving problems is through negotiation.
2. *User-interface unit.* The interface agent is responsible for a communication between user and the workflow engine. It is responsible for providing the interface to the overall system.
3. *Workflow definition unit,* that consists of the workflow definition tool and the preprocessor, which translates user actions into the agent model.

3.2 Expert System as Multiagent System

In the second approach [2], we presented an ES prototype realized as a multi-agent system. It consists of several agents, and each agent is devoted to one part of the problem.

The agents must cooperate during the problem solving and this cooperation is, like a real agency, achieved through communication. Agents are realized as intelligent agents which possess beliefs (realized by using fuzzy logic) and capabilities to perform some actions including inter-agent communication.

The proposed multi-agent ES has been used for creation of the ES for determining of optimal maize hybrid for seeding. It consists of seven interconnected agents which communicate in order to obtain the optimal solution based on given input conditions and requirements.

3.3 Agent-Oriented Workflow Framework in Agricultural Domain

The general Agent-Oriented Workflow Framework presented in Figure 1 is union of the two mentioned approaches. Having agent oriented ES [2], it seems that the best domain for application of AOWF with decision support in an agriculture institution.

The whole business process connected to production and using new hybrids is divided into the following groups:

1. Information and data connected to the growth models for different hybrids.
2. Soil and fertilization data.
3. Long-term meteorological forecast and facts appropriate for maize growing under specific climatic conditions.
4. Statistical data concerning results of variety trials and experimental results in cultivation of different hybrids (during the last 20 years).
5. The maize production data concerning the following facts for every field: preparation of a field plan indicating hybrids and yields; cultivation plan including seed, fertilizers, plant protection and machine operation.
6. Budget/production control takes care of production, plans and budgets to the financial budget for the whole system. For the future production, it is necessary to use empirical data, registered in the former circle, and to adjust the plans and budget in accordance with other elements in the system.
7. Feed-back information for every field during the whole process from sawing to harvesting periods. Based on collected facts, all the necessary changes in Workflow bases are made.

Every recognized group can be represented as an appropriate unit agent in a Workflow engine. They make the essential part of the framework and using that data, knowledge and connections all parts of framework function.

4 Conclusions and the State of the Project

In the paper we presented the general Agent-Oriented Workflow Framework with decision support suitable for different enterprises where information and data flows play important role and affect the process of making decisions.

The Agent-oriented approach offers a number of advantages over more traditional techniques [7, 9, 10]. The research is important because it employs the two emerging fields (software agents and workflow management systems) in achieving robust, useful tool managing an enterprise. It supports process of decision making and helps human expert to choose the final solution.

It is completely new approach in these domains and it unites some kind of information management system and decision support system [11]. Thus, greater productivity and efficiency are more promising characteristics which we expect to get in comparison to the traditional approaches.

It is also a good environment for employing learning agents in order to improve the process quality. An agent could be made capable of learning during its life-time by augmenting or modifying its own functionality as well as improving persistent knowledge.

Natural environment [2, 5] to apply the general framework in our case is Institute for maize hybrid production.

We are in the beginning phase of analyzing processes, information flows, necessary data and knowledge for functioning of Institute and we are going to implement proposed framework using Java programming language, INTRANET configuration and LassMachine system for development and implementation of different multi-agent systems [1].

References

[1] M. Badjonski and M. Ivanović, Java Package for Agent Implementation. In: P. Návrat and H. Ueno (ed.), Knowledge-Based Software Engineering, IOS Press, Amsterdam,1998, pp.43-46.

[2] M. Badjonski and M. Ivanović, Multiagent System for Determination of Optimal Hybrid for Seeding. In: Proc. of 1 European Conference for Information Technology in Agriculture, Denmark, 1997, pp. 401-404.

[3] T. Cai, P.A.Gloor and S. Nog, DartFlow: A Workflow Management System on the Web using Transportable Agents. Technical Report PCS-TR96-286. p. 18.

[4] S. Green, L. Hurst at al., Software Agents: A review. IAG review, May 1997.

[5] M. Ivanović, Z. Budimac, Z. Dudan and S. Stevanović, Using Software Agents in implementation of Workflow Systems. In: Proc. of Baltic DB&IS 2000 Conference, Lithuania, 2000.

[6] M. Kamath and K. Ramamritham, Pragmatic Issues in Coordinated Execution and Failure Handling of Workflows in Distributed Workflow Control Architectures. Work done as part of first author's Ph. D. p. 25.

[7] J. Lorgeou and G.Waksman, Siam, an information service for maize growers to help choice of hybrids and follow-up of their development. In: Proc. of 1st European Conference for Information Technology in Agriculture, Denmark, 1997, pp. 343-346.

[8] M.T. Maliappis, C.P. Yialouris, S.G. Deligeorgis and A.B. Sideridis, EMISP: An Expert Management Information System for Pigs. In: Proc. of 1st European Conference for Information Technology in Agriculture, Denmark, 1997, pp. 325-330.

[9] S.M.F.S. Massruha, C.A.A. Meira et al., FMS: A Software Development Environment for Farm Management Systems. In: Proc. of 1st European Conference for Information Technology in Agriculture, Denmark, 1997, pp. 477-482.

[10] H.H. Pedersen, E. Maegaard and N. Bloch, The Danish integrated farm management system. In: Proc. of 1st European Conference for Information Technology in Agriculture, Denmark, 1997, pp. 483-488.

[11] S.J. Russell and P. Norvig, Artificial Intelligence - A Modern Approach. Prentice-Hall International, 1995.

[12] J. Witschnig, Aspects of modeling Information Flows within an EIS for the Food-industry. In: Proc. of 1st European Conference for Information Technology in Agriculture, Denmark, 1997, pp. 331-334.

[13] M.J. Woolridge and N.R. Jennings, Intelligent Agents: Theory and Practice. *The Knowledge Engineering Review* **10** (1998).

[14] Workflow Management Coalition, International Organization for the Development and Promotion of Workflow standards. Workflow Management Coalition, Avenue Marcel Thiry 204, 1200 Brussels, Belgium. 1995.

Knowledge-Based Software Engineering
T. Hruška and M. Hashimoto (Eds.)
IOS Press, 2000

Mandatory Access Control in Workflow Systems

Daniel CVRČEK
ÚIVT FEI VUT Brno, Božetěchova 2, 612 66 Brno, Czech Republic

Abstract. This paper analysis problems of mandatory access control in strongly distributed information systems that solve computational tasks with long time durability (workflow management systems). We show that problem of mandatory access control may be solved on several levels. There is a strong difference between classification of data the system works with and classification of tasks' definitions. The latter situation is more difficult not only from the theoretical reasons but also from the administration and functional point of view. We are developing procedures for the task execution management that are based on the unified classification of data that are processed. This classification may be used not only for controlling the access to the resources but also for the determination of subjects that are allowed to execute parts of the workflow tasks (task-steps).

1 Introduction

Workflow management systems are primarily destined for commercial applications. This technology possesses special features that allow its implementation in business environment. One can say that it is opposite to classic mandatory access control models that allow very tight access control but the result is that there is not possible to use them in other environments because "classification rules" make usage of such an information system very difficult. But workflow management systems are so valuable that there is a need to show possibility to use them in environments with high security needs - this is the reason why to define mandatory access control in workflow management systems.

The situation is not so easy, because authorization systems shall be viewed at like another layer above mandatory access control in particular autonomous information systems (s-nodes) that are parts of the given workflow system. Workflow management system defines sequences of atomic tasks (database or system resource accesses) so that the whole (workflow) performs some abstract operation (insurance claim, ordering material, creation of a new bank account, ...). The workflow authorization systems must ensure conditions settled for interoperation among s-nodes. Mandatory or discretionary access control (or other) models ensure correct resource accesses in particular s-nodes.

There are, from our point of view, two basic problems. The first one is to define mandatory requirements for inter-operational relations (redefine mandatory access control rules for workflows), the second one is to ensure the stated requirements. Solutions of the problems are demonstrated within frames of two different authorization systems. The first one is the system defined by Wei-Kuang Huang from Rutgers University ([4, 7]) the second one is ours (its basic ideas are based on works of Thomas [8, 9, 10]). Those two models are defined according to rather different concepts. The first model assumes that security requirements are part of the workflows' definitions. It means that processing of workflow steps, atomic tasks, uses processing and security information at once. The second model defines security information separately from the functional information of a workflow. This approach allows implementation of a rather small unit that ensures fulfillment of security demands. There are some other works about authorization systems in workflow systems but they do not feature any integral view on the problem (e.g. [11]).

We show a classification of workflows for the mandatory access control on several levels. We show approaches that solve problems of mandatory access control on the previously defined levels. The results show necessity of two different authorization information that have to be managed during workflows execution.

The following section describes briefly discretionary access control to show its principles and disadvantages. The third section defines mandatory access control. Section 4 divides requirements for mandatory access control in workflow systems into consistent domains and outlines possible solutions. The last, fifth, section is dedicated to definition of tasks in the environment that contains autonomous information systems that have different security classification.

2 Discretionary Access Control

With discretionary access control is the access control for particular data object managed by it owner. A user or any of the user's programs or processes can choose to share objects with other users. The discretionary access control is therefore prone to certain kinds of leakage of information such as Trojan Horse attacks. On the other side, this approach is very flexible. The purpose of discretionary access control in workflow management systems is to provide controlled sharing of information by authorized subjects.

Workflow authorization system is destined for strongly distributed systems with large number of users and s-nodes. The administration of such a system is very difficult and security risks are gained its weight because of benefits that are obtainable by its defeating. The authorization system must support the following features:

1. Synchronize the delegation of authorizations with the execution of workflow.
2. Role-based access control: this is used to express a group if subjects (role) that possess the same authorization in performing the certain tasks.
3. Separation of duties - this imposes constraint to distinguished subjects that belong to the same role but perform different duties.
4. Temporal specification - adds the capability to specify the temporal constraint of an authorization such as the authorization is valid within a time interval.
5. Event-based authorization - provides a conditional delegation of authorization based on the existence of an event or a result of the previous task.

Let's mention two very important aspects of workflow authorization systems. Synchronization of authorizations and workflow processing is crucial for secure workflow execution. There exist several definitions of temporal predicates that restrict access rights but there are always defined for absolute time intervals (e.g. [1]). This is not sufficient for workflow environment because predefined specifications always allow access for more than the time required. The task itself does not need to start yet but it may already possess privileges to access the resources. It is highly appreciated to grant and revoke privileges not according to some predefined moments but to start and end of tasks.

The second aspect is separation of duties. The purpose is not to allow subjects to have sufficient authority to perpetrate a fraud on its own. Since the workflow decomposes a complex activity into a number of smaller well-defined tasks, separation of duties naturally fits into workflow models. Current systems, however, do not support this feature.

3 Mandatory Access Control

Systems incorporating mandatory access control (MAC) are often called multilevel secure (MLS) systems. This arises from the fact that subjects (users and processes) and objects (files) have fixed security attributes that are used by the system to determine whether a subject can access a file or not. Those security attributes are assigned mandatory to all elements of the information system either administratively or automatically and can not be modified by the users or processes on request.

Information is categorized into classifications based on the data sensitivity and subjects obtain security clearance. Subjects are then permitted to access to a specified portion of the information. During determination of access granting the subject's clearance is compared with the classification of the data.

Security classifications are made up of two components. A hierarchical one, called the security level and a non-hierarchical one, called the category. The military security differentiates four security levels (unclassified, confidential, secret and top secret). The categories correspond to the content of information processed in the information system (e.g. Nato, Nuclear, Artillery,). The combination of security level and category forms security classes. Denning showed that security classes form a lattice [2] and presented a set of axioms that security policy must ensure.

The concept of mandatory access controls was first introduced by Bell and LaPadula [3]. The model uses two basic notions (1) subjects (active entities) and (2) objects (anything that holds data). The model, very briefly, does not allow read-up and write-down (security level). Subject acting on security level *secret* can not change content of objects with security level *confidential*. The subjects are in practice processes acting on behalf of users. A user with clearance *secret* must log in with security level *confidential* to be able to work with data classified by the latter security level.

The MAC models prevent Trojan Horse Attack but they are not free of security threats. Sensitive information can be still revealed by covert channels. Covert channels are paths not normally meant for information flow that could nevertheless be used to signal information. Two types of covert channels are identified (1) *covert storage channel* that is any communication path arising in the moment the object is written by a process and other process observers the effect (2) *covert timing channel* results from changes in the system performance that is observable and measurable by another process. The most important property of the covert channels is their bandwidth. Channels exceeding rate of 100 b/s are considered as having a high bandwidth.

Workflow in MLS workflows may belong to several security levels. Dependencies among workflows with the same security level are referred to as intra-level dependencies whereas those among workflows with different security levels are inter-level dependencies. From the security point of view only the latter are important.

Wei-Kuang Huang defines in [4] four levels of execution based on the degree of security and correctness it guarantees.

1. **SSSC-level** (strongly secure, strongly correct) An MLS workflow execution is said to of SSSC-level if it is secure and all the task dependencies are enforced. It assumes complete elimination of covert channels and still enforcing all dependencies.

2. **SSWC-level** (strongly secure, weakly correct) An MLS workflow execution is said to be of SSWC-level if it is secure but all the task dependencies need not be enforced.
3. **WSSC-level** (weakly secure, strongly correct) An MLS workflow execution is said to be of SSWC-level if it enforces all the task dependencies but may allow a low bandwidth covert channels.
4. **WSWC-level** (weakly secure, weakly correct) An MLS workflow execution that does not enforce all the task dependencies and still allows covert channels.

For commercial applications is this classification unusable. Majority of systems used, is supposed to perform workflows correctly and to satisfy security requirements. The author creates the classification for the purpose of redefinition of workflows in running time because of security dependencies that cannot be determined in advance.

4 MAC in Workflow Management Systems

Workflow management systems that implement mandatory access control are studied from various rather detailed aspects (atomicity of tasks [6], modeling MAC in role-based systems [12], ...). We want to analyze more abstract level.

Talking about workflow management systems and mandatory access control we have to see several levels of abstraction due to the workflow system's distributivity. There are at least two criterion we should considered. The first one is sensitivity of data:

1. *Only data are classified* - we are securing only data we are working with. Definitions of tasks are public and there is no reason to suppose them to be sensitive. The classic example may be administration where all the information flows should be transparent.
2. *Workflows' definitions are classified* - the opposite possibility when workflows are viewed as data and access to their definition is granted according to their classification.

The case when workflows are classified opens very interesting problems concerning their distribution, definition of composite tasks and workflows and so.

The second criterion concerns the s-nodes of the distributed information system.

1. *All autonomous systems (s-nodes) are equal from the security viewpoint* - e.g. universities where all centers may be equal because there are users covering all possible security classes in the workflow management system.
2. *Each autonomous system has its own security class* - any form of organization that has got its structure; in the moment there is no uniformity, each node (autonomous system) has got its own security class because only certain data are processed there.

The second case is again very interesting. An autonomous system has to be used to perform certain part of a workflow but it can not see any result of the previous processing and in some cases it can not see the definition of a workflow that does not concert it.

We can talk about another one aspect and it is a scope of dependencies we are solving. The first one describes dependencies inside one node (intra-node dependencies), the second one describes dependencies among nodes (inter-node dependencies). We define four categories according to the first two criterion:

1. WNSN (workflows are not classified, systems are not classified) - this is the simplest situation when there is no need for special treatment of workflows among autonomous systems

2. WNSC (workflows are not classified, systems are classified) - from the security point of view there is no difference regarding to the previous situation, we may use the systems' classifications for optimization of workflows distribution.
3. WCSN (workflows are classified, systems are not classified) - distribution of workflows is without limitations but there is a need for securing confidentiality during the workflow transfer between autonomous systems.
4. WCSC (workflows are classified, systems are classified) - his the most interesting situation because the workflows and systems are classified it means that not all the systems are allowed to see certain workflows' definitions.

All four cases have to solve intra-node dependencies. The WCSC has to solve also inter-node dependecies. To demonstrate the situation let us assume the following situation. One of tasks in the workflow management system solves hiring of new employees - airfield personal. Generally, there are two types of employees, working for civil companies or for the army. The part of the hiring process is check of the candidate career and this differs for the two different customers (civil and army). The army does not even want to show the process used for this check to the world wide. All the environment knows is existence of the procedure, its inputs and results. This situation demonstrates existence of two s-nodes classified as low and high.

4.1 Secrecy vs. Integrity

The mandatory access control can be used not only for the confidentiality of data (no read-up, no write-down) but also for the integrity of data (no read-down, no write-up), see [5]. To make such a model effective it has to be set highest and lowest security level from which is the subject allowed to read (write) objects. Those boundaries allow subjects to access data not only on the same security level but also data that are "slightly" more or less secure. One can see it as a potential weakening of the original mandatory access models but it is a potential way to solve problems with practical usage of an information system when counting with data integrity.

Intra-node dependencies Intra-node dependencies on SSSC-level are extensively solved in [4]. Four categories of high-to-low dependencies are defined according to two basic definitions.

Definition 1: A dependency between two tasks $tw_i \rightarrow tw_j$ is said to be conflicting if there exist at least two conflicting operations $o_i[d]$ and $o_j[d]$, $(i \neq j)$.

Definition 2: A dependency $tw_i \rightarrow tw_j$ is said to be result-dependent if the result of executing the child is different when the dependency is or is not enforced.

The way the inter-level dependencies are solved lies in redefinition of tasks that are defined with Petri-nets and in versioning of data. That redefinition arises from assuring the atomicity of multilevel transactions in relational database management systems. The conflicting, result-independent dependencies (high task reads low data before their modification by another low task) is solved by versioning of data from [6] and by splitting the high task. The read operations are reordered such a way that all reads on low data occur before the first low operation on data items and the task is then divided into partitions based on the data items it is accessing. We assume that this approach is not generally appropriate for the running time of the task, from several reasons.

- There is always an administrator that is the only one competent for the workflows' definitions.
- It is not desirable that system changes definitions of workflows during their execution according to the processed data.
- Definition of workflow should not create sequence when there are no reasons for it. Such relations should be solved by parallel processes.
- This approach solves problem with secrecy of information but says nothing about their integrity

Moreover, there is a problem that we are not generally able to prove equivalence of the original and converted task and any changes in the task's definition are very problematic. This is one of the basic idea in the authorization model that separates functional and security description of the task.

Creation of new tasks is always done by linking elementary, atomic actions. Such actions have defined their classification because we know type of data they are working with. Those information may be used during the task generation to avoid covert channels in this very beginning phase. There is one condition for the previous statement. There has to be defined one and only one general classification of data that is used throughout the workflow management system. We are only checking abidance of the specified rules and in case of their breach is the task execution terminated.

Inter-node dependencies Very interesting area are dependencies among autonomous systems (nodes). We can not find any solution of the problem in the open literature but we thing that this is what the MLS workflow management systems are about. We can look at the problem as generalization of intra-node dependencies with one exception. We do not have to look at underlying access control systems.

We have shown above, that this situation appears in the moment when as tasks as nodes are classified. You can see that this point of view is not important for a common user but for system administrator. The classification of nodes strongly determines the way the tasks are defined and executed.

Definition 3: Classification of the workflow management system $\mathcal{G}$ is a system of sets (equivalency classes) if each node from the set of available nodes is positioned in just one set $\mathcal{G}_i$. Assume there is defined partial-order relation ($\leq$) on $\mathcal{G}$ and there are two sets $\mathcal{G}_o$ and $\mathcal{G}_\infty$ that satisfy the following conditions: $\forall \mathcal{G}_i : \mathcal{G}_i \leq \mathcal{G}_\infty \wedge \mathcal{G}_i \geq \mathcal{G}_o$. The classification of WfMS $\mathcal{G}$ forms then a lattice.

Assume that we have a finite set of tasks that define actions available in the workflow management system. We can define classification of tasks $\mathcal{H}$ the same way as the previous definition.

In the moment we have two classifications $\mathcal{G}$ and $\mathcal{H}$ (algebraic lattices). The function we have used for their definition works always the same way. The function places a node or a task into an equivalence class according to the classification of data it is allowed to process or to its own classification.

We can define an abstract set of data classifications (security levels). We can define two projections e.g. f and g that assign one security level to each equivalency class ($\mathcal{G}_i$ or $\mathcal{H}_j$). In the moment we are able to say that a node from a class $\mathcal{G}_i$ is able to process a task from $\mathcal{H}_j$ iff $f(\mathcal{G}_i) \Leftrightarrow g(\mathcal{H}_j)$. We are even able to define other relations. It may be comparison ('$<$', '$>$', '$\leq$', '$\geq$' or '$\neq$' - incomparability). We can define other mappings that specify sublattices those set may be used for the comparison purposes.

5 Workflows Definitions

The most interesting situation, from the inter-node communication is WSCS. We have already declared that the minimum requirement is the existence of global data classification. This is the necessary condition for any inter-node dependency treatment. The basic assumption is that there are tasks that are processed in several nodes of the workflow system. It means that there must be a way to define those tasks. For the purpose we have to know about existence of tasks that is possible to process on particular nodes. We do not need definitions of the tasks but we need at least know that they exist, way to identify them, their inputs and their results.

Of course that there may be tasks that are internal for the particular node but those have to be assumed as private and cannot be used outside.

We have the following definition of workflow task security information - protection data.

Definition 4: Protection data is a 6-tuple:

$$PD = (\{\alpha | \alpha \in \mathcal{A}\}, id_{task}, id, id_{AU}, \mathcal{U}, \mathcal{G})$$

where $\mathcal{A}$ is a set of authorization units (security information for the particular task steps), id_{task} is an identification of the associated workflow task instance. id is identification this instance of the protection data and id_{AU} is an identification of the last processed authorization unit in this PD. The last two elements of the 6-tuple are an authorization usage log ($\mathcal{U}$) and classification of the PD ($\mathcal{G}$).

And let's define some rules for change of the PD classification - $\mathcal{G}$.

1. $\mathcal{G}_0$ (the initial classification) is defined in the task template (description of the task) and this is derived from the minimum requirements stated by data that are to be processed with the task instances.
2. $\mathcal{G}_i$ (classification after the i-th task-step execution) is maximum from $\mathcal{G}_{i-1}$ and classifications of data actually processed. (Potentially we may assume some other factors).

Now assume the previously described example. There may be a need to define as few tasks as possible. We have to define two tasks for one action only because of different performing of career check. In the situation we have tasks classified we are able to define one task with several contents and selection is done in runtime according to the actual classification of the performed task. The trigger is $\mathcal{G}_i$. That may change during the task processing according to data processed.

This can be said to be a way of dynamic definition of workflow tasks that results from the security considerations. This approach may be used in the inter-node as well in the intra-node context.

6 Conclusion

We have shown a possibility to define workflows the way that is applicable not only in the homogeneous distributed systems but also in the environment that does not offer unified conditions for the workflows execution. The basis for the introduced method is the global data classification. This classification has to be known to all autonomous information systems (s-nodes), that the distributed workflow management system comprises from, and ideally does not change in time.

We have controverted some ideas that assume dynamic reconfiguration of workflows during execution. We say that the approach is applicable only during the workflow's definition because of general security reasons. On the other side, we say that it is possible to use one definition of workflow for different *tasks*, working with distinct classification.

We have defined a way that can be used for determination of possible execution points for the workflows that is based on security classification of workflows and s-nodes. The presented procedure may be basis for the dynamic selection of the proper workflow definition.

References

[1] Bertino E., Bettini C., Ferrari E., and Samarati P. , *A temporal access control mechanism for database systems*, IEEE Transactions on Knowledge and Data Engineering, **8**(1), 1996, p. 67-80.

[2] E.D. Denning, *A lattice model of secure information flow*, Communications of the ACM, May 1976, p. 236-243.

[3] D.E. Bell, L.J. LaPadula, *Secure computer systems: Unified exposition and multics interpretation*, Technical Report MTR-2997, The Mitre Corporation, Bedford, MA, March 1976.

[4] W.K. Huang *Incorporating security into workflow management systems*, PhD thesis, Rutgers University, 1998.

[5] L.C. Dion, *A complete protection model*, Proc. IEEE Symposium on Security and Privacy (Oakland, CA), April 1981

[6] O. Costich and S. Jajodia, *Maintaining multilevel transaction atomicity in mls database systems with Kernelized architecture*, Database Security V: Status and Prospects (North Holland), 1992, p. 173-189

[7] V. Atluri and W.K. Huang, *An Authorization Model for Workflows*, Proceedings of the Fourth European Symposium on Research in Computer Security (Rome, Italy), September 1996.

[8] R.K. Thomas and R.S. Sandhu, *Towards a Task-based Paradigm for Flexible and Adaptable Access Control in Distributed Applications*, Proceedings of the Second New Security Paradigms Workshop (Little Compton, Rhode Island), IEEE Press, 1993.

[9] R.K. Thomas and R.S. Sandhu, *Conceptual Foundations for A Model of Task-based Authorizations*, Proceedings of the IEEE Computer Security Foundations Workshop (New Hampshire), IEEE Press, 1994.

[10] R.K. Thomas and R.S. Sandhu, *Task-based Authorization Controls (TBAC): A Family of Models for Active and Enterprise-oriented Authorization Management*, Proceedings of the IFIP WG11.3 Workshop on Database Security (Lake Tahoe, California), Chapman & Hall, August 1997.

[11] E. Bertino, E. Ferrari, and V. Atluri, *A Flexible Model Supporting the Specification and Enforcement of Role-based Authorizations in Workflow Management Systems*, Proceedings of the Second ACM Workshop on Role-Based Access Control (Fairfax, VA), November 1997.

[12] N. Nyanchama and S.Osborn, *Modeling Mandatory Access Control in Role-based Security Systems*. In Database Security IX: Status and Prospects, 1996, p. 129-144.

Knowledge-Based Software Engineering
T. Hruška and M. Hashimoto (Eds.)
IOS Press, 2000

Information System for Managing the Insurance Business Processes

Elena VIKTOROVA[1], Leonid NOVITSKY[2], Egils GINTERS[3]

[1]*IDC IT, Kr.Valdemara 36, Riga LV-1010, Latvia*
E-mail: idc@balva.lv

[2]*Riga Technical University / IDC IT, Kr.Valdemara 36, Riga LV-1010, Latvia*
E-mail: idc@balva.lv

[3]*Latvian Intelligent Systems, P.O. 26, Sigulda LV-2150, Latvia*
E-mail: egw@lis.lv

Abstract. This paper is devoted to the problems of the development of insurance information system (IIS) *DiasoftINSURANCE/IDC*. Main subsystems and their functions are described.

1 As-is-situation in the Area of IIS Development

First stage of the insurance business (1992-1999) in the field of IT-solutions in the Baltic and New Independent States was characterised by developing and using the sets of separate and incompatible software products to support different insurance business activities (contract-management, accountancy etc).

As premium incomes and number of issued policies rapidly grow the task of creating Integrated Information System is of great importance.

Many software companies offer software tools: *Siemens Nixdorf*, Germany (Insurance – 3000); *IBM*, USA (a kit of modules for insurance); *SAP*, Switzerland (package SAP R/3); *Feilmeier & Junker*, Germany (FJA packages); *Comtec Ltd.*, Israel (TIS – Total Insurance System); *Dr. E.Hackhofer EDV-Software*, Austria (IMS – Insurance Management System); *Colonia Insurance*, Hungary (CEUS); *RISK*, USA (RISK TUTOR – Underwriting support for insurance agents) etc.

The above-mentioned software tools are mainly for data processing to supply the main needs of the insurance business, i.e., policy processing, payment handling and monitoring, reinsurance, claims processing and settlement and contract-management. Most of them are not flexible enough to accommodate the changing needs of the insurance business environment as, ideally, is required of them.

The following conceptions could be used as a basis for developing Insurance Information System (IIS) taking into consideration peculiarities of Central and Eastern Europe insurance market:

- Creating an insurance business model of a company must be the starting point of IIS design.
- IT-solutions have to incorporate modern experience and know-how of leading insurance, reinsurance and financial software companies.

- The term "integrated" means that software system supports all sides of insurance business (contract-management, reinsurance, co-insurance, agents / brokers / commissions, accountancy, insurance reserve, damages / claims, financial management etc.) and provides automatically relationships between them.
- IIS must provide easy modification and extension of existing functions and modes. This statement is very important especially for Eastern insurance market because it is in the phase of formation and is not so stable as, for example, the market of Western Europe
- IIS must support relationships with existing customer-specific applications and distance data exchange.
- Taking into account that a competition in insurance market is very high, time of developing and introducing new information system is restricted for any company. Therefore it could be more efficiently to start the developing process not from the "zero"point, but to choose appropriate basic software product from existing ones and to modify it in accordance with the needs of the company.
- Analysis of the current situation in use IT-solutions in Central and Eastern Europe insurance market shows that even relatively big companies are not ready to make considerable investments to this area yet.
- Rational proportion "expenses / efficiency"must be taken into account starting IIS designing process.
- Choosing software platform (the operating system, Database Management System, etc.) should also be in mind that insurance companies of Central and Eastern Europe are not very large mainly and their computer networks consist of about 30-100 workstations.

Different software tools and advanced IT- solutions were presented during the International Workshop ICTI'98: Information and Communication Technologies for Insurance [1] which was held in Riga (September 9-11, 1998). The following of them were especially appreciated by participants: Insurance Application Architecture IAA from IBM Austrian Research Centre, Software tools for technical risks insurance from Munich Re, agents programs from INGOSSTRAKH etc.

2 Models of Insurance Business Processes

Insurance Information System has to provide a multi-level support of business processes (Figure 1).

Main functions at different business levels:

Front office - Policies issuing, input of primary data in real-time regime;

Back office - Insurance data processing without direct contact with customer (accounting, reinsurance, claims processing etc.);

Reserve accounting - Sum of technical reserves includes three main components: non-paid premium reserve, claim reserve and occurred but not claimed accident reserve;

Financial monitoring - Processing of different insurance values with the aim to monitor financial stability of a company;

Analysis of financial information and forecasting the business processes - Portfolio premium analysis, definition of profitable kinds of insurance, forecasting perspective kinds of insurance.

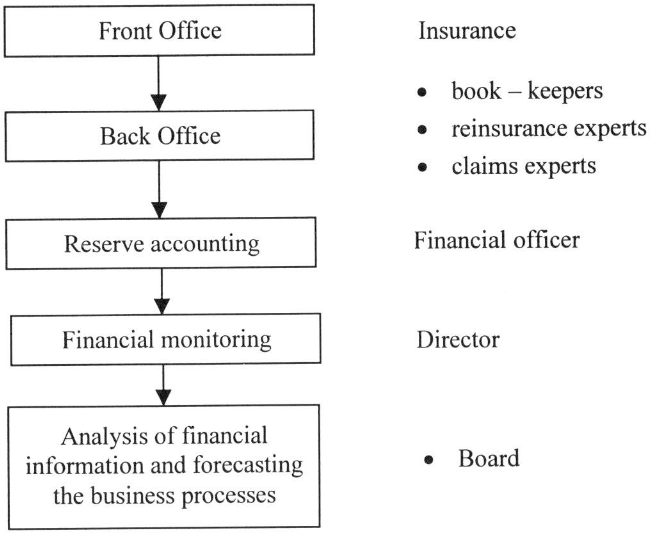

Figure 1: Multi-level support of business processes

A set of business charts, interface tables and Communication Diagrams was created at the first phase of IIS design. The results of this phase were used for further development of software system.

Business System Planning (BSP) method [2] and LIS Technology [3] were used to produce:

- The structure of an insurance company BALVA,
- Business charts (Functions - Processes - Activities),
- Diagrams "Processes-Executors",
- Communication Diagrams and Interface Tables,
- Process Diagrams.

3 Integrated Insurance Information System DiasoftINSURANCE/IDC

The software package *DiasoftINSURANCE* [1] created by the Russian company DIASOFT was used as the basis and instrumental tools for IIS development taking into account peculiarities of the Baltic insurance market (Figure 2).

DiasoftINSURANCE/IDC provides interface "human-computer" in one of three national languages, which could be chosen from the very beginning of the work with system. Standard version provides interface in English, Latvian and Russian. In the stage of adaptation to the customer needs you could change this set of languages (or one of them), making appropriate terminological dictionary.

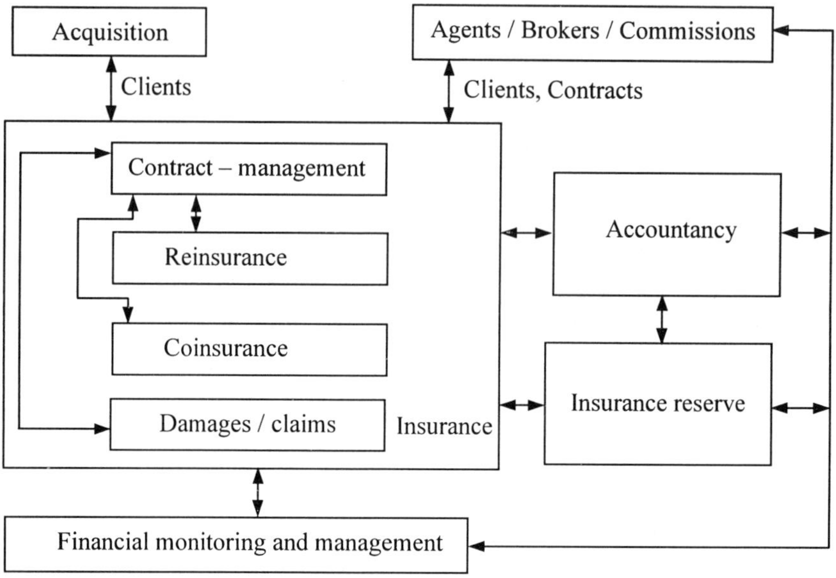

Figure 2: IIS Structural Scheme.

4 Conclusions

DiasoftINSURANCE has the following competition advantages:

- Integrated solution for all kinds of risks insurance and reinsurance business;
- Easy adaptation to the peculiarities of the user by the way of introducing new kinds of insurance;
- Direct relationships between insurance, reinsurance, accountancy, damages / claims and financial management modules;
- User-friendly interface: any user with experience in the insurance business will be able within a short time familiar with menus and screens and will be able to start working from the very beginning.

IIS is running under the operating systems Novell Netware / WINDOWS NT with several DBMS (Btrieve, Scalable SQL, Pervasive SQL).

References

[1] Information and Communication Technologies for Insurance. Proceedings of the International Workshop ICTI'98. Edited by Prof. L.Novitsky. ISBN:9984-552-57-8. Riga, Riga Technical University, 1998 (September 9-11).

[2] Business System Planning. Information System Planning Guide. Pub. No. GE 20-05 27-1. White Plains, N.Y., 1975.

[3] E.Ginters, L.Novitsky, E.Viktorova and E.Bluemel. Data Processing Systems Design. ISBN:9984-552-07-02. Riga, Riga Technical University, 1998.

Knowledge-Based Software Engineering
T. Hruška and M. Hashimoto (Eds.)
IOS Press, 2000

A Petri Net for Workflow Modelling

Dušan KOLÁŘ
ÚIVT FEI VUT Brno, Božetěchova 2, 616 00 Brno, Czech Republic

Abstract. The paper presents a class of Petri nets with limited time features suitable for workflow modelling/representation and shows its features.

1 Introduction

Workflow systems tend to describe a complete way of processing certain input to the required output. During this processing quite a lot of processes may be started, finished, run concurently, and so on. When we design a particular workflow system we concentrate on a robustness of the system and we also want the system to be failsafe. Thus we usually have to check mutual dependencies of particular processes running during processing one case of the workflow system.

Petri nets are a good tool for modelling of concurrent systems. They also offer capabilities for modelling of process synchronization. We can recognize a large variety of Petri net classes introduced already. They can be used for modelling of many systems not only from computer science.

The workflow systems are example of such systems too. A convenience of Petri nets, used as a tool for workflow description and modelling, has been widely shown [1, 2, 5].

Nevertheless, the power of Petri nets usually used for the workflow modelling is poor. On the other hand advanced classes of Petri nets are not too suitable for such a modelling, because any reasoning over these nets is too hard (P-space, very difficult state space reduction, ...), see [11].

In this paper, we show features of another class of Petri nets with features enabling local dircreet timing (delay). We believe that this class of Petri nets will enable deeper reasoning about modelled systems without (or with limited) necessity of state-explosion problem solving.

The next section introduces basic definitions used in P/T Petri nets (may be skipped). Then we present a definition of a new class of Petri nets—τ-nets. Next we show a theorem about time features of such nets. In the end we conclude and state open problems.

2 Definition Overview

This section presents several definitions, which are used further in the paper. The reader, which is familiar with P/T Petri nets can skip to the next section.

Definition: Triple $N_D = (P, T, F)$ is called a *net* if:

1. $P \cap T = \emptyset$
2. $F \subseteq (P \times T) \cup (T \times P)$

The set P denotes *places* of a net N_D, the set T denotes *transitions*, and F denotes the *flow relation* of a net N_D.

Definition: Tuple $N = (P, T, F, W, K, M_0)$ is a *P/T (Place/Transition) Petri net* if:

1. (P, T, F) is a finite net
2. $W : F \to \mathrm{N} \setminus \{0\}$ denotes weight of every edge in the graph
3. $K : P \to \mathrm{N} \cup \{\omega\}$ denotes capacity (even not limited) of every place
4. $M_0 : P \to \mathrm{N} \cup \{\omega\}$ is *initial marking* of a net with respect to the capacity: $\forall\, p \in P : M_0(p) \leq K(p)$. We talk about number of *tokens* present in the place.

Figure 1 shows an example of a simple Petri net. We can see that just the place $P1$ contains a token.

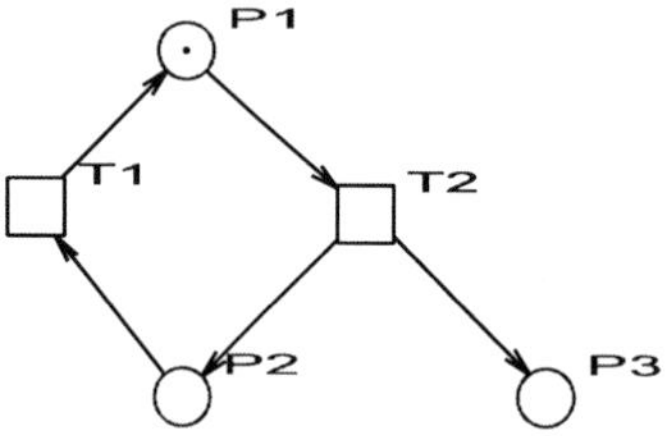

Figure 1. A simple Petri net.

Definition: Let $N = (P, T, F, W, K, M_0)$ be a Petri net, then:

1. $M : P \to \mathrm{N} \cup \{\omega\}$ is *marking* of a Petri net if: $\forall\, p \in P : M(p) \leq K(p)$

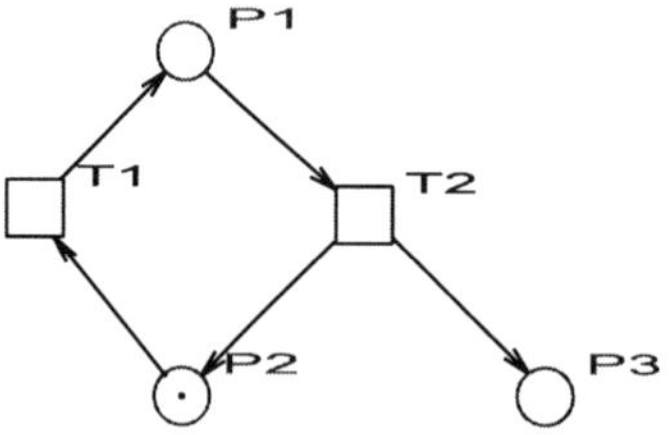

Figure 2. A simple Petri net from figure 1 with a new marking.

Figure 2 shows another marking of the same Petri net.

Definition: Let $N = (P, T, F, W, K, M_0)$ be a Petri net and M is a marking, then a transition t is enabled (*M-enabled*) if:

1. $\forall\, p \in \{q | qFt\} : M(p) \geq W(p, t)$
2. $\forall\, p \in \{q | tFq\} : M(p) \leq K(p) - W(t, p)$

If we take a look at the examples then figure 1 shows a Petri net with enabled transition $T2$ and figure 2 shows a Petri net with enabled transition $T1$.

Definition: If M is a marking of a net N and a transition t is enabled then by firing the transition t we obtain a new marking M' such, that:
$\forall p \in P$:

$$M'(p) = \begin{cases} M(p) - W(p,t), & \text{if } p \in \{q|qFt\} \setminus \{q'|tFq'\} \\ M(p) + W(t,p), & \text{if } p \in \{q'|tFq'\} \setminus \{q|qFt\} \\ M(p) - W(p,t) + W(t,p), & \text{if } p \in \{q|qFt\} \cap \{q'|tFq'\} \\ M(p), & \text{otherwise} \end{cases}$$

Transition firing is denoted further like this: $M[t\rangle M'$.

Fugre 2 shows the Petri net from figure 1 after firing of the the transition $T2$.

Definition: If N is a Petri net with a marking M then $[M\rangle$ is called a *reachability set*, if $[M\rangle$ is the smallest set such, that:

1. $M \in [M\rangle$
2. if $M_1 \in [M\rangle$ and for any t the relation $M_1[t\rangle M_2$ holds then $M_2 \in [M\rangle$

Definition: If N is a Petri net then a place p is called *safe place* if:

1. $\forall\, M \in [M_0\rangle : M(p) \leq 1$

If every place of the net N is safe then N is a *safe Petri net*.

If we consider any of the Petri nets from figures 1, 2 as a Petri net with the initial marking then we can state that they are both safe.

Definition: Let $N = (P, T, F, W, K, M_0)$ is a Petri net. Marking $M \in [M_0\rangle$ is *live* if there is for all $t \in T$ such marking $M' \in [M\rangle$, that transition t is M'-enabled. If all markings from $[M_0\rangle$ are live then the Petri net N is called *live Petri net*.

None of the Petri nets shown on the examples is live, because if a token reaches the place $P3$ there is no transition which can be fired even if there were some before.

3 τ-net

We present a definition of core nets before we define τ-nets. Core nets represent basic properties of the τ-nets just on the field of P/T nets without time representation. As you can see later, the τ-nets are build over such nets.

Definition 1: A Petri net $N = (P, T, F, W, K, M_0)$ is a *core net* if:

1. $\forall\, f \in F : W(f) = 1$
2. $\forall\, p \in P : K(p) = \omega$
3. there is a place $s \in P$ such that $M_0(s) = 1$ and there is no $t \in T$ such that tFs holds; there is no any other place having such properties in the net N
4. there is a place $e \in P$ such that $M_0(e) = 0$ and there is no $t \in T$ such that eFt holds; there is no any other place having such properties in the net N
5. if we create a new net N' from the net N such a way so that we would fuse places s and e then the new net N' will be safe and live

The properties stated for core nets follow from models of workflow or even other process control systems [6].

As we model processes we usually consider starting and finishing of such processes. In the net, there are these states represented by special places s and e. The following definition desrcibes a state, when the process has finished.

Definition: A core Petri net N is *finished*, if its actual marking M_f has the following properties:

1. $M_f(e) = 1$
2. there is no $t \in T$ such that t is M_f-enabled

where e is the place defined in the definition 1.

When a process is working it goes through several states. These states are represented by various markings of the net. A seguence of markings then represents a sequence of states. The definition of firing sequence given here desribes system from the initial state till it is finished.

Definition: A *firing sequence* is any sequence of markings $M_0[t_0\rangle M_1 \dots M_n[t_n\rangle M_f$, $t_i \in T, i \in \{0 \dots n\}$ of a core net N starting with initial marking M_0 and ending with the marking M_f, when the net N is finished.

The process control systems may contain such inner parts, that do depend on the state of the rest of the system. Moreover, process control runs in a time. To verify a system we have to check mutual state coincidence. Nevertheless, if we do not specify exactly the sequence of states the verification is very hard.

Such a complication is usually caused due to time information lack. On the other hand, just a part of the system is usually time-affected. Such a part is represented by the subnet, the definition of which follows.

Definition: Let $N_D = (P, T, F)$ is a net. Triple $A_D = (Q, U, G)$ is a *subnet* of N_D if:

1. $Q \subseteq P, U \subseteq T, G \subseteq F$
2. $|Q| = |U| = |G|$
3. $\forall p \in Q : \exists t \in U : pGt$
4. $\forall t \in U : pGt \wedge p'Gt \Rightarrow p = p'$
5. $\forall p \in Q : pGt \wedge pGt' \Rightarrow t = t'$

The time in the τ-nets is local and discrete. Thus it is represented by a *counter*.

Definition: A counter c is a mutable entity which may carry any single value from the range of $\mathcal{N}_0$, where $\mathcal{N}_0$ stands for natural numbers extended with zero. Actual value of a counter can be obtained via map $value\_of : c \to \mathcal{N}_0$.

In the τ-nets, there the mapping τ represents time delay before appropriate transition may be fired. The mapping υ resents the mapping of timed transitions onto a vector of counters, which carry actual time quantum, which has to pass, to be particular transition fired.

Having the necessary definitions, we can define the τ-net.

Definition: Let $N = (P, T, F, W, K, M_0)$ is a core net and A_D a subnet with respect to (P, T, F). A tuple $N_\tau = (P, T, F, W, K, M_0, A_D, \tau, \upsilon, C)$ is called τ-net if there are defined maps $\tau : G \to \mathcal{N}$, $\upsilon : G \to C$, where $\mathcal{N}$ stands for natural numbers, C is a set of counters, such that $|C| = |G|$, υ is a bijection, τ is defined for all $g \in G$. Moreover,

places s and e are not present in the set Q.
Initial values carried by a counters are defined the following way:

$$\forall g \in G : value\_of(\upsilon(g)) = \tau(g)$$

Figure 3 shows an example. The subnet is marked by a dashed box.

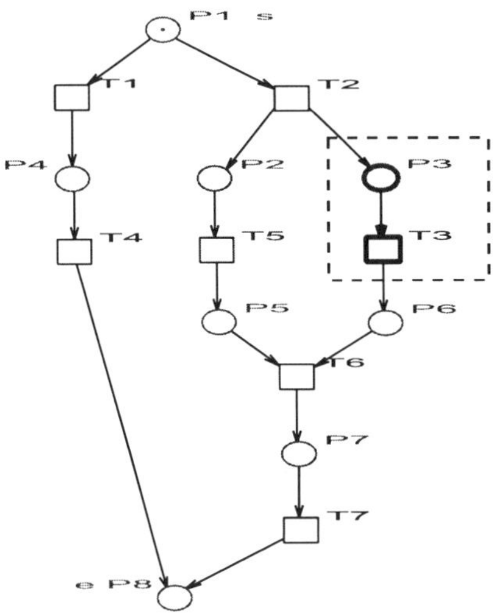

Figure 3. A τ-net.

Next we extend definitions from core nets to the τ-nets.

Definition:

- A τ-net N_τ is *finished* if its core net is finished.
- The definition of firing sequence for τ-net is the same as for core net.

Finally we define a property of the system, which declares, whether the system during its execution was in states, which are time dependent.

Definition: A τ-net N_τ is *finished with a delay* if its core net is finished during firing sequence $M_0[t_0\rangle M_1 \ldots M_n[t_n\rangle M_f$ and $\exists i \in \{0 \ldots n\}, t \in U : t = t_i$.

If we consider our example there are several possibilities, how to reach the state e. Just one of them goes through the subnet.

3.1 Transition Firing in τ-net

The strategy of transition firning in τ-nets is derived from the common one. It just limits the order, in which the transitions may fire. We have to classify transition of the τ-net to specify the order of firing.

Definition 2: Let $N_\tau = (P, T, F, W, K, M_0, A_D, \tau, \upsilon, C)$ is a τ-net then:

1. $T_f = \{t | t \in T, t \notin U, \forall p \in P : pFt \Rightarrow p \notin Q\}$
2. $T_c = \{t | t \in T, t \notin U, \exists p \in Q : pFt\}$
   $P_c = \{p | p \in Q, t \in T_c, pFt \text{ holds}\}$

3. $T_t = U$

T_f represents such transitions, which cannot affect behavior of the timed transitions. T_c represents such transitions, which may be fired instead of the timed transitions (they share certain source-place, such places are in the set P_c). The set T_t contains timed transitions.

Firing algorithm: Let N_τ is a τ-net. Transitions of the net are fired in the order specified by the following algorithm (with respect to marking M):

1. Any $t \in T_f$ which is M-enabled is fired. If there is still some $t' \in T_f$, after firing of the transition t, which is enabled then this step must be repeated again. Let us use a new marking M' after this step is finished.
2. (a) Let $T_{ce} = \{t | t \in T_c, t \text{ is } M'\text{-enabled}\}$. Any $t \in T_{ce}$ is fired, for which there is $p \in P_c, t' \in U : pFt \wedge pGt'$ and pGt' holds for $g \in G$. Set counter $\upsilon(g)$ so that $value\_of(\upsilon(g)) = \tau(g)$.
   (b) Now it must be non-deterministicly deciced, whether this step is to be repeated or not. If it is to proceed to the next step let us assume the net has a marking M''.
3. Let $T_{te} = \{t | t \in T_t, t \text{ is } M''\text{-enabled}\}$.
   Let $G_{te} = \{(p,t) | p \in Q, t \in T_{te} : pGt\}$.
   (a) For all $g \in G_{te}$ the appropriate counter is set, so that: $\forall g \in G_{te}$: $value\_of(\upsilon(g)_{after\_this\_substep}) = value\_of(\upsilon(g)_{before\_this\_substep}) - 1$.
   (b) Let $G_f = \{g | g \in G_{te}, value\_of(\upsilon(g)) = 0\}$.
   (c) All transitions t such, that $\exists p \in Q : (p,t) \in G_f$ are fired.
   (d) For all $g \in G_f$ the appropriate counter is set, so that: $\forall g \in G_f$: $value\_of(\upsilon(g)) = \tau(g)$.

Shortly, transtions without conflict with timed ones are fired as long as possible. Then we select (non-deterministicly) some of the transitions, which are shared among timed and non-timed transitions, and we fire them. In the end, we decrement counter for every enabled timed transition and those with zero time left we fire (and reset the counter). Now the process can be repeated.

4 Properties of τ-net

Let as define a τ-net without conflict transitions/places. The following definition shows how to obtain such a net from the τ-net (spoiling its properties, of course).

Definition: Let $N_\tau = (P, T, F, W, K, M_0, A_D, \tau, \upsilon, C)$ is a τ-net. Let P_c is defined according to the definition 2. Let $T_a = \{t | t \in U, p \in P_c : pGt\}$. A net $N_\tau^c = (P, T', F', W', K, M_0, A'_D, \tau', \upsilon', C')$ is called τ-net *without time conflicts* if:

1. $T' = T \setminus T_a$
2. $F' = F \setminus (\{pFt | p \in P_c, t \in T_a\} \cup \{tFp | p \in P, t \in T_a\})$
3. $W' = W, \forall f \in F'$, undefined otherwise
4. $Q' = Q$
5. $U' = U \setminus T_a$
6. $G' = G \setminus \{pGt | p \in P_c, t \in T_a\}$

7. $\tau' = \tau, \forall g \in G'$, undefined otherwise
8. $\upsilon' = \upsilon, \forall g \in G'$, undefined otherwise
9. $C' \subseteq C$, so that υ may be properly defined

Next we define a net, which we obtain from the τ-net by removing all the timed transitions (removing a subnet).

Definition: Let $N_\tau^c = (P, T, F, W, K, M_0, A_D, \tau, \upsilon, C)$ is a τ-net without time conflicts. A net $N^{\tau c} = (P', T', F', W', K', M_0')$ is called τ-net *without delays* if:

1. $P' = P \setminus Q$
2. $T' = T \setminus (\{t|p \in Q, t \in T : tFp\} \cup \{t|p \in Q, t \in T : pFt\})$
3. $F' = \{(p,t)|p \in P', t \in T' : pFt\} \cup \{(t,p)|p \in P', t \in T' : tFp\}$
4. $W' = W, \forall f \in F'$, undefined otherwise
5. $K' = K, \forall p \in P'$, undefined otherwise
6. $M_0' = M_0, \forall p \in P'$, undefined otherwise

Now we can formulate a theorem about possible delays in the modelled system:

Theorem: A τ-net N_τ represents system, which can be possibly finished without any delay, if the appropriate τ-net without delays $N^{\tau c}$ can be finished.

Proof: Let us assume the contradiction: $N^{\tau c}$ can be finished and the τ-net N_τ always finishes with some delay. It means a transition $t \in U$ is fired (follows from definition). But this is impossible, because all the transitions from the set U are removed from the set T of the net $N^{\tau c}$.

This follows from the definition of a subnet A_D and from the definition of a τ-net without conflicts: all places of the subnet are removed from the τ-net without conflicts and all such transitions, which are in relation with these places. According to the definition of a subnet A_D it means, that all transitions from the set U must be removed. ■

If we consider our example of a τ-net, we can say it *can* be finished without any delay.

5 Conclusion

We have presented a theorem about τ-nets, which are used for modelling of workflow systems, or process control systems in general. The theorem enables to decide (easily) certain time properties of the modelled system.

Nevertheless it is still necessary to study properties of the τ-nets. Especially their properties in obtaining information about possible marking of a set of places.

5.1 Open Items

As open there still remains question about:

- When the net finishes always with zero delay
- If there is alwyas a delay, whether it is possible to deduce upper and lower bound of the limit
- Having two places $p1$, $p2$, are they marked concurrently, in sequence, ...
- ...

Acknowledgements

This work was supported by the research funding No. CEZ: J22/98:262200012.

References

[1] W.M.P. van der Aalst. *The Application of Petri Nets to Workflow Management.* The Journal of Circuits, Systems and Computers, 8(1), pp. 21–66, 1998.

[2] W.M.P. van der Aalst. *Three Good reasons for Using a Petri-net-based Workflow Management System* . In S. Navathe and T. Wakayama, editors, Proceedings of the International Working Conference on Information and Process Integration in Enterprises (IPIC'96), pp. 179–201, Cambridge, Massachusetts, Nov 1996.

[3] M. Češka, L. Motyčková, T. Hruška: Vyčístlitelnost a složitost. VUT v Brně, 2178, červen 1992, Nakladatelství VUT v Brně, ISBN 80-214-0441-8.

[4] M. Heiner: Verification And Optimization of Control Programs By Petri Nets Without State Explosion. Proceedings of ICATPN'97, June 1997, Toulouse, pp. 69–84.

[5] D. Kolář: SFC - A Language for Workflow Description, In: Proceedings of 33rd Spring International Conference MOSIS'99, ISM'99, MARQ, Ostrava, Roznov pod Radhostem, Czech Republic, 1999, pp. 101–108, ISBN 80-85988-31-3.

[6] D. Kolář: SFC Validation via Petri Nets, In: Proceedings of XXIst International Colloquium ASIS'99, MARQ, Ostrava, Krnov, Czech Republic, 1999, pp. 391–396, ISBN 80-85988-41-0.

[7] S. Roch, Prof. P. H. Starke: Manual of INA - Integrated Net Analyzer, Version 2.2, Humboldt-Universität zu Berlin Institut für Informatik, Lehrstuhl für Automaten- und Systemtheorie, Unter den Linden 6, 10099 Berlin, http://http://www.informatik.hu-berlin.de/lehrstuehle/automaten/ina/manual.html.

[8] B. Grahlmann: The PEP Tool, In Proceedings of CAV'97 (Computer Aided Verification), pp. 440–443, Springer-Verlag, LNCS, 1997, vol 1254.

[9] Bartek Kiepuszewski, Ralf Muhlberg, Maria E. Orlowska.*FlowBack: Providing Backward Recovery for Workflow Systems.* SIGMOD Conference 1998, pp. 555-557.

[10] M. Löwe, D. Wikarski, and Y. Han. *Higher-Order Object Nets and Their Application to Workflow Modeling.* Forschungsbericht 95-34, Technische Universität Berlin, Fachbereich Informatik, 1995.

[11] A. Valmari: The State Explosion Problem, In Lectures on Petri Nets I: Basic Models, Edited by W. Reisig and G. Rozenberg, pp. 429–528, Springer-Verlag, LNCS, 1998, vol. 1491.

[12] D. Wikarski. *An Introduction to Modular Process Nets.* TR-96-019, International Computer Science Institute (ICSI) Berkeley, 1996.

Knowledge-Based Software Engineering
T. Hruška and M. Hashimoto (Eds.)
IOS Press, 2000

User Interface for "Kansei" Retrieval System in Virtual Environment

Haruhiko HORIE[1], Shin-ichi SATO[1], Tadashi YAMANOUCHI[1], Tadayuki SOTA[2]

[1]*Mitsubishi Research Institute, Inc. 2-3-6 Otemachi, Chiyoda-ku, Tokyo, 100-8141, Japan*
[2]*Electrotechnical Laboratory, 1-1-4 Umezono, Tsukuba, Ibaraki, 305-8568, Japan*

Abstract. By progress of technology, we are using many picture data daily. However, the user interfaces of the multimedia databases are not almost progressing technically. A user is still looking for the target picture from the file list and the table of the preview picture in a plane window. "Kansei" retrieval system is a multimedia database management system, which put the focus on human's sensitivity. We studied the effective user interface, which used virtual environment for the "Kansei" retrieval system. A user searches intuitively within 3-dimensional virtual space using an image word. A user is shown the result of retrieval dynamically in virtual space. Moreover, a user is shown a user's sensitivity data itself. We propose the user interface for the new retrieval using virtual environment.

1 Introduction

The needs to a multimedia database are increasing today. For example, digital camera users are treating over 1000 picture. The "Kansei" retrieval system with which a multimedia database is searched using human sensitivity can respond to increase of such needs. "Kansei" retrieval system is a multimedia database management system, which put the focus on human's sensitivity. "Kansei" is a Japanese word. It means person's subjectivity, especially the subjective criteria for evaluating multimedia data.

"Kansei" retrieval system can retrieve textures, paints and photos as 2-D objects by using "Kansei" model [1][2][3][4]. It also can retrieve chair model as 3-D object [5]. "Kansei" model is based on the relationship between adjectives and graphical parameters. "Kansei" database management system (Kansei DBMS) is a DBMS, which treats these retrievals in integration [6]. It was enabled to search these various kinds of data systematically by DBMS. In order to use Kansei DBMS and "Kansei" retrieval, the user interface, which can deal with these various kinds of data similarly, is needed.

We studied the effective integrated user interface, which used virtual environment for the "Kansei" retrieval system. We developed the prototype of the "Kansei" retrieval application for supporting the workflow in which a designer coordinates office interior design.

We evaluated the interface of "Kansei" retrieval application. By this, the function of a user interface required for practical "Kansei" retrieval application was clarified.

2 The Requirements for the User Interface

2.1 Conventional Interface of Multimedia Database

The retrieval interface of the conventional multimedia database is mainly retrieval by keyword. A user inputs a key word and gets multimedia data from a database as a retrieval result. Or it searches using file size, a file format, and the time stamp of a file.

The preview picture carries out the list display of the result, or a list display is carried out by the file name. If there are many results, a user needs to page-change or to use scroll-bar. This user interface is not convenient for users.

2.2 Feature of "Kansei" Retrieval System

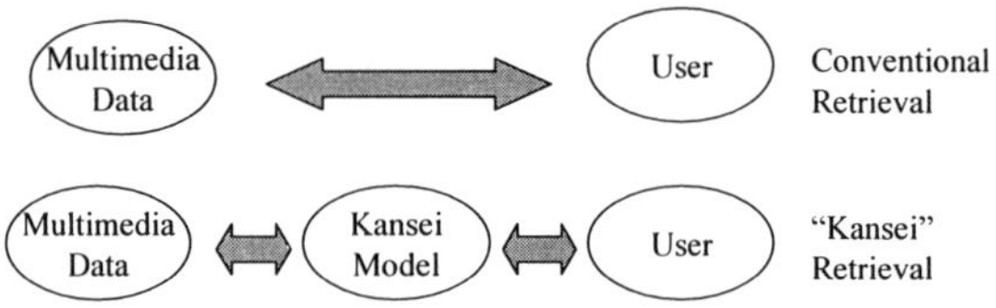

Figure 1: Conventional Retrieval and "Kansei" Retrieval

The feature of "Kansei" retrieval system is searching multimedia data using "Kansei" model (Figure1). We can retrieve multimedia data using image words. A user sends a query like this, "warm 5, soft 7, modern 4". "Kansei" retrieval system interprets by Kansei model and reply multimedia data list of pictures.

2.3 The Requirements for the User Interface of "Kansei" Retrieval System

We studied the requirements for the user interface of "Kansei" retrieval system, which supports designer's work process on prototype system. The number of requirements is mainly two. One is about the input query on Graphical User Interface (GUI). Another is the display method of results on GUI.

(1) GUI for "Kansei" Retrieval Query

It is expected that GUI enable an intuitive query. GUI should satisfy the following requirements.

- Perform simply selection of two or more image words, and a setup of weight of query. Moreover, it can grasp visually for a user.
- Learn the retrieval operation history for every user, and this interface should suit a user.

(2) GUI for Displaying Results of "Kansei" retrieval

In Kansei retrieval, many pictures are shown as a result. While a user grasps each retrieval result visually, he/she should be also able to grasp the "Kansei" model relation between data visually at the display of a retrieval result. When there are many retrieval results, it is required to rearrange legible and to show a user.

- Arrange the retrieval results, which can grasp a lot of retrieval results for a short time.

- The "Kansei" score of the picture of a retrieval result and pictures can be displayed visually.
- They can be re-searched, using 2D picture and 3D object of a retrieval result as a key.

(3) Supporting Design Process

It considers as the system, which supports designer who coordinates office interior design, and the following thing is also required.

- It can be operated, without distinguishing especially multimedia data, such as fine-arts drawing, a scenery photograph, a texture image, and a 3-dimensional solid object (chair, desk, etc).
- Show the history of retrieval and the history of operation visually and follow a user's thinking process.
- Be easy to use all input-and-output interfaces, and unify them.

3 Experiment of User Interface of "Kansei" Image Retrieval System

3.1 The Outline of a Prototype

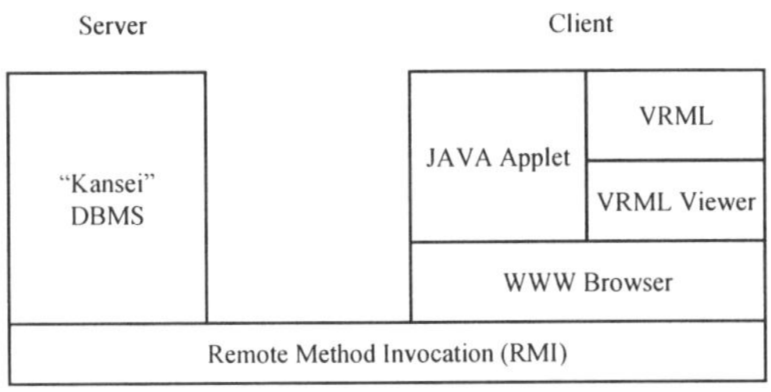

Figure 2: Outline of a Prototype

We made a user interface in virtual space as an experiment in the prototype system of "Kansei" retrieval system, which supports the office interior coordination process. This GUI consists in a VRML world, which operates on JAVA applet and VRML browser (Figure 2). Therefore, it operates on a WWW browser. Netscape Communicator4.0 or upper is required for the browser and Cosmo Player2.0, which is VRML viewer, is also required for it.

"Kansei" retrieval system is operating in the server, and a user connects with a server by the WWW browser of client PC, and uses this prototype system by the interface of VRML and JAVA applet. The server has connected applet to "Kansei" Database Management System ("Kansei" DBMS) using Remote Method Invocation (RMI) technology. "Kansei" DBMS is a kind of object-relational-DBMS, and the "Kansei" model management function and the "Kansei" retrieval algorithm management function were added, and it was extended.

3.2 The Interface for the Office Interior-Design Coordination

We investigated the procedure in which a designer coordinated office interior design. A designer receives an order from a customer, hears an opinion of a customer, and coordinates office interior design. It consists 5 stages, concept making, designing furniture for the office, choosing furniture, arranging furniture layout in office, and the walk-through presentation in the office.

1. A designer takes an opinion of a customer and sets up a unifier concept. The photographs and the pictures suitable for the concept are collected and a new whole image is made in a designer.
2. The designer designs furniture (for example, chair) which suited the whole image.
3. The designer looks for a furniture design of the existing product of the form similar to the designed furniture (for example, chair). And a designer looks for the desk, which matched the goods series of the chair.
4. A designer arranges collected chairs and desks in the room. He asks an opinion and the comment of a customer and changes a layout.
5. A designer shows a customer the walk-through presentation in the room.

Our prototype system is supported 1, 3, 4 and 5. 2 are a designer's privilege.

3.3 GUI for Concept Making

Figure 3: Image Word Retrieval

In our system, image word retrieval interface in virtual space is prepared for concept making. Image word retrieval is the retrieval method of retrieving pictures using image word.

This interface can click an image word icon directly, and can choose it in virtual space. The weight of retrieval of the image word is given by the number of times of a click. The selected image word moves to the right, size becomes large according to the number of times of a click, and the color becomes deep (Figure 3).

This system learns each user's operation history. The image word used last time and the image word used frequently are more displayed on the upper position.

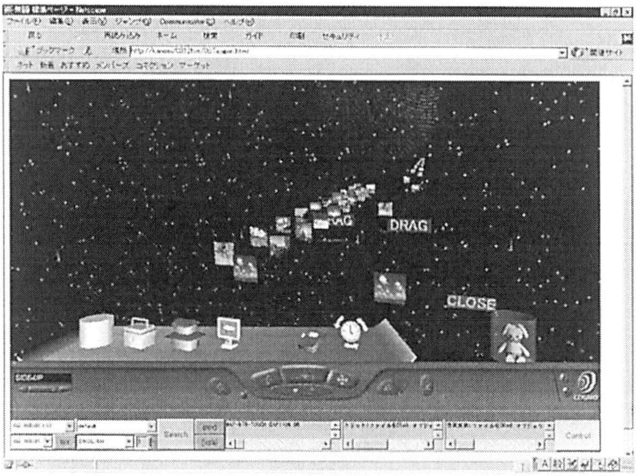

Figure 4: Results of Retrieval

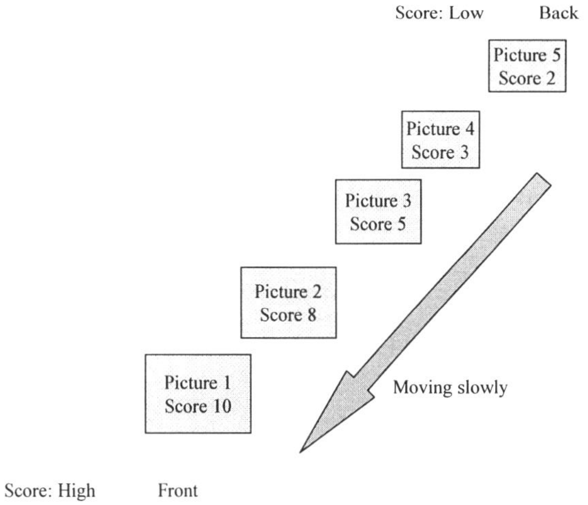

Figure 5: Results of Retrieval (Concept)

A retrieval result is dynamically put on 3-dimensional virtual space (Figure 4). The "Kansei" model in the degree of conformity calculates the picture of each retrieval result. And according to the ranking and score, it is arranged at back from a front (Figure 5).

A user can understand visually the degree of conformity and the ranking to conditions of a retrieval result. Moreover, in order to have a user check many retrieval results for a short time, pictures move to a front automatically from back just like the baggage on conveyor belt of baggage claim of airport. A user can also display two or more retrieval results that changed a few retrieval conditions, side by side. If this changes the conditions of an image word, it can see how a retrieval result changes and can compare.

Figure 6: Basket (Collection of Pictures)

A user can click and collect the pictures of a retrieval result with a mouse. It is put into the picture collected from two or more retrieval results by the picture basket (Figure 6). The selected picture is automatically put into a basket. Basket has many selected pictures from two or more results of retrieval. A User can drag and put In order that a designer may arrange an idea and may get the new way of thinking he drags and moves the icon in a basket, or does similar picture retrieval.

3.4 GUI for Choosing 3D Object

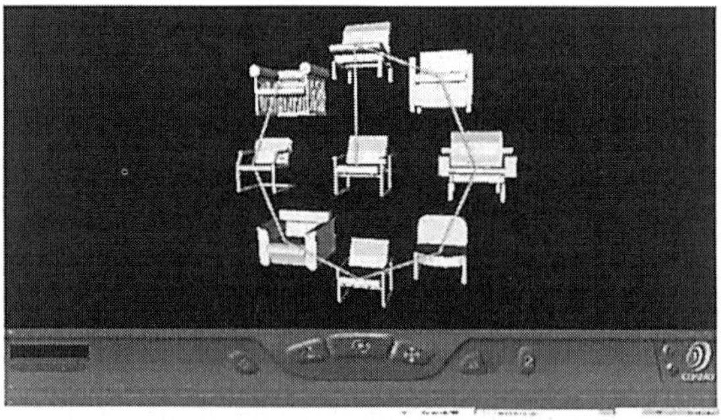

Figure 7: Results of 3D Similar Retrieval

A designer designs office interior design, after agreeing about the concept of a customer and office interior design using this system. A designer begins to design, after agreeing about the concept of a customer and office interior design. A designer designs a chair and a desk using CAD.

This system reads VRML data of the designed chair, and retrieve 3-dimensional solid data of commercial chair products. Figure7 is a display as a result of similar retrieval. "Kansei" retrieval System can retrieve 3D solid model by using "Kansei" model. The key object of "Kansei" retrieval is displayed in the center, and objects of retrieval results are on the circumference of that. It has ranked with the high order of an evaluating point from the center.

If a user chooses an object and clicks a search button, he can use similar retrieval, using the object as a key. The retrieval by the same goods series is also prepared about a commercial product.

3.5 GUI for arranging office layout

Figure 8: Arranging Office Layout

A designer arranges a chair and a desk in the office of virtual space, hearing an opinion of a customer. Moreover, in accordance with the color tone of the room, a color is set as each object (Figure 8).

In this system, arranging the selected object, making the copy of an object, changing direction, the thing that constitutes an object and that a color is changed for every parts, and the scenery besides a window are changeable.

If a user does the point of the arbitrary points on a translucent small room map and they are dragged, he can change the position and the look of a viewpoint.

3.6 GUI for walk-through presentation of the room.

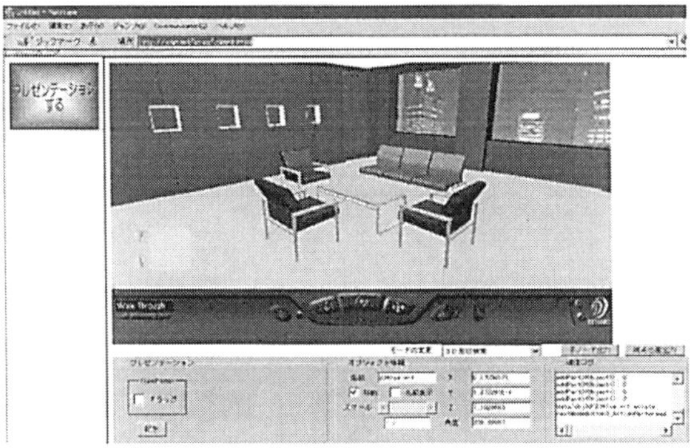

Figure 9: Walk-Through Presentation

A designer will show a customer walk-through of the room, if a coordination of office interior design is completed. Moreover, how when sitting on each chair to be visible can be shown by one-touch (Figure 9).

4 Conclusion

We defined the requirements for the user interface of a user interface of "Kansei" retrieval system. We developed the application of KANSEI retrieval system as an experiment, and verified the function of a user interface for which it is required.

The user interface that we studied is useful in order to utilize a "Kansei" retrieval system effectively. The quantitative evaluation method about the ease of using of "Kansei" retrieval system also needs to be studied.

The study of a "Kansei" Retrieval system progresses, it will also become important to study the user interface for it. We will be advancing study of the user interface as the platform for advancing "Kansei" study.

Acknowledgement

Special thanks to New Energy and Industrial Technology Development Organization (NEDO) for funding. This paper is a part of "Human Media Project" funded by NEDO.

References

[1] T. Kato et al.: "Efficient and Effective Querying by Image Content", Journal of intelligent information Systems,3(3/4);231-262, 1994

[2] T. Shibata et al.: "Modeling of Subjective Interpretation for Street Landscape Image", 9th Int. Conf. Database and Expert Systems Applications, pp.501-510,1998

[3] Y. Kobayashi et al.: "A Trial for subjective Retrieval of Texture Images", Proc. Of the Electronics, Information and Systems Conference(Japan), pp.137-138,1999

[4] H. Kobayashi et al.: "Image Retrieval System using the Combination with KANSEI Features", IEICE, PRMU97-261(Japan)pp.75-80, 1993

[5] M. Suzuki et al.: "3D Object Retrieval based on subjective Measures", Proc. Of Int. Workshop on Database and Expert Systems Applications, pp.850-856, 1998

[6] S. Sato et al : "Proposal for Kansei Database Management System", Proc. of the Electronics, Information and Systems Conference(Japan),pp.139-142, 1999

Knowledge-Based Software Engineering
T. Hruška and M. Hashimoto (Eds.)
IOS Press, 2000

Proposal of Kansei DBMS as a Platform to Organize Kansei Retrieval System

Shin-ichi SATO[1], Haruhiko HORIE[1], Tadashi YAMANOUCHI[1], Tadayuki SOTA[2]

[1]*Mitsubishi Research Institute, Inc.*

[2]*Electrotechnical Laboratory, AIST, MITI*

Abstract. The progress of the computer has enabled us to use multimedia data easily and even a personal computer has been storing many data. It is a problem how to manage these enormous data. There have been some researches to manage these data effectively, and several systems that enable us to retrieve data more intuitively (Kansei retrieval system) have been developed. These kinds of systems will be more important in the future. So, we propose Database Management System as a platform to organize Kansei retrieval systems. We also developed prototype DBMS and organized several Kansei retrieval systems. In this report, we introduce the concept of Kansei DBMS and how to organize Kansei retrieval systems.

1 Introduction

The progress of computer has enabled us to handle multimedia data easily and many multimedia data have being accumulated even in a personal computer. When we consider management of these data, retrieval-by-keyword system will not work well. In addition to the difficulty of assigning appropriate keywords, the time of managing data becomes immense when data increase. Several researches have been performed to provide more appropriate multimedia data retrieval systems, which also reduce cost of data management. There are some examples of the retrieval system which use an image itself as query [1][2]. In recent years, the systems that enables to retrieve suited data for a user's characteristic have been researched [3][4]. These kinds of systems are called "Kansei retrieval system." "Kansei", which is Japanese, means each person's subjectivity, in this case, especially the subjective criteria for evaluating multimedia data. We consider it is meaningful to provide common platform to develop Kansei retrieval systems while they have been developed as monolithic systems. We call this platform "Kansei DBMS." In this research, we examined requirements of Kansei DBMS and constructed prototype system. We also unified some Kansei retrieval systems and verified functions of Kansei DBMS.

2 Concept of Kansei Database Management System

2.1 Model structure of Kansei Retrieval Systems

The Kansei retrieval system enables us to retrieve contents that suit for each person's subjectivity. The results will be different for every individual. The four hierarchies of multimedia perception were hypothesised to implement Kansei retrieval systems [3]. These hierarchies are consisted of the physical, physiological, psychological and cognitive level.

Physical level's data are the contents itself. Physiological level's data are graphical features such as intensity level, edge, contrast and so on. Each person may show different interpretation in classification and similarity measure. This difference among people is taken into consideration in psychological level. In cognitive level, the relation between adjective words and multimedia data is analyzed, considering each person's subjectivity. Each level was defined as a multidimensional space and named as the graphical features' (GF), subjective features' (SF) and unified features' (UF) space.

We defined the model structure of the Kansei retrieval system based on this four hierarchy. Figure 1 indicates the hierarchy of multimedia perception process and the model structure of the Kansei retrieval system.

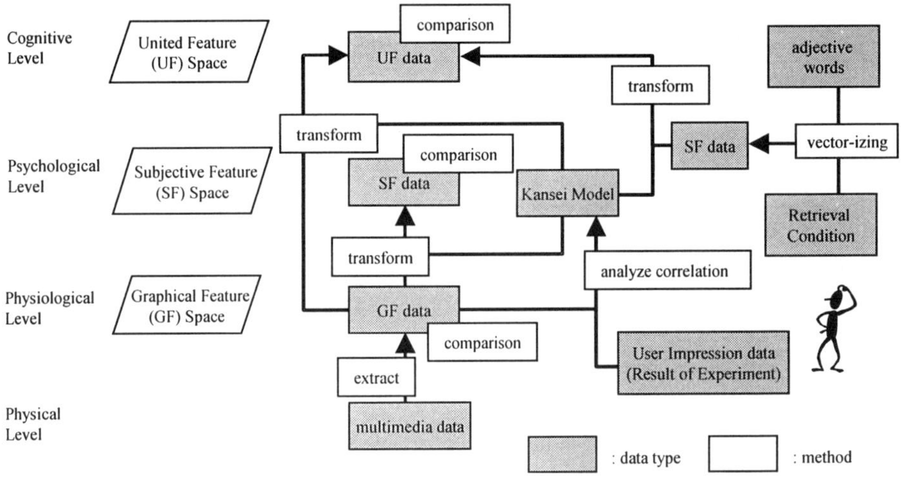

Figure 1: Hierarchy of multimedia perception process and Model structure of Kansei retrieval systems

Here is a typical flow of data processing.

(1) GF data are extracted from multimedia contents as vector data in GF space.

(2) A user answers his/her impressions on sample multimedia data, which are only the part in all data, as the weight vector of adjective words (User Impression data).

(3) The correlation between adjective words and graphical parameters is analyzed statistically, and Kansei model as the personal view model for the user is made.

(4) GF data are transformed to UF data by Kansei model.

(5) User Inputs (Retrieval Condition: adjective words and its weight) are vector-ized and transformed to UF data by Kansei model.

(6) The closer data in UF space will be the result candidates.

In Kansei retrieval systems, we do not have to assign the adjectives to all data. Once the system has learned the correlation between adjective words and GF data, it can automatically estimate the UF data of new unlearned multimedia data. Using the same mechanism, the associative retrieval in SF space can be performed.

2.2 Requirement of Kansei Database Management System

There are several examples of the Kansei retrieval system. These systems are usually monolithic systems and it is difficult to apply the part of another system, although Kansei retrieval systems are composed of many parts as shown in Figure 1. They have to develop every part of Kansei retrieval systems by themselves.

We consider it is important to supply common platform for the Kansei retrieval system in accordance with the model we proposed. It could reduce the development cost and enable to re-use research results. What is required for this platform is the common interfaces to build parts of the Kansei retrieval system as components. Defining data types that specialized and commonly used in Kansei retrieval systems is necessary to define general-purpose interfaces. By using these data types as the arguments, we can keep the consistency of interfaces.

Although the common interfaces need to be general-purpose, it is impossible to design completely general-purpose interfaces since researches about Kansei are still in progress. So, an interface and a data type need to be extensible.

We define this platform as Kansei Database Management System (Kansei DBMS). The managing application of Kansei DBMS is also necessary to manage data, help make algorithms to check the validity of unified algorithms and so on. We expect the Kansei DBMS expand the research about Kansei and help develop practical Kansei retrieval application.

3 Composition of Kansei DBMS

3.1 Composition of Kansei DBMS

We analyzed several Kansei retrieval systems, and designed the common interfaces and data types in accordance with the model structure of the Kansei retrieval system so that most algorithms' methods can be unified as components.

We defined common interfaces to implement functions shown by white squares in Figure 1 and defined grey squares as the expanded data types in the Database. The expanded data types are handled by the libraries (access methods), which enable to Select, Insert, Update and Delete data of these types by various conditions.

Each algorithm should be divided into methods that implement defined interfaces. In the "framework", the flow of algorithms is defined by combining the interfaces to call and it is also described which data to Select/Insert/Update/Delete from the Database using access libraries. Figure 2 indicates the composition of Kansei DBMS.

This composition makes it easier to construct Kansei retrieval system. For example, when someone find a new GF data and want to try Kansei retrieval using that GF data, all they have to develop is a GF data extracting method only. Using a framework and methods implemented already, they can construct the Kansei retrieval system easily.

It is also possible to construct more advanced systems on Kansei DBMS. When someone want to make an advanced or experimental system, they can customize a framework using access functions registered in libraries by which data can be obtained in various conditions. However, it requires further consideration at the present stage how to extend data types and interfaces easily.

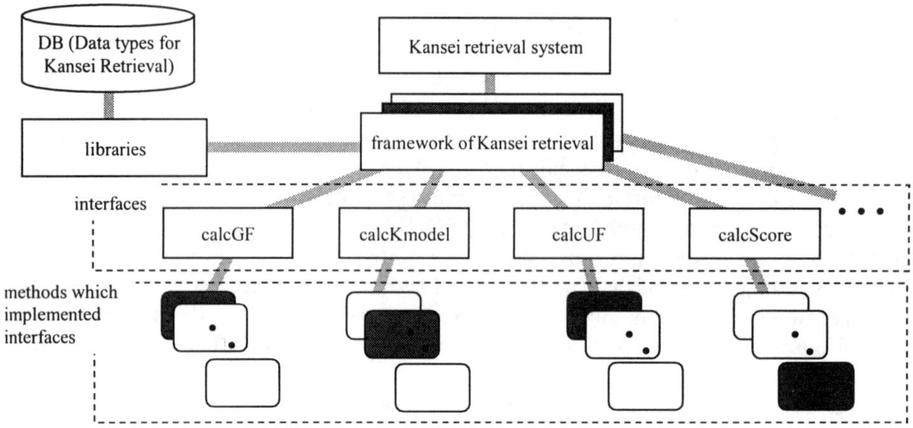

Figure2: Composition of Kansei DBMS

Here is a typical story of developing an algorithm on the Kansei DBMS.

(1) Develop a framework: A framework is just a procedure that described the flow of the algorithm. A developer handles data in the Database using access libraries in the framework and determines interfaces to use. Typical frameworks have already been implemented analyzing some Kansei retrieval systems. So, unless they want to try a new experimental way, they can use one of these frameworks and omit this process.

(2) Implement interfaces: Implementing interfaces is the core part of developing on Kansei DBMS.

(3) Construct algorithm: A developer adopts a framework he/she uses and selects appropriate methods to use in that framework.

Once frameworks and methods are registered, other developers can use them. So, it is rather easy to develop derived Kansei retrieval systems.

If one developer implemented an effective method, he/she can use it by combining with other methods that were registered before. Of course, another developer can try that new method by combining with the methods implemented before.

3.2 Management Application of Kansei DBMS

We developed a web application as a management application of Kansei DBMS. It consists of retrieval interfaces and maintenance interfaces of Kansei DBMS.

The retrieval interfaces are used to confirm the validity of constructed Kansei retrieval system. It will be necessary full-scale GUI application to make practical application of Kansei retrieval system. There are some researches that focused on the GUI of this kind [8]. Our GUI application is simple one just to check the newly constructed retrieval systems. We prepared four kind of retrieval interfaces, which are "Query by Example Image (no consideration of subjectivity)", "Query by Example", "Query by weighted adjective words", "Introspection of adjective words". All GUIs are simple and all results will be displayed just grid like.

The maintenance interface is divided into two main parts. One is the data maintenance interface, through which a user maintains the data that are generated in the process of Kansei retrieval and so on. The other part of maintenance application is the functions to construct Kansei retrieval algorithm. This is the function, which provide GUIs to construct new algorithm by making use of registered frameworks and methods. These functions are not necessary for the user who just wants to use Kansei retrieval systems. We assume that researchers of Kansei use this interface.

4 Prototype System

4.1 Unification of Kansei Retrieval Application

We tried to unify four image retrieval systems, which are pictures [3], landscape photographs [4], texture[5] and photographs [6] retrieval system. One 3D data retrieval system [7] was also tried. These systems were divided and all or part of them was reconstructed as methods that implemented interfaces. It was confirmed most algorithms have been unified correctly and returns the same result as a stand-alone system.

Each procedure should be the method that implements a common interface we defined. Although most procedures have been defined by implementing the interface, only some procedure of one algorithm, which proposes new attributes relevant to Kansei, couldn't at the present stage. It is a future subject to make an interface and a data type extendible.

4.2 Making New Algorithms

There are re-usable frameworks and methods in Kansei DBMS now that several algorithms were unified. So, it is possible to re-use frameworks and/or methods registered by him/herself and other developers. This process can be performed through the management application of Kansei DBMS. Figure 3 indicates the process of making a new algorithm using registered framework and methods.

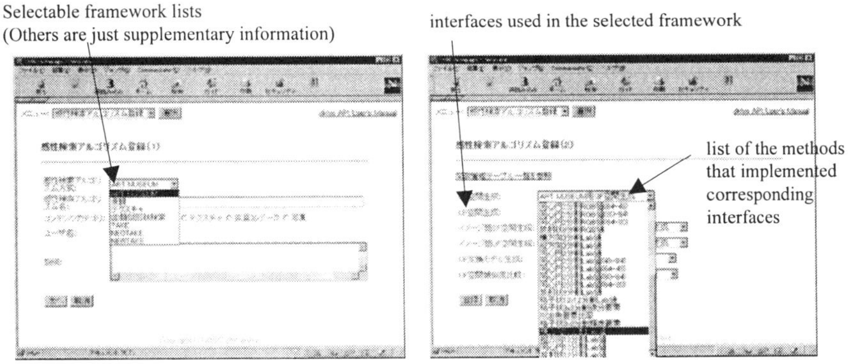

(1) select a framework to use (2) select methods to replace

Figure 3: Process of making new algorithm

This is an example of making an algorithm of "Query by weight adjective words". Figure 3 (1) shows the example of selecting a target framework. After they select a framework, the interfaces to be used in the selected framework and the method lists that implement the corresponding interface are shown. Figure 3 (2) shows the example of selecting the GF extracting method as a part of the retrieval system. Then, new algorithm will come and its validity can also be checked through this web application.

New algorithms can be made like this, re-using many results of researches. We believe that this kind of platform, which enable trial-and-error construction of the algorithm, will help progress the research about Kansei and help develop more effective Kansei retrieval systems.

5 Conclusion

We proposed Kansei DBMS as a platform to develop Kansei retrieval systems. It was confirmed that a new algorithm could be made by combining parts of other algorithms when several algorithms were unified in accordance with the model we proposed.

We will provide researchers of Kansei or Kansei retrieval system with Kansei DBMS and have them evaluate the usability of making new algorithms unifying new methods and a framework. The technique for extending algorithms is necessary at the next stage. And finally, we want to cooperate with the research of GUI application and want to provide more general-purposed platform both for developing Kansei retrieval systems and using Kansei retrieval applications.

Acknowledgments

This research is the result of the "research and development of human media" to which it was commissioned through Laboratories of Image Information Science and Technology from New Energy and Industrial Technology Development Organization as part of a Ministry of International Trade and Industry industrial technology research-and-development system.

References

[1] T. Kato: "Query by Visual Example -Content Based Image Retrieval-", Proc. of International Conference on Extending Database Technology'92, Mar. 1992

[2] C. Faloutsos, et al.: "Efficient and Effective Querying by Image Content", Journal of Intelligent Information Systems, 3(3/4): 231-262, 1994

[3] T. Kato et al.: "Supporting Human-Human Interaction beyond Cultural Backgrounds", CHI97 Basic Research Symposium, March 22-23 1997

[4] T. Shibata et al.: "Modelling of Subjective Interpretation for Street Landscape Image", 9th Int. Conf. Database and Expert Systems Applications, pp.501-510, 1998

[5] Y. Kobayashi et al.: "A Trial for subjective Retrieval of Texture images", Proc. of the Electronics, Information and Systems Conference(Japan), pp.137-138, 1999

[6] H. Kobayashi et al.: "Image Retrieval System using the Combination with KANSEI Features", IEICE, PRMU97-261(Japan) pp.75-80, 1993

[7] M. Suzuki et al.: "3D Object Retrieval based on Subjective Measures", Proc. of Int. Workshop on Database and Expert Systems Applications, pp.850-856, 1998

[8] H. Horie et al: "User Interface for Kansei Database Management System", Proc. of the Electronics, Information and Systems Conference(Japan), pp.143-146, 1999

Knowledge-Based Software Engineering
T. Hruška and M. Hashimoto (Eds.)
IOS Press, 2000

An Interactive Method for Construction and Retrieval of Software Library Collection

Kenro AIHARA, Atsuhiro TAKASU
NII, 2-1-2, Hitotsubashi, Chiyoda-ku, Tokyo 101-8430, Japan
{kenro.aihara,takasu}@nii.ac.jp

Abstract. This paper proposes an HCI approach to supporting development of a directory of software libraries which bridges between software library developers and users. Our basic idea is that designing interaction using an effective visualization of their relations to externalize users' implicit knowledge is critical for our purpose.

We assume that taxonomical thought are one of the most important and skilled operations for us when we organize or store information. We, therefore, use clustering or classification techniques for interactive interface. The proposed system provides two-dimensional space to visualize categories of icons of classes and categories can be customized by SVM.

1 Introduction

Recently many softwares are available on the Internet, and free softwares becomes important resources for computer users and software developers. However, there is still a hurdle for utilizing softwares in software library level, that is, reusing software libraries in software development.

The purpose of this research is to develop a directory of software libraries which bridges between software library developers and users. At the current study, we aims at handling JAVA class libraries. The directory consists of multiple broker agents each of which keeps a class library of specific domain in various levels. Brokers have the following three functions:

- collection of class libraries from the Internet,
- reconfiguration of class libraries, and
- class library selection support.

Each broker selects software libraries specific to the domain of the broker. The software library are usually attached with documents which explain the function and the interface of the library. As for JAVA class library, Javadoc generates document from declarations and comments of the library in a standard format. In our system we use those library documents as the information source of selecting software libraries. Brokers gather documents from the Internet and select documents and related libraries using text categorization technique. All these three functions can improve the reusability of class libraries.

This paper focuses the last function mainly, that is, supporting construction of knowledge bases and selection of appropriate library.

2 Methodology

Integration We deal with JAVA class libraries as content, which are often bundled manuals which are generated by Javadoc. Metadata of classes are attempted to produce automatically from such manuals in the given style and by using information extraction (IE) technologies [2]. We expect that we can extract class hierarchy, related classes, conditions for usage, author, and location for download from such documents.

Instead of assuming complete ontologies for global scheme, we consider to manage local relations declared by administrators as semantical relations between classes. These relations can be not always accepted by all users. They, therefore, must be enabled only in the community which agrees them. Consequently we must manage locality of each relation explicitly and provide such information to users. We would like to emphasize that supporting administrator's declaration of such local relations and management of locality are significant for our approach. This paper considers how to design human-computer interaction for supporting declaration of such relations and retrieval tasks.

Interaction Our basic idea is that it can be effective that the system lets them notice relations between classes for supporting both construction of directories and retrieval tasks. In other words, designing interaction using an effective visualization of their relations to externalize users' implicit knowledge is critical. We believe that functions of visualization and customization must be needed if the system attempts to support externalizing users' implicit knowledge effectively.

Visualization We guess that taxonomical thought are one of the most important and skilled operations for us when we organize or store information. The way of classification may change dynamically according to one's mental and physical situation. On that assumption, we may discuss that clustering or classification techniques are applied to interactive interface.

The proposed system, therefore, provides two-dimensional space to visualize information space. JAVA classes are placed in the space as icon. And the system manages categories of classes. The arrangement of icons are computed by a kind of multi-dimensional scaling method as "similar" classes should be placed close in the space. Similarities are based on term frequency of document attached to each class and relations extracted by IE.

Customization The system is customized in user feedback process. The feedback will be given by users' modification of categories.

It must be noted that customization not only yields improvement of usability or effectivity for the user, but also can be exploited as a nonverbal knowledge of the user. That is to say, a user can use result of customization by another user as a kind of his/her knowledge about classes there.

3 System

Scenario In this section, we show a scenario of the proposed system. Figure 1 illustrates the system architecture. Similarities are defined by term frequency of document here.

At first, the system stores "the document-term matrix" which has entries a weight $f(i, j)$ of term j for document i from a collection. Then the system produces initial categories of documents, "Category Information", by a clustering method. Next, the system shows

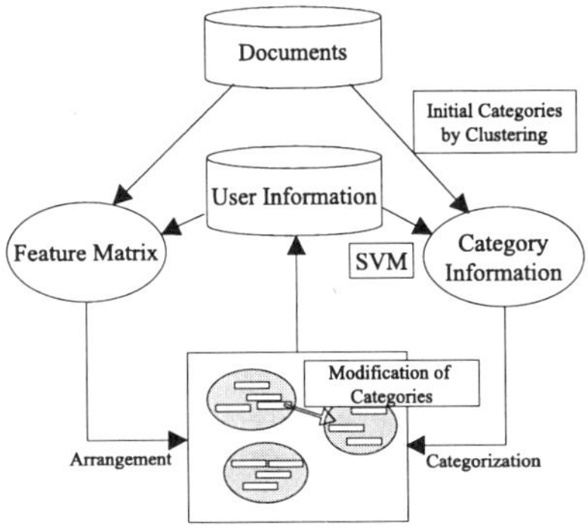

Figure 1: System Architecture

icons in two-dimensional space. Arrangement of icons are computed using similarities of classes. When a user views this arrangement of icons, he/she may recognize an structure of the information space, relation among classes, or any features of classes. He/she may find out familiar classes. The user may also predict the content of a class which placed proximal zone of such known classes.

From previous researches, we know that the user often cannot agree the shown categories. When the user has an unagreeableness in his/her mind, he/she often tries to modify such visualized information as he/she likes[3]. We suppose that that action must include the user's implicit cognition, such an intent which cannot be verbalized by him/herself. The system, therefore, can exploit such actions as the feedback information which is stored in "User Information" of Figure 1. For customization, user feedback is applied to categorization of icons and their arrangement. Thus user feedback information is stored for each user and the system gets customized.

When its user wants to retrieve class or browse documents of class, he/she can use his/her this own customized interface. If a user inputs an query by keywords or an example document of a class, its query vector or the example document would be mapped into an appropriate category.

Categorization The proposed system shows class categories to users. We expect that visualized categories can help users to recognize the shown information space regardless of its user's familiarity of the domain of the information.

Initial Categories Initial categories can be obtained by clustering. Many clustering methods, such hierarchical clustering, graph based clustering, or neural network based clustering, have been proposed. Willet reviewed clustering methods in IR studies [4].

We use a hierarchical clustering and the complete link algorithm. A hierarchical clustering can divide all classes into some sub-clusters according to its dendrogram and sub-cluster can be represented as reference classes. Therefore, the method can keep the number of classes which must be handled at once small. The complete link algorithm computes an inter-cluster similarity as the minimum of the similarities between all pairs of inter-cluster classes. The algorithm merges the pair of clusters with the highest inter-cluster similarity. It, therefore, can produce small and tight clusters. We have to discuss further on which clustering method is the most effective or useful.

Customization Using SVM Let us consider that a user moves a class or a cluster of classes in cluster A into cluster B. The system appends a new attribute to represent the user's intention causing his/her to modify categories well enough in feedback process. The system sets 1 to the value of the attribute of moved class (or classes which belong to the moved category). This attribute can be used for distinguishing between the moved classes and ones in the previous category. It might be difficult to classify them without this appended attribute.

Then, SVM learns the ordinality from the original attributes within the new category. SVM is a classifier for multi-dimensional data to determine a boundary curve between two classes [1]. The boundary can be determined only with vectors in boundary region (so-called "margin") of two classes, so-called "support vectors", in a training examples. SVM, therefore, need to be re-learned only when vectors in boundary change. One of the advantages of SVM is that the boundary can be determined only by its support vectors, namely SVM is robust against changes of all vectors but its support vectors. This advantage is very important for an open collection of class libraries which change constantly. After a user modifies categories, the system re-learns the new boundary of cluster B, B-against-the-rest boundary, by SVM with the incoming classes and support vectors. Thus categories can be customized with user attributes and SVM. The system needs to re-learn not all SVMs of categories but only one of the target category when a new attribute is appended. This feature enables us to append attributes in actuality.

4 Conclusions

This paper introduced an method of developing a directory of software libraries. Our method is human-computer interaction approach and it focuses on designing interaction using an effective visualization of their relations to externalize users' implicit knowledge.

HCI research which should be actually effective for the users need rich real experiments. Therefore, we should implement a usable prototype system and make a great deal of experiments. Definition of similarities and visualization of structural relations among classes are future issues.

Acknowledgements

This research is a part of the research project "Studies on Ubiquitous Information Systems for Utilization of Highly Distributed Information Resources" (JSPS-RFTF96P00602) granted by JSPS (The Japan Society for the Promotion of Science).

References

[1] K. Aihara, and A. Takasu. Customization using support vector machines for information retrieval. In *Proceedings of the Fourth World Multiconference on Systemics, Cybernetics, and Informatics*, to appear, 2000.

[2] B. E. Boser, I. M. Guyon, and V. N. Vapnik. A training algorithm for optimal margin classifiers. In *Proceedings of the Fifth Annual ACM Workshop on Computational Learning Theory*, pages 144–152, 1992.

[3] C. Cardie. Empirical methods in information extraction. *AI Magazine*, 18(4):65–80, 1997.

[4] K. Hori. A system for aiding creative concept formation. *IEEE Transactions on Systems, Man, and Cybernetics*, 24(6):882–894, 1994.

[5] P. Willett. Recent trends in hierarchic document clustering: A critical review. *Information Processing & Management*, 24(4):577–597, 1988.

Knowledge-Based Software Engineering
T. Hruška and M. Hashimoto (Eds.)
IOS Press, 2000

An Object - Oriented Approach in Knowledge Based Software Engineering of an Intelligent GUI

Maria VIRVOU, Katerina KABASSI

Department of Informatics, University of Piraeus
Karaoli & Dimitriou 80, 18534, Piraeus, Greece
E-mail: {mvirvou, kkabassi}@unipi.gr

Abstract. This paper describes an object - oriented approach for the development of a Graphical User Interface that incorporates intelligence and deals with files and folders in a similar way as the Windows 98 Explorer. The system described is called IFM. IFM reasons constantly about users' actions so that it may automatically offer help in case it believes a user may have made an error. IFM has an object – oriented component for the GUI and a knowledge base that is used by its user modelling component for the reasoning. We have used the Rational Unified Process and UML for the development of the whole of IFM, thus integrating the intelligent and the object oriented part. An empirical study and a requirements analysis were conducted during the requirements capture. The results were used for designing the system. After completing the implementation of a second release of IFM, an evaluation took place to find the system's limitations in order to improve it.

1 Introduction

Graphical user interfaces are considered user friendlier than command language interfaces. However, as McGraw [1] points out, they may prove difficult to traverse and use if they are poorly designed; hence in addition to basic user interface guidelines, developers may also want to consider the feasibility and benefits of using AI to enhance the user interface. Intelligent File Manipulator (IFM) is a graphical user interface for file manipulation, similar to the Windows 98/NT Explorer, which also incorporates intelligence [2, 3]. It has the ability to reason about users' actions and aims at providing spontaneous help and advice to users who have made an error with respect to their hypothesised intentions.

However, the development of a user interface is an issue that needs a lot of attention. For example, Sutton and Sprague conducted a survey in IBM in 1978 [4], which revealed that 50% of the designer's time was spent on designing the user interface of a system. The same result was also confirmed by a more recent survey by Myers and Rosson [5] in 1990s. Therefore, as Dix et al. [6] point out, it is definitely worth the effort to provide structure and techniques to understand and improve the interactive design process. If a user interface incorporates AI techniques the difficulty of the design process becomes even greater and so does the need for structure and techniques for the design process.

The prevailing engineering paradigm for user interfaces is the iterative design [7, 4, 8, 9]. Therefore, the classical Waterfall model of life cycle is not appropriate. On the other hand, an object-oriented life cycle model, such as the one suggested by the Rational Unified Process [10, 11], seems more promising since it supports many iterations of the development phases. In addition, UML [12], which is the object-oriented modelling language that is supported by the Rational Unified Process, provides multiple diagrams that may illustrate a lot of the subtleties of the design of a user interface. Not only is it compatible with the object-oriented programming needed for the graphical user interface but it can also provide a powerful language for modelling the knowledge base of the intelligent user interface.

In this paper, we show that UML and the Rational Unified Process may provide a powerful modelling language and a model of life cycle, which can be adapted to the needs of the design process of a GUI that incorporates intelligence, such as IFM. In the life cycle of IFM we have conducted many evaluations and/or empirical studies to ensure that the system addresses real users' needs. Using UML we have modelled these users' needs in the requirements capture. Moreover, we have represented the knowledge base of IFM using class diagrams.

2 Life cycle of IFM

In order to specify all requirements and design of IFM, an iterative development had to be adopted. Therefore the iteration of several phases of the development was considered crucial and the Rational Unified Process [10, 11] formed the basis for the life cycle of the system. According to the Rational Unified Process, during the life cycle of the system the architecture is prototyped, tested, measured and analysed, and then refined in subsequent iterations [13]. On this basis the software life cycle is divided into cycles, each cycle working on a new generation of the product developed. The process divides one development cycle in four consecutive phases: the inception, the elaboration, the construction and the transition phase [10, 11].

During the inception phase, a primary executable release of IFM was developed [2]. Its design originated from another system called RESCUER that was meant to provide assistance to users of command language interfaces, such as the interface of UNIX [14, 15]. In order to enhance the first version of IFM, another iteration of the software life cycle took place. The iteration started with the evaluation of the first prototype. Evaluation is an integral part of the design process and should take place throughout the design phase of the life cycle; most techniques for evaluation at this stage are analytic and involve using an expert to assess the design against cognitive and usability principles [6]. The method selected for the design evaluation was an empirical study that took place in the phase of the elaboration.

In the empirical study expert and novice users of Windows 98/NT, were asked to work with a standard file manipulation program, such as Windows 98/NT Explorer as they would normally do. Each user's actions were recorded using the computer logging method and were then analysed in order to identify the errors that users make while completing certain tasks. Human evaluators, using the video recording method observed the users' actions issued during their interaction with the regular explorer and wrote down their comments about each action. The same protocols were also given to IFM as input, so that we would find out what IFM's limitations were, in comparison with the human evaluators' comments.

The results of this process were models suitable for developing use cases. Use cases are needed for the formation of the so – called use case diagrams, which are incorporated in UML for expressing the system's required functionality. A use case is a description of the system's behaviour during the interaction with an actor [16]. The use cases created resulted in the identification of the misconceptions users have while navigating through a standard "Windows Explorer" and which were not identified by the previous version of IFM.

The limitations of IFM that were identified during the empirical study were analysed and the architecture of IFM was revised. This resulted in the creation of a component diagram, which represents all the implementation modules.

Finally, in the construction phase the primary executable release of IFM was expanded. After completing the second executable release, a formative evaluation took place. The limitations of IFM identified in this evaluation are meant to be addressed in the third executable release of IFM.

3 Primary Executable Release

In the inception phase the primary executable release of IFM [2] was developed, during the preliminary iterations of the life cycle. IFM is a system that constantly reasons about users' actions in order to diagnose problematic situations and give advice concerning the error identified. As Cerri and Loia [17] point out, if error diagnosis is to be performed, a user modelling component should be incorporated into the system. IFM's user modelling component generates hypotheses about users' plans and possible errors or misconceptions. An example of erroneous actions is clicking the wrong command or even the wrong files. However, there may be ambiguities about errors, since there may be different explanations of observed incorrect users' actions [18]. IFM uses a simulator of human error generations and a limited plan recognition mechanism in order to resolve ambiguities about errors.

The simulator of human error generations is based on a cognitive theory that attempts to formalise the reasoning that people use. This theory is called Human Plausible Reasoning [19]. Intelligent File Manipulator adapts this theory to provide a simulation of possible users' errors. The limited plan recognition mechanism is used to improve the system's control. Each action of a user can be considered as expected, neutral, suspect or erroneous, depending on its degree of compatibility with the user's hypothesised intentions. In order to categorise the action in one of the four previous categories we have used a notion called 'instability'. An instability is added when an action results to a new plan and deleted when the action leads to the continuation of a user plan that started earlier. For example, an instability is added when a user selects a copy command. This instability is removed when the user selects the paste command. An example of the system's operation is described below.

The user's initial file store state is shown in figure 1. Folders are represented as boxes and files in plain text. The user intends to move A:\text1.txt into A:\documents1\. However, s/he accidentally attempts to move A:\ text1.txt into A:\documents2\. In this case, he runs the risk of overwriting the file A:\documents2\ text1.txt, which is a destructive action, by moving the file into the wrong folder. IFM would suggest the user to move the file into A:\documents1\ instead of A:\documents2\ for two reasons:

1. The folder A:\documents1\ is empty whereas the folder A:\documents2\ is not.
2. If the command issued by the user is executed it will result in overwriting the file A:\documents2\ text1.txt, which will mean the loss of useful information.

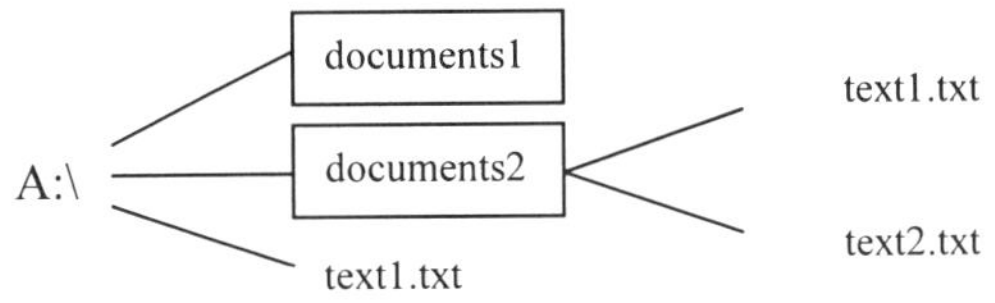

Figure 1. Initial file store state

4 Requirements Capture

For the requirements capture we conducted an empirical study and performed requirements analysis. The empirical study involved end users of a standard explorer, which does not incorporate intelligence, such as the Windows 98/NT explorer. One of the main aims of the empirical study was to categorise as many users' plans as possible and to identify the most frequent errors that expert and novice users may make while interacting with a standard Explorer. In this way, we could identify limitations of IFM. Another important aim of the empirical study was to evaluate IFM's reactions, in comparison to the human expert comments. The results of that comparison were also used in order to identify IFM's limitations so that we would enhance the specifications for a second version of IFM.

4.1 Empirical Study

The empirical study involved 7 novice and 8 expert users. All users were asked to work uninterrupted with a standard explorer such as the Windows 98/NT Explorer as they would normally do. All users' actions were video recorded through computer logging.

Then the protocols collected were given to 10 human experts to comment them. Furthermore, all human experts possessed a first and/or higher degree and had used extensively programs like the one studied or had teaching experience related to the use of such programs. The protocols collected were also given as input to IFM, so that we could record IFM's reactions to these users' actions. Finally, IFM's reactions were compared to the human experts' comments. In this way, we could evaluate IFM in terms of how successful it was at following the users' reasoning as compared to human experts who were also asked to reason about the same users' actions.

By the comparison of the human expert comments to IFM's reactions we found out that in the majority of the cases where IFM had diagnosed an error and generated an advice, its advice was similar to the majority of the experts' advice (range of compatibility of advice: 89% - 100%). Moreover, a lot of limitations of IFM were identified, which resulted in the enhancement of IFM's design, presented in more detail in Section 5.

4.2 Requirements Analysis

The plans recognised during the empirical study were used as input to the requirements analysis. Those plans were carefully studied in order to construct use case diagrams. Use case is a modelling technique used to describe what a new system should do or what an existing system already does [20]. Use case diagrams can represent requirements. In use cases we can identify actors and use cases. An actor can be anyone or anything that interacts with the system. Each actor usually represents a category of users. On the other hand, a use case may represent a functionality of the system.

However, Muller, Haslewanter & Dayton [21] point out that there may be some problems with the use case driven approach. One problem is that the use case model usually is written with the software system as the focus of attention. They mean that the use cases give too little priority to the end users and that each use case has been made up by software engineers to represent user actions. To overcome these problems it is necessary to model the use cases in participation with the end-users [22].

In the development of IFM we constructed use case diagrams as a result of a thorough empirical study that revealed the real users' plans. Sequences of actions. In this way we identified the use cases where users tended to have problems and therefore IFM had to provide assistance.

In particular, we have used use case diagrams to model all actions a user needs to perform to manipulate files. For example, the use case diagram in figure 2 describes the process that must be followed in order to copy or move items, folders or files, from a directory to another. The user must select the directory, where the items are, select the items s/he wants to copy and execute the copy or cut command. The items are then stored in clipboard and the user must select the target directory and execute the paste command. With the execution of that command, IFM identifies the state of the action. If the action is considered as expected or neutral the procedure is completed and the user can see the results of her/his actions to the file store. If the state considered by the system as suspect or erroneous, it searches for alternative actions and present them to the user. IFM's reasoning and interaction with the user about possible errors is represented in the use case called "Use case diagram for moving or copying items".

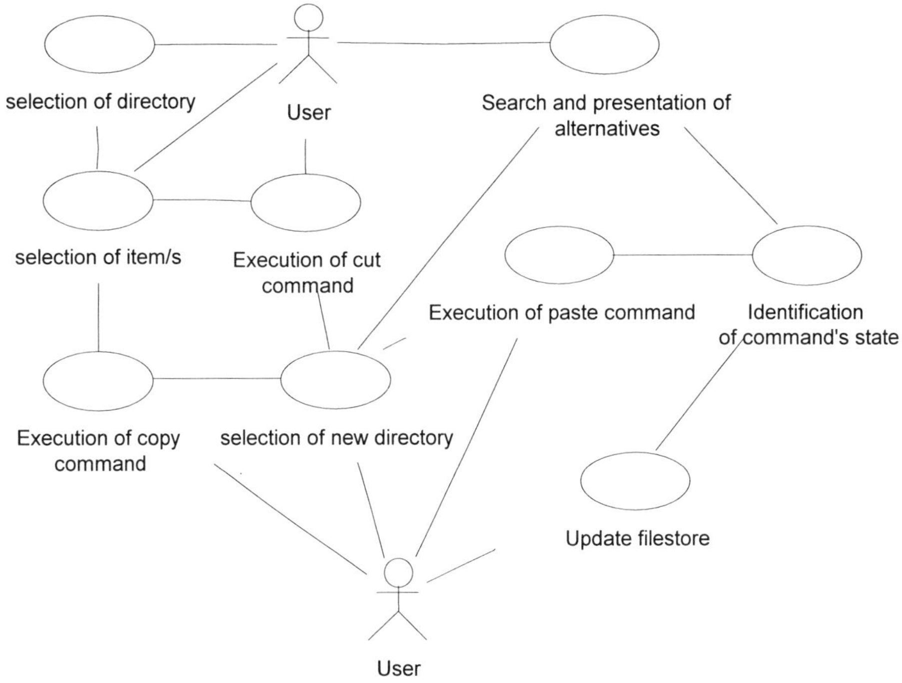

Figure 2. Use case diagram for copying or moving items

5 Analysis and Design

The conclusions drawn from the requirements capture were used as input to analysis and design and therefore led to the extension of IFM's design. Certain observations in the requirements capture resulted in the augmentation of the instabilities used in the primary release of the system. Careful study of the users' errors revealed new categories of errors that had not been taken into account before. Some of these errors were quite important and their identification led to a significant improvement of the system. For example, it was observed that users often deleted folders without being sure about the contents of these folders.

Finally, the empirical study showed that users tend to reproduce the same mistakes over and over again. In order to have more individualised user advice, IFM keeps a long term user model for each user, which consists of long term information about a user [23, 24].

The long term user model holds a profile of the user that may be acquired during several interactions of the user with the system. The long term user model is used in order to diagnose and provide advice in a more individualised way.

The study of users' plans during the requirements analysis revealed the fact that users issued more commands than those included in the domain representation of IFM's primary design. Therefore, the domain representation was extended to include several new commands. These commands had to be represented in hierarchies in the knowledge base of the system.

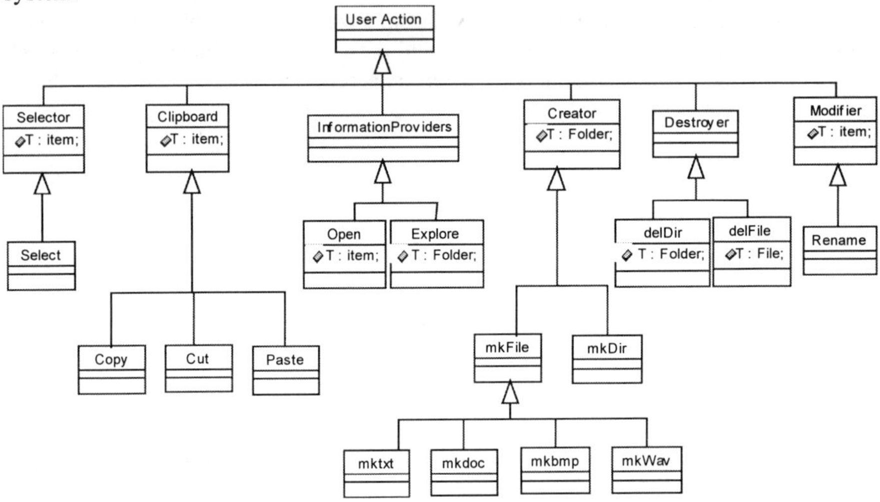

Figure 3. A Class diagram representing part of IFM's knowledge base.

We have found out that UML notation may be quite suitable for modelling our knowledge base. In the case of Prolog, a term may be represented as a class and its arguments as attributes of the specific class. Furthermore, UML relationships can be used to represent predicates (also called *relations*). We can distinguish predicates into three categories according to their semantics. Predicates that correspond to an *isa* relationship can be represented by a UML generalisation, for example isa(selector(T),userAction). Others that correspond to an *ispart* relationship can be represented by a UML aggregation, for example contains(sugar,cake). Finally, UML association represents predicates that cannot be categorised into one of the above categories, for example siblings(bob,mary). A hierarchical, tree-structured knowledge base may be presented by means of generalisations. In particular, in IFM we have used a class diagram in order to represent the structure of the Prolog predicates involved (figure 3). Each term situated in a leaf of the tree structure corresponds to a user's action. Higher-level terms indicate the categorisation of users' actions, namely Selector, Clipboard, Information Providers, Creator, Destroyer and Modifier. The attribute T represents the item involved in user's action. T can be a folder, a file, or either a folder or a file (an item).

6 Implementation

Based on the analysis and design, the implementation of the second release took place. In order to illustrate the implementation modules and their dependencies we use the component diagrams, which show the structure of the code for the implementation. Each component in a component diagram can be a source code component, a binary component, or an executable component [20]. Figure 4 is a component diagram that illustrates the connection between the knowledge-based part of IFM and the object-oriented part.

The knowledge-based part provides the reasoning for the GUI. The component that corresponds to this reasoning is "logic.ql" which is implemented in Prolog. The rest of the components are all implemented in Delphi's Pascal. The component 'main.pas' is the code for the file manipulation system and the identification of user's actions. This component communicates with "logic.ql" in order to create alternative commands to show them to the user. If the system find an alternative that can be considered as expected or neutral, the system informs the user using 'alternatives.pas' and afterwards, the user states her/his next actions. Finally, the component "login.pas" corresponds to the verification of the user.

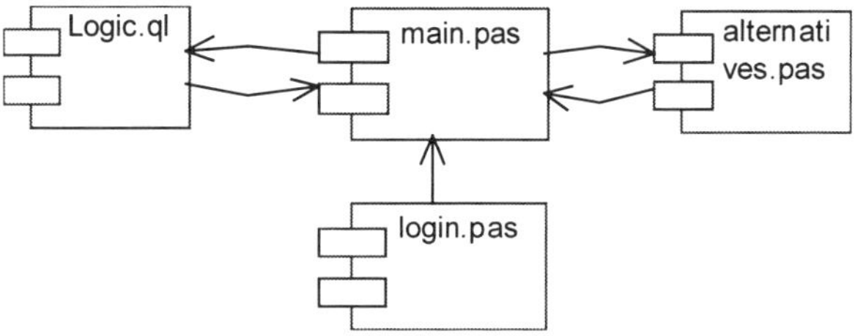

Figure 4. Component diagram

7 Testing IFM

IFM's second executable release was evaluated using half of the protocols collected during the empirical study. Those protocols were used in order to compare human experts' comments to the reactions of the new version of IFM. The results of this testing procedure showed that IFM was quite successful at achieving a high degree of compatibility with the experts' advice. The most important problem derived by the evaluation was that in many cases IFM generated a lot of alternative commands. In most of the cases, the suggestion of the majority of the experts was compatible with one of the alternative commands, generated by IFM. The system should be capable of selecting the most possible ones. This limitation is to be addressed in a subsequent executable release of IFM that will take place in new iterations of the system.

8 Conclusions

IFM is a graphical user interface that incorporates intelligence so that it may address situations where users may have made mistakes that did not intend. A system like this needs multiple iterations of its development cycle so that many evaluations involving users may take place.

The Rational Unified Process has been used as a model of IFM's life cycle and UML has been used for modelling several aspects of the system. The Rational Unified Process has provided a very satisfactory framework for the development of IFM ensuring the necessary multiple evaluations, involving real users. A lot of limitations of the first executable release were identified and addressed in a second release. Currently, further improvements have been specified to be addressed in the next future release. UML's use case diagrams have provided a satisfactory technique for modelling the user's needs that resulted from the multiple evaluations. In addition, the use cases of IFM were specified as a result of empirical studies and/or evaluations which ensures the fact that these use cases really represent user requirements rather than the beliefs of software engineers about users.

Finally, UML has provided a sufficiently powerful modelling language not only for the object-oriented features of IFM but also for the knowledge-based part of it and the integration of both parts.

Acknowledgements

The authors would like to express their appreciation to M. Moundridou for her useful comments.

References

[1] K.L. McGraw. Performance Support Systems: Integrating AI, Hypermedia and CBT to Enhance User Performance. *Journal of Artificial Intelligence in Education*, **5 (1)**, (1994), pp. 3-26.

[2] M. Virvou & A. Stavrianou. User Modelling in a GUI. *Proceedings of the 8th International Conference on Human-Computer Interaction (HCII 99)*, Munich, Germany, **1**, (1999), 262-265.

[3] M. Virvou & K. Kabassi. An Empirical Study Concerning Graphical User Interfaces that Manipulate Files. To appear in *proceedings of World Conference on Educational Multimedia, Hypermedia and Communications (ED-MEDIA 2000),* Montreal, Canada, (2000).

[4] J.A. Sutton & R.H. Sprague Jr. A study of display generation and management in interactive business applications, (Rep. RJ2392), IBM, 1978.

[5] B.A. Myers & M.B. Rosson. Survey on user interface programming. *CHI'92 Conference Proceedings of the Conference on Computer Supported Cooperative Work,* (1990), pp. 195-202.

[6] A. Dix, J. Finlay, G. Abowd & R. Beale. Human-Computer Interaction, NY: Prentice-Hall, 1993.

[7] I. Sommerville, Software Engineering. Addison-Wesley, 1992.

[8] B. Scheiderman. Designing the User Interface. Addison-Wesley, 1998.

[9] D.R. Olsen, Jr. Developing User Interfaces. Morgan Kaufmann Publishers, Inc, 1998.

[10] P. Kruchten. Rational Unified Process-An Introduction, Addison-Wesley, 1999.

[11] T. Quatrani. Visual Modeling with Rational Rose and UML, Addison-Wesley, 1998.

[12] Gr. Booch, J. Rumbaugh & I. Jacobson. The Unified Modeling Language User Guide. Addison-Wesley, 1999.

[13] P. Kruchten. The 4+1 View Model of Architecture. *IEEE Software,* **12 (6)**, (1995), pp. 42-50.

[14] M. Virvou. RESCUER: Intelligent Help for Plausible User Errors. *Proceedings of ED-MEDIA, ED-TELECOM 98, World Conference on Education Multimedia and Educational Telecommunications,* **2**, (1998), 1413-1420.

[15] M. Virvou & B. Du Boulay. Human Plausible Reasoning for Intelligent Help. U*ser Modeling and User Adapted Interaction,* **9**, (1999), pp. 321-375.

[16] I. Jacobson, M. Christerson, P. Jonsson & G. Overgaard. Object-Oriented Software Engineering. A Use Case Driven Approach. Addison-Wesley, Wokingham, England, 1992.

[17] S. A. Cerri & V. Loia. A Concurrent, Distributed Architecture for Diagnostic Reasoning. *User Modeling and User Adapted Interaction*, **7(2)**, (1997), pp. 69-105.

[18] A. Mitrovic, S. Djordjevic-Kajan, L. Stoimenov. INSTRUCT: Modeling students by asking questions. *User Modeling and User Adapted Interaction*, **6(4)**, (1996), pp. 273-302.

[19] A. Collins & R. Michalski. The Logic of Plausible Reasoning: A core Theory. *Cognitive Science* **13**, (1998), pp.1-49.

[20] H.E. Eriksson & M. Penker. UML Toolkit, John Wiley & Sons, Inc, 1998.

[21] M.J. Muller, J.H. Haslwanter & T. Dayton. Participatory Practises in the Software Lifecycle, In M. Helander, T.K. Landauer, & P. Prabhu (Eds.), Handbook of Human-Computer Interaction (pp. 255-297). Elsevier Science B.V., Amsterdam, 1997.

[22] M. Lif. User Interface Modelling – adding usability to use cases (Rep. No 84 CMD). Uppsala University, 1998.

[23] E. Rich. User Modelling via Stereotypes. *Cognitive Science*, **3 (4)**, (1979), pp. 329-354.

[24] J. Jones & M. Virvou. User modelling and advice giving in Intelligent Help Systems for UNIX. I*nformation and Software Technology*, **33**, (1991), pp. 121-133.

Knowledge-Based Software Engineering
T. Hruška and M. Hashimoto (Eds.)
IOS Press, 2000

Domain and User Knowledge in a Web-based Courseware Engineering Course

Lora AROYO[1], Darina DICHEVA[2]

[1]*Faculty of Educational Science and Technology*
University of Twente, P.O. Box 217, 7500 AE Enschede, The Netherlands
aroyo@edte.utwente.nl

[2]*Department of Computer Science*
Winston-Salem State University, N.C. 27110, USA
dichevad@wssumits.wssu.edu

Abstract. AIMS is a knowledge-based system for learning and teaching support within the context of distance education. It is aimed not only at enhancing learner's conceptual knowledge in a specific subject area but also at providing knowledge verification tools for the teacher. The system can be used to aid learning and teaching in different subject areas and to provide user-oriented support in searching course-related information, concept teaching and learning, and conceptual and task-oriented domain structuring. AIMS has an agent-based system architecture, which accommodates a team of agents mediating the process of providing information to the individual user. Each of those agents is an active system entity characterised by a set of specific roles with respect to the main system functionality. In this paper we present a general view on AIMS with an emphasis on its agent-based architecture and the domain and user knowledge.

1 Introduction

Knowledge-based systems (KBSs) refer to software programs that use explicitly stated knowledge to reason and provide solutions. KBSs can be very beneficial to decision-makers in problems that are described with large volumes of data, different sources and a related task to fulfill. They provide means to support the process of problem analysis and decision-making. Vital issue in this context is the notion of 'intelligence' – what is it and how is it realized. It closely relates to the topics of knowledge and its management - representation, storage, sharing, and maintenance. When we refer to knowledge it is to both the system knowledge of the domain and of its users. Thus it concerns modeling activities in both aspects. Various applications have been implemented in trying to capture and mimic the human expertise in this context. Numerous expert systems were built and applied in various application areas, mainly in medicine, natural languages, geology, etc. A large number of knowledge representation schemes and languages were developed in order to provide most appropriate tools. In this research we adopt the view that the system's intelligence is represented and mediated via a set of software entities referred to as 'intelligent agents'. They appear to be a very convenient tool for supporting a large number of cognitive tasks, as well as for implementing the system architecture processes. They have already proved to be quite a suitable software solution for knowledge-based systems. Our target in this research is to contribute to the rather popular lately strive to introducing agents for different activities related to education and to defend their effectiveness and actual contribution to the complex process of teaching and learning. We aim at designing agents that do a good job within educational environment and more specifically in respect to information support there for both instructors and learners. We discuss some general principles used in agents' design. The major issues among them point to creating a common environment for them to 'live', to show how agents perform actions to fulfill a task, how do they learn and how do they communicate among each other and with other system entities.

In this paper we present AIMS, a knowledge-based system for learning and teaching support within the context of distance education. It is aimed not only at enhancing learner's conceptual knowledge in a specific subject area but also at providing knowledge verification tools for the teacher. The system can be used to aid learning and teaching in different subject areas and to provide user-oriented support in searching course-related information, concept teaching and learning, and conceptual and task-oriented domain structuring. AIMS has an agent-based system architecture, which accommodates a team of agents mediating the process of providing information to the individual user.

While AIMS is a knowledge-based system, it offers support not only in the process of problem analysis and decision making, but also in the overall process of subject matter understanding, structuring and task-oriented searching within it. It helps the users to come to the solution of their problems, but it doesn't contain the solution itself. It contains explicit knowledge of the subject domain, builds up knowledge about the user and supports him or her in the process of finding, collecting and organizing the information necessary to perform a course task or assignment.

We start this paper with a general overview of AIMS, emphasizing the agent-based architecture and the way it realizes a knowledge-based approach for informational support within learning environments. Further on, we describe the system implementation and show the possibilities where agents can play roles within the general AIMS framework. We also present some conclusions and further topics for discussion.

2 AIMS: an Agent-based Intelligent Tool for Informational Support

The main goal behind AIMS is to present an integrated working environment for both instructors and students, which will facilitate the process of preparing and taking on-line courses in an intelligent and efficient way. AIMS is created to support the students from the Faculty of Educational Science and Technology, University of Twente, participating in the course of 'Courseware Engineering'. The intention is to integrate AIMS in the web-based course environment already created for this course. As we aim at a general course support tool, there are possibilities foreseen to facilitate importing of different subject domains or to create different courses in the same subject domain. Several experiments, within the scope of different computer-supported courses, have already been performed. They have evaluated the student's attitude towards AIMS interface and the effectiveness of its conceptual support for the learning process. The tool could be also successfully used for in-company training needs including course authoring and information handling support.

AIMS stands for Agent-based Information Management System that aims at providing combined adaptive information support for students and instructors within the context of on-line course environments. The main goal is to improve the usability and maintenance of information in such environments. We envisage the management of information as concerning two mutually complementing processes: these of retrieving the right information and visualizing it in the right way. Thus the focus of the work is on information search, retrieval, and effective presentation to the user. An important educational constraint is that we consider supporting learners to deal efficiently with information only within a specific subject domain and course in respect to certain educational goals (tasks).

AIMS targets to support the knowledge crystallization task, which is characterized by the use of large amounts of heterogeneous information, ill-structured problem solving, and a well-defined task [1]. This point of view is related to externalization rather than visualization, stressing on the cognitive role of *interactive* visual representations [2]. The process of knowledge crystallization involves getting insights about data relevant to the task in hand, so that the user will be able to fulfill it and achieve better results.

2.1 Agent-based architecture

AIMS is built as an agent-based architecture. The agents' behaviour is modeled in correspondence with the main activities involved in the process of task-based information retrieval. Agents have their tasks and strategies. Tasks define agents' responsibilities and communication means and entities within the system. Strategies define methods and rules for performing actions related to the overall informational support task. Among agents' tasks are maintaining subject domain, course, library and user models, performing search activities, and presenting the search results to the user.

Agents' co-operation abilities to communicate with each other and change their behavior depending on the user's action, to exchange messages, and to act even when there is no explicit user request for an action, contribute to the overall system efficiency. The agents perform their tasks by working in parallel as separate but coordinated processes.

As mediators between the users and the information content, agents are contributing to the general system adaptiveness. Their collaborative intelligent behaviour results in an intelligent user-oriented information support for learners and instructors. The general architecture of AIMS as an agent-based information support system is elaborated elsewhere [3, 4]. In this paper we will focus on the issues related to building, representation, and visualization of both domain and user knowledge.

2.2 Domain knowledge: representation and authoring

One of the milestones of the proposed approach is building subject domain ontology and using it for information structuring and classification. On a conceptual level we define three main models for representing system's information and domain knowledge: domain model, course model, and library model.

Domain Model

The domain model defines the subject domain ontology and is represented as a concept map (CM) of domain concepts and links between them. There are numerous definitions of concept mapping depending on its various applications, but for the purposes of this paper we will concentrate on the concept mapping in the context of memory, perception and meta-cognition [5] as a formalism for structural knowledge representation [6]. The most widely accepted definition of concept mapping is as a technique of graphically representing concepts and their hierarchical interrelationship. They are organised in a spatial configuration of nodes and links in a given knowledge domain. The valuable thing in our context is that concept mapping allows the learners to connect new ideas to knowledge that

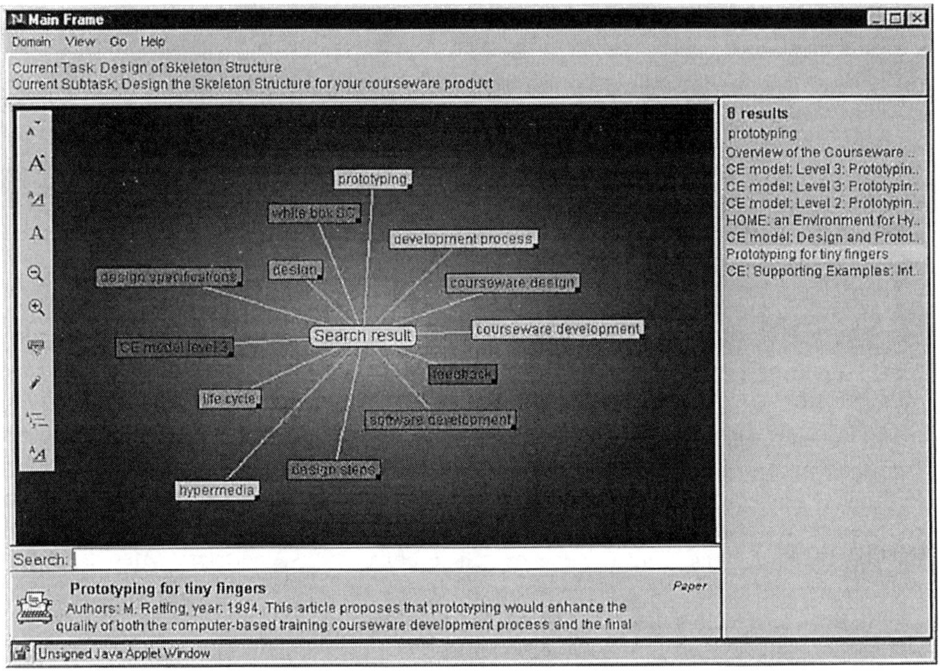

Figure 1. AIMS Domain Browsing and Search Environment for Learners

they already have and to organize them in a logical structure. This way it allows them to see more complex relationships between ideas than just sequence and hierarchy [7]. It is simple and intuitive, visual form of knowledge representation [8] well applicable for subject domain structuring and course task presentation. The link types we use are based on the generic selection of link types defined in [9]. There could be a number of instances of the subject domain model, each describing a different subject domain within AIMS.

The use of CMs as a basic mechanism for information structuring allows for an effective visual presentation of the subject domain, since CMs furnish simple and intuitive visual form of knowledge representation. In AIMS, information visualization targets the presentation of the subject domain structure and the overlaying structures of the course and user models. As part of the supporting information search functionality AIMS also proposes combined visualization of the search results. Same technique is used for presenting the course components, such as tasks and subtasks and the user model. Information search results are also partly presented with this graphical approach. The result documents are still organized in the traditional way of textual list-based presentation, but are related to a result concept map of domain terms used in those documents (see Fig. 1). Some meta-data is provided in order to support a better and quicker overall search result comprehension. Meta-data in the form of short descriptive information and structured tags is also used in order to describe the context of the domain terms and links [10].

Course Model

The course model defines the structure of a course and includes course topics, course tasks and course evaluation items. Since the main goal of AIMS is to provide a task-based information support, a series of tasks are associated with each course. Course tasks are predefined and correspond to course assignments a student is supposed to perform. The main idea is that the system uses a task to constrain the information provided to the learner in support of his or her efforts to complete this task. The system keeps track of the status of all course tasks - which have been successfully completed by the user, which are not attempted or have been started but not completed yet. The tasks are represented in terms of domain concepts and contain some additional information, such as task description, task status, etc. Course evaluation items correspond to different forms of student evaluation over the timeline of the course, such as instructor's tests, student's self-evaluation of his or her knowledge of domain terms, etc. They are used for a run-time evaluation of the current learner's knowledge on a specific course topic and for consecutive adaptation of the system's behavior and information presentation.

Library Model

The library model provides means for representing and maintaining a whole collection of information related to different courses and domains. Its main variables are course materials and domain related documents together with their characteristics. The library documents are related to domain terms and through them - to the course tasks and topics.

Responsible for building the system domain knowledge is the domain expert (course instructor). In AIMS, the domain expert's work is supported by three editors: domain, course, and library editor.

Domain Editor

The domain editor is aimed at providing support for the instructors to build and maintain the AIMS subject domain knowledge (see Fig. 2). Its functions cover building a new domain structure, that is, building a domain concept map and linking relevant documents to it, as well as editing and updating an existing domain structure, including terms, links, and documents. There could be a number of different subject domains within AIMS. The Domain editor contains four different sections: *Domain Info, Domain Concepts, Domain Link Types and Domain Related Documents*. 'Domain Info' gives general information about the domain including domain name, author(s), creation and last modification dates, and short description. 'Domain Concepts' provides facilities for creating new and modifying existing domain concepts. Each concept is defined in terms of name, short description, synonyms, spelling and writing forms, and classification level. The labeled links between concepts are created and modified in the 'Domain Link Types' section. When linking two concepts the user can either select a link type from a predefined list or create a new one. In 'Domain Related Documents' the user can create links between domain concepts and documents by selecting a concept and linking it to a document from a list of existing AIMS library documents (with a certain weight indicating how relevant is the documents to this concept).

Course Editor

The course editor is aimed at facilitating the instructor to build the structure of a specific course and organize along going tasks, course materials, and reference documents. Since the main goal of AIMS is to provide a task-based information support, a series of tasks are associated with each course. Course tasks are pre-defined and correspond to course assignments the student is supposed to perform. The main idea is that the system uses a task

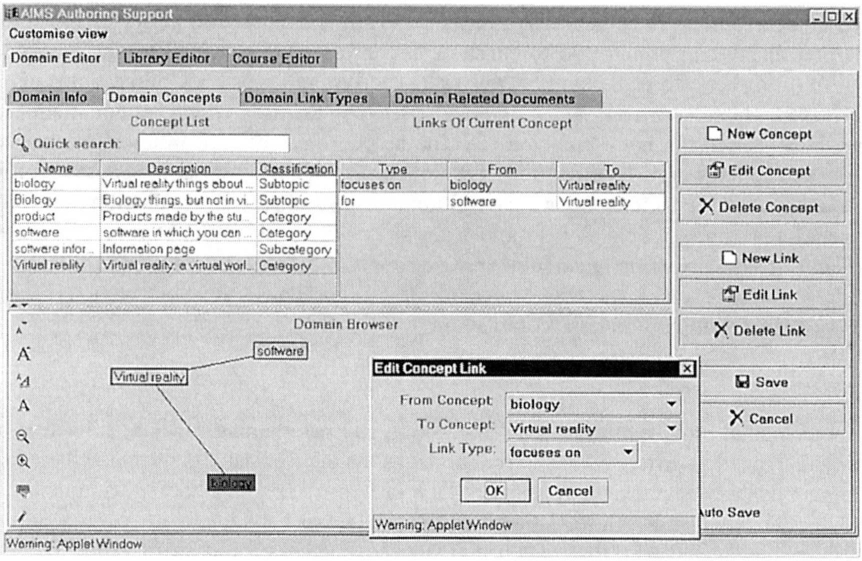

Figure 2. AIMS Domain Authoring Environment for Instructors

to constrain the information provided to the learner in support of his or her efforts to complete this task. Each course task is associated with a list of domain terms, which the student must know to perform successfully the task.

Library Editor

The library editor provides means for maintaining a collection of information related to different courses and domains. Each document in the AIMS library is described by a document name, author, year of publication, location (URL or library index), short description, and list of weighted keywords. Documents have also a presentation format (text, audio, video, EXE, ZIP, etc.) and instructional format (example, definition, description, procedure, etc.).

2.3 User knowledge

User modeling provides grounds for system adaptiveness. In AIMS, the user model (UM) refers to the learner (not to the instructor) and is related to his or her activities in the on-line course environment, such as:

- performing a course task,
- browsing the domain,
- searching for a term,
- visiting documents related to a term,
- requesting for terms related to a specified term, etc.

User Model

The user model is an *overlay* of the domain, course, and library models, enhanced with tags indicating user's knowledge and interests and course tasks status. Thus, it is represented in terms of domain concepts, course tasks, and library documents and related status indicators.

AIMS uses UM to provide user-oriented support for information searching in the context of an educational task, as well as for refining and adapting the search results to user's interests and course tasks. It is an *open* model, that is, built jointly by the user and the system. The user can enter information about his or her *knowledge* of or *interest* to a specific term on system's request or on his own initiative, while browsing the conceptual presentation of the subject domain or in the process of searching documents.

Building UM: system's perspective

The main source of system information about the user model is the user behavior. The system monitors user performance and collects information from sources like search expression entries, course task dialogue, search result scan, and usage and browsing the domain concept map. On the basis of this information the system makes its conclusions about the user knowledge of and interest to terms and documents. Maintaining the user model involves incorporating new facts, checking that they are consistent with previously learned or inferred facts and resolving any discrepancies and contradictions.

Building UM: user's perspective

Every user logs in the system with his or her personal username and password. The user's account contains additional information about the user type (student, instructor or administrator) and provides adaptive access to the AIMS environment. When a student logs in and selects a course, he or she is presented with a list of tasks in the current course along with their current status. The task status represents student's work on the task – 'completed', 'not completed', 'not visited' or 'forbidden'. Forbidden tasks are those, which require knowledge from previously performed tasks that are still 'not completed' by the student. The student can either select a task to work on or enter the AIMS environment in 'no-task mode'. The latter allows him or her to explore the subject domain and perform task independent search queries. When the user selects a task to work on, he or she is presented with a list of domain terms related to this task. The student is asked to indicate his or her knowledge status for each of them. This information is used later for adapting system's behaviour. All user data is stored in the user model and is used by the user agent within the AIMS architecture.

3 Conclusions

This paper describes an approach to integrated information handling support in web-based course environments for both learners and instructors. It provides learners with an easy access to and an attractive visual presentation of information related directly to the course tasks as well as with a conceptual view of the whole subject domain. Instructors are facilitated with a domain- and course- authoring environment, which helps them to build a general view of a specific subject domain and over it - course structures.

Several pilot experiments have been performed at the Eindhoven Technical University and the Antwerp University, the Netherlands, for evaluating AIMS browser and editor GUI functionality, user-friendliness, and learning effectiveness. The purpose of these formative evaluations was to validate the proposed AIMS approach and to identify any problematic aspects in order to improve it.

In the last experiment, conducted in the Faculty of Educational Science and Technology, University of Twente, The Netherlands, AIMS is being effectively applied within the framework of the design for the "Courseware Engineering" course. The course topics and tasks were clearly defined by the instructor with the help of AIMS authoring support tools and AIMS information search and browsing tool is used to support students conceptually. Within this experiment we focus on one aspect of a course design: encouraging students to integrate new design concepts, procedures, and methods with their existing conceptual knowledge in different educational areas as well as the field of software design and implementation. To accomplish this goal we rely on the role of concepts in learning of design, and in particular, we focus on central conceptual structure of the domain and its cross-linking with the task-oriented view of a course structure. In this experiment we explore how conceptual support, represented by concept maps, can help students to build connections between the 'dry' domain concepts and the topics in the course structure (context rich and task oriented), as well as between formal task descriptions and informal conceptual knowledge.

The results of all experiments will be summarized and will serve as a basis for developing a new improved version of the system.

Acknowledgements

We would like to thank our student Ivan Velev for his implementation efforts in realizing the AIMS prototype and Prof. Paul De Bra for his efforts and support in preparing and conducting the AIMS experiments within his courses.

References

[1] Card, S. K., Mackinlay, J.,D. & Shneiderman, B. (1999). Using Vision to Think, *Information Visualisation,* Morgan Kaufmann Publishers, Inc., California, pp.579 - 581.

[2] Tweede, L. (1997). Characterising Interactive Externalisation. *Proceedings of CHI'97, ACM Conference on Human Factors in Computing Systems*, Atlanta, pp. 375-382.

[3] Aroyo, L., Diana, I. & Dicheva, D. (1998). Agents to Make Your Information Meaningful and Visible: An Agent-based Visual Information Management System. In *Proceedings of WebNet'98 Conference*, Orlando, USA.

[4] Aroyo, L. & Dicheva, D. (1999). Information Retrieval and Visualisation within the Context of an Agent-based Information Management System. In *Proceeding of ED-MEDIA '99*, Seattle, Washington, 195-200.

[5] McAleese, R. (1994). A Theoretical View on Concept Mapping. In *Educational Psychology Interactive*, Readings in Educational Psychology, William G. Huitt (Ed.)

[6] Jonassen, D. & Marra, R. (1994). Concept Mapping and Other Formalisms as Mindtools for Representing Knowledge. In *Educational Psychology Interactive*, Readings in Educational Psychology, William G. Huitt (Ed.)

[7] Hale, S. (1997). Concept Mapping. http://www.dc.peachnet.edu/~shale/humanities/composition/handouts/concept.html

[8] Kremer, R. (1997). Multi-user Interactive Concept Maps for the Learning Web. In *Proceeding of ED-MEDIA '97*, June 16-19, 1997, Calgary, Canada.

[9] Lambiotte, J. G., Dansereau, D. F., Cross, D. R., & Reynolds, S. B. (1989). Multirelational semantic maps. *Educational Psychology Review*, 1(4), 331-367.

[10] Aroyo, L. & Dicheva, D. (2000). Conceptual Visualisation in a Task-Based Information Support System. *ED-MEDIA 2000*, Montreal, Canada.

Knowledge-Based Software Engineering
T. Hruška and M. Hashimoto (Eds.)
IOS Press, 2000

Adaptive Presentation of the Educational Module Information using XML

Mária BIELIKOVÁ
Slovak University of Technology
Department of Computer Science and Engineering
Ilkovičova 3, 812 19 Bratislava, Slovakia
bielik@elf.stuba.sk, http://www.dcs.elf.stuba.sk/~bielik/

Abstract. Educational module information indicates module characteristics and enables to answer such questions as "What is this module about?" or "Who is the reader of this module?" In this paper we describe the proposed framework for representation and adaptive presentation of the module hypermedia information. It is based on the XML (eXtensible Markup Language). Our work deals with adaptation of provided information during the module running. Adaptation is based primarily on the context of presentation. We experimented with the proposed approach and implemented a software prototype, which enables time view and user view of the module information. All presented data are stored in a database. Each element has associated constraints at the level of presentation, intended group of readers and presentation time represented by XML.

1 Introduction

The explosive growth of the World Wide Web as a medium for information dissemination caused several new problems, which have to be solved. The problems are often linked to continuously increasing amount of information that we are faced with. In this paper we deal with a problem of adaptive presentation of information represented as hypermedia.

Issues of adaptive presentation have received attention of the Web community only recently. Adaptive presentation is one of the generally recognised ways of adaptation in adaptive hypermedia [5]. It uses some data about the user (e.g., his knowledge about a particular problem, his previous visits) or about the context of the presentation (e.g., time) to present the content, which is the most interesting for the user. Another way of adaptation in hypermedia is adaptive navigation, which focuses on link adaptation.

In the process of design a method of adaptive presentation an application area should be considered. In our case we concentrate on educational hypermedia. The shift is away from a relatively static, localised paradigm of teaching and learning towards an interactive, dynamic, and non-localised paradigm [2]. Educational hypermedia typically deal with relatively small hyperspace. For adaptation they use the fact that students have often different goals and strategies of learning. A piece of educational material is often unclear for a novice and at the same time trivial and boring for an advanced student.

Methods and techniques of adaptive hypermedia are largely designed and evaluated within educational environments. They often focus on the educational materials, e.g. adaptive hypermedia books [6]. Summary of methods and techniques used in adaptive hypermedia (including educational) is given and discussed extensively by Peter Brusilovsky [5]. Described methods are based on a user model. They adapt the content and/or the navigation according to the user characteristics and requirements. Irrelevant information and links that overload the user's memory and screen is hidden, labelled as not recommended, or removed. Often additional information related to recommendations is presented by different colours [8].

Only little attention is devoted to delivering information about a module, its objectives, reader, lab requirements, schedule of lectures, conditions to obtain a grade etc. This kind of information is necessary for any kind of education delivery. Usually it is presented on the paper (on whiteboards at the departments), or electronically in the form of non-structured document files or as HTML hypertext document on the Web.

The content of the presented module information is usually solid. Each overlooked word can cause student later problems to fulfil requirements to obtain a grade. Although reading all available information can be useful in some cases, we have experience that for most students it is helpful to see details when they are current (i.e., needed). Such information can be represented by a presentation context. The presentation context is defined as a collection of data, which depends on the current state of the presentation but not on the data about the user.

Appropriate module information depends more on time of information reading (the context) instead of a detailed user model based on the knowledge related to the particular module content. Adaptation presented information according the current context would improve presentation and administration of such information.

The context model does not depend on the user model. For the purposes of module information, the context can be reduced to consider time of information reading. The context can contain also data about used browser or language. In this case we need several variants of the presented document and have to deal with the problem of hypermedia document version management. Methods and techniques for version management are discussed elsewhere [1]. Variants of content, which correspond to the particular user model, can be also considered.

2 Representation of the Module Information

The module information is represented by XML (eXtensible Markup Language). XML is a data format suitable for storing structured and semistructured text intended for dissemination and ultimate publication, perhaps on a variety media [4]. XML document contains chunks of the required information (elements) named and stored separately. Using XML allows interpretation of data of different documents without needing to adapt the application (i.e., interpreter of XML module data).

Each element has defined adaptation conditions in the form of required values of defined attributes. Elements can form an arbitrary hierarchy and can be named by the user (who is responsible for the module development). Presentation of information copies this hierarchy. In order to present 'pages' with reasonable length, some elements with long text and/or many offsprings can be displayed by the use of links.

Granularity of a document (the degree to which element's content is organised into offspring elements) is determined by a developer. The presentation method only requires to declare conditions (as predefined attributes of elements) and content of elements. Some elements however, do not have content in the form of text – they just name the hierarchy. This kind of elements is useful when the presentation is divided into several pages.

Each module has its own Document Type Definition (DTD) which defines the elements allowed in a particular document of module type. Several modules can define common DTD.

Bellow is an example of part of DTD declaration:

```
<!DOCTYPE Module [
  <!ELEMENT Module (Header, Body, Foot)>
  <!ELEMENT Header (Module-name, Module-Abbreviation?,
                    Study-Type?)>
  <!ELEMENT Module-name (#PCDATA)>
    ...
  <!ELEMENT Body (Info?, Objectives, Syllabus, Labs, Faq?)>
    ...
  <!ELEMENT Foot (Modification-date, Administrator-name?)>
...  ]>
```

A major decision in producing adaptive hypermedia systems is the decision about structuring information in such a way that it will be possible to adapt presentation. In our approach, the XML element according to the module data type definition is the smallest information chunk that can be adapted. However, the structure of the module information and the structure of the content to be adapted and presented can be of different granularity. Developer can define tags, which reflect the structure of presented information (e.g., paragraph tag <p>), but are not related to the structure of the module information.

Actual data related to the particular module are represented by the XML document according to its DTD. Each element contains several conditions, which define the model of presentation according to a given context. Attributes and their values within each element represent conditions. We have experimented with attributes related to the type of user, granularity of presentation, time and splitting of the presented information to several pages. Some of the used attributes are described in the next section. Set of available attribute-value pairs can be enhanced. In this case, their interpretation should also be defined.

3 Adapting the Module Information

We use the conditional text technique for adaptation [5]. With this technique, all information about a module is linked to the condition at the level of a user model or context model. When presenting information in the particular context and for the particular user, the system presents only information with the condition evaluated to be true. A simple example is hiding detailed information about the lab exercises in the first week of semester. The purpose of hiding this information is not to disable view of the information but prevent information overload in the first week of semester. Solution to this requirement is to disable some information in short or medium views in the first week, but enable it in the full view. Later, when information is current, it is presented also in short or medium views. This technique requires to set all the required conditions by administrator (or teacher) of the module. When the presentation of the module information is required, attributes of each element are evaluated and compared against the current context and adapted module information is displayed.

We don't use link removal for one concept. The main reason for this decision is the purpose of the system: presentation of administrative information related to the module. For this purpose, hiding or link/ content removal after "reading" something is not necessary.

We have developed a software prototype for adaptive presentation of a module information [7]. The software prototype uses the following data about the current state: group of the user, granularity of presentation and context represented by the current time. In order to reduce the amount of information displayed at once, two additional attributes are related with each element – *link* and *include*. Values of these attributes determine creation of links and splitting of some information into several parts presented independently and reached by hypertext links. Important simplification of representation of conditions concerning the current state is achieved by ordering possible attribute values representing the current state.

Bellow is an example of meta-data related to the element `syllabus`:

```
<syllabus description="Syllabus"
        from="01/01/2000" to=""
        user_operator=">=" user="guest"
        mode_operator="=" mode="medium"
        visible="yes" link="yes" include="no">
    <B>Background:</B>
    A brief history of expert systems; the expert system
    concept;
    ...
</syllabus>
```

All meta-data defined in the element `syllabus` are evaluated according to the current state. If date of presentation is after the 1st of January 2000, the element `syllabus` is presented to any user (*user* >= *guest*) who have selected the medium granularity (*mode* = *medium*). When the element is presented, the text "Syllabus" is displayed. This text is marked as link (*link* = *yes*), which results in hiding the actual text of syllabus into the separate page (reachable through this link). When the link attribute is set to "no", all text defined for this element is displayed.

Within our tool information about the modules can be presented in a consistent form. For example, all pages include a standard tool bar for navigating to the particular sections of the information. Form consistency is achieved by generating pages according to the defined style, which determines a page layout. Developers can combine text with the HTML tags in the content of the particular element.

The system recognises two types of links (similarly to [3]):

- links to the absolute URL (external) are represented by `<A>` tag with `HREF` attribute in the content of any element,
- conditional links are investigated by comparing the current state to actual representation of a particular element.

Figure 1 illustrates the part of appearance of presented information for the module Knowledge-Based Systems. Each page starts with a generated header, which contains text defined in the first element named `module` (the only parent of the hierarchy) and current date, and is automatically included in every page. The page content is generated according to the XML definition of the module information and the current context. Each page

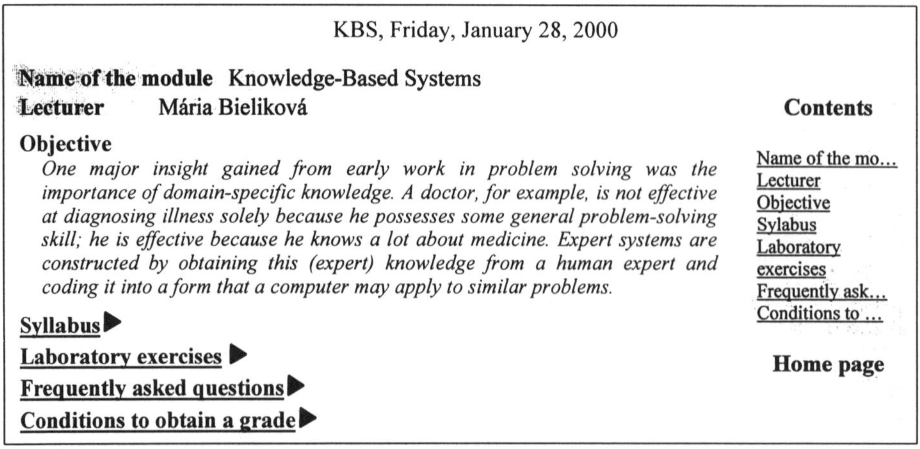

Figure 1. Example of module information presentation.

contains frame on the right hand side, which serves as a content navigation within the current page. Different data formatting can be expressed by a style sheet. Alternative style sheets can be applied at any time, changing the format to suite intended audience (e.g., format of the university web pages) and the capabilities of the used publishing media. Pages are assembled from these parts by means of PHP3 scripts.

We also developed a tool for supporting the design of adaptive hyperdocument, including definition of elements, conditions of their adaptation and the content. A developer can create and modify hierarchy of elements and define meta-data and the content of each element.

Figure 2 illustrates part of the hierarchy for the Knowledge-Based Systems module. On the left side the names of elements are displayed. A developer of the module uses the buttons on the right side, which serve for content modification (Chg), inserting a new element into the next hierarchy level (Ins), adding a new element into the same level of the hierarchy (Add), and deleting element from the hierarchy (Del).

Information related to a new module can be developed by the use of predefined templates or from the scratch. The element `module` is the starting element, which cannot be deleted. This element is the only element on the first level of the hierarchy (action add element on the same level is also not allowed). An experienced user can view and modify the XML code of module information.

Design and implementation of a prototype was oriented mainly toward prototyping the proposed framework for adaptive presentation of the module information. However, an effective use of such system in the Web environment requires effective storing and manipulation of the data about several modules, the data about users, and also requires some level of security (mainly at the level of authentication for modification of XML documents related to the particular module). Due to aims of the prototype development, the problem of security was not solved. Data manipulation efficiency is tackled by the design and implementation of relational database, which serves for storing the whole content of data elements together with the data about users and developers. We used the database server MySQL.

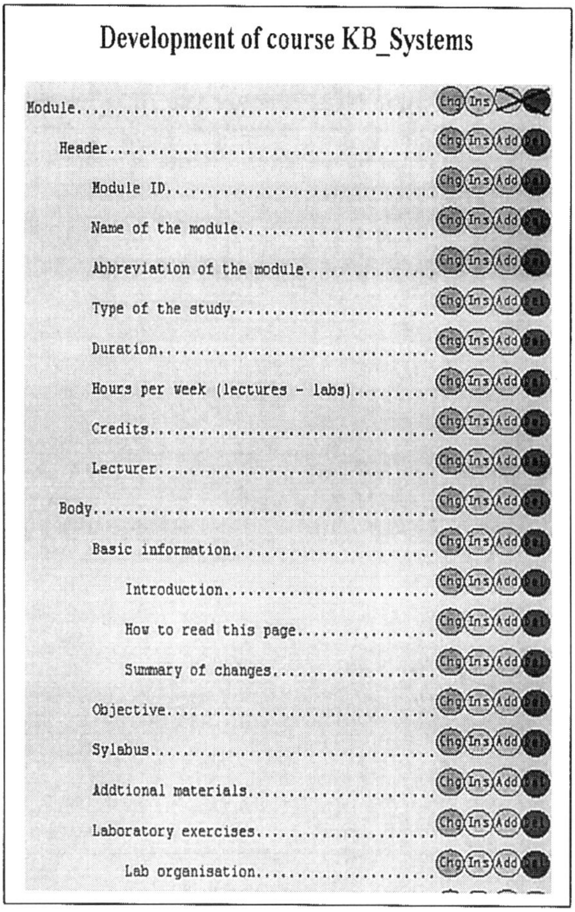

Figure 2. Example hierarchy of elements.

4 Conclusions

The paper is focused on the problem of adaptive presentation of organisational aspects of an educational module. It investigates three possible adaptive ways to help the users: hiding information according to the current time, considering type of a user and choice of the granularity of information (time, user and info views).

We use the conditional content adaptation technique for adaptation, similarly like the AHA system [3]. Unlike AHA system, where conditionals are encoded in the structured HTML comments, we represent conditions as attribute-value pairs in XML. Conditions are expressed declaratively as values of attributes. They are interpreted in our prototype by the PHP3 scripts. In [8], a similar approach is used, where constraints are expressed in the form of typed first-order logic, which allows for expressing complex conditions declaratively.

The main contribution of our work is the proposal of a flexible representation of an educational module organisational data using XML and considering the current context in adaptation of presentation.

An important feature of the good administrative module system is not only the adaptive presentation based on the current context, but also keeping modifications introduced to the pages. In traditional learning environments, the modification of the module material is not frequent and usually not interesting for a student (student receives package with learning material, and modifications are usually incorporated into a new version of learning material used in the next module run). A modification is frequent and important in presentation of organizational aspects of the module. The proposed representation of the module information allows support of modification management. We work on extension of the adaptive presentation, which will also consider recent modifications of the module information.

Acknowledgements

The work reported here was partially supported by Slovak Science Grant Agency, grant No. 1/7611/20.

References

[1] M. Bieliková and P. Návrat. Modelling Versioned Hypertext Documents. In: Proc. of System Configuration Management, SCM-8 Symposium, Brussels, Belgium, July 1998. B. Magnusson (Ed.), Springer Berlin, LNCS 1439, pages 188-197, 1998.

[2] C.M. Boroni, F.W. Goosey, M.T. Grinder and R.J. Ross. A Paradigm Shift! The Internet, the Web, Browsers, Java, and the Future of Computer Science Education. *SIGCSE Bulletin*, (1998) 145-152.

[3] P. De Bra and L. Calvi. AHA: A Generic Adaptive Hypermedia System. In: Proc. of the 2nd Workshop on Adaptived Hypertext and Hypermedia, Hypertext'98, Pittsburg USA, June 1998. Available on line from http://wwwis.win.tue.nl/ah98/DeBra.html.

[4] N. Bradley. The XML companion. Addison Wesley, Harlow, England. 1998. 440p.

[5] P. Brusilovsky. Methods and Techniques of Adaptive Hypermedia. *User Modeling and User Adapted Interaction* **6**, 2-3 (1996) 87-129.

[6] P. Brusilovsky and E. Schwarz. User as Student: Towards an Adaptive Interface for Advanced Web-Based Applications. In: Proc. of the 6th Int. Conf. User Modeling, A. Jameson, C. Paris, C. Tasso (Eds.), Springer Wien-New York, CSIM, pp. 177-188, 1997. Available on-line from http://um.org.

[7] L. Drobný. Web-Based Presentation of the Information about University Modules. Slovak University of Technology, Diploma Thesis, 1999. (in Slovak)

[8] P. Fröhlich and W. Nejdl. A Database-Oriented Approach to the Design of Educational Hyperbooks. In: Proc. of the workshop "Intelligent Educational Systems on the World Wide Web", 8th World Conference of the AIED Society, Kobe, Japan, 1997.

[9] G. Weber and M. Specht. User modeling and Adaptive Navigation Support in WWW-Based Tutoring Systems. In: Proc. of the 6th Int. Conf. User Modeling, A. Jameson, C. Paris, C. Tasso (Eds.), Springer, CSIM, pp. 289-300, 1997. Available on-line from http://um.org.

Knowledge-Based Software Engineering
T. Hruška and M. Hashimoto (Eds.)
IOS Press, 2000

Modeling of an Educational Domain

Gennadiy ATANOV

Donetsk Institute of Social Education; DISO, Donetsk, 83000, Ukraine
E-mail: atanov@dongu.donetsk.ua

Abstract. The paper develops a topic of construction of the normative student model. The subject student model is a part of it representing a sum of demands to the curriculum of the subject, to students' knowledge and skills, and a semantic model of the domain. The subject student models pick out the educational domains from all the multitude of the domains, so the subject model is a model of an educational domain. Examples in physics are given.

1 Introduction

A fundamental concept of modern didactics is the student (learner) model. In the widest sense, the student model is our knowledge about a student. There are two sides here: (1) knowledge about how the student is, and (2) knowledge about how we want to see him/her. The first knowledge is determined by the way of analyzes of student's behavior, and it is a behavioral student model. It changes with the student's change therefore it is also called dynamic one. Mechanism of construction of this model is the cognitive diagnostics [8,9].

Knowledge about how we want to see students, that is, demands to their final state is a normative student model. As a rule, this knowledge is various. It consists of demands to personal qualities of future specialists, their professional qualities and skills, their knowledge and skills in different subjects, characteristics of their physical and psychological state, and so on. The final aim of teaching is achievement of such a state when the behavioral student model concurs with the normative one.

2 The subject student model

A part of the normative student model determining domain knowledge is a subject student model [3]. In knowledge engineering, it is called expert knowledge, or domain model [5,6]. The subject student model picks out the educational domains from all the multitude of the domains, so the subject model is a model of an educational domain.

The final aim of instruction is formation of way of acting. The way of acting is realized via skills in the practical activity [7]. The mechanism of this is operation with knowledge being displayed in the behavior of a person. Therefore, in a wide sense, skills are attributed to knowledge, namely behavior one [9]. Thus, the subject student model has to contain skills that are to be formed in the process of instruction. Let us call a list of such skills as the operation subject student model.

The declarative component of the domain knowledge [5,6] makes up a semantic part of it, namely the semantic student model.

One of the distinctive properties of knowledge is that it has a structure, giving us more or less extended ideas about what the subject knowledge is. A usual way here is a thematic approach when themes are enumerated. Let us call a list of themes liable to studying as the thematic subject student model.

It is very important methodologically to determine which role either knowledge plays and which functions it carries. It can be done with the help of a list of functional rubrics determining the functional knowledge. The functional knowledge makes up the functional subject student model.

In such a way, we suggest a four component subject student model consisting of thematic, functional, operation, and semantic parts [1-3].

3 The thematic subject student model

The thematic subject student model is known for a long time. In essence, it is a usual curriculum of the course. It is just built according to the thematic principle; sections and themes liable to studying are enumerated in it. The model reflects the structure of the course. It is always not knowledge itself but its names. In fact, this is a define characteristic of the subject knowledge, a knowledge about the subject knowledge, that is, metaknowledge.

It is a natural and convenient model for planning and organization of the instructional process. The more, it is an obligatory normative document. Nevertheless, it is excessively general to use it for diagnostics.

4 The functional subject student model

The functional subject student model shows which role either knowledge plays; and it is also metaknowledge. It has a define structure in the horizontal direction, which may be given with the help of some rubrics. The role of knowledge and its functions depend on a particular subject. For example, we picked out the following rubrics for physics courses: *concepts, wordings, laws, properties, consequences, conclusions, reasons, formulas, equations, models, methods, and algorithms* [3]. The rubrics have a filling that, nevertheless, also does not reflect semantic of the subject and is metaknowledge.

It is the subject student model that allows working out in details what students must know. Let us give an example from the molecular physics. Students have to know: definitions of the concepts: *mole, thermodynamic system, pressure, temperature, density, concentration, ideal gas, equation of state*, and so on; wording and consequences of: *Pascal's law, Maxwell's and Bolzmann's distributions, Kirchhoff's law*, etc.; deductions of: *the mine equation of kinetic theory, equation of the adiabatic process, law of atmospheres*, etc.

5 The operation subject student model

As it was noted, the operation subject student model is a list of skills liable to mastering by students. Let us note that skills in education make up a hierarchical system [2]. It consists of five groups of skills: fundamental, methodological, general, inter-subject, subject. Subject skills take the highest position in the hierarchy of skills.

We pick out three classes of the subject physical skills: general, particular, and experimental. The general skills are, on the first hand, methodological ones. Spectrum of the particular skills is far wider, for example, there are more than 200 them in the list in physics. According to the contents of the instructional material, the following skills are picked out: *to find, to determine, to fix, to build, to obtain, to calculate, to compute, to estimate, to distinguish, to pick out, to sort, to take into account, to represent, to traverse, to decompose, to compose, to generalize, to put in practice, to use, to formulate.*

There is a fragment of the list of the skills below:

3.1. General skills

To analyze physical processes and phenomena, to estimate orders of physics magnitudes and determine essential factors, to build physical models, to build mathematical models of particular physical processes and phenomena, to determine boundaries of applicability of the models, and so on.

3.2. Particular skills

3.2.2. Molecular Physics and Thermodynamics

To estimate quantity of particles and their mass in particular conditions, to determine parameters of state of gas, to determine number of degrees of freedom and molecular mass of a gas and mixture of gases, to determine possibility of the use of the model of an ideal gas, to make use functions of distribution to find average values of physics magnitudes, etc.

Experimental skills are divided into three groups: *to measure physical magnitudes*; *to reproduce independently physical phenomena and processes; experimental particular skills.*

There is a hierarchical structure of the subject skills corresponding to the development of the subject in instruction. Besides that all of them also have a definite structure in the horizontal dimension because they are complicated, or composed, skills. In order to master them, a wide spectrum of skills both of the lower levels and subject is necessary. For example, skill *to solve physical problems* is composed of ten simpler skills*: to pick out the necessary information from the condition of a problem to solve it, to code the condition of the problem in a word form, to draw a picture to the problem, to choice a rational method of solving*, and so on.

6 The semantic subject student model

Semantic knowledge in different subjects is contained in textbooks, other training literature. There are two parts in the content of any textbook: CON-1 and CON-2 [7]. CON-1 is knowledge making up the content of a domain directly, CON-2 is knowledge attending the CON-1 (for example, knowledge from other subjects, interpretations, explanations, examples from life). In fact, it is the CON-1 that is the semantic knowledge of a domain. Nevertheless, this knowledge is not picked out especially, it is distributed all around the textbook, interacts with another knowledge, and is not formalized.

Semantic knowledge represents the declarative component of the subject knowledge as the procedural knowledge is realized in skills (operational knowledge). Thus to construct a semantic student model on the basis of a textbook, it is necessary to pick out domain facts from it and group them in a definite order. According to their structure, facts may be of a great variety. As a rule, they are compound ones. Nevertheless, elementary facts may be picked out that, appearing in different relationships, form the compound facts. General questions of representation of facts in instruction are considered in works [4]. For example, expression "*Translational motion is the motion that all the point of a solid body have identical trajectory*" is a compound fact as it can be represented as a set of the following elementary facts: (1) *a solid body moves; (2) all the point of the body have identical trajectory; some motion is called the translational one.*

One can easily see that the elementary facts do not carry any semantic loading of the domain although they contain domain terms. Only on gathering together in a compound fact they acquire some domain sense. Such compound facts are finished thoughts and they are represented by finished sentences, or expressions. Let us call them the *semantic* facts. As a matter of fact, the semantic facts are a unit of the domain knowledge, as smaller portions of it have no domain sense. The objects of the expression are concepts, phenomena, processes, laws, principles, theorems, conclusions, consequences, reasons, properties, rules, and so on.

It is the full set of the semantic facts that is the semantic subject student model. The order of their disposition is subordinated to the logic of the development of the course.

Such a semantic subject student model was firstly constructed in Gas Dynamics and than in Physics [1]. Those were very small brochures because there were no calculations, proofs, and explanation in them. Nevertheless, they contained all the statements of the courses. These brochures received the title *semantic synopsis.* As an example, there is a fragment from a physics semantic synopsis below:

3.1. The elementary work of a force is defined as the scalar product of the elementary displacement of the point of the force application.

3.2. The work of a force is defined as a line integral from the elementary work along the trajectory of the point of the force application.

3.3. The unit of the work is one joule that is equal to a work done by a force of one newton on a displacement of one meter.

In the opinion of instructors and students, the synopsis turned out an effective means while consolidating the instructional material, preparing to seminars. It helps to size up the structure of the instructional material, pick out and easily memorize the most essential its moments. It is very important that student remember them for a longer time.

The synopsis allows carrying out fast and regular control students' knowledge during a lecture. In this case, the expressions serve as a base for the open type test tasks being created by missing some keywords in the expressions. Students note a great value of the synopsis while preparing to the examinations when there is a danger do not pick out and master the main statements of the course.

7 Conclusion

An approach to construction of the subject student model as a part of the normative one is described. The model consists of four components: thematic, functional, operation, and semantic. The thematic model gives ideas about the structure of the subject, the semantic one reflects its content, functional one determine what students have to know, and operation one does what students have to be able. The approach allows constructing more detailed current student models and reaching the main aim of teaching, namely forming the way of acting, more successfully.

References

[1] Atanov, G.A., Belaya, T.D., Beshevly, B.I., etc. The base synopsis in physics. Kyiv, NMK VO, 1993.

[2] Atanov, G.A., Efros, T.I. System of skills in instruction as a part of the learner model. Proc. of the Intern. Conf. on Computer Assistant Learning CAL-97. Exeter, UK, 1997, pp. 369-372.

[3] Atanov, G.A., Martynovitch, N.N., Tokiy, V.V. Curriculum of Physics Course as a Student Model. Proc. of the Int. Conf. on Computer Technologies in Education ICCTE'93. Kiev, Ukraine, 1993.

[4] Atanov, G.A., Pustynnikova, I.N. Representation and Structuring of Domain Knowledge by the Semantic Networks and Productions Methods. Proc. of the 8th Intern. PEG Conf.: Meeting the Challenge of the New Technologies. Sozopol, Bulgaria, 1997, pp. 392 - 393.

[5] Brachman, J., Levesque, H.J., Reiter, R. Knowledge representation. MIT Press, 1992.

[6] Dean, T.L., Allen, J., Aloimonous, J. Artificial intelligence: Theory and practice. Benjamin/Cummings, 1994.

[7] Mashbits, E.I. Psychological and pedagogical problems of computer assistant learning. Pedagogika, Moscow, 1988 (in Russian).

[8] Self, J. Dynamics of Learner Models. Artificial Intelligence and Education. IOS Press, Amsterdam, 1994.

[9] Wenger, E. Artificial intelligence and tutoring systems. Computational approaches to the communication of knowledge. Morgan Kaufmann. Los Altos, 1987.

Knowledge-Based Software Engineering
T. Hruška and M. Hashimoto (Eds.)
IOS Press, 2000

AEGIS: Automatic Exercise Generator with Tagged Documents based on the Intelligence of Students

Takayoshi SHOUDAI, Akira SUGANUMA, and Tsunenori MINE
Graduate School of Information Science and Electrical Engineering Kyushu University
6-1 Kasuga-koen, Kasuga 816-8580, Japan
{shoudai@i, suga@is, mine@is}.kyushu-u.ac.jp

Abstract. This paper proposes AEGIS (Automatic Exercise Generator based on the Intelligence of Students) that generates exercises of various levels according to each student's achievement level, marks his/her answers, and returns the marked results to him/her, automatically. The aim of this system is to help the students understand the lecture.

1 Introduction

As the Internet has come into wide use, WWW environments provide lots of opportunities to various fields. In the educational domain, Web data are being exploited as useful materials. We have been developing Web-based self-teaching systems and constructing the tools for helping students understand their subjects [4, 5, 7, 6].

We are currently focusing on automatic students' achievement level evaluators that generate exercises from tagged documents, present them to students and mark their answers automatically. Several automatic quiz generating systems have been proposed so far. Browning et al. proposed Tutorial Mark-up Language to generate questions automatically [1, 2]. Carbone et al. proposed CADAL Quiz [3], which generates a multiple-choice quiz from a question database. After marking students' answers, CADAL Quiz returns the results to the students and tutors. Both of them, however, restrict the question type only to a multiple-choice quiz and do not describe the effect to make the difficulty level of question type change based on the students' achievement level.

This paper proposes AEGIS (Automatic Exercise Generator based on the Intelligence of Students) which generates the three question-types, that is, multiple-choice question, fill-the-gap question, and error-correcting question, from the same tagged data. Guessing the achievement level of each student from his/her trial history, AEGIS selects the most suitable question-type and exercise for him/her. After marking his/her answer to the exercise, AEGIS returns the result to him/her with its explanation.

2 Question-Types

Because any computer can not well understand demonstrative answers unless those are written according to some instructions, the question-types must be restricted. Thus we consider the following three question-types:

Multiple-choice question. Students choose the correct answer from a given candidate list.

Example. Complete the sentence. Choose your answer from the list.

Data structures need to be studied ____ order to understand the algorithms.

(1) an (2) in (3) on (4) at (5) by

Fill-the-Gap question. Students try to fill the correct answer in the blank of a given sentence with no help.

Example. Put in the right word.

Data structures need to be studied ____ order to understand the algorithms.

Error-correcting question. Students have to find the wrong expression in a given sentence and correct it.

Example. Right or wrong? Correct the sentence if it is wrong.

Data structures need to be studied an order to understand the algorithms.

All of these question-types can be constructed from a sentence by replacing one or more consecutive words with a blank or a wrong expression. We call the region replaced with either a blank or wrong expression *hidden region*. We note that these three question-types have different difficulties even if they are constructed from the same *hidden region*.

3 Automatic Exercise Generating

The exercise generating process from teaching materials is summarized as follows: (1) Setting a *hidden region*: Teachers choose the most suitable *hidden region* for their intentions. (2) Selecting a paragraph or sentence(s) from teaching materials: The sentences before and after *hidden regions* are often of importance to ask students the unique answer of the question. We call the paragraph or sentence(s) a *question region*. The question region may have more than one *hidden regions*. (3) Constructing a candidate list: A multiple-choice question requires a couple of distractors to construct a list of answer candidates. These three steps are deeply related to the teachers' intentions. In order to embed their intentions into the teaching materials, we define the three kinds of tags: QUESTION, DEL, and LABEL.

QUESTION This tag surrounds a question region and has an attribute SUBJECT to specify the subject or topic of the question region.

DEL This tag indicates a *hidden region*. All we have to do for making some fill-the-gap questions is to replace the *hidden region* with a blank. CAND is an attribute of DEL which is used to embed a candidate list directly into the DEL tag.

LABEL This tag has an attribute NAME that specifies the dependency relations with *hidden regions*.

We define the additional attributes of DEL to generate an exercise that is suitable for the achievement level of each student.

LEVEL LEVEL specifies the lowest and highest levels of the exercises generated from the *hidden region* and its value is a pair of integers between 1 and 10.

GROUP GROUP specifies the dependency relation between *hidden regions* and holds the uniqueness of the correct answer. This is used to adjust the exercise level.

REF REF specifies the dependency relation between a *hidden region* and the expressions other than the *hidden region*. This attribute works together with a LABEL tag.

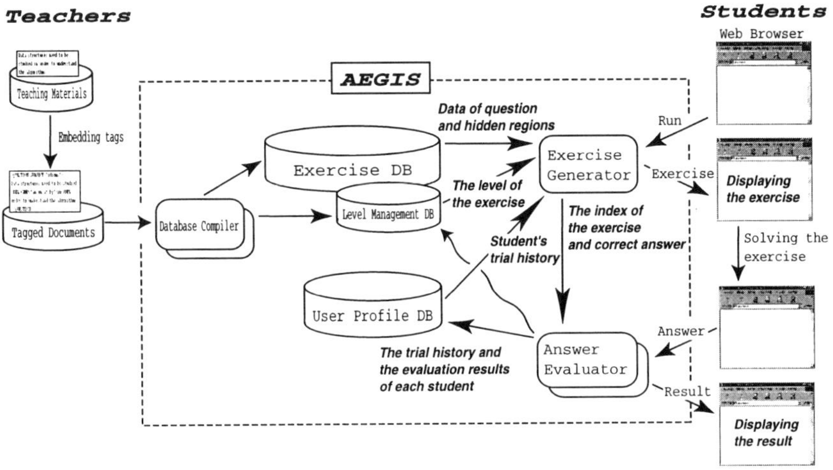

Figure 1: Overview of AEGIS

⟨QUESTION SUBJECT="arithmetic operations"⟩ This program computes the multiplication and division for two input integers and shows the answer.

```
program enzan;
var x,y:integer;
   seki,shou:integer;
begin
   write('Input two integers : ');
   readln(x,y);
   seki:=⟨DEL CAND="x,xy,x×y,x mul y" LEVEL="1,5"⟩x*y⟨/DEL⟩;
   shou:=⟨DEL CAND="x/y,x÷y,xdivy,x mod y" LEVEL="1,5"⟩x div y⟨/DEL⟩;
   writeln('Seki:',seki);
   writeln('Shou:',shou)
end.⟨/QUESTION⟩
```

Figure 2: Example of teaching materials with tags

4 AEGIS system

AEGIS consists of three databases and two main database managers (Fig. 1). The three databases are called *Exercise DB*, *User Profile DB*, and *Level Management DB* respectively. Teaching materials with the tags in Section 3 are compiled into the Exercise DB and Level Management DB. All of the question regions are indexed sequentially and each *hidden region* is labeled with its own subindex of the index of each question region. The level of a *hidden region* is stored in the Level Management DB together with the index of the *hidden region*. User Profile DB keeps students' personal trial histories including their current achievement level. The two DB managers are called *Exercise Generator* and *Answer Evaluator*. They also make communications with the users (students) through Web browsers after being invoked through CGI (Common Gateway Interface). AEGIS system determines whether or not the *hidden region* is worth being transformed into the exercise by examining the student's *Profile DB* and *Level Management DB*.

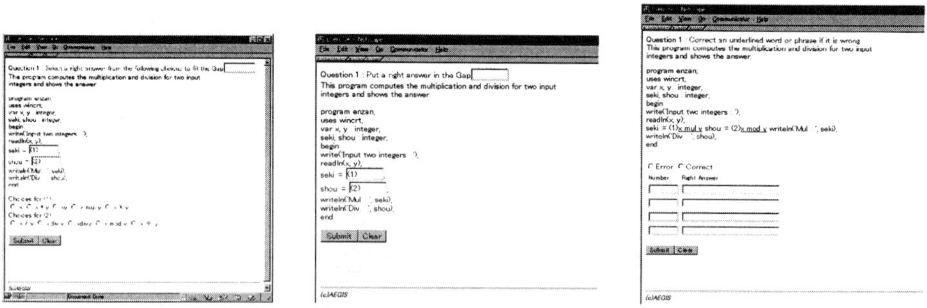

(a) Multiple-Choice (b) Fill-the-Gap (c) Error-Correcting

Figure 3: Three questions generated from the document in Fig. 2

5 Conclusions

We discussed our new Web-aided system AEGIS. It works fine as an educational tool for every student and helps him/her to understand every subject if teachers can prepare their teaching materials as tagged documents. Fig. 2 shows an example of teaching materials with the tags. This example is a piece of the teaching materials in the elementary course of computer literacy at Kyushu University, Japan. Fig. 3 shows the three question-types generated from the document shown in Fig. 2. We are now preparing to apply AEGIS system in the real classes at our university in order to develop reasonable methods for the level management.

References

[1] P. Browning, J. Williams, D. Brickley, and H. Missou. Question Delivery over the Web using TML. CAA, 1997.
http://www.ilrt.bris.ac.uk/netquest/liveserver/qbanks/demos/paul/lboro/ohp1.html

[2] P. Browning. TUTORIAL MARKUP LANGUAGE - A CBA SYSTEM. 1998.
http://www.soton.ac.uk/~ukgec/workshop/5-cba/minutes.htm#TUTORIAL

[3] A. Carbone and P. Schendzielorz. A Web-Based Quiz Generator for Use in Tutorials and Assessment. Global J. of Engng. Educ., Vol.I, No.3, 1997.
http://www.eng.monash.edu.au/usicee/gjee/vol1no3/paper20.htm

[4] R. Fujimoto, A. Suganuma, and T. Mine. Development of a classroom management system on the web. In *Proc. of Int. Conf. on Computers in Education, ICCE'99*, volume 2, pages 756–759, 1999.

[5] R. Fujimoto, Y. Tsutsumi, and A. Suganuma. Cacce: Computer aided cooperative classroom environment. In *World Conference on Educational Multimedia, Hypermedia & Telecommunications*, page 1686, 1999.

[6] T. Mine, D. Nagano, K. Baba, T. Shoudai, and S. Hirokawa. On-web visualizing a mechanism of a single chip computer for computer literacy courses. In *Proc. of Int. Conf. on Computers in Education, ICCE'98*, volume 2, pages 496–499, 1998.

[7] H. Sato, T. Mine, T. Shoudai, H. Arimura, and S. Hirokawa. On web visualizing how programs run for teaching 2300 students. In *Proc. of Int. Conf. on Computers in Education, ICCE'97*, pages 952–954, 1997.

Knowledge-Based Software Engineering
T. Hruška and M. Hashimoto (Eds.)
IOS Press, 2000

Knowledge-Based Neural Network: a Method to Support Learners in Building Neural Network Models

Toshio OKAMOTO, Safia BELKADA

AI & Knowledge Computing Lab, The Graduate School of Information Systems,
University of Electro-Communications
Chofu-shi, Chofugaoka 1-5-1, Tokyo 182-8585.
{okamoto, safia}@ai.is.uec.ac.jp

Abstract. This paper describes our ongoing research on the DiscoverNet system that provides an interactive simulation-based learning environment, for discovery- and self-learning. We chose 'neural networks' as domain application. DiscoverNet allows users to build their neural networks by blending theory and praxis within a simulation environment. In this paper, we especially focus on the virtual assistant embedded in the system that is responsible for the educational orientation during the design and training of a neural network. The framework we use for the virtual assistant module to give advice is concentrated on connectionist theory refinement. To diagnose a neural model made by a user, the assistant constructs a script file during the learner's manipulations of neural objects, using a set of inference rules to help determine the network's topology and initial weight values. The assistant examines which information is lacking or wrong and sends it to the user together with the initial network, to show the user's misconceptions.

1 Introduction

In symbolic machine learning, methods such as ID3 are widely used and have shown a good reliability. However more recently, sub-symbolic, neural network methods are being developed, as promising alternative to knowledge refinement. Knowledge-based systems often suffer from the knowledge acquisition bottleneck. A neural network model, on the other hand, can be trained to perform reasonably well - based on the training data sets - but they cannot readily incorporate domain knowledge or provide explanation of the results. Hybrid systems made of a combination of the two approaches cited above, have shown to outperform both approaches, when used separately.

There are different approaches to construct a hybrid intelligent systems which aim to exploit the features of both knowledge-based system and neural network methods [1,2,4]. One way is to translate the domain theory into a neural network and thereby determine the neural network's topology, than refine the reformulated rules using backpropagation. The knowledge-based neural network (KBNN) algorithm falls in this category [3].

In this paper we propose a framework based on the hybrid approach, integrating a knowledge-based system with the neural network paradigm, to support learning neural networks within an interactive simulation-based environment for discovery and self-learning.

DiscoverNet allows learners to build their neural network simulators [4], by blending theory and praxis within a simulation environment, and facilitate learning through a tutoring program. In the following sections, we focus on the virtual assistant embedded in the system that is responsible for the educational orientation during the neural network simulator design. To diagnose a model made by a learner, the virtual assistant constructs a script file during the learner's manipulations of objects, using a set of inference rules to help determine the network's topology, and initial weight values. Then, the assistant translates the script file into a set of nodes represented as an AND/OR dependency tree. From the tree we choose a proper index and examine whether the architecture and the corresponding parameters can be approximated in the space of neural network topologies. An initial neural network is constructed and trained. The assistant examines which information is lacking or wrong and sends it to the learner together with the initial network, showing his/her misconceptions.

The paper is organized as follows: Section 2 provides a brief description of neural networks followed by a computational description of the advice process. In Section 3, we illustrate the domain knowledge representation of the neural networks and in Section 4 we describe the basic features of the system, and its underlying simulation environment.

2 Learning With The Virtual Assistant

2.1 Neural Network Models

A neural network model is formally defined by a quadruple $< S, W, L, F >$, where W is a set of weights (w_{ji}), L is a set of learning algorithms (l_a), F is a set of activation functions (f_{act}), and S is further defined by a pair (N, C), where N is a set of nodes (n_i) and C a set of connections (c_i).

Assume n nodes in a neural network model. We have the following definitions:

$$
\begin{aligned}
N &= \{n_i | 1 \leq n\} \\
C &\subseteq \{(n_i \rightarrow n_j) \mid 1 \leq (i, j) \leq n\} \\
W &\subseteq \{(n_i \rightarrow n_j, w_{ji}) \mid 1 \leq (i, j) \leq n\} \\
L &= \{l_{a1}, l_{a2} \ldots\} \\
F &= \{f_{act1}, f_{act2} \ldots\}
\end{aligned} \qquad (2.1)
$$

Neural networks (NNs) are often classified as a single layer or multilayer. The number of links between the slabs of nodes defines the number of layers in the NN. Each node is connected to other nodes by means of direct communication links, each with an associated weight. The weights represent information being used by the model to solve a problem. Each learning algorithm is a mapping that transforms one neural network state, which is defined by the set of W, to another neural network state. For the most typical neural network setting, training is accomplished by presenting a sequence of vectors or patterns. The weights are then adjusted according to a learning algorithm by summing its weighted inputs and applying an activation function. Typically, the same activation function is used for all units in any particular layer.

For instance, let F be a set of activation functions $F=\{f\}$, and X_i, Y_j a sets of input, respectively output units. Assume that $xi \in X_i$ and $yj \in Y_j$. The output, y_j, is expressed as:

$$y_{inj} = \Sigma x_i w_{ii} \qquad (2.2)$$

$$y_j = f_{act}(y_{inj}) \qquad (2.3)$$

2.2 Learning With The Consultant Module

In this section, we analyze the approach used for the virtual assistant (VA). The VA gives advice to the user considering different possible concept descriptions, by integrating a knowledge-based system with the neural network that helps the former to refine the initial domain knowledge, and adapting the KBNN algorithm [3] with a new method to support the advice process. The VA deals with two main parts: the advice algorithm and the Rule Base.

2.2.1 The Advice Process

In the following we examine the computational approach of the advice process by using our algorithm, which has two phases:

1. Searching through space of neural network topologies *H*.
2. Training the neural network and providing feedback information.

The Figure 1 shows the advice process in the virtual assistant. VA diagnoses a neural model made by the learner by constructing a script file during the learner's manipulations of objects (considered as initial domain knowledge). The algorithm uses the initial knowledge to help guide its searching through the space *H* and give a starting point in the weights space. The Algorithm tries to translate the script file into a set of nodes represented as an AND/OR dependency tree. From the tree the assistant chooses a proper index related to the learning algorithm and examines whether the architecture and the corresponding parameters can be approximated in the space *H*. The following algorithm describes the searching method:

(i) Assume $I <S_2, W_2, L_2, F_2>$ is a set of instances representing the initial knowledge (user input).

(ii) Select $h <S_1, W_1, L_1, F_1>$ with q layers in H,

(iii) $I = I^+ \cup I^-$: I^+ is the set of instances satisfying h, and I^- ,those that do not satisfy h;

(iv) Map $h <S_1, W_1, L_1, F_1>$ *with* $I <S_2, W_2, L_2, F_2>$

(v) Compute the probability P to choose the best initial weights in h to be included in I.

$$P_i = \frac{\sum_{(j,i)\in I} |w_{ji}|}{\sum_{(j,i)\in I} |w_{ji}| + \sum_{(j,i)\in H} |w_{ji}|}$$

, where $wji \in I$ is weight value from node i to node j. The probability of belonging to the instance I^- is (1-this probability). The assistant tends to assign most of the nodes that are heavily linked together. This helps to minimize the destruction of the design model I made by the user, since nodes belonging to the designed model are connected by heavily linked weights.

(vi) I can be mapped to h *if* $card(I) = card(h)$ and $P_i \neq 0$.

That is, h can induce all possible partitions of I instance if the dimension of h is the same as that of I.

The induced network is a fully connected neural network with $L = \{l\}$, where l is the learning algorithm chosen by the user. $F = \{f_1, f2...fq\}$, where F is the set of activation functions. The weights' values are confined to the range from –1 to –1; that is, $-1 \leq w_{ji} \leq 1$ for all weights w_{ji}, $1 \leq (i, j) \leq n$, where w_{ji} is the weight associated with the connection pointing from node i to node j. Then, the assistant optimizes the induced neural network as follows:

(i) Neurons chosen by the learner are initialized with heavy weight connections,

(ii) Lightweight connections are added to the network to facilitate the correction of the student's network,

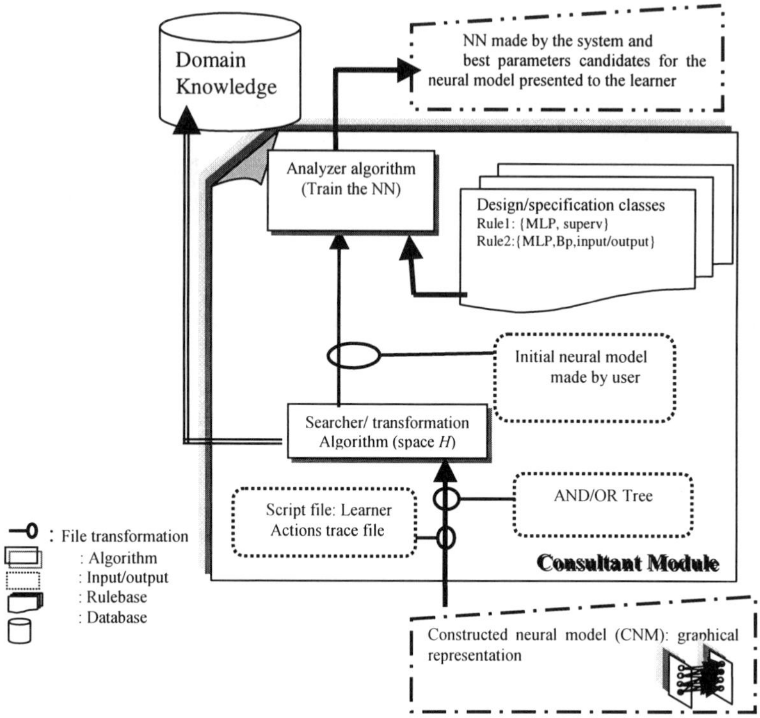

Figure 1. The Description of the Process Steps in the Virtual Assistant

(iii) Additional input neurons may be automatically added by the system to the network, to incorporate features, which do not appear in the network made by the learner,

(iv) The assistant initializes the weights and biases if needed (i.e., if not already initiaized by the learner),

(v) The assistant examines which information is lacking or wrong and sends it to the learner together with the initial network showing his/her misconceptions.

2.2.2 Description of the Rule Base

A rule-based system captures the decision-making of the design. The decision-making rules consist of packages of classes that attempt to identify objects or decide on actions:

(i) ***Design*** classes contain a set of rules, which describe the construction of a neural net work model according to what constraints should be given in the design stage and what information is desired (figure 2).

(ii) For each ***Design*** class we define a set of rules that describe a specific neural network model and we name it ***Specification*** class.

```
Rule MLFFwithBP = new Rule(rb, "MLFF_with_BP",
new Clause(supervisedType,cEquals, "Norecurrent") ,
new Clause(activfunc,cEquals, "nolinear"),
new Clause(learning,cEquals, "Backpropagation"),
new Clause(training,cEquals, "batch_training")) ;
....
```

Figure 2. Definition of rules in the Design class

```
RuleVariable supervisedType = new RuleVariable("Supervised_Type") ;
RuleVariable learning = new RuleVariable("learning") ;
RuleVariable activfunc = new RuleVariable("ActivFunc") ;
learning.setLabels("Delta_rule Error_correction Competitive_learning Backpropagation") ;
```

Figure 3. Definition of rule's variables in the specification class

(iii) ***Advisor*** classes manage the communication between the user and the whole system. The Figure 3 shows an example of the rule-based system.

3 Representation of the Initial Domain Knowledge

The Model of the domain knowledge consists of a set of classes; the architecture of each class has two levels. The object knowledge level is based on objects and contains the core of formal and procedural concepts related to the neural network models. The user creates instances of a class when s/he manipulates objects. For instance, in the feedforward neural networks [4], the initial instances are the creation of activation functions instances, matrix weight instances, and control parameters instances. The user can interactively create instances and specify the values associated with the relevant functions. The structural knowledge level allows the exploration of the design stage by defining concepts and relations (e.g., learning algorithm…) over object knowledge. The structural knowledge is a set of rules defined on sets of instances from the domain knowledge. The modeling of the domain knowledge of neural network consists of hierarchical relations between various neural network models as described in Figure 4. We construct models of knowledge for various neural network models and various design models for a particular knowledge model.

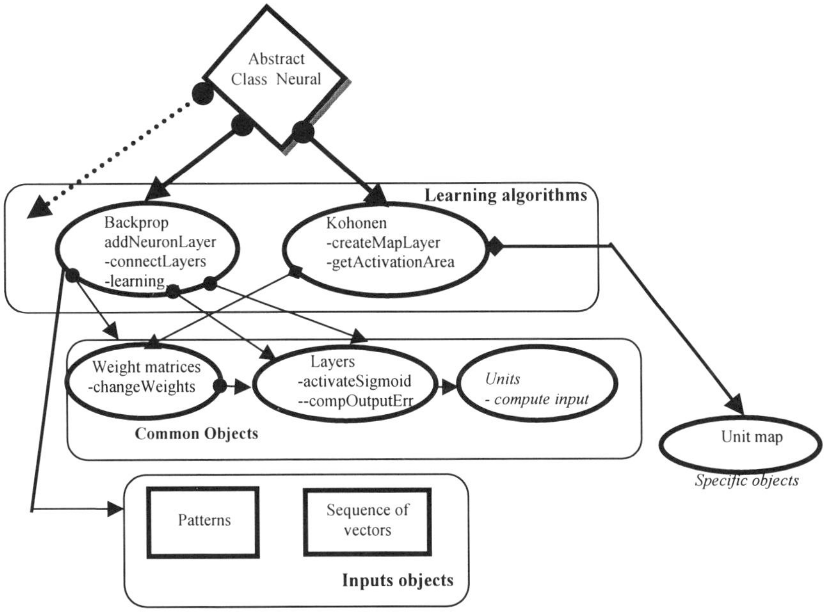

Figure 4. Representation of the Domain Knowledge

4 Simulation-Based Learning Environment

With DiscoverNet the user designs a neural network model through different manipulations of objects existing in the library and different requests to the system for helps and hints. Figure 5 shows a simplified control flow of DiscoverNet, which consists of three main parts:

(i) **Adaptive user interface**: it consists of the learning and authoring environment related to the design of the neural network models. It is in this part also, where the user model representing the individual's understanding level is first analyzed and built.

(ii) **Knowledge based neural network**: it accumulates neural network models. Each neural model consists of a respective architecture and learning algorithm and a set of parameters [7]. The selection of appropriate parameters and architecture for a given application is made after many trials.

(iii) **Virtual assistant** (VA): it manages the communication between different parts and gives assistance to the user whenever it is needed.

(iv) In Figure 5, the **design database** stores representations of the design description made by the user of the solving procedures of one specific application.

(v) The **object library** contains components of neural networks.

(vi) The system gradually builds a **user model**, and uses it for the analysis and understanding of the real user's needs. Especially, this model is used by the virtual assistant, to generate useful guidance and correct the user mistakes.

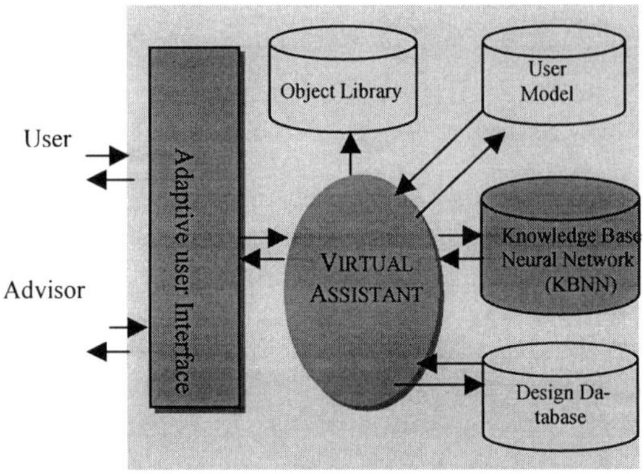

Figure 5. Simulation-Based Learning Environment

4.1 Sample Assistance Process

At the start of the session, the main screen pops up as shown by Figure 6, upper screen. The user builds his/her network by assembling objects. The system constrains the network to be physically possible, by graphical representation restrictions. When the design is satisfactorily completed, the user is required to train the network by specifying a learning algorithm accompanied with its specific parameters. The environment shows the output data of the network and the corresponding graph. In fact, to build a neural model, starting with the data, the user constructs the topology of his/her neural model and specifies its initial weight matrices and learning parameters. Each layer of the constructed model has to contain vectors of data for input/output units. When the learning algorithm is selected from a list of options contained within menus, the training session can be started. At the end of the training session, the output pattern of the data and the corresponding graph are shown in the simulation environment.

Since the selection of appropriate parameters is crucial for a fast convergence of the algorithm [8], the user may impose some constraints on the parameters. It is practical that the user specifies how much correction should be applied to the weights by tuning the parameters.

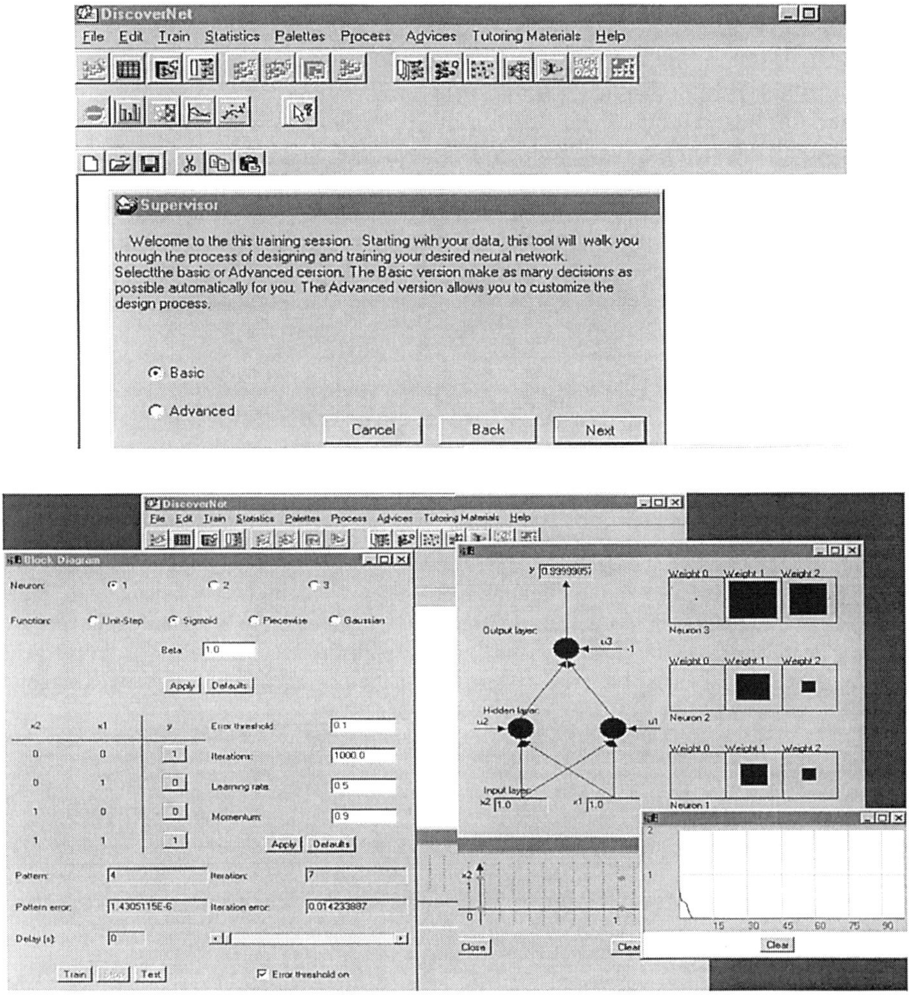

Figure 6. Neural Network Design Session

As can be seen in the upper screen shown in figure 6, the user can specify parameters such as the external activation function type, other learning parameters, such as the error threshold and/ or the number of iterations to perform, the learning rate, momentum and others. The user can also specify the pairs of I/O values directly. This particular figure displays the situation of a beginner user, simulating XOR. The architecture of the network is presented on the right side of the lower display in figure 6. The weights and their dynamical changes during training are displayed next to the network architecture. Below, the time display of the training error can be followed, as well as the spatial representation of the XOR problem considered.

5 Conclusion

In this paper, we presented a method to teach students Neural Network basics, as well as more advanced theory, moreover, to support them with interactive, adaptive advices during their learning process. For this purpose, we built and are refining a CAD system with an attached knowledge-based neural network learning support tool.

Our approach consists of constructing assistant script classes to follow the learner's design steps; a script defines the sequences of assistance. An initial neural network can be projected on the space of topologies *H,* only if it matches approximately one or more rules of the space *H*, otherwise the initial neural network cannot be trained. We backed up our approach with convincing results given by the knowledge based neural network approach. In the KBNN approach, some prior domain knowledge is used, but complete initial knowledge is not required. The initial knowledge is translated into a primary neural network, than refined into correct and complete knowledge. During this process, the student's attention is drawn to the mistakes s/he made, and more insight in the structure and laws of neural networks is given to him/ her, by this learning-by-doing and discovery learning type of educational strategy.

We presented an object-oriented approach for the design of a simulation-based learning environment for discovery learning. The system also contains an assistant that contributes in the learning stage. In this paper, we focused on the description of the advice process algorithm of the assistant. As the first step, in order to study the feasibility of such a system, we considered the typical components and building blocks of the feedforward neural network and Kohonen Feature Map network. We chose these models because they are the most commonly used, and the equations that describe the models are simple, compared to other models. The system is implemented with Java.

For future research, we plan to integrate other types of neural networks, and start gathering data on students training in our environment, to evaluate the system. Moreover, we plan to extend our system to lead a better dialogue with the user, as well as to implement more functionality for each of the two system stages, the beginner and the advanced stage.

References

[1] Pazzani, M., & Kibler, D.: The utility of knowledge in inductive learning. Machine Learning, 9, 57-94, 1992.

[2] Fu, L. et al: Integration of neural heuristics into knowledge-based inference, Connection Science, 1, 325-340, 1989.

[3] Towell, G.G., Shavlik, J.W., and Noordewier, M.O.: Refinement of approximately correct domain theories by knowledge-based neural networks. proceedings of the eighth national conference on Artificial intelligence, pages 861-866, Boston, MA. MIT Press, 1990.

[4] Stephen, I.G.: Neural network learning and expert system, A Bradford book, the MIT Press Cambridge, Massachusetts London, England, 1999.

[5] Haykin, S.: Neural Networks: A comprehensive Foundation, New York, Macmillan, 1994.

[6] Belkada, S., Cristea, A., Okamoto, T.:Development of an intelligent simulation-based learning environment to design and tutor neural networks, Paper presented in the seventh international conference on computer in Education (ICCE99), vol.2, pages 291-298, Tokyo,1999.

[7] Chenoweth, T., Obradovic, Z.: A multi-component nonlinear prediction system for the Sp 500 Index". Neurocomputing, J., vol. 10, no3.3, 275-290, 1996.

[8] Venkateswaran, R., Obradovic, Z.: Efficient learning through cooperation, in Proceeding world Congress, Neural Networks, San Diego, CA, vol.3, pages 390-395, 1997.

Knowledge-Based Software Engineering
T. Hruška and M. Hashimoto (Eds.)
IOS Press, 2000

Multi-Media German Teaching Material on the WWW for the German Learner in Japan

Jiro KURIYAMA[1], Yuji IMOTO[2], Katsuaki NAKAGAWA[3], Masa-aki HASHIMOTO[4]

[1]*kuriyama@lai.kyutech.ac.jp, Dept. of Human Science*
[2]*imoto@ai.kyutech.ac.jp, Dept. of Artificial Intelligence*
[3]*nakagawa@lai.kyutech.ac.jp, Dept. of Human Science*
[4]*hashimoto@ai.kyutech.ac.jp, Dept. of Artificial Intelligence*
Kyushu Institute of Technology: Kawazu 680 - 4, Iizuka, Fukuoka 820-8502 Japan

Abstract. This paper introduces a multi-media German language-learning program on the WWW for the distance teaching supported by the databese system and the server-client sysytem. The paper describes mainly the structure of this program. Users can learn the German language by means of German pronunciation exercises, pictures, and movies in both the German and Japanese alphabets.

1 Introduction

Foreign languages are some of the most popular subjects of study among Japanese students. However, there are not as many opportunities for students of German to speak with native German speakers in the streets of Japan. In addition, there are numerous American videos and books in Japan, but not enough German ones. At universities, many German teachers teach German through the "Grammar-Translation method," which emphasizes the memorization of the rules of German grammar such as " ich lerne, du lernst, er lernt," or " der Vater, des Vaters, dem Vater, den Vater."

Students learn such rules very well. However, when they eventually meet a native German speaker, they cannot utter a word in German. This happens because they have had no experience speaking German in their classes.

In the "communicative method," instructors teach listening to and speaking foreign languages as in daily-life. By applying this method to the teaching of German, we try to offer German learners a chance to listen to native German speakers through the WWW. Using this method, learners can improve not only their listening, but also their writing and reading skills. Our program does not neglect the teaching of grammatical rules. However, our main purpose is not that students memorize the rules, but that they get used to understanding the German spoken in the streets instead. Students following this program will have the motivation and courage to speak German even in unprepared situations.

The importance of practice in using a foreign language is recognized by all. In this program, students are given many opportunities to do listening, writing, and reading exercises in German. Using the WWW and following our program, learners can practice German in their free time. A series of tests has been prepared so that students can evaluate their own listening, reading, and writing skills in German.

2 Level of the material

This program is intended for beginner students of German. Therefore, only words and sentences used for basic communication are used. The sentence structure is not complex. The material contains conversations between two speakers, a native German woman and a Japanese man. While the female speaker speaks German at normal conversational speed, the male speaker uses a somewhat slower speech to facilitate understanding by Japanese students. The program has 10 lessons. Lesson As the lessons progress, the level of difficulty increases. However, priority is always given to the most common phrases of the German language.

3 Structure and Contents of the material

Our program consists of 4 steps. In the first step, we show a scene with two people in a movie (Cf. 3.1 Introduction). Next, words and expressions used in this lesson are explained in Japanese and German (Cf. 3.2 Explanation). After that, there is an exercise section (Cf. 3.3 Exercise). Lastly, a test is presented (Cf. 3.4 Test).

3.1 Introduction

In this step, learners can hear a conversation between two people. The scene of the lesson is in a movie, students can read the German text of the conversation. Students should carefully listen to the conversation several times until they can understand the pronunciation of both the native German and the Japanese speakers and understand the topic of their conversation.

In order to help students who have no previous knowledge of German, our program provides a translation and a short summary of the German text. This can be accessed by clicking the number appearing before the sentence of the German text. In this description, students read the exact meaning and use of expressions in German sentences.

3.2 Explanation

In the second step, "Explanation," students increase their skill and knowledge about the content of the lesson. They look at a picture and hear the Japanese and German expressions and the pronunciation of the German expressions at the same time . By looking at the picture, they can understand what it means, and by clicking on the pronunciation button, they can hear the pronunciation of the German sentences, phrases, or words and recognize their spelling at the same time.

In the first step, "Introduction," the material does not offer numerous words or expressions because the step is intended to provide only common phrases of every-day use such as "Guten Morgen!" as a greeting. However, in everyday life, people sometimes use expressions such as "Guten Tag!" or " Guten Abend!" In order to cover for this lack, the second step of the program gives a supplement to the words and phrases shown in the first step. Since students become apprehensive about their learning ability when they encounter too many words, phrases, or expressions during the early stages of learning, new expressions are limited to 40.

Figure 1. A scene of the third step, "Exercise"

3.3 Exercise

After learners understand how to pronounce the expressions and spell the phrases in the lesson they are doing, they must practice listening to and writing the German language. The third step, "Exercises," is divided into three parts to provide sufficient practice in the four skills: speaking, listening, reading, and writing, which are necessary for mastery of a foreign language.

Section 1: Learners read the Japanese words, phrases, and expressions that they learned in the previous step and translate them into German. In this section, they judge their own ability at understanding the meaning of vocabulary and expressions.

Section 2: Students hear the pronunciation of the German words that they spelled in the previous step and write them in German. In this section, they assess their own listening ability (Figure 1).

Section 3: Students see the picture of the German daily-life scene they checked in the previous step and write German sentences describing the scene.

Each of the words and expressions appearing in the second step (Explanation") is used once in each of sections 1, 2, or 3.

After each student response, the program indicates whether a student's answer is right or wrong. After three failed attempts, the correct answer is automatically provided. If students feel they do not understand or do not have sufficient ability at this step, they can go back to the previous steps "Introduction" or/and "Explanation" before moving on to the next step "Test."

3.4 Test

The content of this material progressively increases the students' knowledge of German as lessons advance from 1 to 10. The expressions and contents of the advanced lessons are planned to allow the students to move on only if they have mastered the contents of the previous lessons. Therefore, they must pass the "Test" step before they progress to the next lesson.

The structure and the succession of the step "Test" are basically the same as those of the step "Exercise". However, there are two differences: 1) The time for the test is limited to 20 minutes, even though the instructor can change the length of the time allowed for the test. 2) Students can not see whether their answers are right or wrong.

Each question is weighted differently. Students answering a few difficult questions correctly receive a better score on the test than students who correctly answer a higher number of easier questions. The maximum score of the test is 100 points. Each of the three sections is weighted at 33% of the whole number of possible points. In order to move on to the next lesson, each student must receive a score of 60% or better on the test.

4 Evaluation

The test results are provided to students both individually and on a graph which compares students' scores. This comparative graph shows the position of a student with respect to all students using this program and encourages him/her to learn diligently and actively.

5 Conclusion

We have produced a German teaching program to be used on the WWW. This material can be characterized as a sample of the multimedia material available to distanced beginner learners of the German language.

References

[1] K. Arnold, J. Gosling: *The Java Programming Language*, Second Edition, Addison-Wesley, 1997.

[2] Y. Imoto , K. Nakagawa, J. Kuriyama, K. Kakizaki, and M. Hashimoto: Modeling and Implementation of a German-Language CAI System, *Technical Report of IEICE*, KBSE98-13, pp. 25 – 32.

Author Index